INTO ONE'S OWN

INTO ONE'S OWN

From Youth To
Adulthood In The
United States
1920-1975

JOHN MODELL

UNIVERSITY OF CALIFORNIA PRESS
Berkeley   Los Angeles   Oxford

University of California Press
Berkeley and Los Angeles, California

University of California Press, Ltd.
Oxford, England

Copyright © 1989 by The Regents of the University of California

Library of Congress Cataloging-in-Publication Data

Modell, John.
    Into one's own : from youth to adulthood in the United States,
1920–1975 / John Modell.
        p.   cm.
    Bibliography: p.
    ISBN 0-520-07641-9 (alk. paper)
    1. Youth—United States—History—20th century.   2. Young adults—
United States—History—20th century.   3. Marriage—United States—
History—20th century.   I. Title.
HQ796.M5718   1989
305.2'3—dc19   88-30637
                                                                                CIP

Printed in the United States of America

1 2 3 4 5 6 7 8 9

For Judith

CONTENTS

TABLES

FIGURES

xi

ACKNOWLEDGMENTS

When one has worked as long and hard on an intellectual project as I have on this book, one builds up a lengthy list of people who have contributed to it. The extent of a list of "intellectual contributors" risks numbness in any readers it might have, and its close overlap with a list of one's friends and the difficulty of deciding at years' remove whether someone's contribution was to the book in particular or to its author's thinking in general produce a dilemma, whether one's inclination is to be inclusive or exclusive.

I have elected to acknowledge here only the most prominent, direct, and purposive contributions to the project, for I am sure that readers will realize that I am both thankful to and proud of the larger list of people I might have included.

Some of my debts are to institutions. The John Simon Guggenheim Foundation provided a fellowship during which this book "spun off" a related project. Among specialized libraries, the Institute for Sex Research, University of Indiana, the Minnesota Historical Society, and the Social Welfare History Archives, University of Minnesota, were especially generous in their efforts on my behalf. Both of my home institution libraries, at the University Minnesota and at Carnegie Mellon University, were supportive, assiduous, and resourceful: without their help, the book couldn't have been. Let the name of Erika Linke, who (coincidentally) departed my initial institution for my current one just when I did, and who has been exceptionally helpful at both, stand for that of a half-dozen librarians to whom I am indebted.

The History Departments at Minnesota and at Carnegie Mellon were both wonderful places for me to work and think. The Minnesota Family Study Center, University of Minnesota, was too. These were daily settings and always mattered a great deal to me, but so, also, in different ways, did the occasional and varying institutional contexts provided to me by the Committee on Child Development Research and Public Policy of the National Research Council (National Academy of Science), the Social Science Research Council, and the Social Science History Association. To cite these institutions is in part shorthand for listing the many individuals I've met thanks to them.

Tanya Rogers, for two years my secretary, was the best person at any job that I've ever seen. For this book, she typed and carried out some data entry. I thank her.

Copy editor Sheila Berg has done all that she can to make me sound less like a second-rate Tobias Smollett and more like a writer from my own century. It's not welcome help, exactly, but thanks are due.

Stanley Holwitz of the University of California Press, my editor, has offered patient, shrewd, and encouraging advice to me over quite a long time. That he's been a fan of the idea of this book has mattered to me.

Machine-readable data would have served me hardly at all had I not had the intelligent assistance, in sequence, of Phil Voxland, Director of the Social Sciences Research Facilities Center, University of Minnesota, and John Stuckey, then Director of Computing at the College of Humanities and Social Sciences, Carnegie Mellon University.

In the process of collaboration on closely-related projects, I was taught much of what I know by John Campbell, Glen H. Elder, Jr., Frank F. Furstenberg, Jr., Tamara K. Hareven, Theodore Hershberg, the late Reuben Hill, Duane Steffey, and Douglas Strong.

The manuscript was read critically and indispensably in its final form by Glen Elder, Doug Gower, Carol Z. Stearns, Peter Stearns, and Viviana Zelizer. This was an enormous chore, and I appreciate it greatly.

Department of History
Carnegie Mellon University
Pittsburgh, PA 15213
August 20, 1988

1
DEFINING ONE'S OWN

At sixteen, Sylvia rejected the hand of the boy next door. Her mother made the decision easy, reminding her that she was too young to know what love was. When Sylvia was eighteen, her mother prompted her to reject the suit of a poor but ambitious young man with whom Sylvia thought she really was in love. At nineteen, Sylvia considered but finally rejected the proposal of a young man of wealth and family, whom she did not love. "When Sylvia was twenty-five she was much lovelier than she had been at nineteen. At least, so her mother said. . . . Somehow, the men she met [now] were not so eager for matrimony. Most of them were earning smallish incomes, most of them had someone dependent upon them, most of them, when they did consider marriage, looked for a girl who had some earning power."[1] For a period, Sylvia rejected the logic of this proposition but eventually acceded. Her rebellion was episodic and individual.

This story in *The Ladies' Home Journal* in 1941 presenting the workings of the marriage market was typical of the genre that was a staple of the monthly woman's fiction mill. Marriage at some age, Americans held and still hold, is clearly too young; love at sixteen is either impossible or empirically unrecognizable. The winnowing process of courtship, however, rapidly reduces the pool of eligibles to those with special demands or disqualifications. The corrosion of age on woman's physical allure begins its cruel work; and the great, if lessening, social disadvantages of the single female allow even the bachelor dregs to demand not only beauty but economic resources. In this account, the events leading to marriage are presented as essentially a learning process. The literary token of the accomplishment of this process was a *recognizable* expression of *true* love, and marriage was the melodramatic climax or humorous resolution toward which the action tended. The protagonist's uncertainty about marriage was followed by a declaration of intention to marry, after a learning process in which both sexuality and *some* kind of nonsexual "rightness" were discovered to unite the couple. This learning process was formally analogous to the "search" phase of the "marriage market" as abstracted by economistic model builders.[2]

In 1941, Sylvia knew that her mother knew the rules of the game all too well. But in more recent decades, the path has become obscured—indeed, contested—and in many of its particulars. Most obviously, it has become an embarrassment to present marriage itself as a happy ending, not so much because marriage is not a happy event but because so often it is no longer an ending. The impact of divorce and serial marriage on parenthood, on children, indeed on the kinship system as a whole, is under wide debate today.[3] The search for "the" husband in women's fiction today has dissolved into a variety of quests with less-determinate patterns: for physical gratification, for love, for self, for security, for "fulfillment." These may take longer to find; and both men and women may gain the capacity to contribute to them only slowly and, indeed, may develop them only rather late.

At the same time, entry into marriage in American society, no less than earlier in the century, is still said to depend on love, which in our culture is understood to be spontaneous. But love ordinarily has an explicitly age-graded aspect: "puppy" love is different from "mature" love. "If you've never been kissed, you've never been ardently loved, before you are twenty-six, then beware! Love, at eighteen may be just a lark, a game, but at twenty-six, the starved senses, suddenly aroused, whirl with a giddiness that blinds clear thinking."[4] A second culturally defined dimension of marital love, roughly distinguishing "fleshly" from what might be called "obligational" love, has also usually been thought to be influenced by the chronological ages of the lovers and their ages relative to one another.[5] Thus have age norms of marriage been intertwined, as in Sylvia's case, with the ways people are supposed to *feel* toward each other and the forms these feelings are encouraged to take.

Two decades after the exposition of the conventions by which Sylvia finally learned to live, two best-selling books roundly condemned contemporary patterns of early marriage as a special bane to American middle-class women. Debate over the shape of the way young people should approach marriage had moved from the personal to the political. Today we view Helen Gurley Brown's *Sex and the Single Girl* as a period piece and honor Betty Friedan's *The Feminine Mystique* as the opening (or reopening) gun in a heroic battle to realign the genders. Both books offered arresting arguments that women's personal fulfillment was sabotaged by early pursuit of marriage and parenthood. But their prescriptions differed radically.[6]

> I think a single woman's biggest problem is coping with the people who are trying to marry her off! . . . Finding *him* is all she can think about or talk about when . . . her years as a single women can be too rewarding to rush out of. . . . I think marriage is insurance for the *worst* years of your life. During your best years you don't need a husband. You do need a man of course every step of the way, and they are often cheaper emotionally and a lot more fun by the dozen.[7]

> The problem that has no name—which is simply the fact that American women are kept from growing to their full human capacities—is taking a far greater toll on the physical and mental health of our country than any known disease. . . . If we continue to produce millions of young mothers who stop their growth and education short of identity, . . . we are committing, quite simply, genocide, starting with the mass burial of American women. . . . We need a drastic reshaping of the cultural image of femininity to reach maturity, identity, completeness of self, without conflict with sexual fulfillment, . . . to stop the early-marriage movement, stop girls from growing up wanting to be 'just a housewife.'[8]

At the time these tracts appeared, the age at which women were marrying had *already* been moving upward for half a decade. What is important is not demographic precision, however, but the passion with which the authors spoke to and as women, yet from startlingly different perspectives and with such contrasting tone: one recalling the coyness of such Hollywood confections as the Tony Curtis-Natalie Wood *Sex and the Single Girl*, the other foreshadowing changes we even now are assimilating. Women who faced the world quite differently sensed that there was something wrong with young women's life course and that *as women* they had a stake in rectifying it.

Brown took on herself the major task of promoting an open and enthusiastic recognition of female sexuality, so that in its various guises it is seen as suffusing the life of the "mature" single woman. "Theoretically a 'nice' single woman has no sex life," she remarks. "What nonsense! She has a better sex life than most of her married friends. . . . Since for a female getting there is at *least* half the fun, a single woman has reason to prize the luxury of taking long, gossamer, attenuated, pulsating trips before finally arriving in bed. A married woman and her husband have precious little time and energy for romance."[9] But Brown's transvaluation is accomplished by promoting the single-girl phase as a period of almost single-minded focus on *fun* with men, however varied, exquisite, and (but for that last time when the right man comes along) transitory. "Liking men is sexy. It is by and large just about the sexiest thing you can do. . . . And there is quite a lot more to it than simply wagging your tail every time a man pats you on the head. You must wag your tail, or course, . . . but there are about five thousand more aggressive ways to demonstrate liking. . . . You must spend time plotting how to make him happier. Not just him . . . *them!*"[10] Sexiness, practically, inheres in plotting, luring, tempting, challenging, especially at the workplace, and, above all, *enjoying* men. All this is a learned skill, one substantial enough to rightly command a longish time in its practice, a period brought to an end only by a marriage on the terms that Brown understands it.

For Friedan, this kind of sexual triumph, on the ideological level, is no solution; it is part of the problem. Once, she argues, women did have to liberate their sexuality from the pedestal, but postwar gender ideology had already changed this before she (or Brown) wrote. "The split in the new image opens a different fissure—the feminine woman, whose goodness includes the desires of the flesh, and the career woman, whose evil includes every desire of the separate self." [11] And this separate self is exactly what Friedan believed women deserved as their birthright, and needed for their mental health—contradicting the popular psychology of the day that (like Brown) saw women's problem in sexual neuroses. Education and then employment would save women, not lustier, more extensive courtship habits.

Contemporary married life seemed dreary to both Friedan and Brown, and both believed that it would be far less dreary if it were entered into later. The postponement of marriage had for both authors the secondary advantage of superior choice of mate, and the primary advantage of prior "fulfillment" for the woman. "Those who glom on to men so that they can collapse with relief, spend the rest of their days shining up their status symbol and figure they never have to reach, stretch, learn, grow, face dragons or make a living again are the ones to be pitied. They, in my opinion, are the unfulfilled ones." (And this is *Brown* speaking.) [12] The two authors each sought to revise the life course of American women, in the belief that the content and value of marriage (and, explicitly in both cases, parenthood) are in part determined by the courses women took on the way there.

Both authors would extend schooling, the extent of which both saw as far too subject to foreshortening by women in the interest of early marriage. Both would make the occupational life a far lengthier and less casual part of women's life courses, although Friedan advised that women seek vocation in the classic sense, while Brown advised frequent job changes or at best a shallow careerism to facilitate the pursuit of fun with men. And they agreed that sexuality must be recognized and accepted outside of marriage, lest it drive toward one that was poorly timed. While the prophetic quality of these prescriptions may (in hindsight) be more a matter of simple observation, the fact is that the scenarios Friedan and Brown proposed do describe in many ways how life was to change in the next decade and a half. How people grow up—the life course—has been a subject for debate through much of our century. The debate, however, more commonly addresses directly the *content* of phases of the life course rather than their proper timing or sequencing. Recent debate on marriage provides a case in point.

HOW TO MARRY

Typically, pre-World War II fictions played with the age norms of marriage by setting youthfully eager wishes off against essentially *external* hindrances, which delayed marriage. The culmination of true love was postponed because, while the flesh was eager, the economy often made it impossible for couples to fulfill with sufficient certainty the obligations of true love. In the prosperous postwar period, however, the willing flesh of the enamored arrived at marriage (younger) after conquering not external hindrances but the actors' own doubts and confusions, characteristically placed within the sexual realm. A typical didactic fiction in a 1957 issue of *True Love Stories*, "Engagement Jitters," provides a case in point.

> Diane Glazer had met Raymond Tappan eighteen months before. Their courtship was in no way unusual; as their interest in one another grew, so did the number of their dates. They'd been going steady a little over a year when Ray asked Diane to marry him. He was twenty, his military training was behind him, his future as a clerk in the post office promising. Diane had suffered no doubts when Ray proposed. She loved him, he loved her; what could be simpler? Of course she'd marry him! In six months, a June wedding? Of course! . . . But as the date of the wedding grew nearer, Diane found some of her excitement dying down. . . . Before, when Ray had kissed her, she'd always had to fight her raging emotions. Now sometimes, she wanted to run when he drew her into his arms. Oh sure, they'd talked frankly about sex. . . . but talking and doing were two different things! And the doing part was only a few weeks away.[13]

Correspondingly, when Hannah Stone and Abraham Stone added a new section on ideal marriage age to their virtual catechism on health in marriage in the "completely revised" postwar edition of their well-known *Marriage Manual* (1937), their prescription moved the offset against premature lust from the external realm to the internal. "The best age for marriage is the age at which emotional and social maturity is attained. In general . . . the early twenties are the best years for marriage." But "the extent of a person's maturity in thinking and behavior" outranked both "chronological age" and "the economic situation" in indicating when to marry.[14]

In retrospect, we are hard put to determine whether the ideal marriage age had shifted downward because people grew up emotionally quicker, or vice versa, or whether the removal of material hindrances to marriage allowed many people to marry younger, encouraging a simultaneous change in the age people considered best for marriage and the way people at a given age felt about themselves. In fact, one cannot say in the abstract, for material circumstances, values, feelings, and institutional arrangements are all thoroughly intertwined. Transitions like marriage often demand a certain material wherewithal, and under some conditions, changes in material circumstances may be granted a certain primacy, on the assumption of institutional constancy, as in the matter of parental underwriting of marriage. But just as this volume will discern changes in the material environment, it will also show institutional changes as well as normative and even emotional ones. My purpose is not to disentangle cause so much as it is to portray in some richness the way in which the push "into one's own" was repeatedly revised over a half-century.

A series of life course *transitions*, including marriage, similarly freighted and indeed interrelated, are the subject of this book. Sequentially, marriage is at the center of the events I will explore; it is preceded by the inception of what roughly can be called dating and by the initiation of sexual intimacy.[15] As courtship "leads to" marriage, so marriage "leads to" parenthood, the fourth transition treated here. (First marriage is by no means ultimate marriage since the 1960s; thus, my account of "family-building" also treats divorce.)

The path into one's own is somewhat vaguely bordered, but it is no less bordered for that fact. In twentieth-century America, for instance, as elsewhere and at other times, powerful social forms have gathered about life course transitions which are distinctly but not precisely prescriptive in content.[16] The most obvious is the wedding, a ritual that in twentieth-century America has always seemed somehow anachronistic, but which, as "tradition," has always seemed to renew itself. *Bride's Magazine*'s 1973 revision of its *Bride's Book of Etiquette* instructs readers that "most wedding customs evolved from a wish to symbolize all the good things the union meant to the couple and the community. . . . Those that continue to symbolize the same good intentions . . . will flourish. . . . Other, older traditions are gradually outgrown and eventually abandoned. . . . Do look over some of these time-honored customs and choose those that appeal to you and your families' sentiments." [17] The wedding is the particular ritual whose form symbolizes compliance with widely held values, *including those regarding appropriate timing*.

Religious weddings, especially large church weddings, constitute in the contemporary American context a form of communal ritual oversight of the marriage. [18] Couples marrying in religious ceremonies have been markedly more concentrated in the modal age-at-marriage categories than those marrying in civil ceremonies. This pattern, if anything, *intensified over time* between 1961 and 1974. [19] Reeves's data on marriages in New Haven indicate a marked trend toward a somewhat enlarged proportion of civil marriages among all marriages from 1870 to 1940 but rising only to about 18 percent. [20] Long-term annual observations for the city of Philadelphia indicate a slow, gradual increase in secular weddings from an initial figure of about 2 percent around the turn of the century to a peak of around 8 percent in the early 1920s, followed by another decline, to about 5 percent in 1937, at the end of the series. [21] National data for 1939, 1940, and 1948 show that at this time about a quarter of marriages were civil. [22] When the national vital registration system began to regularly record type of ceremony in 1960, the proportion of civil marriages was slightly lower than this. The trend since then has been a very gradual increase. [23] The data, taken together, indicate that during the twentieth century, there have been modest changes in fashion in type of ceremony, but nothing more than this. In view of the dramatic changes in the timing, structuring, and terminability of marriages during this period, the stability in the ritual is remarkable. As a passage from one stage of life to another—although both stages may have developed new content—marriage continued to matter, to the community as to the bride and groom. Continuity in ritual provided resources that in part offset circumstantial changes in the way young people came into their own.

Obtaining systematic information on weddings themselves over time requires a certain resourcefulness. Newspaper reports of weddings offer such an insight into trends in ritual surrounding the entry to married life. Wedding notices are stylized, their contents partly editorial whim and partly the preference of the family member who reports the wedding to the paper, so we read not so much a report on *what happened* as an account of *what should have happened*.[24] But exactly this quality is what interests us about the wedding *as a ritual*, and from this perspective, stylized stories in local newspapers serve nobly. To respond to the indeterminate but not improbable inclusiveness bias of wedding notices, and especially the possibility that this has changed over time, I have drawn clusters of wedding stories from consecutive late spring and early summer issues from 1925 to 1975 of three newspapers from places varying in population size, on the grounds that the smaller the town, the likelier the incorporation of people of lesser means. The three newspapers, all from Minnesota, included a metropolitan but localistic newspaper, the St. Paul *Pioneer Press*, a small-town daily, the Albert Lea *Times*, and a small-town weekly, the Thief River Falls *Tribune*.[25]

As though in response to the plasticity of marriage *timing*—a central theme of this book—there has been a distinct secular trend toward increasing *elaboration* of the rituals surrounding these events. One of the more prominent aspects of this trend has been a growing emphasis (in the wedding notices) on large ceremonies. To accommodate expanded attendance, weddings have been shifted from weekdays (6 in 10 in the 1920s in all three towns) to weekends (8 in 10 by the 1970s). Newspaper accounts more and more have included the names and origins of wedding guests from beyond the vicinity. By 1957, they often listed "honored guests" from afar.

Concurrently, the number of *named offices* in the wedding expanded markedly, as formalities became more elaborate. And the *reception* has emerged as a central part of the wedding story. "A wedding is a solemn ceremony and the reception that fol-

Table 1. Wedding Receptions in Minnesota Newspapers

	% with Reception Mentioned	*Where Place of Reception Is Mentioned, Proportion Held in (in percentages)*			*Number of Articles*
		Private Home	*Hall, Club, Restaurant*	*Church-Related Building*	
St. Paul					
1925–26	72	90	10	0	105
1932–33	78	66	25	9	58
1941	80	43	47	11	61
1946	79	33	35	33	58
1957	92	20	58	22	60
1969	92	6	66	28	57
Albert Lea					
1925–26	78	95	5	0	27
1932–33	63	61	28	11	30
1941	86	63	22	14	58
1946–47	88	27	28	47	60
1957	98	10	16	75	59
1975	96	9	24	67	50
Thief River Falls					
1922–25	79	96	4	0	33
1940–41	87	67	18	15	39
1946	93	70	11	19	30
1957	97	15	21	64	35
1973	100	6	24	70	54

SOURCE: See discussion in text.

lows should be joyous. It's traditional to gather friends and relatives to celebrate the happy day."[26] Table 1 details two aspects of the reception trend. The first shows that gradually (in each newspaper) the reception became an obligatory part of the story, and thus, putatively, of a ritually complete wedding. At the same time, the reception moved from the home of the bridal family to church parlors in the small towns and to private clubs or restaurants in St. Paul. The reception's rise points to the secularization of the wedding ritual (even as the proportion of religious *ceremonies* has remained roughly stable) and its increasingly public orientation. Surely, this shift does not bespeak a lessening of social oversight over the marriage but a shift— or, more properly, a broadening—in its focus. Indeed, nuptial couples now were twice on inspection, twice required to be grave, then joyous and sociable before they left on their honeymoons, symbolic of their separateness.

The trend of officiants within the formal portion of the wedding has been distinctly toward the masculine, a tendency tied to the move toward elaborate weddings, and also their increasingly public orientation. A marked rise in the prevalence and number of ushers represents the most striking instance. Ushers, typically, were of the generation of the couple who saw fit to affirm the value of an orderly passage into marriage. In Albert Lea, for example, wedding stories in 1925 mentioned an average of three wedding officiants but in the period from 1973 to 1975, no fewer than nine. Girls and women, however, have increasingly filled a burgeoning, imaginative list of reception roles—"coffee pourer" and the like—that scarcely ever were assigned to men. In the case of both wedding and reception officiants, nonrelatives have gained in numbers more quickly than have relatives, but there have also been growing numbers of relatives in official roles. When we categorize relatives with stated wedding roles according to whether they are relatives of the bride or the groom, we find consistently heavier participation from the brides' side. The wedding in American culture— no less so in 1975 than in 1925—was to be arranged by the bride's side of the family, as etiquette books insisted. As ever, the bride had more at stake, and she accordingly convened more of her kin. But at the same time, the community's ritual stake had seemingly grown.

Although the rather steady trends in ritual oversight do not correspond to the ups and downs in the fragility of marriages, at least as registered by divorce rates, it certainly is plausible that a growing *awareness* of the voluntary nature of both entrance into and departure from the married state occasioned the evidence of enlarged ritual communal concern.

DEFINING SYLVIA'S CHOICES

The timing of transitions in lives is individually determined in our society—to a degree, probably increasingly so (as in the case of marriage), but not entirely. At the same time, the location of the transition point along the life course is socially recognized, monitored, and sanctioned, although the timing of some transitions is obviously more strongly sanctioned than that of others. When I was of an age to protest such matters, a popular song lamented that "they tried to tell us we're too young, too young to really be in love." "They" cared not because they believed that young people's emotions were of real concern to them but because "in love" has been a significant marker in twentieth-century American lives, with attendant rights and privileges, with consequences for related and subsequent action.[27]

Analogously, if less sublimely, the licensing of automobile drivers, which at two distinct points in the course of life has been a matter of concern to me, is and has long been an age-graded, gender-differentiated, societally sanctioned phenomenon. It is also a phenomenon with an unremarked recent history that is indicative of the ways the life course may change. For boys initially and increasingly for girls, the capacity to drive virtually defined a life course stage. That is, driving was not simply a privilege with obvious utility but also definitive of *a stage in one's life*, although admittedly one without a particular name attached to it. Excellent national data since World War II on drivers' licenses by age[28] reveal that the growing availability of automobiles encouraged more and more boys, younger and younger, to take out licenses. The steepest increase was at age fifteen to seventeen, when most American boys in the late 1940s became licensed drivers. For girls, the age-grading pattern was always less steep, taking more years for an entire cohort of girls to become drivers. But over time girls, have increasingly approached boys' pace of transition to licenseship, the convergence occurring initially at the older teen ages and more recently at the younger ages. Over time, the steepness of age-grading for girls has come to approach that of boys. This narrowed the age span during which in any boy-girl couple the boy alone would possess this legal, practical, and symbolic competence, a point of some symbolic and perhaps practical consequence for gender relationships.

There is more to the story than adolescents' own choices, as in the case of many of life's highly freighted transitional moments. For adults controlled the governments that licensed drivers, and their response to adolescents' increased material resources was symptomatic of the often quiet debate over the nature of the adolescent years that has been carried on in twentieth-century America. In the early 1960s, there was a broad movement to limit the freedom of children to drive by raising the legal age for licensing. Some states came to offer two age-graded licenses, a full and an aptly named "junior" license. By the late 1960s, at just about the point when adolescent boys were about as completely licensed as they would become, adults relented and began to add their full normative sanction to an early transition to driverhood. Often, adults now inserted the completion of school-sponsored drivers' training courses as an intermediate stage of adult-organized socialization to the road.[29]

In American society, as in most societies, although with varying emphasis, age is an important social marker. Yet age (even in combination with gender) is not ordinarily—in our society—a status to which *in and of itself* particular rights and privileges are due, certainly after early childhood and before retirement. Rather, chronological age provides the most important single cue for *a series of transitions* that mark the departure from a prior status or relationship to a major social institution and the entry into a subsequent status or relationship. Two major American institutions affecting young adults, formal education and the armed forces, are explicitly age stratified. Many occupations build age increments of income into the normal careers they imply.[30] The paths through life have been, accordingly, marked by traditions, entered into by individuals attendant on more or less clear cues and sanctions.

On the one hand, on-time transitions are, as a matter of course, culturally prepared, cushioned by anticipatory socialization and by supportive institutional arrangements.[31] On the other hand, and correspondingly, individuals moving too slowly or too quickly through a particular transition are often admonished, where they are not restrained by administrative regulations or by positive law itself: a too-early retiree will receive no Social Security benefits for some years; youths seeking to marry too young may be told by the state to get their parents' permission, or they may not be allowed to marry even with their parents' consent; school "dropouts" are so stigmatized that they will feel they have failed to complete an expected transition rather than having simply chosen to spend those years at work instead of in school. The violation of these norms may be quite powerfully sanctioned. School dropout offers an example of a norm for which strong sanctioning has developed recently and rapidly. In 1964, 9 percent of white male high school graduates ages 16 to 24 not in college were unemployed, compared to 14 percent of like high school dropouts. Among blacks, the comparable figures were 19 percent and 18 percent, respectively. But by 1976, this "price" of dropping out had risen from 5 percent for whites and -1 percent for blacks to 11 percent for whites (9 percent vs. 20 percent) and 10 percent for blacks (22 percent vs. 32 percent).[32]

The life course perspective holds that while biographical sequences are not by any means wholly determinate, they are determined to a degree, and in two senses. First, the steps one has already taken make more probable particular future outcomes: if I marry at 21, I am more likely to have a child by 25 than if I marry at 23. Second, both the timing and the sequencing of important life events are to a degree socially determined, whether structurally, normatively, or both: if married men, or fathers, are deferred from military service in their early twenties, and military service is a life stage neither greatly honored nor highly rewarded, there will be added incentive to marry at 21 rather than at 25.[33] The life course perspective argues that the determinate elements of these patterns constitute objective "social facts" and, no less, that individuals live and experience their own biographies as aware actors, who do not merely receive these patterns as in the nature of things, but *construct and evaluate them as they move along*, looking both forward and back. Culture, in this view, although both a set of symbols and a structure of belief and thus not equal to the sum of individual outlooks, is in substantial measure responsive to this sum.

Under current assumptions, conformity with the social and

cultural cues promoting timely movement through the life course is expected to be directly satisfying to the actor. When, on balance, this seemingly does not happen—as has been documented commonly happens when married couples first become parents—troubled commentary is heard. In 1926, Margaret Sanger expressed the conventional understanding of the motivation to parenthood among happily married wives in terms of a "maternal desire . . . intensified and matured, . . . the road by which she travels onward toward completely rounded self-development, . . . the unfolding and realization of her higher nature."[34] A decade later, however, Lewis Terman was embarrassed to report on the basis of his extensive empirical investigation, *Psychological Factors in Marital Happiness,* that "the widespread belief" that Sanger and others reflected was not on the average borne out by the facts. Nevertheless, it was "reasonable to suppose that the presence of children is capable of affecting the happiness of a given marriage in either direction."[35]

Another decade later, Evelyn Millis Duvall and Reuben Hill reasserted that "for the couple ready for this step, having a baby is a supremely satisfying experience," a position for which at least one fine height-of-the-baby-boom study found some empirical justification.[36] But data from the late 1960s and 1970s showed that this was no longer true—if it ever was—for the average American couple. Summarizing the results of many studies, including a soundly based study of their own, Norval Glenn and Sara McLanahan concluded that in view of the fact that "in American society children tend to lower their parents' marital and global happiness," it was "ironic that most Americans want to have children" and that they do so.[37] The irony, of course, hinges entirely on the individualistic—and arguably hedonistic—assumptions governing our interpretation of life course transitions. Such assumptions, however useful they may be in simplifying interpretation of motivation, fly in the face of evidence that even in a relatively short number of years, contraception, by changing the material circumstances of *choice*, has participated in a redefinition of the "should" that has surely always played a part in the motivation to become a parent.[38]

Some transitions are typically more age determinate than others. On the whole, transitions earlier in the life course—where state bureaucracies are given greater sway—have tended to occur more uniformly to members of a given cohort than those occurring later.[39] And for some elements of the population, some life course transitions have been relatively more loosely timed. An instance of this, relevant to the account to follow, has to do with the timing of marriage, which has always been considerably more closely supervised (and, correspondingly, more nearly uniform) for women than for men. Intuitively, one can see how this fact is related to other aspects of the asymmetry between the genders. And thus it should not be too surprising that the gender differential in this regard has been declining recently. How culturally influenced the marriage transition is, for both men and women, is attested to by the near-disappearance of the category "bachelor" as a culturally recognized (if not universal) life course stage for men and the development during the past two decades of a closely parallel popular understanding of a rather extended unmarried adult state—"living with"—for members of both genders.[40]

Indeed, the very concept of a life course "stage" like bachelorhood implies cultural notions about the content of that stage and about its place within one or more of the trajectories its occupants are presumed to be working out. We here witnessed, for instance, the passing of one strongly supported middle-class norm, that of men's economic independence at marriage.[41] It must be remembered, however, that if culture sets some of the terms for the staging of the life course, it does not set them all—certainly for individuals, but perhaps for whole cohorts. Gunhild Hagestad's insight, that "some of us find ourselves in life stages for which our society has no clear culturally shared expectations" is important for understanding the recent social history of the American people and useful for interpreting the materials presented below. "Demographic change [for instance] may have been so rapid and so dramatic that we have experienced 'cultural lags'" in the construction of normatively defined "stages."[42]

CONSTRUCTING A HISTORY OF THE LIFE COURSE

Increasing attention has been given to the life course over the past two decades by an interdisciplinary grouping of scholars.

Their concerns have evolved from a focus on the *cohort* among demographers,[43] the relevance of the notion of *age stratification* to social gerontologists,[44] and a concern for *life span psychology* among students of human development.[45] Somewhat more recently, it became evident to workers in several of these fields that if they were genuinely to import a processual orientation to social science, *historical change* could no longer be ignored, as was so characteristic of American social science at the time. "Career lines are structured by the realities of historical times and circumstance; by the opportunities, normative pressures, and adaptive requirements of altered situations; and by those expectations, commitments, and resources which are brought to these situations."[46] Both historical events and trends affect individuals differently according to life course stage, sometimes affecting the life course itself in the process. "Processes commonly denoted as [individual] development . . . [are] social products to be understood within the particular features of a specific societal and historical context." In that context, the analyst seeks "the causal bases of age stratification within the social system that lead to some level of age-graded events for a collectivity at a particular historical moment and to broad similarities in individual life courses or psychological biographies during that period."[47]

From a historical life course standpoint, structure may—sometimes—be seen in dynamic perspective. "The important contribution that historical research makes is in specifying and examining diachronic changes, which often have a more direct impact on the life course than macrosocial changes. Most importantly, historians can identify the convergence of socioeconomic and cultural forces, which are characteristic of a specific time period and which more directly influence the timing of life transitions than more large-scale or long-term linear developments."[48] *Children of the Great Depression* (1974) is justly viewed as the pioneering empirical exploration of this fundamental insight.[49] It examines life courses of children who in varying ways faced the Depression's rigors and provides an acute treatment of many of the theoretical issues. Especially eloquent has been Elder's insistence that the historically oriented life course approach be explicitly connected with the *agentic* perspective on individual experience and choice carried within the sociological discipline by the "Chicago school" variant developed by W. I. Thomas and carried on by Herbert Blumer and Everett C. Hughes.[50]

Martin Kohli has argued in an exceptionally thought-provoking essay that not only have particular stages changed historically but also *the salience of the life course itself*.[51] The "chronologization" of life, he maintains, has grown apace with modernity (or capitalist development), as "part of the more general process in which individuals are set free from the bonds of status, locality and family." Such a process is of quite long standing, of course, and yet there now appear signs of reversals—the kinds of indefinition that individuals themselves must resolve, which Hagestad refers to. Kohli admits there are many hints that *individuation*, not chronologization, has become the dominant trend over the last decade or two. Nevertheless, he maintains, "the successful institutionalization of the life course is the basis for the present individualizing departure from it."

Presented narratively, the burden of my account is to demonstrate concretely the power of such insights as Kohli's. The chapters that follow show a life course segment rendered (somewhat ironically) more salient and, in some respects, more determinate by the increasingly explicit debate that has emerged over its construction. The number of contestants in this debate has been progressively enlarged, so that over the twentieth century, teenagers *qua* age group have come to articulate—and to have articulated for them, especially in music—a distinctive view of how they wish to grow up. This is not to say that teenagers differed from adults in what they wanted to grow up *into*, but, instead, about how and when. I show, thus, how dating, a contested institution constructed by "kids," was connected with the institution of marriage in a way that by the 1970s seemed decidedly conservative. As I also show, increasingly self-conscious considerations of gender played a part in the debate about dating, marriage, and the youthful life course as a whole. It is apparent, too, that a distinctive organization of the youthful life course has more lately emerged among the inner-city black poor, a subject for debate within the black community and for denunciation outside it.

We currently are witness to an adult effort to condemn large portions of American youth as a "postponed generation."[52] Explaining the inappropriateness of youth's hesitant passage through the life course by "scarcity," Susan Littwin describes a generation of middle-class young people who had learned to "paint or run a mock constitutional convention or jog six miles," only to learn that in the hard world beyond adolescence "no one cared." "It is hard enough to establish an adult identity, even in the best of times," she argues, employing a characteristic translation of roles into a psychological state. "What today's twenty-to-thirty-year-olds have elected to do is continue the identity search while avoiding reality," that is, the signals of the current job market, "and that makes it exceedingly slow work."[53] The reader can hardly fail to detect like themes in neo-conservative condemnation of the mutual failing of one another by schools and students.

My examination of transitions is embedded in a more inclusive study of the life course in which transitions are seen from the perspective of their *sequence*. Determinate sequences underlie the "career," or, in the less evocative terminology that Elder for that reason prefers, *trajectories*. Within a given culture, those transitions seen as part of the same trajectory commonly have a normatively prescribed (or at least preferred) sequence. "Through cultural and structural forces, established career lines present individuals with particular constraints, incentives, and options as they work out their trajectories."[54] Through this perspective, one is led to link the examination of the socially and culturally structured circumstances individuals find themselves in, with their chosen responses to those circumstances. Individuals understand their own situations in terms of the process— their relative efficaciousness in it, the extent of positive or negative sanctions they have received—by which they have arrived at their present stage.

Often quite prominent in popular debates about the life course are disagreements not about timing but about the sequencing of transitions, about the appropriate shape of trajectories, about what it means when a handful of actors, or growing numbers of actors, violate what is ordinarily done in relating one change in their lives to another. Such an argument often has a less arbitrary sound than that over the timing transitions, being couched in terms of "competence" rather than "maturity"—something presumably an attribute of the individual rather than something substantially derived from the social definition of the individual's chronological age. Consistent with the individualistic trend of our times, however, sequencing arguments have commonly faded on the demonstration of effective "competence" by those claiming the right to out-of-sequence transitions.

An important example is the blurring of the once well-guarded normative sequence of leaving school and entry into the labor force. The decades since World War II have seen a massive expansion of the employment rate (and the hours of work) among high school (and college) boys and girls, at the same time as out-of-school boys and girls *of the same ages* are suffering *increasing* unemployment. In the interest of reducing the risk of "dropping out"—a distasteful transition—schools have adopted a number of mechanisms that permit and even encourage tentative entry to the labor force before graduation.[55]

The increasingly embarrassed giggle that accompanies contemporary use of the term "virgin" (in the context of persons, not derived uses applied to materials) is likewise evidence of massively lessened vigilance regarding the sequence of coitus and marriage, especially for women. To recur to popular music, whether one wishes to take "love" literally or metaphorically, it is apparent that the "love and marriage . . . go together like a horse and carriage" sequencing formula of my adolescence has been uncoupled, to be reassembled every which way. Many hope that the fear of heterosexually transmitted AIDS will return this sequence to its earlier state.

The life course perspective brings together historians' concern with *experience* and the recognition that aggregates like "populations" do not have intentions. It allows us to take advantage of the fact that samples of populations leave accounts of how they feel about their actions. Obviously, this is a very broad perspective, and not one that proposes a singular methodology. But it does propose that students of the life course focus their attention in a number of ways.

1. As a necessary step toward simplifying, we reduce what is in fact a continuous moment-to-moment development to a series

of what, *a priori*, are defined as transitions: marriage, parenthood, and military service are typical.

2. These transitions are seen as involving changes in individuals' social roles, to accord with changed statuses as defined by social institutions. Thus, becoming a father involves acting in a particular kind of reciprocal relationship with an infant and involves being known publicly as one who should perform a certain set of obligations that pertain to occupying the status of "father" in the institution "family."

3. The cultural meaning attached to such roles and statuses is not fixed, but, in part, changes according to the experience of the actors who are living in them. That "fatherhood" no longer brings draft deferral somewhat changes what it means to fathers.

4. The experience of a given status is not divorced from the other sets of roles and statuses occupied simultaneously by the actors: the experience of "motherhood" is different for mothers who are simultaneously wives and those who are not.

The empirical emphasis of students of the life course has been substantially, although not entirely, on concerns usually associated with social psychology, especially having to do with the learning of life stage roles. A number of scholars within the discipline of sociology, however, especially in its more demographic reaches, have worked with life course concepts in such a way that they move toward aggregate concerns that are in some ways more akin to the kind of questions posed by historians (which I emphasize in the chapters that follow). Sandra Hofferth, for instance, has apportioned the aggregate experience of recent cohorts, subdivided by race, to time in childhood spent in incompleted, completed, and broken families.[56] Peter Uhlenberg, in a number of superb studies that take up particular transitions and sequences, has estimated the prevalence, timing, and variation in timing of these transitions over historical time, alerting scholars to the truly marked changes in the modal life experiences of historical populations.[57] Dennis Hogan's ambitious *Transitions and Social Change*[58] is based almost exclusively on a single large retrospective interview survey of the transitions of American men from youth to adulthood, covering in a very different way the same general subject of this volume. Hogan has looked closely at the individual level at both the timing and sequencing of transitions and is as concerned with the *amount and sources of variation* within the single-year birth cohorts he examines as with *central tendencies*. In addition, he has sought to explain these statistically with a number of independent "historical" variables characterizing succeeding birth cohorts.

My interest has long been in the Janus-faced relationship of these changes in the aggregate to the choices as faced by the individuals making them. In reviewing Elder's path-breaking *Children of the Great Depression* in 1975, I argued that for all Elder's concern to place individual development in historical context, in the end he was most interested in the one-way relationship between the two—in the impact of large-scale historical change on the way individuals' lives were lived. I argued that a social-historical approach to the life course might be no less interested in the way those altered individual experiences *aggregated* to constitute a new *context* for others living through these changes. I maintained that when Elder examined the impact of the Great Depression on the subsequent lives of children and youth at the time by comparing those whose families had suffered substantial declines in income with those whose families had not suffered declines, he implicitly assumed that the *direct* impact of economic deprivation markedly outweighed the *indirect* impact—that which might be felt by *all* families who *observed* others' plights, who *anticipated* hardship, who *compared* their situations not with the period before the Depression but with what might have been. That Elder found differences on the level of individual families implies nothing about the existence or magnitude of universal, contextual effects.[59] Even "kids" can make history, as their choices aggregate into behavioral patterns and, rationalized, become normative. It will be shown how dating, in the 1920s a liberating invention largely of girls' making, became by the 1960s a vehicle that often constrained girls in the choices they now were permitted to make.

The amount of certainty and determinism in the environment of individuals has varied historically,[60] and I find it a fascinating paradox that the relaxation of certainty in the material environment may possibly give one's community the freedom to impose a regime of individual decision-making that in fact may be more, rather than less, externally determined in the perception of the individual.[61] The early commitment of young members of the postwar cohort to marriage or childbirth had not in itself committed other members to similar prompt action. Rather, change in cohort behavior was essentially the sum of annual responses to period phenomena: That is, memory was not cohort-specific. But the kinds of period phenomena I show to have had an impact on the timing of vital events were sometimes subtle enough that actors did not always understand themselves to be responding to them. In fact, their response was not to them directly but to changed circumstances underlying the balance of prudence, idealism, and optimism that characterizes individuals' decisions to form a family. As environments have gradually shifted, so have Americans' sense of how one "ought" to form a family, but these shifts did not affect particular cohorts uniquely, bringing about a society that on the level of belief was stratified by date of birth (or marriage, or parenthood) about values regarding family formation. Yet environment did not impinge uniformly on people of different ages, and herein lay the mechanism by which characteristic timing patterns in the life course changed.

Were these kinds of changes over time in the experience of cohorts a product of some initial cohort characteristic— whether predisposition or powerful early experience or radically different upbringing—or did historical experience occurring over the life course of the cohorts produce the distinctive life course curves? This question amounts to trying to decipher the impact on age-graded behavior of "cohort" and "period" processes.[62] The original impetus for this line of questioning came from the discovery in the early 1950s[63] that the accelerated birth schedules of that period were not a reversion to older large-family norms but instead constituted a long-lasting revision of the tempo of Americans' childbearing, a new style of family formation possibly related to a new style of family.[64]

"Period" effects were overall the most important in explaining those aspects of the life course that concern me here. In no instance did the kind of circumstances that typically have differential effects on persons of different ages—say, the unemployment produced by economic depression or the severe dislocation of a large call to military conscription—set a whole cohort into a distinctive timing pattern that was sustained through its life course. Social history does not exclusively study cause and effect, but it ought to sort them out when possible. I am arguing here that a set of environments promoting early marriage and childbirth (for example) made possible the articulation and, no doubt, the practice of a variety of normative schedules that were not themselves innovations but rationalizations. Indeed, as we shall see, these rationalizations typically were drawn from elements already present within the set of ideas explaining (and, admittedly, setting outer limits to) family-formation behavior in recent times.

Even though it is apparent that the marriage and parenthood "schedules" of cohorts changed very markedly, it also seems to be the case that it was the environment for marriage and childbirth that changed lastingly, that this changed environment eventually affected members of virtually all cohorts undergoing either of these transitions, and that new life course schedules tended to come into effect which influenced *all subsequent birth cohorts*—at least until another "period" phenomenon contributed to the establishment of a new pattern. This is not to say that the heightened early pace of vital events had no impact on the lives of cohort members in subsequent years. It does mean, however, that the sets of actors' perceptions, values, and understandings that arose as part of these new schedules were not unique to particular cohorts but were shared by all of an age to be married or become a parent.

DEMOGRAPHY AND THE SOCIAL HISTORY OF THE
LIFE COURSE

This volume is about the summing up of multiply caused, individually engaged lines of action that altogether amount to a change in the way a whole cohort of individuals face the world. I would like to know with certainty whether (as I suspect, and as I will argue based on admittedly modest evidence) as dating became an institutionalized stage in the adolescent life course, an introduction to heterosexual physical pleasure became a more rapid and more certain concomitant of courtship.

This must inevitably be "latent history," in Bernard Bailyn's sense, history that emphasizes themes—certainly the aggregate themes—that were not necessarily important or perhaps even present in the minds of the participants. The debates over aspects of the life course that I discuss as often as not *followed* behavioral change; or, a quietly institutionalized pattern like engagement may change with no explicit cultural debate at all. The justification of writing latent history is that the themes it takes up are important in some sense that contemporaries did not recognize but that we can now recognize in hindsight. The justification here is that the life course, as a socially organized process of growing up, is an abstraction that allows us to focus a variety of simultaneously acting demographic, material, and cultural developments on one coherent aspect of experience of contemporaries. I hope this effort will enable us to see how sometimes subtle shifts in the way the sequence of life course events has been organized have brought individuals to the stage of parenthood, and to antecedent stages, differently prepared and with different understandings of what that stage entails. "One's own," along with the process of achieving it, has changed.

At the core of this book lies a demographic approach, sometimes applied unconventionally, one not massively different in its logic from that employed by the aggregate-level, neatly demographic empiricists, like Hofferth, Uhlenberg, or Hogan, although far more informal. In this vein I seek to discover, and thereafter to explain, group and over-time variations in *rates of transitions*—for example, annual rates of marriage among the unmarried, of first parenthood among those married during the previous year, or, by extension, of first premarital coitus among single virgins. Around this core, as much as evidence and imagination have permitted, I have tried to build a double contextual framework—of the fit of the individual transitions into the socially constructed life course and of the fit of this life course into the material and institutional imperatives of the day, as they impinged on individuals.

My commitment is to understand the life course as a series of individual decisions that are not determined but are nevertheless structured by external phenomena, including the prior behaviors of others in the same cohort. I argue that in the twentieth century, the youthful life course of Americans has been quite malleable. This is not so startling, however; in early modern England, the age of marriage moved sharply downward in response to the shift from a landed to a protoindustrial economic base.[65] What is special about the American situation in the twentieth century is the variety of forces to which life course timing responds, most notably, in the realm of beliefs. Especially striking in this account are the subcultural and institutional structures erected by young people themselves, which have played a substantial part in setting the timetable for coming into one's own. This underlines much of the enlarged *salience* of the youthful life course and explains, too, some of the heat of the on-and-off debate over it. For the way one grows up is closely related to what one becomes.

Demographers proceed by confining their measures as much as possible to those "at risk" of experiencing that which is of analytic interest, as I try to do here. Thus, although Alfred Kinsey's extraordinary data on sexual behavior permit me to measure a fair amount of important information on "petting," enabling an estimate of annual rates of transition into the status of "having petted," for instance, they unfortunately do *not* permit me to estimate like rates based only on those who are dating—even though (with some exceptions, of course) only those dating are really "at risk" of petting. Likewise, demographers proceed by progressively "refining" their measures. As much as possible, they measure what they are interested in for narrower and narrower groups, so that they may discover differential rates and seek reasons for these. So do I, although I am often constrained by the modest evidence available.

Because two of the transitions centrally treated in this book are commonly understood as demographic phenomena, and because my most secure and therefore more primary methods are demographic, this book focuses more than it otherwise might on *marriage* and *parenthood*, and somewhat less on other elements of the youthful life course. Marriage ("nuptiality" is the demographers' technical term for its study) has been widely studied and in recent times has been well documented. I focus on *first* marriage, with some reflections on departure or non-departure from it by way of divorce.[66]

My treatment of parenthood is something of a twist on the best-studied, best-documented aspect of demography, "fertility." While demographers are mainly interested in one particular product of the act of giving birth, the babies who will eventually replenish the population, I am interested in a different product, the parents who came into being with the birth of their first child. This means that only nonparents are at risk of becoming parents and that only firstborn children can be counted when I compile the rates according to which those at-risk couples become actual parents. Although most demographers' analysis of fertility is thus of no direct use to me, fertility data has been commonly enough tabulated by parity (birth order) that I can base my argument about the transition to parenthood quite solidly. Unfortunately, only in recent years has reliable information linking first-parity birth data to time since marriage been widely available, for where this is available, it permits me my preferred way of examining fertility—as the subsequent transition of a married couple, after however many years of marriage, into parenthood.

On the whole, marriage serves as the centerpiece around which I array other life course transitions, especially as I work to establish the relationship of the timing of one event to prior and subsequent events. In this account, then, divorce is by and large examined in a demographer's life course style as an event terminating a marriage after however many years, or, more in keeping with the marriage-centric tendencies of this book, non-divorce in any given year after a first marriage is seen as indication of the survival of that marriage. By the same token, the intent of my perspective moves me toward seeking to make statements about the extent to which coitus and other, less culturally freighted aspects of sexual exploration have preceded marriage. Were there consistent, reliable data, I would wish to know (changes in) the proportion of dating couples who had already petted who went on to coitus, as well as the proportion of individuals who had dated by ages 12, 13, 14, and so on, who had petted by ages 14, 15, 16, and so on, and who had had coitus by 16, 17, 18, and so on. I have to make do. By and large, I have chosen to relax my standards of certainty rather than my descriptive and analytic ambitions. But because the data are invariably weak as they approach the edges of my account, I use the solid core as an anchor.

Because this is a social-historical account, not a demographic one, the circumstances in which transitions are accomplished are of particular interest. Especially interesting are the institutionalized structures and rites that commonly surround transitional events. In a subsequent chapter, I make an effort to study *engagement* at a particular historical juncture at which the partly institutionalized life course stage was under pressure. Because of that pressure, I believe, documentary materials were produced from which the historian could discern at least a speculative account. But engagement also proved one of my most conspicuous failures in research, for I had—quite erroneously—imagined that both secondary and primary sources would be readily available. In fact, neither are (again apart from the normative, and even these are slim).[67] Perhaps we can take this lack of interest as indicative of a lack of importance placed on engagement by twentieth-century American culture, but both the Kinsey data and a variety of studies of marital happiness indicated that both the fact and the length of an engagement have mattered to the kind of marriage that eventuates.[68] This suggests that the event has a place in the analysis of the life course.

The preponderance of evidence presented here is quantitative. At first glance, this may not seem to be consistent entirely with my shared focus on material, institutional, and cultural considerations facing individuals constructing their life courses or with my wish to imaginatively reconstruct the contents of life course transitions, but I believe that it is. The reason for my having made a more determined search for quantitative materials than for (say) diaries and letters that might directly reveal individuals' own constructions of their situation lies in the nature of the life course as I understand it. My first concern here has necessarily been to *describe* in considerable detail and with as much precision as possible the *range* of options that individuals might have taken and the *distribution* of the options actually elected. Only after having assessed the overall, aggregate structure of "experience" in this sense do I move to the macroscopic level, to the level of material circumstance, institutional arrangement, and cultural prescription.

The *optimal* kind of document for my quantitative use *sometimes* exists, for it is a kind of document that has come to be in exceptionally high demand as social science has moved toward seeking processual views, namely, the *individual-based, longitudinal* record that allows one to describe transitions, sequences, and, sometimes, actors' perspectives on these. With such records, one can examine the delicate weave of individuals' trajectories through the structures that, from one perspective, help form them, and, from another, that they help to create. But such data do not exist, not remotely, for the earlier periods that I treat in this book. Therefore, I must use a variant of the historian's craft, must make do with all sorts of unconventional and admittedly imperfect evidence, used—sometimes—unconventionally.

And to do this, I must proceed first by pressing hard against the available *aggregate*, quantitative materials to pull from them plausible suggestions of *portions* of the careers of the individuals. To try to read the behavioral options of individuals out of the observed behavior of a cohort (or, worse, a cross-section of individuals at different ages viewed at a single point in time) is, formally speaking, a perversion of the data.[69] But, then, historians always pervert data. An operational definition of a historian's methodological skill, I believe, would be the ability to find in the shards of the past something that their creators did not intend to express by having created them. One can do so as responsibly as possible, seeking, as would a demographer, the most precisely constructed "at-risk" measures that can be discerned there. The quantitatively sophisticated reader will recognize that I am using many kinds of data here as though demographic, around which interpretation will be arrayed.

The story I am telling is a national story. Regional variation is not one of the phenomena I am particularly interested in exploring, even where the data are available, except where such variation allows inferences about change at the national level. But often I must have recourse to local data, for, very often, that is all that is available. Most census data, but not all, pertain to the national level, but it has only been quite recent that vital-registration data have been uniformly available on this level. A good deal of the social research that I cite or on which I carry out "secondary analysis"[70] in pursuit of my story is local. My assumption is that good samples that are representative of identifiable local populations preclude thereby the largest dangers, but sometimes I have been forced even to relax these cautions. Usually, however, I use local data—like the Minnesota wedding reports—either to provide *time series* information that otherwise is not available where the trends are presumably produced by responses to the same kind of macroscopic changes affecting the nation generally or to examine *systematic variation within* the data. Insofar as national trends outweigh place-to-place variation, I believe I am generally on safe ground, that the range of phenomena I find out about is important, and that we can informally take into consideration the fact that my materials are derived from wherever they could be found. But I have regularly taken the more aggressively interpretive path in preference to the more cautious.

The variety of social science data sources that are available to the resourceful historian of the twentieth century is surprising. Wherever possible, of course, I have attempted to reanalyze the original data, not because I mistrust previous analysts but because many of my purposes are "perversely" demographic, or to make close comparisons to other materials of no interest at the time of the first analysis, or in some other way run athwart others' purposes. More of such raw data tend to be available the more recent the period on which one seeks information and, generally, the richer the survey, although I was fortunate to be able to use the raw data from three superb and *very* old studies: an extraordinary commercial survey of youth taken in 1939, the Indianapolis Fertility Study of 1941, and Alfred Kinsey's Study of Sexual Behavior, gathered from the late 1930s into the early 1960s. More often than not, however, raw data are not available,[71] but often enough even published data-arrays reveal other things than initially seen, or of interest. In this category, large numbers of publications of the Census Bureau have been most useful, as were, also, a number of social inquiries carried out under WPA aegis in the mid-1930s.[72]

While I have, where possible, utilized public opinion survey research as an important clue to cultural change and relied in later chapters rather heavily on others' syntheses of such materials, I have also carried out a fair amount of primary research in a number of unconventional nonquantitative sources. In the examination of the changing nature of wedding ritual, presented above, I quantified a type of "belletristic" evidence. In another instance, I systematically examined another stylized belletristic source—lovelorn letters—with respect to the evolving vocabulary for describing "dating" relationships of young people. And in surveying a substantial amount of imaginative but tasteless short fiction describing courtship, I read with an eye closely attuned to the formal structuring of courtship problematics in those stories and the diction used to engage readers' emotions in the events of the fiction. But I sometimes simply read "culture" as historians ordinarily do—in a nontechnical sense in which descriptive, hortatory, normative, and personal documents are intuitively scanned for "what was at issue" at that time and place. In this vein, the documentation pertaining to cultural conflicts and difficult-to-resolve issues related to family formation was of particular interest to me. My reliance on such materials lessened with the greater availability of social science data for more recent periods.

On the whole, I feel that such informal procedures as I used with the cultural materials are justifiable in the main because I have assessed them in the light of the behavioral, "demographic" core of my account, which was independently gathered. This, of course, was the evidentiary strategy of my research in the first place. But neither author nor reader should blink at the fact that the fundamental criterion for accepting the interpretation that this book constitutes is *that it is intuitively plausible* in view of a large and varied body of evidence. That is, despite all the numbers, this book is history, not social science; it is a piece of conventional history about an unconventionally chosen subject, employing unconventional evidence. It is an effort at writing a history of an aspect of social change the conceptualization for which is drawn from social science and the data for which have typically been provided by social scientists.

I had initially hoped to explore three aspects of *differential* experience systematically: by gender, by race, and by social class. It is apparent that males and females, blacks and whites, working-class and middle-class people grew up according to somewhat different schedules at any given time, and often with somewhat different values. But my account has not turned out to be systematically comparative in this sense. I have succeeded best with regard to gender, which is the most important differentiator and also, happily, the one for which evidence is easily the fullest.

But demographic data is not always available broken down by race, and belletristic evidence is slight for blacks. Indeed, because Afro-American history is now beginning to develop the broader outlines of a social history, the kinds of relatively intimate questions raised in this book are as yet quite obscure, the evidence required to elicit answers to them not in the least obviously available. Where I have been able, I have made racial comparisons, interpreting these differences in the light of the broader general trends (pertaining, I am often afraid, especially to the white majority). And the evidence on social class, while often more readily available than that on race, is also more difficult to interpret, with a variety of indices of class roiling the question about exactly whom one is talking about. Again, where possible, I have detailed and discussed socioeconomic differentials, but, as with blacks, I have never felt confident of interpreting these *within the distinctive social history of particular classes*, rather than as somewhat simple comparisons to more aggregate trends. The largest reason, in life course terms, to have developed the race and class differentials fully is to test the intuitive hypothesis that while class differentials are declining, the experience of the two races in this important aspect of social and personal life *is becoming more distinctive*. But to carry these accounts beyond the essentially demographic terms in which scholarship so far has taken them is beyond my capacity at this point.

This book is conventionally historical in that, after two general chapters, it uses periodization, not just to define chapters but to allow me to focus attention on different portions of the life course at different historical periods and to argue for varying causes, from period to period. Obviously, "periodization" is a radical simplification, subserving stylistic purposes no less than more analytic purposes. The formal assumption behind periodization is that the periods can be treated as more or less internally homogeneous with regard to some important underlying dimension or trend, or at any rate as more alike in this regard than they are like the periods that precede and follow.

The 1920s, not unusually, are treated as a distinct period. The Great Depression serves as a second period for my account and World War II as a third. The "baby boom" constitutes a fourth period, one a bit more unconventional than the others in that it is periodized according to somewhat uncommon criteria. A fifth chronological chapter treats the period that runs from the end of the "baby boom" to 1975, at which point, roughly speaking, many of the family formation phenomena under study began to change once again. The "periods" I treat are short, far shorter than those in most social-historical accounts. I have arranged the account, first, to emphasize my substantive argument about just how malleable the youthful life course has become and how subject it is to a shifting debate. But I have periodized also to highlight the ways in which material or institutional change—which largely defines all but the most recent period—intertwines with the more manifest and more commonly remarked cultural change. And I have exercised my historian's right to leave the most recent phase of development to others.

I have emphasized in each chronological chapter a single contested or sharply modified transition around which to organize a larger part of the story than might have been available to contemporaries. Frankly, I do this partly for the modest drama it brings to the longish and complicated story I tell here. For, despite this selective emphasis, it is the argument of the life course approach that the sequence of events is cut of a single cloth. In the first "period" chapter, focusing on the 1920s, I elect to emphasize the evolution of an institution that governed (and brought progressively earlier into the lives of individuals) the transition to heterosexual erotic and emotional exploration: dating. In the chapter on the Great Depression, as dating continued to develop and diffuse, my emphasis shifts to a phase of the life course that lost much of its meaning: engagement. The following chapter, dealing with World War II, looks closely at the way military service affected entry into marriage. In turn, the focus shifts to parenthood, appropriately enough, in treating the baby boom decades that followed World War II. The final chronological chapter, dealing with the challenge to and repudiation of the baby boom in many of its salient aspects actually has several emphases, notably, the freeing of sexuality from the "timing" elements previously contained within the institutions of dating and marriage.

2

THE CHANGING LIFE COURSE
OF AMERICA'S YOUTH

The transitions into which the life course can be analyzed are deeply embedded in the material, institutional, and cultural circumstances in which they are accomplished. This will be the subject of subsequent chapters. As background, this chapter lays out a number of trends and patterns seen across the half-century examined in this book, trends in the very transitions on which the analysis will henceforth focus as well as in closely related contexts. The materials presented here are highly aggregate, and the treatment is descriptive and fairly close to the underlying data.

The sequence of discussion essentially follows the sequence of the typical life course. The data presented will show that:

- schooling has come to extend later into the life course, but gainful employment, receding for a while, has advanced in recent decades.
- for young men, military service, which greatly affects the timing of marriage as well as the departure from school and entry into the civilian labor force, initially rare, became common for a generation before once again becoming rare.
- premarital coitus, first with fiancés and then among other intimates, became more common, first slowly and then more rapidly; no less significant, women's patterns have converged on men's. Premarital conceptions followed a different path, growing somewhat earlier than the major expansion of female premarital coitus and being especially prominent among black women.
- marriage, long moving earlier in the life course, turned around (as Friedan and Brown had hoped) and did so ear-

lier for women than for men. In addition, the determinants
of marriage timing have changed.
• parenthood trends have generally followed nuptiality
trends, but the relationship of these two transitions has
changed in that the sequencing of pregnancy and marriage
has become less determinate, and the average interval between the two has changed markedly from period to
period.
• divorce propensity has grown unevenly, but rapidly, without
the typical timing of divorce within marriage changing
much and with no trend in the strong relationship of the
age at marriage to probabilities of divorce. But an initially
negative relationship of divorce and parenthood has largely
disappeared.
• overall, many of women's life course patterns have come
more nearly to approximate men's. But many patterns of
blacks and whites have become less similar to one another.

LEAVING SCHOOL, BEGINNING WORK, AND MILITARY SERVICE

The median age of leaving school and of entry to gainful employment has risen in parallel from about 16 in 1920 to 18 or
19 in 1980. Transitions like that from out of school into work
typically imply changes of roles that themselves determine substantial elements of one's daily rounds, perspectives, and obligations. Requiring the learning both of a cognitive and an
emotional sort, life course transitions of this magnitude are
commonly psychologically demanding, because of the need to
learn new ways. In the years following the Great War, educators
resumed their effort, begun decades before, to extend the influence of the school into late adolescence. Proportions of adolescents entering high school increased rapidly, so that four in
five boys and five in six girls did so by the early 1940s. By 1980,
virtually all did. The proportions of young people who graduated from high school increased right along with increased access to high school. The proportion of boys and girls who were
graduated from high school increased from some 16 percent
around 1920 to about half by 1940, and to 67 to 85 percent

between the immediate post-World War II high school cohort and those of the late 1960s and early 1970s, after which the figure stabilized. And through the 1960s, for increasing proportions of high-schoolers, graduation led to college.[1] Since World War II, however, the age of school departure has become rather less narrowly defined, with a more substantial proportion of eligible young people than previously remaining enrolled in school until their early twenties.[2] As schooling has pressed later in the lives of many Americans, entry to the labor force has come earlier for a substantial minority of the youthful population and *earlier also than the initial departure of a substantial minority from school.*

Thus, there has been a secular trend since the 1920s to push later in life the ages of a full transition from school to work, while, since World War II, there has been an accompanying loosening up of the age at which *at the latest* young people leave school and of the age at which *at the earliest* they enter gainful employment.[3] These trends exist for both genders. The transition thus involves an increasing number of people who *simultaneously* find themselves in school and at work, as table 2 documents. Growing from a low proportion among boys and a very low proportion among girls, rapidly and regularly increasing proportions of those who were either in school or at work were simultaneously engaged in *both*, rising to over one in four for boys at 16 and girls at 17, which reflects a phase in late adolescence that for increasing numbers was complicated by the simultaneous occupancy of roles that many have said might have implied conflicting demands. Here we find an increasing tendency to learn the new without exchanging it for the old and, as such, a subtle but significant change in the construction of the life course.

More than any other important youthful life course commitment, military service has varied irregularly from cohort to cohort because of the sporadic wartime mobilization.[4] Before World War II, the demands of military service on young people were minimal. The standing army was small in the 1920s and 1930s, and service was entirely voluntary. Conscription began in 1940, and because of the relatively small cohorts that came of age during the war and then again during the Korean con-

Table 2. Proportion of Those Either Enrolled at School or in the Labor Force Who Are Involved in Both, by Age and Sex, 1930–70 (in percentages)

	Male			Female		
	1930	1950	1970	1930	1950	1970
At age						
14–15	7.2	13.3	13.1	3.2	4.7	6.5
16	9.9	17.8	26.5	5.1	9.0	16.3
17	9.0	18.7	26.4	5.4	13.2	26.4
18	7.1	13.4	29.3	5.7	11.2	22.9
19	5.5	9.5	21.9	5.9	9.3	18.2
20	4.3	7.6	19.2	5.6	8.0	16.1
21–24	2.8	7.8	13.3	4.3	5.4	9.0

SOURCES: Calculated from *Census 1930–1*, 1182–1183, and *Census 1970–4*, 97–98.

Table 3. Proportions of Men Serving in the Military by Service in War or Otherwise and Year of Birth (in percentages)

	All Service	War Service	Peacetime Only
1901–05	16.5	13.3	3.2
1906–10	24.3	22.0	2.3
1911–15	35.6	34.0	1.6
1916–20	57.3	56.5	0.8
1921–25	74.2	73.5	0.6
1926–30	72.3	69.2	3.2
1930–34	64.9	54.2	10.7
1935–39	42.3	14.2	28.1
1940–44	36.1	23.9	12.3
1945–49	39.2	38.1	1.1
1950–54	17.0	14.7	2.3

SOURCES: Calculated from *Census 1960–6*, 1; *Census 1970–5*, 1; U.S. Veterans Administration, *Veterans in the United States: A Statistical Portrait from the 1980 Census* (Washington, D.C.: Office of Information Management and Statistics, 1984), table 1; and census tabulations of age by sex.

NOTE: All men's veteran status determined between ages of 35 and 44 except the two earliest (at 50–59) and the two youngest (at 25–34) cohorts.

flict, large proportions of young men passed through the military at one time or another during the following three decades, until the peacetime draft was abolished in 1973. During 1953, the last year of war in Korea, very nearly one in two at the peak age of 20 served. Military manpower needs stabilized and were satisfied increasingly smoothly by the growing cohorts attaining military age. Vietnam, by the end of the 1960s, produced a new phase, particularly affecting those who had recently finished high school and who did not go on to college. A third of all male 20-year-olds served during 1968—high but not rivaling the Korean demand. But after Vietnamization and then the ending of the draft, the proportions of young men called on to serve in the military dropped to levels lower than at any time since World War II. After conscription was replaced by a volunteer army, authorities had to depend substantially on the material benefits they offered to induce young people to commit a phase of their lives to the service. For adolescents, the military became just another job option, as indicated in table 3, which summarizes the military experience of successive cohorts of American males.

PREMARITAL COITUS

Something of a consensus on periodization has emerged among students of premarital sexuality. They record two sexual "revolutions," one in the first two decades of the twentieth century, and a second spanning from the mid-1960s and the late 1970s. Catherine Chilman, reviewing the literature on adolescent sexual behavior, sees continuity across the two revolutions.

> Sharp changes in the United States toward greater sexual liberalism occurred in the early 1900s and were reflected in the more emancipated behaviors of a sizable proportion of middle- and upper-class women in the 1920s. . . . As women became more emancipated from earlier puritanical prescriptions, men became more emancipated too, especially in terms of greater freedom to have premarital and extramarital sex relations on a more equalitarian, companionship basis with women in their own reference groups. This trend toward increased sexual liberalization has

strengthened recently, especially since the mid-1960s. . . . It is probable . . . that further liberalization of attitudes, if not of behaviors, had taken place between the 1920s and the 1960s, especially as a result of upheavals caused by World War II.[5]

Our understanding of the first revolution rests heavily on the retrospective accounts of premarital sexual behavior tabulated by Alfred Kinsey and his associates.[6] The Kinsey data presented in table 4 reveal a general increase in premarital coitus for both white men and women, with the greater increase having occurred among fiancées among women, nonaffianced friends among men. Throughout this period, many men apparently engaged in occasional casual premarital coitus with relatively promiscuous women, who constituted a relatively small portion of the female population. The persistent, perhaps increasing gender difference is the outstanding datum in the table and will bear contrasting with patterns seen in the second "sexual revolution." The modest changes in *incidence* of premarital coitus in the early figures, too, was accompanied by a decline in the *variance* in age at which individuals experienced coitus for the first time.[7]

The second sexual revolution is better documented, and revealed that 1960s women were different from their predecessors. A late 1950s Midwest study, replicated in 1968, saw women's rates of coitus increase from 21 percent to 34 percent, while men's rates were stable.[8] These figures were virtually duplicated by a probability sample of students in nonreligious colleges taken in 1965 and in a 1967 national sample of college students.[9] The 1967 sample was tabulated by class at school and indicates an initiation by sophomore year of nearly all the young men who were going to be sexually initiated at any time during college. For young women, however, the rise was steady, year by year. A thorough, representative national study of girls' sexuality in 1971 revealed that by that date, the high-school years were a time of steadily increasing coital incidence, to the point where one-third of the eighteen-year-old white girls had had intercourse and four in ten of the nineteen-year-olds.[10] Replications of this survey have shown a continued enlarge-

Table 4. Proportion of Ever-Married Persons Having Had
Premarital Coitus with Fiancées and with Others
(excluding Prostitutes), by Birth Cohort and Sex
(in percentages)

Birth Cohort	Approx. Period of Premarital Coitus	Males		Females	
		Fiancées	Others	Fiancées	Others
< 1900	< 1920	45.4	66.3	31.1	15.3
1900–09	1920s	61.1	71.9	40.2	27.2
1910–19	1930s	50.2	76.5	41.2	18.9
1920–24	early 1940s	57.6	81.6	33.7	21.1
1925+	mid-1940s+	48.0	80.1	38.4	22.1

SOURCE: Computed from Kinsey Sex Histories, standardized for year of interview and educational level.

ment of the field of adolescent girls who had had coitus from the early 1970s to the mid-1970s and again to the late 1970s.[11]

Substantial proportions of firstborn children in America have long been premaritally conceived, but this proportion has changed markedly.[12] Careful tabulations of retrospective family formation schedules gathered in 1975[13] allow us to examine closely the early months of marriage to see how fertility and marriage were sequenced. Figure 1 represents the proportions of women married at 18–21 or at 22 or older who became mothers at such a time that premarital pregnancy was clearly indicated, for five-year *marriage* cohorts beginning with women first married between 1930 and 1934.[14] Both the racial differentials and the time trends are quite large. A marked rise in antenuptial pregnancy among both whites and blacks seems to date from about the late 1950s, so that while about one in eight 1930s white marriages were preceded by pregnancy, close to one in five 1960s white marriages were. For blacks, corresponding figures differed by age but indicate, overall, a rise of from about one in three black marriages preceded by pregnancy to over one in two. Among blacks, premarital pregnancy characterized young brides rather than older brides, but among

Percent
Probability

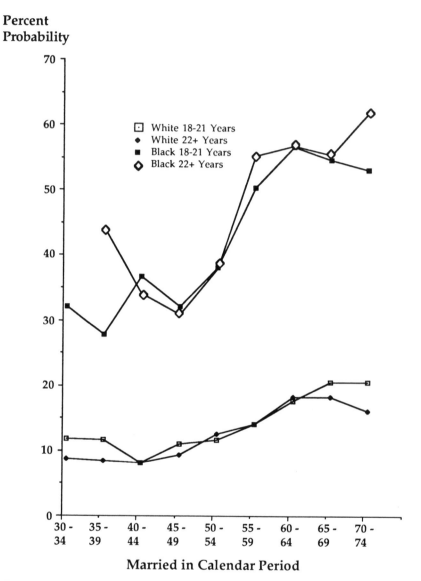

Figure 1. Proportions of Women Married at 18–21 or 22 and Older Who Had a Child within 8 Months of Marriage

whites, the relationship with age was quite weak.[15] The heightened emphasis on marriage (and, ideally, *subsequent* parenthood) for young white women in the baby boom did seem to argue subtly for a corresponding relaxation of the ban on premarital conception. There was, however, a striking downturn in premarital conception during the last decade on which the table bears, a period known for its considerable liberation of female sexuality. The availability of legal abortion probably explains the downturn more than does any tendency toward other prudent behaviors; but the downturn points also to a reduction in the favorable attitude toward parenthood, as reflected in the cumulative-parenthood graphs just examined.

Further understanding of the normative aspect of the sequencing of marriage and fertility can be obtained by examining the subject of illegitimacy, using data from another retrospective family-formation survey carried out by the Current Population Survey to analyze births to mothers (not just wives) at ages 15–19 and ages 20–24 during successive four-year periods.[16] By dividing antenuptial pregnancies into those that come to term *before* and *after* marriage, we find that the former have been *far* more common among black than white women, even when the larger component of antenuptial pregnancies among black women altogether is taken into account. Between the late 1930s and the late 1960s, the legitimization ratio for both races remained roughly steady, but in recent years, among whites and even more so among blacks, younger girls became sharply less prone to legitimizing their pregnancies through marriage before parenthood. Or, to put it another way, as the normatively defined schedule of marriage moved once again toward a later preferred date, higher and higher proportions of *younger* girls who had become pregnant could not or would not marry promptly, and to a greater extent than among women somewhat older. Single parenthood became more acceptable, illegitimacy less of a curse—changes evidently more quickly remarked by relatively young girls than by their elders. And this was particularly true among black girls. By the 1975–1978 period, *seven in eight births to black teenagers were outside of marriage.* The differential, and the trend, is great enough to suggest a distinctive normative element to at least this element of the black life course.

MARRIAGE

Over our period, the phase of life in which marriage is typically contracted converged with that of the school-to-work transition. For men, the entire period in the 1960s saw a general, if uneven, decline in the median age at first marriage and a marked contraction (certainly during the 1940s and perhaps beyond) of the period of years over which a great majority of young men contracted their first marriages. Bachelorhood became a less and less prevalent stage, and whatever bachelorhood there was became something that happened at a relatively young age. For women, these trends were present until the late 1950s, when there was some reversal. What this means in practical terms is that for increasing proportions of young men and women, the processes of leaving school, entering the labor force, and entering marriage occurred at nearly the same time.

Thus, in 1930 fewer than 1 percent of young women ages 16–19 who were in school were married, as compared with nearly *half* of those who had left school.[17] By ages 20–24, at which point 85 percent of young women out of school were married, a minute 6 percent of those few who remained in school were married. For women, and generally for men, too, schooling and marriage were virtually exclusive statuses in 1930. By 1970, the proportion of women in school and married at 16–19 had risen slightly although the proportion for those who had left school had *declined*.[18] And at 20–24, while the proportion married among those out of school was only three-fourths as high as it had been in 1930, the proportion married among the considerably enlarged group still in school had *increased threefold*. The rather determinate sequence of school departure and marriage of 1930 had weakened.

Labor force entry and marriage had not so unequivocally become less determinately sequenced as had departure from school and labor force entry and marriage. At 20–24, proportions married among those men not in the labor force increased by about twofold from 1940 to 1970, a more rapid increase than that among men in the labor force.[19] Among women, the change was enormous, but reflected not so much the destruction of determinate sequencing of the transitions of the life course as new assumptions about appropriate roles for married women. Essentially, the propensity of women in the labor force to be married saw such an increase between these years that it almost effaced the initially radical difference in this propensity between themselves and women of like ages who were not working.

Young men and women, then, while facing a set of developmental tasks that was not markedly different over the years in question, accomplished them with timing and sequencing that had changed. In part, these behavioral changes simply reflected different constraints and resources facing the participants. But in part, they reflected and even encouraged changed outlooks on "growing up," as experienced. They also reflected institutional change.

Figures 2 and 3 present the *annual likelihood of marriage* among young white men and young white women still unmarried, at given ages.[20] We here examine first marriage at a relatively early age (taken as 19 for males, 17 for females), at two ages at the beginning and end of roughly the most typical marriage ages (22 and 25 for males, 20 and 23 for females), and at an age taken as somewhat old (28 for males, 26 for females). Turning first to white males, and looking first at marriage at the youngest age shown, we see in Figure 2 a pattern of only very modest change through the mid-1960s. A brief downward deflection at the beginning of the Depression and another in the last two years of World War II breaks a slowly upward-drifting pattern, as youthful marriage for white men became just slightly more prevalent, the most notable period of increase coming in the decade following the end of World War II. The marked downward trend in the mid-1960s[21] reflects a marked and persistent backing away from youthful marriage on the part of white males, to the point where the annual probabilities of marriage of any unmarried 19-year-old were less by 1979 than they had been fifty years earlier, before the great restructuring of this part of the life course around World War II.

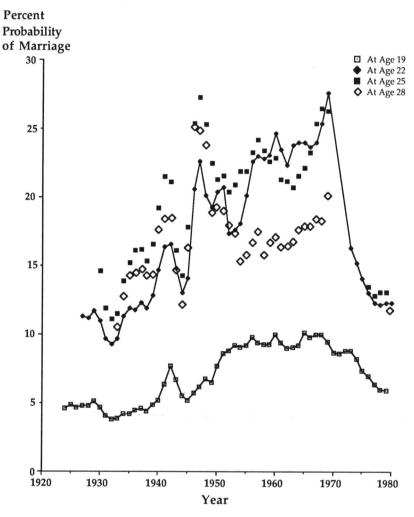

Figure 2. Annual Likelihood of Marriage among Young Unmarried White Males

We see even more striking changes in men's nuptial patterns at the older ages, especially those in the central ages at which first marriage was the most probable. At 22 and at 25, the graph moves up quite steeply from a less than 10 percent probability in the earliest years considered to more than a 20 percent probability by the mid-1960s. Once again, from the perspective of the young people themselves, this quantitative

Percent
Probability
of Marriage

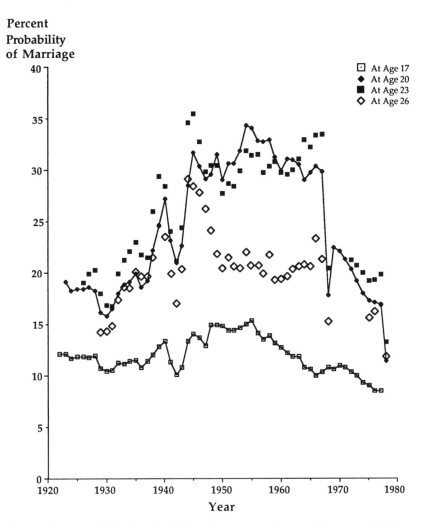

Figure 3. Annual Likelihood of Marriage among Young Unmarried White Females

change represents a real modification of experience. Young men entered on courtship—indeed, life more generally—with different expectations when they knew from experience that there was a one in five chance of marrying in the year than when they knew that there was merely one chance in ten.

The marked upward trend was broken by sharp downturns. The Depression mattered a great deal, although the tendency

toward postponement of marriage at these two ages was reversed by the middle of the 1930s. The sharp upward spike in
World War II was prominent at both these ages. The postwar
spike was even more so. The era following the Korean conflict
constituted another upward spike, and a lasting one, so that by
the time Vietnam came to influence the choices of young white
men, the movement up to a probability of marriage in a given
year of more than one in four for unmarried white men at 22
and 25 was only a slight upward deviation from tendency. The
end of Vietnam, however, represented the end of an era in
family-formation patterns. The decline in marriage probabilities for white men at the central marriage ages was nothing
short of spectacular. White men in their young twenties clearly
looked forward differently after Vietnam. Less and less of their
youthful life course came to be organized around marriage
plans and preparations.

Nonwhite single men, in a general way, changed over the
period much as did white single men, but their temporal variations were *even more extensive*. The Depression and the war had
a greater impact on all ages: the marriage boom associated with
the 1950s and early 1960s was very apparent. And the collapse
in marriage probabilities after the mid-1960s was a highly
prominent trend among black men. The suddenness of the decline is clearly pointed out by a decline from about one in four
single black men at 22 marrying during each Vietnam year to a
mere one in ten marrying by the early 1970s. This perspective
helps link the crisis of black teenage unemployment to the crisis
of the black family.

The data for white females shown in figure 3 closely parallels that for white males, except for an earlier decline in marriage probabilities among younger women starting in the late
1950s. The peaks and troughs present in the male graph are
once again present, but white females exhibited one markedly
new tendency: the still-single "older" women *lost considerably
in marriageability* under the baby boom marriage regime. The
"sorting" of women into the marriageable and the future spin-
sters occurred early and vigorously in the baby boom, one of
that period's experiential meanings. The minority that failed to
"pass muster" at the age when most succeeded were *as though*

stigmatized thereby. Men, too, married at somewhat more uniform ages during the baby boom, but this was far truer among white women. There are clear signs of a shockingly more broad definition of "old maid" during the late 1940s and early 1950s. This pattern persisted to the mid-1970s: among white women, marriage was for the young only.

Nonwhite women, like their nonwhite male counterparts, experienced considerably more year-to-year fluctuation than did whites, owing presumably to their greater vulnerability to external circumstances. Early marriage disappeared far earlier and dramatically than for white women. And, for black women, as for their men, the period since the late 1960s has been a period of general deterioration of marriage possibilities.

Detailed New York State marriage-registration data allow us to explore the question of interannual variability in nuptiality, with close attention to age.[22] All age groups varied very considerably from year to year in numbers who married, average annual variation exceeding 10 percent. There were, moreover, consistent differences by age—consistent also for both women and men—in the extent of variation in this variability. Those who married older were *more* likely to postpone marriages in one year, and, perhaps, to accelerate them the next, as circumstances became less or more propitious for marriage. Young people, it seemed, were relatively inflexible, perhaps pushed by inner urges that they had not learned to weigh against less intimate concerns, perhaps pushed by premarital conceptions.

When observations are subdivided into the period extending from the 1920s to World War II, and into the period beginning with that war to 1967 (when the data series ends), the variability of annual marriages is seen to be far greater in the latter period, despite the rigors of the Depression. More important yet, *the relationship of age to the variability of interannual variation was present only in the later era.* In earlier times, it seems, younger people had to exercise about the same degree of prudence that older people did. (Lower rates of premarital pregnancy, and hence of marriage promoted by necessity rather than by choice, in the usual sense, probably also played something of a role.)

To a significant degree, the year-to-year variations in cohort first-marriage experience as well as the pronounced secular trends can be explained with reference to a number of measurable, intuitively comprehensible circumstances, both demographic and economic. These differ somewhat by gender, and from the prewar to the postwar period, but they basically tell a consistent story. Most of these circumstances influenced the initial nuptiality of the young most of all, for their resources were generally the least and their buffering from external circumstances the least substantial. Thus, in certain years, because of the volatility of fertility rates in this century and the tendency for men to marry women somewhat younger than themselves, men were occasionally in short supply, slightly accelerating their marriages while retarding those of young women. In like fashion, military calls have varied markedly. When they are high, this has ordinarily been a signal to young people to marry sooner, rather than later. Marriage has been a life experience that we consider highly consequential for the individuals directly involved, consequential as well (if less so) for the two families thereby joined, and consequential for subsequent demography and for the nature of aggregate demand for goods. The paths that have led two individuals to join together in marriage at given points in their own lives have been in a sense prepared by others, by institutions and by rules that the partners have played by in getting to the altar.

In years when jobs were relatively plentiful, and wage income relatively high, marriages were solemnized rather than postponed. On the one hand, a concomitant of twentieth-century prosperity has been increasing job opportunities for women, and their work lives in one way encouraged, but in another way discouraged, nuptiality. On the other hand, women's premarital incomes have made possible earlier marriage: it is, indeed, the dynamic aspect of growing disposable income per capita that is most closely related to marriage trends. At the same time, gainful employment—the possibility of decent independent livelihood outside of marriage—has on the individual level tended to predispose women not to hasten into marriage. On balance, younger first marriages were promoted by women's gainful employment, while older ones were retarded.

These striking age-to-age differences in determinants of marriage probabilities are strictly a product of the postwar. In the prewar period, one single model seems to suffice for men and women of all ages—a rather simple economic model. The constantly shifting age relationships characteristic of the postwar period was not characteristic of the prewar and, arguably, not in periods previous to that. The age-differentiation of the postwar, and the great awareness of age-related phenomena, was a product of the way the environment impinged so variably on people of different ages. After World War II, young men but not older men were strongly influenced in their marriage decisions by the military draft, and by higher current incomes per capita. For older men, the draft operated mildly to encourage marriage, while current income had no particular impact. Younger women, unaffected directly by the draft in their marriage behavior, were affected by current and relative income, as were the older men; for them, these relationships were more or less the same in the older age group, except that for them the draft encouraged marriage.

PARENTHOOD

In the minds of most Americans for much of the twentieth century, marriage not followed by childbirth within a few years was somehow lacking, and partly for this reason the age probabilities of first childbirth—certainly for whites—have generally resembled those for first marriage, slightly lagged, and at a somewhat lower level. Childbirth rates have shown more extreme downward cohort-to-cohort movement than rates of first marriage (notably in the 1909 and 1944 cohorts), a reflection of the far more irreversible economic impact of childbirth. However, marriage—and again this is understandable in commonsense terms—seems to have been sometimes but not always as upwardly "flexible" as first childbirth. This was so especially among the early and mid-twenties in pre-World War II cohorts. Such external events as economic downturns have affected not only the way couples passed through courtship into marriage but also the way they committed themselves to parenthood, once married. Military service and the circumstances surrounding the draft call seem not to have encouraged couples to become parents so much as it encouraged marriage.

Parenthood patterns for white and black women are substantially different variants of the same family. On the whole (the difference was especially apparent for the earliest cohorts but remain visible in later years), black women initially had a far more rapid pace of childbearing but trailed off very substantially by their mid-twenties. The tendency toward early childbearing among nonwhite women, perhaps a product of ignorance of and then disregard for birth control, fairly well characterized *all* the cohorts, from the earliest to the most recent—in contrast to the far more varied teenage-fertility patterns among the cohorts of white women. The slope representing movement into parenthood was generally steeper for white women than for black women; and there was for them no particular trend in this regard. More white women were more nearly universally mothers by age 34 than were black women, a fact that was true for all cohorts examined here but especially true for the 1926 and 1936 birth cohorts, which participated in the extensive baby boom of the years following World War II. Whites participated more fully than nonwhites in this striking episode in the reordering of the life courses of young people.

Tsui's calculations of the average number of months elapsing between first marriage and first childbirth for white women still married offer a summary perspective on the relationship between the timing of marriage and the timing of parenthood.[23] She shows that the rapid decline in average interval continued to the late 1950s, followed by the near plateau into the mid-1960s, and an increase that was even sharper than the rate of decline that followed in the late 1960s and early 1970s. The years of decline in first birth interval were years of especially steep decline in this measure *for those marrying oldest.* Marital careers had once been sharply defined by the point in the life course at which couples took the plunge into marriage, the cautious distinguished from the incautious. But by the post-World War II period, this was no longer so, for in the war years, the average first birth interval of those marrying under 25 actually increased, sometimes owing to the draft and other war-related inconveniences. For those who married at older ages in those years, however, and presumably less often subject to the draft, jobs and prosperity allowed considerably earlier parenthood.

The sharp increase in average pauses between marriage and first childbirth in the 1965–1974 period again brought about differentiation by age at marriage, but with a new twist. In the new arrangement, those marrying youngest were anomalous, because some fairly substantial proportion of their marriages followed antenuptial conceptions. But for the other three, the pace of first births on average now ran in the opposite direction to the youthfulness of marriages. Almost as though couples had, at marriage, both a distinct fertility target and an age beyond which childbirth was thought undesirable, and as though "child-free" years were now valued as a distinctive stage within marriage, it was now younger-marrying couples who postponed first births, while older-marrying couples did so only to a lesser extent, perhaps for fear that they not attain their fertility targets or their preferred date for leaving a childbearing stage.

There is very little reliable data that describe the differential pace of parenthood by the age of marriage of the partners for the earlier years of this century. One source, although only imperfectly comparable, is available in the retrospective fertility questions on the 1910, 1940, and 1950 censuses, and is displayed in table 5. When we tabulate for *current* ages of white and black women of under 20, 20–24, and 25–29,[24] we find that for marriages contracted late in the first decade of the twentieth century by native white women, there was a considerably higher propensity to become parents in the first few years of marriage than there was to be for marriages contracted late in the Great Depression and even in the half-decade following the conclusion of World War II. These turn-of-the-century couples showed the same marked relationship that baby boom couples showed between youthful marriage and prompt parenthood. The data on both white and black women indicate, in short, that the Depression seems to have brought primarily a general slowing-down of patterns of transition from marriage into parenthood, although those who married older (and there were somewhat more of these) postponed parenthood a bit more commonly than those who married relatively young. After the Depression, however, the hesitancy shown by those black women who married older seems to have persisted far more than for white women, whose passage to parenthood al-

Table 5. Proportion of Women Married 3–4 Years and in Intact
Marriages Who Have Had a Child, by Race and Current
Age, 1910, 1940, and 1950 (in percentages)

Age of first marriage****	White Women			Black Women		
	*1910**	*1940**	*1950***	*1910*	*1940*	*1950****
20–24	86.2	74.7	79.1	79.0	61.6	75.9
25–29	76.7	59.2	73.6	67.6	45.6	58.0
30–34	68.3	51.1	59.2	62.0	39.2	50.9

*Native white women only.
**All white women living with their first husbands.
***All nonwhite women living with their first husbands.
****The ages at marriage reflect current ages of 20–24, 25–29, and 30–34 at census date and the 3–4 years since marriage.
SOURCES: Calculated from *Census 1940–3*, tables 1, 2, 3, 4; *Census 1950–4*, tables 18, 19.

most returned to its 1910 swiftness.[25] By the time of the baby boom, however, this racial distinctiveness was effaced. It seems to have taken nearly a decade after the war's end, however, for the most "prudent" among black women to abandon the highly cautious attitude toward parenthood that the Depression had instilled—considerably longer than it took white women.

Figure 4 examines trends in immediate transitions from marriage into parenthood, those that occur between the ninth and twelfth month, "wedding-bed conceptions" and their near cousins. The graph suggests that this kind of an unguided or eager initial approach to pregnancy early in marriage described a curvilinear pattern, rising from the depths among Depression marriage to maxima among marriages during or just after the baby boom. The turning away from early parenthood was considerably more abrupt than its earlier expansion. Throughout, those who married older were either better armed with knowledge about birth-control techniques or else less eager to become parents right away, or both. And, throughout, black women who entered marriage without being pregnant were slower thereafter to become pregnant than their white counterparts.

Percent
Probability

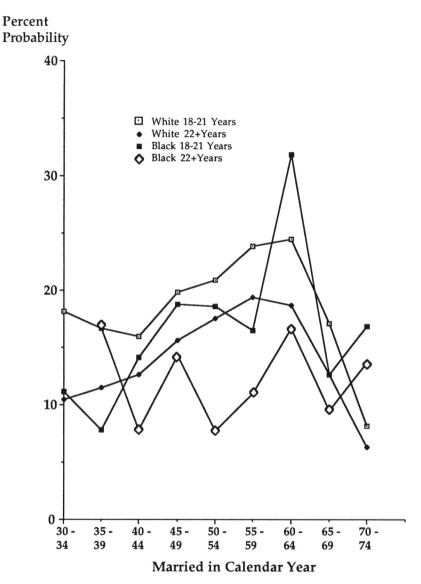

Figure 4. Trends in Transition from Marriage into Parenthood between the Ninth and Twelfth Month of Marriage

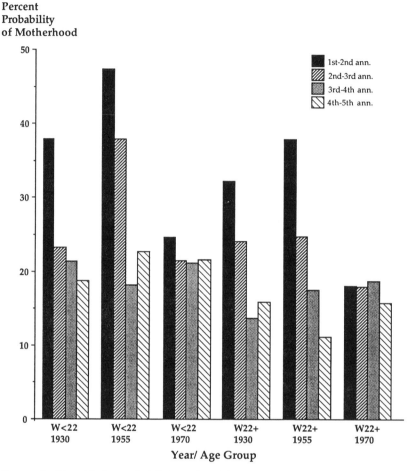

Figure 5. First-Birth Probabilities of White Women between Successive Anniversaries

When we examine first-birth probabilities of women between successive anniversaries of their marriages, the historical patterns speak even more eloquently of the short-term malleability of the youthful life course. The 1975 retrospective data allow us to examine marriage cohorts from the early Depression on. To simplify, figure 5 shows this story only for white women and only for three marriage cohorts, with separate tabulations for those who married "young" (under 22) and those who married "old" (22 or older). Several generalizations obtain quite generally:

- The transition to parenthood is more likely in the second year of marriage than in subsequent years. The reason for this was rarely, if ever, biological. Rather, the relationship is to be explained by the unique standing of motherhood among women who had married younger, strongly influenced by the cultural prescription of marriage and parenthood, and before they had a chance to develop other interests and roles.[26]
- Couples who married younger were considerably more likely to become parents promptly, but this difference waned over time.
- After the second year, however, the rate of decline of the likelihood of marriage is slight: once couples made a "decision" to become parents promptly or not to become parents promptly, normative scheduling became less pressing on them. A marriage cohort moved gradually into parenthood for idiosyncratic or circumstantial reasons. (The baby boom marriage cohort was something of an exception here—for reasons I will consider below.)

Beyond these generalizations, the most striking phenomena that figure 5 indicates are two differences between the baby boom marriage cohort and those earlier and subsequent. Most evident, of course, is the increased probability of parenthood at almost every point in the marital career. But equally significant was the extent to which the third year of marriage continued to be one of relatively eager motherhood for brides of this cohort. Indeed, we can fairly say that for the baby boom marriage cohort alone, prompt parenthood was a transition that was virtually enjoined on them. Most couples' effort to accomplish this in the first few years of marriage left only normatively or biologically "deficient" couples still childless at their fourth wedding anniversaries. As we shall shortly see, later in this chapter and elsewhere, as the baby boom faded, so did the normatively promoted connection between parenthood and a lasting marriage. That is, timing of parenthood after marriage became more volitional, just as would even the sequencing of the two events.

Figure 5 is particularly eloquent in this regard in its representatives of the 1970 marriage cohort. For both younger and older women who married then, the pact of the transition into parenthood was not only slower *but also less differentiated over the years that followed marriage*—the exact obverse of the baby boom. Correspondingly, the age at marriage mattered less to the pace of transition into parenthood than it once had. The disappearance of this formerly pronounced pattern could possibly be explained by a spread of contraceptive knowledge and capacity, and no doubt this played a part. But considerably more striking is a normative explanation that also deserves weight: both in the 1930s and in the 1950s, marriage was essentially *supposed to* be followed by prompt parenthood, the marriage being understood as completed, perfected, by the arrival of a child. But by the 1970s, with new definitions of marriage abroad and divorce considerably more prominent, both in a statistical sense and as an understood and frequent contingency of marriage, couples moved into parenthood both more slowly and more evenly.

Black women's patterns, not shown here, differed from those of white women in some significant ways. If black women who married young were considerably more likely than their white counterparts to become pregnant before marriage, as we have earlier seen, they were and remained considerably less likely to become mothers at later dates in their marriages. Black women who married later were, as has already been suggested, far less likely to become mothers than were their white counterparts. In these respects, the Depression cohort particularly affected blacks. And for older black women, *there was no "baby boom" to speak of.*

Taking together the seeming reluctance of childless married black women to become mothers, the considerably greater black premarital conception rate, and the far more accelerated youthful fertility rate for all black women than for whites, we can see that even in the earliest period this book treats, the entry into adulthood for black women differed from that of white women, both in timing and sequencing. Indeed, throughout the period discussed here, blacks differed so markedly in the way they typically constructed their life courses, that it at least suggests a subculturally distinctive (but no less dynamically changing, and in some of the same ways as for whites) normative structure. (Such a subculture would clearly not necessarily encompass the entire black community, but it surely must incorporate substantial numbers.) No less, however, we must recognize how much more subject to circumstantial pressures blacks have been as they have negotiated their own life courses. The flexibility of the black family structure has been often remarked, with differing evaluation. Their life courses, too, were flexible. Some reflection will suggest that these two observations are in fact related.

DIVORCE

Marriage and the onset of coital activity have become less closely interconnected with time, as have also marriage and parenthood. These trends are intuitively consistent with the well-known rise in divorce, which implies that whereas formerly for most people (in contemplating marriage, and in enacting it) one's first marriage was one's final marriage, this has become decreasingly true. Divorce, moreover, has changed its relationship to the life course, notably, its relationship to the age pattern at which marriage was initially contracted.

The general upward tendency of divorces during much of the twentieth century was not steady but included lengthy periods of approximate plateau in this rate, which followed the rather sudden upturns that account for much of the secular upward trend. World War I marriages brought such a sharp increase, which was followed by a plateau that lasted up to about the middle of the Great Depression, at which time increasing numbers of marriages begun incautiously in the face of highly challenging material circumstances earlier in that decade began to fail. On top of this rising rate, failed World War II marriages pushed the divorce rate to a new peak in 1946. But at this point, the rate *declined*, rather persistently, reaching a low in 1958 that resembled the level of divorce in 1940.[27] The decade and more of steady decline was at this point replaced by an initially slow increase in divorce that picked up headway around 1963 and accelerated into the mid-1970s. Black marriages, initially hugely more prone to divorce than that of whites, were less subject to the upward trend. Glenn and Supanic note that "every recent study that has focused on black-white differences in divorce (or divorce and separation) in the United States has found more marital dissolution among the blacks." In their own sample, from the early 1970s, they discovered that "the correlates of divorce/separation" of the two races "seem to differ in important ways" and could not be reduced substantially by racial differences in demographic or socioeconomic characteristics.[28]

Preston and McDonald partition change in marriage-cohort divorce rates into a trend component and the episodic deviation therefrom.[29] They concede that the pronounced underlying upward trend in divorce rates is not amenable to the kind of explanation they offer for deviations from that underlying trend. Upward deviations, they discover, are in part products of the destabilizing circumstances surrounding the couple at the initial solemnization of the marital tie: marriages contracted in depression or war have been prone to impermanence. Stress may have made it hard for the couple to establish a satisfactory relationship during the early days of the marriage, or material resources or social support may have been lacking. When the wars ended, when the depressions passed, the upward deviations in divorce rates receded. This argument accords well with the interpretive summary of Glenn and Supanic: common features of these dimensions conducing, in the early 1970s, to relatively unstable marriage were those—residence in mobile regions and communities, absence of religious affiliation, and attendance at service—that suggest relatively little integration into social groups that might help to hold the marriage together.[30]

Through the whole period examined in this book, with a slight moderation for wartime marriages, marriages contracted young were considerably more likely to eventuate in divorce.[31] Early, the fragility of marriages contracted relatively young was recognized, documented in empirical investigation, and warned against. For both whites and blacks, men and women, younger marriages were considerably more prone to divorce than were others, and it is hard to discern any trend in this relationship. Glenn and Supanic established that in the 1970s, among a list of nine aspects of background, circumstance of marriage, and current circumstance, age at first marriage was by far the most important predictor of divorce for women and one of two overwhelmingly important predictors (along with religious commitment) for men.[32] Marriages entered into at a young age, on average, undergo relative economic privation early on, just as their patterns are being established; persons less "mature" are presumably less able to recognize what a lasting marital relationship will require; and, insofar as marriages contracted "too" young are deemed ill-advised, social support for such marriages is compromised by doubts.

Recent national data[33] show more precisely wherein the stigma of prior divorce has lessened as divorce has become progressively incorporated in the American marriage system.[34] Thus, in 1961, 3.5 times as many divorced men who remarried at 25–34 married women who had previously been divorced as did single men marrying at 25–34. For remarrying divorcees, the ratio was a bit lower, 2.9 times as many marrying divorced men. So, quite clearly, "endogamy" among the divorced was the pattern in 1961. And so it was also by 1978 (the most recent data available), but by that date the ratio for remarrying men at this age had dropped to 2.8. For women, it had dropped to 2.4. This is rapid change. Acceptance of the legitimacy of divorce as a necessary component of a marriage system incorporating large volitional elements has encouraged acceptance of divorced people as legitimate—if not quite yet fully fledged—reentrants to the not-yet-quite-integrated marriage pool.[35]

Over this period of time, *how long* it ordinarily took failing marriages to fail changed very little, even though the proportion of couples choosing to terminate their marriage has risen greatly. Typically, six or seven years has been the median duration of a first marriage that ends in divorce, while three to thirteen years' duration encompasses the central 50 percent of all marriage durations.[36] The 1920s saw a slight lengthening of the median duration of marriages terminated by divorce, but by 1948, the average was below what it had been at the beginning of the 1920s. The median length of marriage terminated by divorce climbed again, peaking in 1963 at 7.5 years (the highest recorded figure since the early years of the century) before gradually moving downward during the divorce "boom" that ensued at about this time.[37] This stability, however, disguises an important trend that is quite relevant to the life course: divorces of childless couples have come *more quickly* than they used to, while the couples with children who eventually elected to divorce waited *somewhat longer* to do so.

Even while the trend in overall divorce rate held fairly steady over much of the first nearly fifty years we are examining, there was a change in the life course location of divorce that foreshadowed the large change in the incidence of divorce that was shortly to come. Gradually, parenthood became less of a hindrance to divorce (while still remaining a substantial hindrance, to be sure). The statistics indicate *directly* the proportion of divorces that are of couples who have children, leaving us to infer from this the divorce-proneness of married couples with and without children. Only couples with children are at risk of divorcing after having had children, after all, and those who have become parents are no longer at risk of divorcing without having any children. We must therefore gather some estimate of trends in the proportion of *all* married couples *who had children of their own under 18 years old living in their families*, so as to compare it at least roughly to the trends in proportions of divorces that are of parents.[38] Such data became available only in 1940, but what they reveal makes interpretation easy: proportions of currently married couples who were parents varied only slightly, changes in age structure offsetting those of the timing of fertility.

Divorce registration was spotty and irregular until recently, and the patterns we discern there may be inaccurate in detail. But it is the gross patterns that are relevant to the case at hand. In 1916, three in eight couples divorcing reported that they had one or more children.[39] By 1922, this proportion had dropped slightly, one in three couples who were divorced in the year reporting that they had a child. But during the decade of the 1920s and into the 1930s (when the data series was dropped), this proportion rose gradually to just slightly above the point it had been in 1916.[40] When the data series picked up again in 1950, the proportion of divorcing couples who had children was up to 46 percent. By about 1957, the proportion crossed the 50 percent mark and continued to rise, passing to the 60 percent level by 1963. And at roughly this point, *before* divorce rates *per se* rose at a pace and to a level that tended to suggest even to dispassionate observers a change in the nature of the institution of marriage, *the level stuck.* In 1975, the proportion of divorcing couples who were parents was 59 percent.[41] The trends, then, indicate an increasing integration between parenthood and a commitment to permanent marriage, at least between the 1930s and the mid-1960s. During this period, there was no lasting pattern of childlessness among couples, but there was a decided increase in proportion of divorces granted to parents. After this period, the same trend in effect continued, but with a different surface manifestation, as proportion of divorcing couples who were parents held steady even as the proportion of all couples at risk of divorce *declined* rather dramatically. Thus, in 1930, where between about 38 and 40 percent of all couples divorcing were parents,[42] 59 percent of all married couples in that year were.[43] Thus (ignoring age), propensities to divorce were at this time perhaps two-thirds as great for couples with no children, compared to couples with children. In 1975, however, 59 percent of divorcing couples had children, while 54 percent of all married couples—*a smaller proportion*—had children. Once again ignoring age, the presence of children acted almost as though *no hindrance* to divorce.

Table 6, based on retrospective data, provides some historical depth. It shows the disposition of marriages by divorce in succeeding decades, examining the racially varying propensity at different stages of existing marriages for divorce to be constrained by the presence of children. Thus, we see that on the whole, parenthood has militated against divorce, at least in the aggregate, but that this relationship is relatively weak for both whites and blacks in the first two years of marriage and then, again, fades somewhat. More striking are the racial differentials: historically, *and especially more recently*, black divorce rates have exceeded white rates by more for the childless than for

Table 6. Average Annual Proportion of Women's Marriages
Ending in Divorce, by Year of Divorce, Whether Wife
Has Living Child, and Race (per 1,000)

		Whites		Blacks	
Divorces during		Parent	Not	Parent	Not
1st–2nd	1940–49	16	16	31	25
year of	1950–59	12	12	18	18
marriage	1960–66	13	25	10	15
3rd–5th	1940–49	12	10	25	18
year of	1950–59	17	13	24	17
marriage	1960–66	16	15	29	13
6th–10th	1940–49	16	9	15	18
year of	1950–59	9	8	17	19
marriage	1960–66	13	9	24	13
11th–15	1940–49	9	7	11	14
year of	1950–59	12	6	25	9
marriage	1960–66	10	8	12	14

SOURCE: Calculated from *Census CPS P20-223*, table 4.

parents, suggesting real racial differences in the way this aspect
of the life course has been constructed. Black divorce rates
among the childless considerably exceeded that for whites in
marriages in existence in the 1940s, almost but not quite as
much as black rates exceeded rates for whites where no children were involved. But increasingly, the presence of a child
has seemingly brought a constraint on black couples which cut
down considerably on their readiness (or ability) to seek divorce. By contrast, among the childless, blacks' rates of divorce
have grown to exceed whites' by even more, over the period to
which the data pertain. Interpretation is probably premature,
but it is hard not to perceive in this weave of patterns the continued existence of a "conventional" life course pattern, more
characteristic of whites than blacks, of women who marry older
rather than younger, in which divorce is still seen to violate the
most approved family-building patterns. But, as demonstrated
above, the trend data point clearly to the declining relevance.

We will return later to the notion that increasingly blacks have evolved a variant, and distinctive, life course, which characterizes some but not all of that race and very few not of that race.

Divorce, in this sense, had worked its way fully into the family-building sequence and was now a life course event that could "legitimately" take place indifferently before or after parenthood. In fact, while this trend seems certain, the story is probably even more complicated, depending in fact on *prior aspects of the life course* of the members of the couple. Thus, Moore and Waite, employing longitudinal data referring to 1968 through 1972, show that the impact of children on marriages then varied according to *both* wives' age at marriage and the interval before parenthood. They show, further, that the circumstances—or the rules—of the life courses of black and white people were sufficiently differentiated at this date that some patterns varied markedly by race.[44] They argue that, contrary to what they had anticipated, "early childbearing does not seem to increase the probability of marital break-up among whites, quite the opposite." But, for blacks, "there is a strong association between teenage childbearing and marriage break-up" which is *not* simply a product of the also-significant relationship of youthful marriage and subsequent divorce, which obtains for blacks as for whites.[45] They further show that while the "presence of children under three years of age has *no influence* on marital stability among brides 18 or younger and significantly *increases* the likelihood of dissolution for those 19–20 at first marriage, . . . [it] has *a significant inhibiting effect* among those who delayed first marriage until at least 21."[46]

CONCLUSION

Divorce, the usually voluntary ending of one marriage as often as not followed by entry into another, is an appropriate place to end this introductory chapter on trends. Nothing so well as the periodic alternation of spectacular upward lunges and level plateaus of divorce rates suggests the sometimes dramatic ways in which the aggregated choices—constrained, often anguished choices, but choices nevertheless—have modified the normative expectations surrounding the youthful life course. No less, the new incorporation of divorce into the understanding of marriage, together with the greatly enlarged prevalence and widespread expectation of coital experimentation before marriage, points to the way in which the meanings of phases of life have changed in the current century.

And yet, as we saw, the ritual of the wedding has become, if anything, increasingly encrusted by "tradition." If individual volition is more commonly reflected in the circumstances in which marriage is undertaken and exited, this does not point to a loss of the cultural or institutional importance of marriage in the life course. It may, as Kohli has suggested, point to an enlarged pressure on increasingly self-aware individuals to harmonize what they understand to be what they themselves want with what they understand to be the social prescription for people *like* themselves. This paradox may well lie at the base of the current interest in life schedules to which this book, among others, responds.

3

MODERN YOUTH: THE 1920s

CULTURAL INNOVATION

That the 1920s was not a decade of unalloyed prosperity as myth proposes should not blind us to the pervasiveness of cultural themes reflecting a sense of growing plenty that fed and was fed by a focus on the post-Victorian sense of individualized satisfaction. If some elements of the consumer economy lagged, many evolved rapidly.[1] New expectations and elements of a revised organization of the youthful life course emerged from an enlarging and increasingly self-confident middle class, ineluctably intertwined.

In the 1920s, the United States moved a long way toward reducing the enormous heterogeneity that had been created by the headlong development of an urban nation and had for half a century focused the nation's cultural and political energies. Immigration, to take the most obvious example, severely constricted by the Great War, was now sharply reduced by statute. The proportions of the foreign-born who were passing through their childbearing years declined sharply, not compensated for by a comparable increase in second-generation "ethnic" youth. Emigration and death, in addition to cultural adaptation, both consciously foisted and unplanned, worked their effects on the foreign-born community. As the "second generation" of the last great stream of immigration grew up in the 1920s, the once-acute sense that heterogeneity was a "problem" for American democracy began to fade. Evidences of ethnic and cultural discontinuities, to be sure, were still numerous; but a sense of gradual assimilation had begun to overwhelm more conflictual imagery.

The twenties began with a sharp depression, as overoptimistic entrepreneurs failed to anticipate the degree of retardation the changeover to a peacetime economy would entail, and pre-cipitated a sharp depression. By 1922, however, the economy had largely recovered and in short order had absorbed the substantial enlargement in production capacity that war mobilization had produced. With productive capacity so near to ability to consume (given current organization of demand and wants), the precise recognition and imaginative reformation of demand and those financial and informational services that subserved the closer coordination of activity, became crucial economic skills. Among the rewards for economic growth for many, then, was the accession to white-collar jobs that offered shorter hours, cleaner conditions, and prestige.[2]

When Robert Lynd and Helen Merrill Lynd traveled to "Middletown" (Muncie, Indiana) in 1923 to discover how the twentieth century had changed the now-booming American industrial heartland, changes in women's lives seemed to the Lynds to lie at the center of what felt new and different. Wives were more able than before to support themselves and better informed about sex and contraception; but the bread winner/homemaker dichotomy had remained firm. Despite the absence of any sign of change in the ideologies in which this distinction was embedded, behavior had changed in response to the pervasive seeking after material well-being for oneself and one's family and the increasingly favorable evaluation of such motives. As new wants—for an automobile, for a tract house, for commercialized leisure—came to motivate family getting and spending, the coordination of daily life in the family changed, as did the family bonds that subtly drew on these patterns.[3]

Even economically comfortable families seemed to the Lynds less able than before to derive unquestioned satisfaction from "the plans for today and tomorrow, the pleasures of this half-hour."[4] The heroic economic performance of goods in the household appliance, health, cleanliness, beauty, recreation, and entertainment categories during the 1920s points out dramatically the newness of the consumer preference schedule that was emerging. Otis Pease plausibly finds a new cultural theme in the "conspicuous preoccupation with leisure and the

enjoyment of consumption. . . . Leisure to consume and to enjoy material goods was an effective guarantee of happiness. . . .
[Advertising copywriters] looked on themselves, in effect, as
crusaders for the liberation of a middle-class people from the
tyranny of Puritanism, parsimoniousness, and material asceti-
cism."[5] The expansion of national, branded products presenting their case in national periodicals led to advertising cam-
paigns of great skill and impact. The world of objects and
possessions burned brightly in many of these 1920s publications, with new graphic techniques complementing a profound
shift in advertising philosophy—toward evoking a favorable
aura that might be associated with the product.[6] A new standard of living was being defined, whether one thinks of advertising as manipulative or as merely educating the values inherent in the new goods being distributed. "Consumer durables"
came to occupy a far larger corner of the daily routine, setting
a kind of standard of interest and excitement in acquisition.
"There is probably today a greater variation from house to
house in the actual inventory list of family possessions and of
activities by family members than at any previous era in man's
history. The consumer's problem is one of selection to a degree
never before known."[7]

By the 1920s, Americans lived with an internal monologue
about the short-run satisfaction of wishes. To be sure, there
were voices that upheld self-denial for its own sake, but to
young people, these voices increasingly sounded anachronistic.[8] The psychology of advertising at this time recognized just
this and identified the sexual as prominent among these wishes.
"Advertisers should realize that appeals to the physical aspect
of the sex instinct will get attention without question but will
lead only to such action as is in accord with man's selfish wants.
It is only when the psychological aspect is aroused that man
wants to do something for his wife, sweetheart, mother or sister."[9] Among the goods merchandised so successfully by the
new methods were clothing, accessories, and toilet goods, all
depending on links to sexual expressiveness. American young
men and women had, of course, long prepared themselves for
one another's eyes, but the new emphasis on "aura" had a

profound effect on many who beheld them, proposing legitimacy and propriety for an open and unashamed focus on self-
presentation.

Contemporaries were momentarily exercised over a rapid
expansion of consumer debt. So startling was this development
that two-thirds of a sample of Oregon credit buyers raised mor-
alistic objections to such borrowing against the future.[10] Within
the decade, consumer borrowing had become pervasive and
was understood as a normal, neutral way of increasing purchasing power.[11]

For many youth of the middle and more prosperous working
classes, the material prosperity of the period meant they grew
up with access to a family car, the enlarged range of casual social intercourse offered by the telephone, and the beginning of
a "by rights" claim to discretionary spending within the family
budget.[12] A parents' group secretary's report reflects nicely
both the dimensions engendered in the older generation, and
their resolution of the matter.

> In the young days of many of us, clothes meant quality, but that's
> not so now-a-days—at least the main thing is style, and continuous
> change in terms of color and style. Quality doesn't count for so
> much. Clothes are cheaper too. But with our early induced feeling
> for quality we can't understand this constant buying of cheaper
> clothes, and think it wasteful. . . . We need to reorganize our think-
> ing. Why not more dresses as an expression of the individual?[13]

Childbearing and even child rearing were postponed by
some women who now could work gainfully, achieving a range
of material comfort so that family life could embody the new
sense of domesticity. As before, "child-bearing is . . . to Middletown a moral obligation. Indeed, in this urban life of alluring
alternative choices, . . . there is perhaps a more self-conscious
weighting of the question with moral emphasis." When Middle-
towners reduced their fertility, they only shifted their emphasis
"somewhat from child-bearing to child-rearing." By this point
in a marriage, "in general, a high degree of companionship [be-
tween marriage partners] is not regarded as essential for marriage," although hopes for a lifetime of "being in love" were
seemingly on the rise.[14] Divorce became more imaginable for

women, and this now began to be a consideration in their initial choice of marriage partners, and marriage timing. "Apparently this growing flexibility in attitude toward the marriage institution reacts back upon itself; one factor in the increasing frequency of divorce is probably the growing habituation to it."[15] It was not so much that marriages were less successful than before as that people were prepared—and women, with more gainful employment open to them, more able—to sever ties that had not proven satisfying. When the Lynds revisited Middletown in 1935, they noted "a growing belief" among youth "that marriage need not be final since divorce is no longer a serious disgrace."[16]

In Middletown, marriage age continued to move downward, but not because unions had become more impetuous. Rather, young people responded to the ability to postpone fertility, the availability of remunerative work for wives, and the replacement of communitywide socializing by an increasingly privatized life.[17] Weddings in Middletown were now often only a "brief ceremonial exchange of verbal pledges," but bride and groom were by convention and generally in fact linked by being "in love."[18] In a sense, their courtship was now the better suited to exactly that value. "Sexually, their awareness of their maturity is augmented by the maturity of their social rituals," which still went on with subtle parental guidance. The Lynds' account suggests that a rather callous approach to the opposite sex was gradually being replaced by a deeper way of knowing, accomplished perhaps under the influence of the "personal intimacy" now permissible.[19]

The 1910s and early 1920s were characterized by a "dance craze," which contributed to a new definition of appropriate heterosexual relationships among young people. Before the 1910s, open-admission dances had most characteristically been held by ethnic, neighborhood, and other established social organizations, largely catering to their own members, who, knowing one another, restrained one another's tendencies to overstep moral rules. But in 1911, a dance "palace" was opened in New York City, an arrangement that spread rapidly, especially in the early 1920s.[20]

The dance halls dazzled and featured lively jazz, the surroundings and the music (sometimes aided by liquor) encouraged the easy and spontaneous contact between unacquainted or slightly acquainted members of the opposite sex. The music was sensual, offering a rhythm in which two bodies moved smoothly to that music, together.

> Into these halls come many types seeking many ends. There are those fascinated by the promise of a thrill, college boys whose purpose is to "sow wild oats," high school girls and boys in search of sophistication, the repressed and inhibited in conventional grundies, and frustrated women who seek Bohemianism. The majority, however, are not cases requiring social therapy. They find here a means of social contact. Here they may mingle freely with others in an emotionally charged atmosphere.[21]

The new dances of the era (sometimes called "tough dancing") were less formalized in the steps they demanded of participants, correspondingly offering room for expressiveness of body movement, in keeping with the jazz-derived rhythms that underlay them. "The dances fostered an unheard-of casualness between partners, permitted greater options in holds and distances, and symbolized the high value placed on mutual heterosexual intimacy and attraction." Working-class boys and girls ordinarily came separately to the dance hall, seeking out partners during the evening. But middle-class youth drawn into this world typically arrived at the dance palace in boy-girl couples, their dance-floor intimacy part of a longer-term "career" as a couple.[22]

Identifying the *openness* of sensual expression as the common element, an authority on adolescence explained the rapid spreading of petting among young people by the *overt* public acceptance of the new dances. "Some of the modern dances and petting are parallel forms of excitement and experience in sexual affairs."[23] Despite the obvious risks, high schools were quick to institute dances, in an effort of varying success to take the play away from commercial dance halls and roadhouses.[24] The meaning of dancing was, in the main, recreation and structured sociability, but inherently suggestive and potentially explosive. Boys, as a group, found it in their interest to press dancing in a sexual direction, which suited girls' purposes insofar as the dancing also served as a declaration of generational freedom; but for them, the sexualization of dancing also inched the terms of the boy-girl negotiation that much closer to "going too far," at which point they had more to lose.

The morally innovative meaning of the movies was also apparent to adolescents.

> It is important to consider that the movies do not come merely as a film that is thrown on a screen; their witnessing is an experience which is undergone in a very complex setting. There is the darkened theater . . . ; there is the music which is capable not merely of being suggestive and in some degree interpretive of the film but is also designed to raise the pitch of excitement, to facilitate shock and to heighten the emotional effect of the picture; there are the furnishings—sometimes gaudy and gorgeous, which help to tone the experience.[25]

Between 1921 and 1930, average weekly attendance at motion pictures increased rapidly. A weekly movie habit, or more, was typical of unmarried youth, who characteristically attended with age-peers, except among those exceptional boys and girls whose "moral habits" were considered especially "high" by adult standards.[26] Even in rural areas—at least those that were neither geographically isolated nor poverty-stricken—teenage patterns of recreation were no less transformed by this form of commercial entertainment.[27] Films were very special events for their new fans in the 1920s, if hardly rare ones, and in their content no less than in the emotional "tone" their purveyance suggested a larger world of possibility to their viewers.

> A movie is judged by the thrill it produces. . . . The scenes which make the greatest appeal to the boys are usually those which satisfy some desire which is in them. The scenes which appeal most to the girls are those which correspond but apparently do not satisfy some desire they have. The boys seem to be content with the things as they see them on the screen while the girls only long for the things that they see there.[28]

Mary Pickford and Douglas Fairbanks, by easy stages, and then the morally ambivalent dramas of Cecil B. DeMille led Americans to accept the body as a legitimate locus of pleasure and

gratification as a worthwhile and even necessary aspect of marriage, replacing the compartmentalization of sex implied by
the risqué short films characteristic of the previous era of the
American industry.[29]

One student of contemporary motion pictures counted five
and one-half love scenes per film. In love films in which the
circumstances surrounding love could be determined, just under half the occasions of initial love were love at first sight and
more than half the remaining occasions were at second or third
sight. The formal needs of movie dramaturgy explained much
of this, but there was a strong cumulative impact on young
people's sense of the timing and sequencing of the emotional
structure of the life course. Among the "goals of the leading
characters," of 115 motion pictures studied, "winning another's
love" was a clear goal in 70 percent. "Marriage for love" was
present in 36 percent of the movies, "illicit love" in 19 percent.
These three motives alone accounted for 45 percent of all goals
detectable.[30] For the more impressionable young viewers, the
films provided explicit content for sex fantasies and instruction
in lovemaking techniques.[31] *True Confessions*, in working out its
formula for morally subversive moralizing, moved from literally true confessions through a slick presentation of movie stars'
glamorous, too-worldly lives, to a mixture of mythic confession
and movie-star revelation.

If sexuality was purveyed commercially to youth in the 1920s
in deliciously small doses, so also in what was deemed to be
denatured form it was increasingly supplied *gratis*, by adult authorities. Right education about sexuality was an occasion for
progressive educators to address children on a subject not
perhaps of their own choice but under the circumstances, compelling.[32] The sex-education movement, in fact, had grown
from the successful suppression of officially—or unofficially—
tolerated segregated urban vice districts during World War I.
Ironically, the movement thus triumphant had ramified considerably beyond the suppression of prostitution, shattering in the
process "the conspiracy of silence" about sexuality that had co-
existed with tolerated but circumscribed vice.[33] To banish vice,
vice must be discussed, and thereby sexuality must be discussed, as a question of policy. The young conscripts of World

War I received a broadened range of official information regarding venereal diseases. Volunteer social hygienists told them yet more, placing their sexual drives into a larger context that moralized them but stopped short of the repressive levels of the prewar period. As tolerated prostitution was vanquished, the "social purity" movement expanded its concerns to include venereal disease, and thereby, sex education. At this point, a long-lasting alliance was struck up with those promoting the notion of eugenic contraception, who sought to diffuse the motive and means of family limitation among the immigrant and working-class population.

By the 1920s, sex educationists were increasingly eager to free their subject from a narrow focus on the biological aspects of sexuality and to incorporate larger psychological and guidance components.[34] Sexuality and the study of sexuality became a national fascination, as science and scandal.[35] In the early 1920s, a large sample of junior high students was asked their opinion of taking a "course dealing with marriage, home and parenthood." At this time, only 46 percent of the girls and 41 percent of the boys who offered an opinion supported the courses—and a majority of the boys and one in three girls ventured no opinion at all. But by the mid-1930s, seven in ten Maryland 16-year-olds believed that the schools should incorporate sex education, one-quarter of these feeling that *elementary school* was the appropriate level. (Girls were slightly more in favor of sex education, especially early, than boys.) The only remaining pockets of opposition were among those youth who had dropped out of school at an early age.[36] One would not call the viewpoint of this movement "modern" today, certainly not in the sense of an explicit embracing of sexuality as a good. But as a public movement, as a group of respectable propagandists with scientific and religious authority to speak publicly on issues that for some time had been hushed, it certainly was a "modernizing" movement.[37]

Before the end of the 1920s, it had become conventional wisdom in substantial segments of the population that adult sexual expression was not merely permissible, but "a duty toward one's 'mental health' or 'whole personality,'" one that had a "pivotal place . . . in marriage."[38] Thus, the U.S. Children's Bureau cautioned parents that in responding to their developing children's questions about sex, "no attempt should be made to bolster up good, sound advice with statements of dangers which, in the first place, may not exist and, in the second place, serve no other purpose than the creation of unreasonable fears at the time and may well become handicaps to him later in life."[39] By 1941, the American Association of School Administrators would seek to assume a moral entrepreneurship in the realm of the now thoroughly acceptable field by urging "that the school offer leadership to the entire community, and especially to parents, on problems of marriage and parenthood."[40] A systematic study of the results of a "personal improvement" curriculum offered within Home Economics in a Pittsburgh high school in the mid-1930s provides evidence that the curriculum *was* effective in promoting girls' "social skills," adding to the like impact of simply growing older. At the same time, the special curriculum contributed most to the social skills of daughters of middle-class parents. Further, *self-perception* of social competence proved to be largely independent of social skills, while exposure to the special curriculum seems to have increased working-class girls' self-consciousness at their own social failings even as their objective social skills increased.[41]

THE HIGH SCHOOL AND THE
TRANSITION TO ADULTHOOD

In a setting of increasing disposable wealth, decreasing population heterogeneity, and an enlarged emphasis on the individual's ability to choose his or her own way of life, the idea of universal high school "took" as a broad-gauge instrument of socialization. The schooling explosion of the 1920s was characterized by a greater extension of schooling among most of those groups previously least exposed to schooling (and especially in urban places where high schooling was already relatively prudent): an educated population was presented as no less a public good than a private one.[42] To be sure, even at the end of the 1920s, native whites of native parentage received more schooling than nonwhites and than the foreign-born and their children, but the differences had narrowed significantly. Table 7

Table 7. Proportion Having Completed at Least One Year of High
School, Cohorts of High School Age around 1918 and 1928,
by Sex, Race, and Urban Proportion of Population in State of
Residence (in percentages)

	Most Rural		*Rather Rural*		*Middling*		*Rather Urban*		*Most Urban*	
	Male	*Female*	*Male*	*Female*	*Male*	*Female*	*Male*	*Female*	*Male*	*Female*
White										
1918	38.7	47.0	43.7	52.2	44.8	52.6	37.3	52.0	46.7	48.5
1928	51.4	59.7	55.7	63.7	64.2	70.9	66.9	69.5	64.6	65.1
Nonwhite										
1918	8.2	12.7	10.0	12.4	21.3	28.9	22.5	27.8	25.4	28.4
1928	13.0	20.8	16.5	24.9	36.9	45.5	42.7	48.1	40.4	45.3

SOURCE: Census—*Population Trends*, table 6.
NOTE: Proportion urban in state calculated as of 1960. Urban/rural differentials will be somewhat exaggerated by differential *migration* of the more educated to more-urban areas between
1918–1926 and 1960. More-urban states in 1960, however, by and large will have also been more
urban in 1918–1926.

suggests the pace and location of high school attendance by
contrasting the schooling of the birth cohorts who were of high
school age in the late 1910s and the late 1920s, subdivided by
race, sex, and the degree of urbanization of the state in which
they lived. In the decade, high school experience (about twice
as common as high school *graduation*) became modal for whites
in all categories, especially (and most rapidly) in the most urbanized states. And in the most urbanized states, too, high
schools began to reach a majority of black youth. Starting considerably below females in both high school attendance and
graduation, males caught up slightly during the decade, but
only in the more urbanized states. In those places, as well, the
rate for nonwhites grew the most rapidly, and converged the
most rapidly on the rate for whites.

The enlargement of the high school experience proved to be
of particular importance to young women, both because they
found in the high school an especially consequential social setting and because they learned there employable skills that were
to be useful immediately and were to draw them back into the

labor force in later decades. As Claudia Goldin's fine cohort analysis of women's work patterns shows,

> although change in the labor force participation rates of married women did accelerate [only] after World War II, many of the pre-conditions for the expansion had been set decades before. . . . New social norms of the 1920s may have influenced the decisions of many young women to delay leaving the labor force until their first pregnancy, rather than with marriage. . . . This change may have . . . provided that critical break on which future change was founded.[43]

Each year in the decade saw greater numbers of both boys and girls graduating from high school. Between 1922 and 1924 there were annual increases of no less than 2.5 percent in the proportion of all 17-year-olds graduating.[44] The reduction of child labor in good part preceded the school increase, especially at the youngest ages—through 15—for both boys and girls. In Philadelphia, the proportion of white boys and girls out of school and in gainful employment at 15 declined from nearly half in 1915 to one in six in 1925, at which point it leveled off. The proportion of white boys and girls out of school *without* work, although far lower, dropped even more precipitously. Black boys and girls, far less likely to be gainfully employed but somewhat more likely to be at home without work, showed parallel trends. Both public schooling and Philadelphia's strong parochial school system eagerly took up those who moved out of the labor force. The school trend slowed considerably in Philadelphia in the second half of the decade, but pushed up again in the Depression, never to be reversed thereafter, except briefly during World War II. In 1932, only about 5 percent of Philadelphia's 15-year-olds were out of school.[45] In Pittsburgh, the numbers of boys at work at age 14 declined by two-thirds between 1923 and 1929, while the numbers of boys still enrolled at school at 15 increased by half. Girls had previously been less given to work, more given to school. In the seven-year period, enrollment gained and work declined by 40 percent. The distribution of what jobs there were shifted sharply away from adultlike work in heavy industry toward service, clerking, and message carrying.[46]

In 1910, half of all boys of 15 had been gainfully employed, nationally. By 1930, the proportion was down to one in six. Girls at work at 15 declined from one in four to one in twelve. These figures bespeak a change in the operation of the family economy so rapid that it must have been felt quite consciously. The age at which children would begin "paying back" their parents for the investments they had made in them was postponed over this period for two years or longer, the greater part of this change coming in the 1920s. Communities proudly established more and more high schools, formally training their adolescents for a new kind of work life and participating in a democratization of secondary education that brought in students of less-favored socioeconomic background as well as students of less promising scholastic aptitude.[47] Only the fact that parents were having fewer children allowed them, and their communities, to support the new youthful life course that was elaborated at this time. These patterns coincided with, and were intensified by, the development of nearly purely residential suburban areas much given to high-quality schooling, where parents had clearly made a choice about the kind of youthful life courses their children were to have.[48]

In the 1920s, age homogenization within grades was a self-conscious policy of many high school administrators, accomplished even as the schools expanded rapidly to include students from families that were close enough to the economic margin to require supplementary income from their children from time to time.[49] Failure to promote increasingly was seen to encourage dropping out, and this was seen as unfortunate. A dramatic example of the progress of age homogenization is found in the school system of heavily working-class Duluth, Minnesota. Among sixteen-year-olds attending Duluth public schools in 1920–21, only 25 percent of the boys and 36 percent of the girls were to be found in a single grade; five years of policies promoting age homogenization brought these figures to 33 percent and 40 percent. By the mid-1930s, they had been brought up to 42 percent and 54 percent.[50]

The 1930 census affords a full picture of children's passage out of school and into the work force at decade's end. Figure 6, presenting the story for males, shows that by that date, after

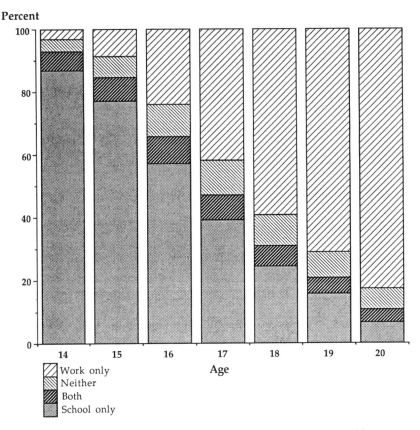

Figure 6. Boys' Passage Out of School and into the Work Force, 1930

the innovations of the past decades, the movement from school into work began apace for boys only between 15 and 16. School and extended gainful work were rather rarely pursued simultaneously. Nor did many more boys at any age emerge from school without promptly completing the transition to the work force. The proportion of boys enrolled in school who were at the same time in the work force rose from about one in seven at age 16 to nearly two in five at age 20, but the proportionate rise was more the product of leaving school than of finding jobs. Even at 16, fewer than one in three boys who had left school were not yet at work, a proportion that had dropped to about one in twelve by age 20. By 20 (by which age fewer than one in eight young men were married), eight in ten had entered into adult labor force status.

Figure 7 presents like data for girls and young women. The dominant trend here, as with boys, is that as they get older, there is a movement away from exclusive attention to schooling. The level of enrollment at each age, and the inflection points, in fact, are very similar to boys' levels. Boys, however, quite clearly had a single complementary activity: work. When boys moved from school, they ordinarily tried to move directly into work, but the "idle" proportion among girls was considerably greater and increased with age. The proportion of girls neither in school nor at work, in fact, was at each age almost identical

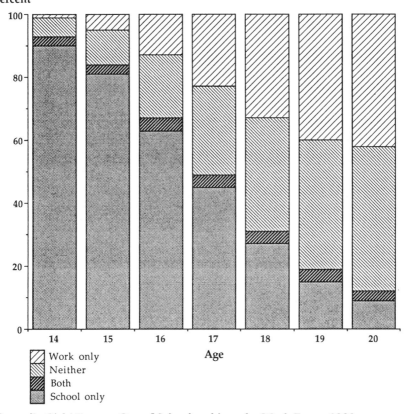

Figure 7. Girls' Passage Out of School and into the Work Force, 1930

with that of girls at work. As it happens, the census data includes marital status for girls (but not for boys), which allows us to examine the extent to which the "idle" girls were generally married or, alternatively, helping around the parental home. The data indicate that only by age 19 were more than half the "idle" girls married. At age 17, by contrast, only three in ten girls who were neither at school nor at work were married. At this age, the "idle" constituted nearly one in four girls.

Dropping out of school, then, was itself in a sense normative for girls, rather than being immediately propelled by an immediate transition to wife or worker. Although the 1920s saw a very significant intertwining of courtship with schooling, it is equally clear that a subsequent—and far more elusive—phase of the female life course typically supervened before marriage. At the same time, the graph reminds us that gainful employment was quite common but far from universal for late-adolescent girls. For this reason, therefore, we may understand why girls less than half as frequently as boys *both* worked and attended school. Among the concomitants of recent economic developments was a noteworthy rise in women working at sales and clerical jobs.[51] At this date, however, married women worked, essentially, under necessity: with no pressing family need for income, being a homemaker was commonly prescribed. Yet the concept of necessity was being broadened.[52] The decade saw more, and more prominent, exceptions to that rule, and they seem to have conveyed to contemporaries a sense of a norm that was changing.[53]

We can detect emergent in the decade a new sense of life course organization closely connected to extended education, a sequence of events deliberately geared toward material accumulation and personal gratification, in which middle-class women's work was seen as far more compatible with marriage than formerly. The new pattern can be seen to advantage in the data collected in 1941 from native white Protestant couples in Indianapolis who had married in the years 1927 to 1929. These data reveal a close, but by no means perfect, connection among the young people's socioeconomic background, their own educational attainment, and their labor force experience. Socioeconomic background and educational attainment helped determine a cluster of subsequent behaviors, including the age at which women married, the frequency with which they had worked before marriage and after marriage, and as we shall see later, the timing (and means of managing the timing) of their transition to parenthood. Thus, among women who graduated from high school, only 14 percent had married at 18 or younger, a figure contrasting strongly with the 53 percent of the girls who did not finish high school who had married by 18. Among women who did not complete high school, although they married younger, 21 percent never worked before marriage, a figure exceeding the 15 percent among those who did complete high school. After marriage, however, these patterns were to reverse: 52 percent of women who had not graduated from high school but 58 percent of the graduates worked shortly after the marriage.

School and marriage were incompatible statuses for women during this period, and work and marriage, if decreasingly so, were substantially incompatible as well. There is really no secure way of estimating the separate "contribution" to young women's marriage of leaving school, entering work, and simply growing older. Table 8 shows the proportions of young women in 1930 who were married, for each single year of age, according to school and work status. It is apparent that age had a large direct effect on marriage-proneness, apart from its indirect effect through discouraging school enrollment and, conversely, encouraging gainful employment. Even among those in school, as among those out of school both in and out of work, proportions married increased with each single year of age. The whole sequence is best described as an occasionally varying sequence of transitions, school leaving coming first and proportions attending school falling dramatically between the ages of 15 and 18. Leaving school can be said to have precipitated some openness to marriage, but not overmuch, with a greater effect on promoting gainful employment. After age 17, the proportions of young women out of school who were gainfully employed leveled off at a shade under half, but this was to a growing extent a product of the competition between work and marriage: of those who were out of school *and unmarried*, the proportion at work increased year by year, reaching a majority

Table 8. Proportion of Young Women Married, by School Enrollment
          and Labor Force Status, 1930 (in percentages)

	14	15	16	17	18	19	20
Young Women in School							
Not working	0.1	0.2	0.5	0.9	1.5	2.2	3.3
Working	0.0	0.1	0.2	0.4	0.7	0.9	1.2
Young Women not in School							
Not working	3.6	9.2	17.7	30.6	45.7	58.5	68.1
Working	1.9	2.9	3.4	4.6	9.5	10.2	14.1
in School	92.9	84.5	66.8	48.8	29.4	18.8	11.7
% of those not in School							
who Work	19.9	27.7	38.9	46.0	49.6	49.1	47.4
% of those not in School and							
Unmarried							
who Work	20.2	29.1	42.8	54.0	62.1	67.6	70.8

SOURCE: Derived, with some interpolations, from Census 1930–1, 1180–1181.

by age 17 and two in three by age 19. The increasing proportions married of the entire group—38 percent by age 20—was
drawn substantially from those who had completed the entire
series of transitions, or who promptly left school or work when
they married.

The exfoliating high school was already a hotbed of anxieties
and longings when the automobile, World War I, and a new
definition of adolescence banished the chaperone and direct
parental oversight of courtship. "Who has not observed the
various ways in which the high school girl, while not admitting
her motive even to her self, endeavors to draw the regard of
her male companions?" asked psychologist Phyllis Blanchard in
1920. The high school, Blanchard observed, was a haven of
"incessant giggling" produced by girls' "new consciousness of
sexual differences" and the rigors of new "social situations for
which she as yet feels herself lacking in poise. . . . With the
dawn of adolescence comes a new self-consciousness as the awakening sexual and social instincts induce comparison with others and emphasize personal deficiencies hitherto discarded."[54]
The old term "calf-love" no longer seemed to describe behavior

adequately and now seemed too dismissive. "If a child is the product either of a modern home or of a coeducational school of today, his adolescent fixations, if any, are likely to be directed heterosexually to a person of approximately his own age," wrote a researcher in 1934, contrasting his findings to those made in the first decades of the century. Child study experts observing adolescents in these settings discovered that girls now directed their early amorousness toward far more plausible love-objects, and shortly developed a vocabulary with which to engage them.[55]

THE DATING SYSTEM

"The outside world of today has no use for flimsy worshipers of petty idols such as 'popularity,'" thundered a Minneapolis Central High editorialist in 1923, but popularity was the universally understood term for what the great majority of high schoolers sought to a greater or lesser degree. Popularity and cliquishness were closely related and tied closely to dating: both were parts of a new system of social relations governed informally but firmly *by young people themselves.* Well before the adult world took much notice, most boys and girls from their midteens on came to organize their social lives around an institution not of their elders' making.[56] This was so even before they evolved the dating system. As early as the turn of the century, in places where high schooling was common enough that it enrolled a socially heterogeneous student body, it was there that students "transferred emotional ties from the family to the peer group. Students felt compelled to present themselves to win approval from their classmates," in activities in which they "carved out personalities derived from the role models of their parents and teachers, but infused with unique youthful styles to win popularity or prestige."[57] Not all youth saw dating in the same light, to be sure, even in the high schools. Material wherewithal made a difference; so also did cultural heritage. And asymmetries of gender roles were the armature around which the dating system would evolve.

A fine historical account of the emergence of the dating system first suggested by Paula Fass and recently elaborated by

Beth L. Bailey[58] understands dating as one among many of the achievements of a self-conscious generation, acting in part over and against its predecessors:

> It was not caprice . . . that made them question traditional proprieties in sexual morality and in such areas as smoking, drinking, and dancing. These the young defined as the private sector, as a sphere for personal expression to be governed by need and taste rather than by laws and morals. . . . The young knew that their patterns and attitudes provided a margin of difference between them and their elders, and gave them a vehicle for group cohesion.[59]

Fass and Bailey demonstrate that the symbols of generational revolt were preeminently borne by women and that they took the form of the narrowing of the differences in the behaviors of the two genders: language, clothing, smoking, hair style, and social intercourse between the sexes, the latter constituting a modest challenge to the double standard of sexual propriety. If "freedom" or autonomy seemed to contemporaries to be at stake, in retrospect, youth—and young women in particular— seem to have proposed no fundamental changes in the moral order, only the lifting of limitations, based on age and gender, on their own right to choose among conventional options. They challenged received definitions of authority, not morality, positioning themselves to take advantage of the alluring but hardly revolutionary range of new consumer choice created by an expanding economy. As Bailey astutely notes, "sex became the central public symbol of youth culture, a fundamental part of the definition that separated youth from age."[60] If sex was now "as frankly discussed as automobiles or the advantage of cold storage over moth balls, why should our elders consider our interest in this subject a sign of unnaturalness or perversion? Should it not constitute the chief concern of those in whose hands the future generation lies?"[61]

Young people, however, did attend to what their elders said in condemnation and alarm, and they formed their own responses partly in opposition to them with sex no less symbolic to them as to their parents. "In forging the new conventions and living with them, the meaning of youth's sexual experience was transformed."[62] If young people in rejecting received courtship procedures also rejected traditional romanticism, they by no means rejected marriage or marriage based on love. The new dating system, as they understood it, was an institutional framework that subserved exactly this end.

While the Fass-Bailey description of the dating scene is persuasive, its focus on collegians slights evidence that the dating system evolved simultaneously among high school students. This part of the system affected more people and coincided with the phase of heterosexual awakening in participants' lives. Both the age homogenization of the high schools and their expansion promoted the evolution of a dating system, since dating depended on freely entered short-term agreements between near equals, differentiated mainly by gender and overseen by the opinion of mutually valued, interrelated sets of age peers. Age, with its correlated experience, earning capacity, was the kind of differentiator that could render too unequal the negotiation of dating's core. (In parallel with cultural expectations governing marriage, girls could date somewhat older boys.) Age homogenization limited exploitation and permitted the girls to move somewhat beyond the constrictive safety provided by adherence to the double standard.

The defining characteristic of the new dating system and, what is more critical here, of the graduated series of dates that might lead to a more lasting commitment between young men and women was that a date was away from home, proposed and paid for by the boy, unchaperoned, and not subject to detailed parental veto; it depended on the free election of the participants. "An invitation to go out on a date," as Bailey maintains, "was an invitation into man's world—not simply because dating took place in the public sphere (commonly defined as belonging to men), though that was part of it, but because dating moved courtship into the world of the economy," where the boy's money paid for the date.[63] Certainly, *some* American boys and girls of the middle classes had coupled in every imaginable way without parental awareness before dating was practiced, but encounters of this sort lacked the continuity and regularity that the full evolution of the dating system after World War I would permit. (Bailey offers some evidence of "dating"—for instance, the use of the word—among select groups as early as the mid-1910s.)[64] Under the older system, there was no normatively sanctioned way for an adolescent to get "serious" about someone of the opposite sex without submitting the relationship for parental approval. Chaperonage asserted parents' oversight of what boys and girls might do together, and the home visit assured girls' parents of some control over whom their daughters might be seeing. Both were important, and both vanished with dating, which substituted peer oversight. Not the occurrence of emotional or physical intimacy but the question of whose advice guided young people in developing heterosexual ties was the critical difference between dating and the practice of "calling" and "keeping company" that it was rapidly supplanting in the 1920s.

Parents with cars or the wherewithal to get them indeed found them near the core of their conflicts with their children, as indicated in *Middletown*, where the automobile was the most visible sign of change. The Lynds note that "social fitness" and possession of an auto were closely linked in the minds of local high schoolers, explaining their exigency when addressing their parents on the subject. When, in the next paragraph, the Lynds explored changes in youth standards of sexual behavior, automobiles, along with movies, were cited as causes, or near-causes.[65] In this matter, conventional accounts have taken the Lynds too literally, affected perhaps by the fascination automobiles have long held for boys in "wild" phases, sexual and otherwise.[66] The far more mundane telephone would seem to have been a more crucial piece of dating technology, and the motion picture and the motion picture theater even more so.

Cars certainly were important to boys and girls who dated, and permitted much explicitly sexual behavior to transpire, but it is doubtful if the automobile importantly promoted the change that dating (or petting) constituted. For one thing, there simply were not enough cars to go around. Even in San Jose, California, at the end of the decade, nearly one in three high school junior boys never drove, and nearly as many again had the family car only "seldom."[67] The car was in fact only the most conspicuous of the heightened consumption patterns that were associated with dating. Cars were no more literally prescribed than was any other unique item or gesture. It was in large cities, where cars remained notably fewer than in the countryside and small towns, that dating evolved; there, the streetcar sufficed as a means of moving about on dates. Transportation was less important than the availability of somewhere to go to that the girl was willing to go to, and able to convince her parents to let her go to, a legitimate but individualized activity. Thus, a sociologist's inquiry into cultural change in the 1920s that compared rural with county-seat life observed that it was in the *rural* areas—where dating was not yet practiced—that parents saw the automobile as a threat to their authority.[68]

The elaboration of dating as a system began in the first quarter of this century and spread apace during the 1920s and 1930s from its initially urban and middle-class center. A large study of schoolchildren in Kansas City, Kansas, and nearby communities in 1923–1926 found that among boys of 13, "having dates" (as the questionnaire collected from the subjects put it) was the tenth most favored activity (football was tops) and advanced to the fifth most favored by age 17. Girls at 13 (who liked reading best) were even more fond of dating, and retained their lead over boys in this regard, with dating the fourth leading activity at age 17. In a San Jose, California, high school, two-thirds of the sophomore boys and three-fourths of senior boys were dating in 1930. Data collected in 1933 from a large sample of high school girls (oversampled among Catholic schools) found that half of the freshmen and 84 percent of the seniors had begun dating. Blumenthal's 1932 ethnography of isolated "Mineville" found the dating system in operation.[69]

A careful study of upstate New York rural girls in 1933 revealed that the institution had begun to make its way into the countryside. Only 33 percent of the girls aged 15 to 17 had never yet dated, and an additional 49 percent did not yet date "consistently." At ages 18 to 20, a somewhat greater proportion, 58 percent, were not yet consistent daters, suggesting that dates had arrived there quite recently. For each younger cohort of girls interviewed, dating had begun younger, as the institution diffused. These girls, when they dated, went to movies, dances, and parties and motor rides, just as did urban youth.[70] But in less prosperous rural locations, social life devoted exclusively to youth was exceptionally truncated. In the countryside, parents' capacity to exercise close supervision was often too great; many farm youth were even said to seek the city partly on this account.[71]

Urban working-class youth seem to have had quite sufficient distance from parental oversight to erect a dating system, but other matters at first militated against it. The sociological accounts of Donovan on waitresses, Thrasher on the boy gang, and Thomas on girl delinquents discuss non-middle-class milieus of the 1920s which lacked both material wherewithal and peer groups with wide enough consensus to oversee dating. Here, dating in the sense we are discussing clearly did not organize heterosexual contact.[72] Nor did it in factories and shops with mixed work forces, sexualized as byplay became there, precisely because females were at such a disadvantage in the work world that they ordinarily shied away from the kind of exploratory gestures characteristic of dating.[73] Whyte's Boston observations in the mid-1930s pointed out the continued existence of ethnic working-class settings in which highly asymmetrical assumptions about gender roles rendered dating inappropriate.[74] Working-class children at first could not control the time, place, or tempo of boy-girl contacts. They also lacked both the wherewithal for the "good time" dating asked of the boy and the effective, school-based, same-age peer group that oversaw behavior within the dating system.[75]

Information on black youth is rare, but a suggestive account can be put together which argues that lower-class urban blacks, at any rate, had *not* by the early 1930s elaborated a dating system on the order of that developed by whites. In Kansas City, Kansas, in 1926, although black children did date a bit in their teens, boys and girls both omitted dating from their list of favorite activities.[76] Instead, black boys and girls socialized commonly in large mixed-age settings of various sorts, some of which did but others of which did not offer the kinds of protections against boys' sexually threatening behavior that were provided by the elaborated dating system, as among whites.[77] Such protections were both lacking and—for a subset of girls who were striving for "respectability"—necessary because talk of sexual matters—and not just as fantasy—was prevalent among both black boys and girls. A proper seventeen-year-old Washington girl of lower-class background told an investigator:

> We girls often discuss boys and having relations with them. All my girls friends think about the same as I do. They don't want to have any now. I know it's natural, and I don't object if people want to do it. But, you see, my mother trusts me and lets me go with boys because she thinks I won't go wrong.[78]

Among urban black youth, relative license in sexual matters for boys, and a sharp discomfort caused by such license on the part of a self-consciously "respectable" grouping of the girls, fit with a marriage schedule that was appreciably earlier than for whites. The highly restrained attitude toward sexuality within dating that later marriage permitted seemed out of place to blacks who would shortly begin marrying, even without pregnancy. An eighteen-year-old boy in Cincinnati offered to a social investigator a plaint that, with moving naiveté, incorporated prompt marriage.

> She has subthing of mine. I ask her to let me walk home with her but she said no. I have not got the nevers to ask her do she love me. I am going to stop school and get a job and I am going to ask her to marry me. she look like the morning star. she look like a sweet rose in a valley. I love her so my heart ach. it dance around. no Jive.[79]

In more realistic contact with the severe family economic circumstances that promoted early marriage was a fifteen-year-old girl.

> My father has no regular job and I have some more little sisters and a brother. Friends have told me I ought to marry. But I want to go through high school. I haves a good home and very kind sweet loving parents. There is a boy who loves me and ask me to marry. But I refuse.[80]

Among middle-class whites, the fully evolved date itself had a compelling logic quite distinct from that of prior forms of courtship: it was a step in an ongoing negotiation, with rules defined and deviations punished by age peers. The logic of the date anchored it in modest pleasures and centered the choices it occasioned in the daters themselves (within limits imposed by the peer culture). The home visit or chaperoned dance, in essence, had been either purely sociable—part of a group occasion—or explicitly related to courtship. The date might turn out to be either of these, or both, or, most commonly, something else again, but what it turned out to be depended on how well the negotiation at its core went, a negotiation regarding short-term gratification. By definition, boys planned and paid for "a good time" and asked of their girls a bit of physical intimacy. How a boy pled his case, how his date responded, and the future of the pair as a couple depended not only on the boy's sense of his investment and the girl's scale of values but also on the public commitment each was willing to make to the other and their capacity for emotional intimacy, which "modern" girls (like their nineteenth-century predecessors) wanted badly, and often missed, in their consorts.[81]

A charming 1929 story in *The Ladies' Home Journal* celebrated the diffusion of the date and its code by a nice reversal. When a rich and attractive, but somewhat behindhand, girl coolly plans to hone her date-related skills on the young handyman at her summer place—the better to succeed with her chosen suitor—her conventionalized behaviors work *too* well: her wiles capture both the handyman and her designated boyfriend. But the handyman captures her—and turns out to be working his way through college, and thus acceptable and, at the story's conclusion, accepted.[82]

The developing internal logic of the date can be discerned in the statements of those whose dating experiences seemed to them imperfect enough that they wrote to newspaper advice columnists.[83] In the broad shifts in vocabulary, usage, and assumption contained in these published letters can be seen the progressive definition of the institution of dating as it spread. Internal evidence points to regular editing (even apart from selectivity) by the columnists, and scuttlebutt suggests some fabrication; newspaper readerships were narrower than the full range of the population, and only readers possessing both a sense of moderate anguish and a yen for disclosure would even consider writing. However, if the letters had not smacked of verisimilitude, the advice proffered would have read as a parody of itself; and to judge from the generally sober (while distinctly adolescent) tone of the great majority of the letters examined that dealt with problems in the early stages of boy-girl relationships, adolescent readers were in fact reached. That parodies appeared frequently in the high school newspapers attests to the intense, if ambivalent, interest of young readers.

Urban youth were not yet entirely familiar with dating in 1920: even the simplest rules of the dating system might not be well understood. Doris Blake's early correspondents often asked about when boys might be and should be invited to girls' homes, reflecting the transition from the older tradition. But it was the goodnight kiss that provided the most common perplexity at this early date. W. A. wrote to Blake, "I am a girl seventeen years of age. I have been going with a young man three years my senior, whom I love and admire very much. . . . Is 11 o'clock too late to arrive home from a show or some other place? Is it all right to allow him to kiss me good night, even though we are not engaged?" Within a few years, kissing would imply to all only the most evanescent commitment.[84]

The growing recognition that dates should incorporate an ambiguous mixture of physical pleasure and self-restraint did not by itself remove all the perplexities of daters. They had still to learn how to "read" the dating situation. R. S., for instance, could not quite fathom the implications of the behavior of the young man "that I care for." "He has declared his love for me also. But he goes to visit other girls and takes them to places and has never yet taken me anywhere. He's forever praising those girls. All this makes me doubt that he really cares for me. Do you think he does?" R. S. simply did not know whether "caring for" is in any way articulated to the dating system, and while she obviously intuited that there was such a thing as a boy's "line," she lacked confidence in her ability to discern it in action. Only over time were symbol and gesture fitted into a changing code of dating that was a thoroughly known part of the developing culture of adolescence. "I am 16, good looking and a good sport. A is 17, bashful, and not very good looking. His friends say he likes me"; "I am a young boy of 16 and am in love with a girl 5 months my junior. So far I have not told the girl anything but have confided in two of my boy friends. One of these boys went back and told her. As a result she was just a bit peeved."[85]

Culture, as always, though supportive, could also be confining, as when the peer group's influence extended too far into the dating situation. "Heartbroken" was a girl of sixteen, dating a boy of seventeen in 1925: "I love this fellow very much and I know he loves me. When we are at a party or a dance he is always with me, and he always asks to take me home, and I let him. He is very nice, but when he is with a bunch of boys he just says hello and keeps right on going. I would like to know the reason for this (he is very bashful), because I love him." Or a jealousy composed of confused frustration might appear a product of divergent definitions of the two partners over the degree of articulation of the dating system with intimacy, on the one hand, and the peer popularity system, on the other: "My friend's chum is keeping him away from me because my sister doesn't care to go out with him."[86]

The reader of adolescent lovelorn letters from this period can hardly fail to observe the generally shallow connotation of the word "love." The notion, of course, was by 1920 carried into teenage courtship parlance through the insipid romantic fiction of stage, screen, and print, so teenagers had good authority for feeling "love" easily and often. In the 1920 letters, the vocabulary is limited to a few variant usages of "love" and occasional references to "care for." By 1925, the range of expression had widened a bit, with a new verb or two enlarging the capacity for discrimination and a raft of new, conventionalized intensive adverbs. By 1930, even the brief letters to Blake indicate a concern for emotional precision. Connie wrote Blake that her fellow "never told me he even cared for me." "Doubtful" reported to Blake that her "fellow says he loves me. I like him as a friend." Blue Peggy, seventeen years old, wrote to Martha Carr that she felt left out because while "several of my girl friends have fellows and seem so in love," she herself "can't seem to get enthused" over her "several boy friends." In Blue Peggy's view, being "in love" was something one might be but at least should "seem" to be at seventeen, and such a seeming might be approached through enthusiasm in dating, if only she could experience even that.[87]

In the 1930–31 letters, "steady" relationships of one kind or another, including references to "going steady," virtually absent before, were quite common. Lacking such a defined stage, earlier daters like Tootsie had been confused:

> I am a young girl of 17 and am really in love with a young man of 19. I have known him for over a year. We are not exactly engaged, but he has promised not to go with any other girls, nor I with any other boys. I am in a suburb now and am attending school. He goes to a university. I love this boy with all my heart. But some time it is such a temptation to go out with the boys.[88]

A few years later, a metropolitan seventeen-year-old would have known that going steady was easy to begin or terminate and that it combined clear behavioral prescriptions with undefined emotional commitment and was in fact merely the boundary between casual dating and the steep and demanding road to marriage, rather than the first step on that road. Tootsie could have negotiated with her young man for gradually enhanced emotional intimacy without such risk of irrevocable sexual intimacy or premature marriage, which was possible in an overheated, unstable relationship of "not exactly" engagement.

The main architects of the dating system were middle-class girls.[89] Girls had more to gain by the establishment of dating, because the new version of the double standard that it put in place was considerably less restrictive to them than the one it replaced. Before dating, parents had tended to construe strictly girls' obligation to enter marriage untainted by even a hint of scandal, and they supervised courting accordingly, limiting both its occasion and the set of eligibles. The boy who came calling had not only to be prepared to behave himself but he also had to pass *prima facie* muster as a boy who by reputation *would* behave himself. Under the double standard, however, boys' reputations were both subject to repair and of far less interest to their own families. Girls were far more constrained by parental oversight.

Despite their substantially united front toward their parents' generation, boys and girls had by no means identical interests in the new dating scheme. The female physical-growth spurt came earlier and provided a convenient sign for what contemporaries believed (and thereby encouraged) to be girls' earlier awareness of the opposite sex as objects of interest. Contemporary accounts of adolescent behavior had boys entering the high school ages still in a "gang state," while girls had long before turned to "fancies . . . of men and boys, and of herself as the center of attraction and interest. . . . She becomes interested in dress and personal adornment . . . [and] ruin[s] her healthy skin with rouge and lipstick."[90] Furthermore, girls more often than boys remained through high school to graduation. If there were more girls in high school potentially to be seeking dates, so also higher proportions of them, particularly among the freshmen and sophomores, presumably hoped to date. Accordingly, girls sought to limit competition by defining its terms, and they sought to enlarge the pool of eligible boys. There was, of course, the alternative possibility for a girl to be a collegian's or an employed boy's "townie," but such a choice took the date outside its familiar negotiating balance and outside the supportive structure of peer-group gossip.[91] Gossip and the clique system operated to limit the terms of competition among girls, most particularly by regulating the amount of physical gratification with which they could reward their dates. Commonly, such gossip took the form of "catty" statements that anyone could get boys by giving a good deal of sex: doing so would only counterfeit popularity.

The date, as a bargain, was unromantic but affectionate. In dating, *style* mattered a great deal. Performance was far more important than the unmediated expression of feelings. The very ordinariness of dating placed practical limits on the amount of romantic idealization that courtship could now support.[92] The success of the dating system encouraged a set of rules, rules of performance more than of feeling, rules that even young boys and girls could learn. Thus, Ernie, thirteen, stoutly denied in 1931 that "I want to call on girls and take them out" but admitted to having girlfriends and that in defiance of his parents' wishes he liked "to have friendly talks with girls over the telephone." "Every boy my age likes to have money to spend and to dress up," Ernie lectured a love advisor in 1931.[93]

THE GENDERED RECONSTRUCTION OF SEXUALITY

Petting, that delicate standoff between sensual indulgence and constraint, was almost universal in the sense that all daters petted at some time but not in the sense that all couples petted. Graduated physical intimacy became an accepted part of lasting teen relationships, both a marker of affection and a spur to increased commitment. The sexual histories collected by Kinsey and his associates point to a distinct sexualization of noncoital relations far more pronounced than the often-remarked increase in premarital coitus also recorded. The Kinsey data here point to an increase between the pre-World War I and postwar adolescent cohorts—from 29 percent to 43 percent of girls who petted before sixteen and an increase from 41 percent of boys to 51 percent.[94]

A decided reduction in the typical age at which petting began was coupled with a marked increase, especially in women, in orgasm achieved by petting. Unconventional sex practices, like fellatio and cunnilingus, likewise increased, as did premarital coitus, especially with eventual marriage partners. Overall, the increase of sexualization of the whole path to marriage is inescapable, although qualitatively the downward extension of erotic petting was the most pronounced and the most significant in restructuring the life course.[95] One particularly acute observer of campus mores understood the enlargement of sensuality in the lives of students as an offset, engineered by girls, to the economically based reluctance to marry that young college men were expressing, and in this sense it was a reassertion of older values regarding marriage rather than an abrupt assertion of moral innovation. "Since petting leads to 'dates,' and dates lead to more dates and to real romance [i.e., marriage], one must pet or be left behind."[96] It was not thoughts of future bliss that bound two people together but mutual gratification in the present. "The modern lover daydreams not merely of a lifelong companionship, but of a lifelong state of being in love."[97]

In American middle-class ideology before the 1920s, the

deferral of sexual pleasure until marriage had provided the pledge that cemented love unions—the chastity of the bride and the definition by the groom of his prior sexual experiences, if any, as the unfortunate yielding to instinctive drives and the temptation of "bad" women of no account. Adherents of the older structure of values maintained that "in the general wreck" of prewar values, "the wreck of love is conspicuous and typical. . . . Sex, we learned, was not so awesome as once we had thought. God does not care so much about it as we had formerly been led to suppose; but neither, as a result, do we. Love is becoming gradually so accessible, so un-mysterious, and so free that its value is trivial."[98] Edward Sapir defined this concern presciently: "Sex as self-realization unconsciously destroys its own object by making of it no more than a tool to a selfish end."[99] But by the 1920s, modest sexual pleasure was little more than one of several commonplace "thrills" available to young people. "The adolescent convention of petting is used not as a preliminary to the sex act but as a pseudo-substitute for it, as a means of working off tense emotions."[100] Dating, and even petting, fit appropriately into a view of adolescent development that favored "an emotional attitude of free, wholesome contact with members of the opposite sex" during the teen years, when not thwarted by "psychologically inept efforts [by adults] to create inhibitions in the young" as by the "over-idealization of womankind . . . as . . . almost too delicate to touch."[101]

Many young women of the postwar generation asserted in word and gesture that they were sexual beings quite like men— *and not ashamed of it.* Paula Fass sees this insinuation in the most characteristic and explosive aspects of the "new woman's" appearance. Bobbed hair, flattened breasts, shortened skirts created "a well-poised tension between the informal boyish companion and the purposely erotic vamp. . . . Smoking implied a promiscuous equality between men and women and was an indicator that women could enjoy the same vulgar habits and ultimately also the same vices as men." Such signs could assert sexuality as long as they could play off against the double standard, focusing on the *right* to be openly sexual rather than the still-outrageous notion of actually behaving with "masculine" lustfulness.[102] Sociologist Joseph Folsom, from his vantage point at Vassar College, argued that a "woman may conscientiously allow herself to *feel* passion to the same extent as the man, if she controls its expression."[103]

The double standard was not overthrown but modified. Rearguard actions, like the bills submitted in a number of state legislatures regulating the cut and material of women's dresses, so patently attacked symptoms alone that they invited ridicule that pressed the argument further than most defenders were ready to face. "Why should men be permitted to tell us how to dress? Why should women always have to protect their 'feelings'? Why are not men made to control their 'feelings' just as women are? Why should the fact that a girl has legs arouse the wrong kind of impulses in a man? Does he think we travel on wheels?"[104]

When asked for a stark statement of personal preference, sizable majorities of sophisticated young men and women (2/3 of the men and 7/8 of the women in one 1920s college study, half of the men and 2/3 of the women in another) rejected the dual standard.[105] Girls could now express themselves sexually. Indeed, as Folsom remarked, "a new method of adjustment [of gender relations] has begun, namely, the education of women to find greater pleasure in sex." The great majority of contemporary testimony, however, indicates that even while girls who seemed unawakened sexually were made the butt of humor, girls (not boys) who (even if in love) proceeded to coitus and spoke too widely of the fact were devalued. "Our newer mores permit us to *experiment* widely with human emotions, yet they do not permit us to observe freely the results of these experiments."[106] Young men of the times were "for the most part disposed to try to face the problem of sexual urgencies before marriage, and of responsibility, like the problems, on a more nearly mutual basis. To some extent, nevertheless, they too are likely to hope and expect that the girl will prove more worthy than they feel they can hope to be."[107]

In time, the "modern" perspective became mere common sense.

> Not so very long ago make-up was associated with prostitutes and the kind of women who laid themselves out to attract men and

parents still associate the use of cosmetics with that class—and though latterly make-up is part of the general effect of the costume. . . . Leader thinks that's all there too it—The whole design counts—it's a matter of taste. . . . It's surely not necessary to consider the moral end of it. Fashions change. . . . But we are ruled by fashions. . . . It is better to conform to the prevailing style—as well as possible—take it out of the realm of right and wrong.[108]

The advice subtly moved beyond appearances.

However difficult it may be for parents who are themselves neurotically afraid of sex to accept the healthy conditions of our unsegregated modern adolescence, we cannot oblige them to turn back the clock to the patriarchal era. Our world needs adults who have grown up emotionally and who can be enough in love with their mates to stay in love without economic and social pressures. Petting-parties . . . are for Phyllis a natural and wholesome part of growing up emotionally into womanhood.[109]

These cultural assumptions underlay a dating system in which boys were by convention assumed to be always on the lookout for some petting, but girls were conventionally assumed to get far less physical pleasure on the whole from the act itself.[110] Boys pursued; girls rewarded boys who were affectionate, restrained, and provided a pleasant time; girls rewarded boys moderately. When girls were fond of petting, they found that their peer group (aided by boy gossip) stood in the way of their being too easy. Even for girls in love, peer pressure set limits to lovemaking. Thus, a high school girl noted in 1929, "The girl who permits liberties is certainly popular with boys, but her popularity never lasts very long with any one boy. You know the saying, 'Just a toy to play with, not the kind they choose to grow old and grey with.' "[111] Boys' behavior could be modified. "Even freshmen girls know . . . that a boy who considers himself a gentleman may have standards that vary according to those of the girl with whom he may be," wrote a high school dean of women.[112] Dating, thus, operated still within a double standard of sexual conduct that demanded of girls the strength to say no and the strength of mind to prevent matters from coming to such a pass.

In dating, physical pleasure was defined as properly a token of affection and commitment. Through dating, girls considerably before marriage could discover patterns of emotional intimacy with boys congruent with those the female subculture had long valued, but without ultimate commitment, physical or marital.[113] Nor need the task of finding a good mate be forgotten, for the dating system elaborated a series of stages that led toward engagement and beyond. The tender interpersonal qualities sought in a good date, while not identical to those of a good mate, were nevertheless among the desirable traits. For female readers slow to pick up the detailed, subtle relationship among sexuality, emotional intimacy, popularity, and eventual marriage, "A High School Boy" in *True Confessions* explicated the ideal girlfriend and acceptable variants. "The kind of girl that will kiss you and let you know that the kiss means something and that that's all there is, there isn't any more, is one of the square shooters and if you can get her to marry you you're lucky, and you needn't ask any questions."[114]

The terms of the dating exchange were widely understood among the young but not entirely uniformly. Petting was particularly often at the heart of misunderstanding, especially in that it incorporated a partial revision of the deeply inculcated double standard.[115] Certain adolescents, like "Miss Dateless," found themselves essentially outside of the dating pool because they failed or refused to recognize that this fundamental exchange in dating was normatively governed and structured by a sense of the emotions appropriate to age and stage.

> I am 20 years old and, to use the slang expression, "hard up for dates." I am rather small, but have my share of good looks. I am inevitably cheerful, like sports of all kind and like to talk of them. I am interested in good music. . . . But—I sit at home without the boys. I think one of the reasons is that I am not common enough. I let a boy know it if he gets fresh with me and scratch him off my list. I use cosmetics, but sometimes look pale near some of these "clowns." However, they get "dates."[116]

Other girls, who yielded too readily to the combined pressures of boys' entreaties and the clear-cut injunction to date and—to a degree—enjoy physical "thrills," were devalued as dates for being too easy. A popular and spirited girl, whose friend had inadvertently become the butt of boyish ribaldry ("they called her the 'lemon' because they said she was made to squeeze"), castigated the boys for their insensitivity. She recalled that she "told those boys just what I thought of them, and they hadn't a word to say when I got through, either." But then, her friend's behavior was to be explained by inexperience and excused because "she hasn't any mother." [117]

The formal extracurricular life of the high school quickly came to be articulated with the gender-structured dynamics of the dating system. "It is a well-known fact that club pins are an absolute necessity when a young man wishes to plight his time-enduring regard for some lady; but, even considering this, it ought not be necessary to have more than three or four." [118] Beyond visible symbols, word of mouth was powerful where everybody was likely to know everybody. "Why should we have so many idle gossipers in the school? . . . Much to our dislike we have many social groups and this lowers cooperation within the student body." [119] Gossip, of course, while lowering cooperation, also regulated behavior—reassuringly for the most part, oppressively on occasion. Trends in fashion were sharply defined and served to mark out those who qualified for the dating pool. A "bobbed hair census" at Little Falls (Minnesota) High in 1923 indicated the strength of fashion: in each of the four classes, more than three girls in four had adopted this hair style, so rich in affirmation of modernity. [120] Even among "subfreshmen," 65 percent had already caught on.

A ritualized jousting and chiding of the boy population in general (sometimes, happily for the historian, in the high school newspaper) served to bring marginal boys into the dating pool. Chiding served to educate boys to the proper ways of behaving toward girls, so that the rules of the dating system might be learned even by the more backward among them:

> Boys, is it fair to make the girls come to a school entertainment unescorted? So far, I have not been to an entertainment without seeing three-fourths of the girls come without escorts. The most disgusting thing about it is, that the boys act as though they did

not realize the predicament they've placed the girls in. . . . I believe the faculty should make a rule that no girls come to the parties unescorted and that no boy be admitted without a young lady.[121]

Or:

> What has come over the boys of this school? . . . Is it the lack of carfare? I am sure that we girls would be happy to supply that . . . instead of going home alone after 11 o'clock. Fewer girls will be allowed to attend parties at school, since they must return late alone. Just because a boy is gentleman enough to take a girl home, is no reason that he is in love with her. All we want is common courtesy, not husbands.[122]

Boys must be taught the nonbinding quality of a date, to distinguish it from the courtship system that dating was replacing. The complaint was not misdirected, for an earnest correspondent responded in the next issue:

> There are many reasons. Not that the young man has not the price of carfare, or is too stingy, but that the girls of to-day are too different from those of yesterday. He has not as yet become acquainted with their ways. It will take a long time unless the girls do their part and bring the boys out of that bashful state which is keeping them from mixing in with the girls and being treated as equals. Therefore, act as though you wanted to be taken home, and I am sure you will not be disappointed.[123]

"Bashful" was the word. Throughout the decade, female correspondents in high school newspapers would resurrect it as an adjective of mild condescension addressed to the boys they hoped to recruit to the pool of dating eligibles:

> As usual, only senior and junior girls are to be present, but boys of the lower classes are allowed to come. In that case the senior and junior girls must wait to be invited before they can attend. It would be unfortunate to have these girls left out and, weird as it may seem, the task of inviting them is up to the boys—bashful and otherwise. Let's have as many junior and senior girls asked as possible, boys.[124]

The public nature of the high school dance—aside from fueling the competitive element of the dating system—served girls' purposes ideally. In the 1923–1926 Kansas City study, boys consistently ranked social dancing below "having 'dates' " while girls consistently ranked it above. When the Alexandria (Minnesota) High School in 1927 circulated a questionnaire to its students regarding more parties and, for the first time, school dances, both boys and girls voted overwhelmingly for more parties, but boys only split evenly on dances, which girls supported by five to two.[125] "Stags" posed a problem, however, and girls pressed for the elimination of stags and the establishment of fixed-partner dates at school dances and no doubt elsewhere. For girls, the stag arrangement and its attendant "cutting in" at dances was an invitation to humiliation or boredom and left all the power of decision making in the hands of boys, who not rarely looked after one another's interests and gave no thought to the wallflowers the system inevitably created. "Just fancy knowing that a boy is dancing past the stagline and waving a five-dollar bill behind your back as an offer to anyone who'll come and take you away?"[126]

Occasionally rebelling verbally against "girls who have dates four or five out of the seven days of the week" and the "sort of contest" among girls "to see who can get the most dates in one week," boys accepted the new regime.[127] For them, it was something of a gain, in the sensual pleasures of petting, in the tenderness of occasional intimate conversation, in the articulation of "popularity" with the bumptiously democratic tone (and stratified structure) of the new, expanded, age-homogenized high schools. " 'It's just that I like to take her places,' explained one among the many suitors of Bette, the most popular date in the junior class. 'You're sure to have a good time with her. She's never a liability, you know that she'll be the belle of the ball. But really I'm not crazy about her.' "[128]

Were the interests of middle-class girls harmed by the new institution they had promoted? Considerable evidence from the 1950s, to be discussed below, indicates that dating overwhelmed most other concerns for many high school girls—and many college girls—thereby perpetuating disadvantages in other realms to which schooling was relevant, especially the world of work. But domesticity hardly seems to have been the gender issue in the 1920s and 1930s that it was to become a generation later. A more serious charge against the new dating mechanism concerns girls' sexual vulnerability. We have seen it to be the case that premarital coitus, both with fiancées and with others, did increase in the first cohort of girls within the new dating regime, at which point knowledge of birth control technique was obviously too shallow to offer reliable protection to many. But the evidence presented on age at marriage and pregnancy status at marriage do not point to forced marriages owing to pregnancy, nor to numbers of women condemned to spinsterhood through youthful loss of virginity and subsequent consignment to the category of "soiled goods." On balance, it seems that moral innovation did bring female sexuality into the arena of boy-girl relations in a new way but not without peer-group safeguards, imperfect but because quickly institutionalized perhaps no less effective than the foregone familial mechanisms that sometimes failed in the face of passion.

THE TRANSITION TO MARRIAGE

Youthful emotions were given more play in the heightened pace of courtship, which continued selectively into the 1920s. Details are shown in table 9, which presents *proportions married* at young and average ages for marriage, from which can be derived a sense of a cohort's movement into marriage.[129] For both young men and young women, the table shows, the most prominent continued downward trend of marriage age was among the native whites of native parentage who lived in cities, the prime locus of economic and cultural innovation— including the new dating system. Urban marriage ages moved downward, approaching those of rural people of like nativity. By contrast, the downward movement of marriage age for second-generation Americans and for blacks, like those of rural native whites of native parentage, essentially ceased.

The continuing eagerness of young people for marriage was a matter of some relief to contemporary students of manners and morals, for it spoke to a considerable continuity of values at a point of apparent upheaval. Blanchard and Manasses, thus, reported that their survey revealed that "the modern girl seems to want marriage most of anything in life." In their college sam-

Table 9. Proportions Ever Married, by Sex, Age Group, and
Social Characteristics, 1910–1930 (in percentages)

	Males		Females	
	20–24	*25–34*	*15–19*	*20–24*
Native white of native parentage Urban				
1910	23.6	62.7	9.1	44.5
1920	29.6	68.7	11.9	49.8
1930	31.0	73.3	12.3	52.0
Rural				
1910	30.0	72.4	15.7	59.7
1920	32.9	73.6	15.0	60.4
1930	32.7	73.1	16.2	61.5
Native white of foreign or mixed parentage				
1910	15.8	56.1	5.6	37.2
1920	18.7	59.9	6.5	40.8
1930	17.9	63.6	6.0	41.5
Black				
1910	40.3	74.9	18.8	65.1
1920	45.1	74.9	21.3	68.4
1930	45.3	76.2	22.1	66.9

SOURCES: Calculated from Census 1920–1, 391–393; Census 1930–1, 848–850.
NOTE: Data are available for foreign-born whites, but in a strict sense these, and those for the children of the foreign-born, are not commensurable across censuses in the same way that natives are, since they are highly subject to changing migration patterns, recent or remote.

ple, nine in ten supported wives' work to permit timely marriage, but only half this proportion when wives' earnings "are not necessary."[130] At the same time, they noted that this old-fashioned concern led to innovation, for girls now were choosing to remain at work after marriage "in order to achieve an earlier mating."[131] New material circumstances, innovations in courtship practices, and changing prescriptions for prudence promoted a confusion about the right age to marry. Young people—"modern" urban girls particularly—seemed to press for a downward revision of the marriage schedule. Thus, an advice book, in some alarm, told young women not to rush, reminding them quite inaccurately that "marriages are being made much later than they were a few generations ago."[132] Correspondingly, "A Family Doctor" worried "with changing economic conditions, just how are we going to tide young people over the years when they are physically ready to marry but not yet ready financially." The author leaned even harder on young men, drawing on their sense of economic prudence to construct a right basis for assessing marriage. "If men entered into marriage as carefully and deliberately as most of them enter into business deals, the outcome would be more certain of success."[133]

With girls newly able to display their charm and sex appeal unashamedly and in new social settings, boys had to be more careful not to fall too quickly. "She intends to marry at a more specific date if she can bring it about, have a definite number of children at desirable intervals, and earn a definite sum toward the upkeep where she needs to. . . . And she is determined to have more of a grip on the bank account than her mother, to help to swell it with her own earnings, married or single, and to do so in chiffon stockings and silk underwear."[134] Success in entrancing men and designing one's own marriage, however, ran the risk not only of overprudent men but of experienced, exploitative ones. A popular short story on this theme, evoking the mythic opposition between country tradition and urban oversophistication, places a charming, capable young woman between the contrary pulls of a professionally ambitious spinster—her supervisor at the department store—and a good man from her old hometown. Ultimately, success at the department store required a too-blatant use of her body (in dress modeling). The plot resolves itself, on these grounds, in favor of the boy next door, and prompt marriage.[135]

Figures 8 and 9 show the changes over the decades of the 1910s and the 1920s in proportions of men and women who had married by successive single years of age.[136] Among men, it is apparent, the most substantial gains in proportions married in the 1910s had occurred at the younger ages—the late teens

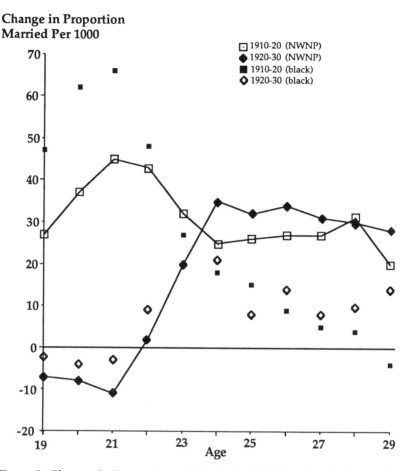

Figure 8. Changes in Proportions of Men Who Had Married, by Successive Single Years of Age, 1910s and 1920s

and early twenties—for both native whites of native parentage and for blacks (native whites of foreign parentage followed essentially the same path as native whites of native parentage, here and elsewhere). Black women, too, had moved toward earlier marriage again—in the 1910s, especially at 17 to 20 or so. Native white women of native parentage were more likely to be married in 1920, too, but not especially so at the youngest ages. But we should not make too much of the age-specificity of the decline: the strongest point is its *substantial generality across groups* and the *amplitude* of the change in the 1910s. Thus, even after leveling off after the youngest ages, about 2.5 percent more young men were married at any given age in 1920 than in 1910.

The 1920-to-1930 trends are trickier. On the whole, the 1920s represent a dampened continuation of the downward movement in marriage age. By far the greater proportion of

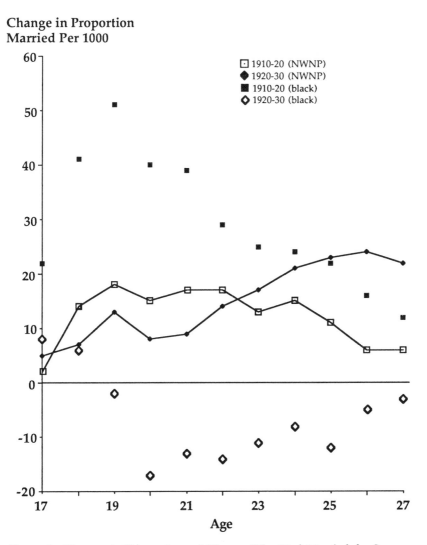

Figure 9. Changes in Proportions of Women Who Had Married, by Successive Single Years of Age, 1910s and 1920s

men married after age 21, and after that age, the 1930 data show even greater proportions married at single years of age than did the 1920 data. This is the case for both native whites of native parentage and for blacks. Since virtually all of marriages for people this young would have occurred at the very end of the decade, it is possible that the earliest phases of the Depression could have caused the observed downturn. More likely, however, is that just as 1920 was a period in which relatively young marriages for men became notably more common, the end of the decade saw a return to the previous pattern.

Beyond age 23, however, the 1920s saw an increase in the pace of men's marriage that was about as great as that in the 1910s. There can be no doubt (given the age schedule of men's marriages) that most of these marriages were taking place in the latter half of the decade, so it is safe to conclude that except for the relatively young ages, the 1920s were a decade in which, rather regularly, younger cohorts could look forward to somewhat younger marriages than their immediate predecessors and to distinctly younger marriages than in the generation of their parents.

Close examination of the year-to-year changes over the 1920s in numbers of first marriages of young men and women at selected single years of age in New York State (exclusive of New York City) reveals a rather complicated pattern. Among women, the most rapid increase before about 1926 was in young marriages—at ages up to about 20. After mid-decade, however, this trend reversed, and it was marriages between the ages of 20 and 25 that increased the most rapidly, particularly at age 21. For men, trends were gradual throughout the decade, toward younger marriages, at ages that increasingly approached those of women.[137]

When we examine figure 9, we find that most of the trends for women in the 1910s and 1920s resemble men's. For older white women, nuptiality was increasing even more rapidly in the 1920s than in the 1910s. For black women, however, things were different. The decade's marked black migration from southern agriculture to northern urban centers definitively interrupted the increases in nuptiality that had characterized the previous decade. If the 1910s had brought a great enlargement of marriage probabilities for black women, the 1920s was a decade of return to prior patterns. But these black women provide the only marked example in which the 1920s saw a clear reversal of the downward movement of the marriage transition that had lasted over a generation.[138]

Because states differed from one another in the characteristics that may have promoted early marriage, we can enrich our sense of what lay behind the new life course scheduling by examining what was associated on a state-to-state basis with continuing nuptiality increase in the 1920s. The simplest and also the most powerful way to analyze these data is to examine proportions ever-married for the single age group 20–24, encompassing a critical half-decade of marrying for both male and female cohorts. (To avoid confounding with differential inmigration patterns, I examine only native whites of native parentage. No analysis of black marriage patterns is feasible by this method at this time, because black marriage patterns were considerably differentiated by region, and the period was one of great interregional migration among black people.) The analysis here, to be sure, is not causal, but, literally, only tells us what characteristics of states—rather large and heterogeneous places at that—were associated with increasingly earlier marriage in the years just prior to 1930.[139] But by including as a predictor variable the extent of downward edging of the marriage age in the 1910s, we will be able to see not only what characteristics conduced earlier marriage but also which of these were especially relevant to the shifts, discussed above, in the trends that were already extant by the 1920s.

Earlier marriage during the 1920s was facilitated by whatever promoted relatively rapid population growth.[140] The balance of migration—surely in a decade during which traditional channels of overseas migration were substantially plugged by restrictive legislation—probably indicates well the kinds of possibilities for starting a life on one's own that were reflected also in decisions to marry earlier rather than later. On balance, then, we may conclude that the prosperity of the 1920s conduced to couples taking the plunge into marriage. Two other easily measured factors were also reflected in the state-to-state patterns for males. The first—best measured by the proportion foreign born in the population—suggests what inspection confirms: the states of the industrial belt of the Middle Atlantic and Midwest where large numbers of foreign-born persons resided more often than one would otherwise expect showed small or no statewide increases in proportions of men marrying young, a pattern strongly contrasting with the continued drop in marriage age in the homogeneously white areas in the Mountain and Western states (but not in the agriculturally depressed South). A second factor improving male marriage prospects depended not on improved resources in the hands of the potential groom but rather on improvements in the marriage market itself. Across the nation, ratios of native white males of native parentage to native white females of native parentage (taken as indicative of a single marriage pool) was in 1920 strongly skewed in favor of males in a considerable number of states, especially in the West, a product largely of "frontier" patterns of long-distance interstate migration. By 1930, this skewing had on balance considerably declined, and the state-to-state variance was markedly reduced.[141] The approach of states to sex parity among native whites of native parentage "explained" just about as much of the downward movement of male marriage ages as did population increase or proportions foreign born. We need not insist on the details of the model; but we should recognize that both the *means* to contract marriage younger and *easier access to appropriate mates* explain how men came, on balance, to continue their trend toward earlier marriage in the 1920s. In states that were among the faster in population growth *and also* among those in which the sex ratio moved most rapidly toward parity, 2.2 percent more of the males at 20–24, on average, were married in 1930 than had been in 1920. At the other end of the distribution, in those states where population growth was slower *and* in which sex ratios among native whites did not move rapidly toward parity, or moved away from it, about 0.7 percent *fewer* men were married at 20–24 in 1930 than had been a decade earlier.

For women, the "market" for acceptable mates also improved, and in such a way that accounted for about as much of the continued if modest decline in women's marriage age in the 1920s as did population increase. But women were of course not aided by the general movement toward parity in sex ratio that had been important for men. Rather, what improved women's marriage-market opportunities was an institutional change—the great expansion of the high school. Women at this time married on average between two and three years younger than men; and as high schooling became typical within the population, the age of school-leaving came close enough to marriage age that the high school and its informal social life became a critical arena for increasing numbers of girls to contract marriages. Accordingly, when states like California, New York, and Ohio added to the school rolls something like 25 percent of the 16- and 17-year-olds during the 1920s, it is not surprising that for women at ages 20–24, the proportions who were married increased rather markedly. In states that were among the faster half in population growth *and* the half in which school was extended the fastest, the average increase in the proportion married at 20–24 was 2.1 percent; in the states below par in population growth *and* school extension, the comparable proportion was a *reduction* by 1.6 percent in the proportion married. In assessing the significance of these patterns, it is worth considering that, outside of those alluded to, regional patterns did not appear; nor did proportion urban or pace or urbanization; nor did initial values of youthful-marriage proportions explain trends; nor did the trends in the 1920s merely continue on a state-to-state basis the trends of the previous decade. That is, marriage age dropped *where circumstances facilitated it.*

These factors, statistically significant, certainly do not deny the emergence of new values that addressed the right construction of the life course. But the state data do not seem to "require" normative change, suggesting rather that the sometimes-realized but always-intriguing possibility of earlier marriages for "modern" urban young people emerged out of the new material and social circumstances of the decade.

PARENTHOOD

The decade of the 1920s was a period of overall fertility decline, a continuation and intensification of prior trends. In several respects, these years were marked with a sharpening of the differences in family behavior between classes and between rural and urban residents. Strongly associated with the fertility decline, among white women, was the spread of secondary and higher education. Black women, too, reduced their fertility, but for them, the decline was also quite steep *within* groups divided by educational attainment, as it was only among the more well-educated whites. On the whole, these patterns of decline for whites (blacks were not so tabulated) held in both urban and in rural nonfarm areas, although they were attenuated among farm women.[142]

When we turn from overall fertility to the timing of *initial* parenthood, the pattern becomes more complex. Decline in first-childbirth rates was sharpest among women already somewhat on the old side to be having a first child—those 24 or 25 and up.[143] By contrast, among those 18 or under, there was but little overall reduction in initial fertility. Indeed, something of a peak in first-parity fertility was attained by young women around 1925. While, overall, the 1920s were a period in which the likelihood of becoming a young mother at first grew, then declined markedly, for older women not yet mothers the pattern was one of slow decline for the first half of the decade followed by rapid decline in the second half.

Corresponding to and complementing the rise in nuptiality in the first part of the 1920s was a tendency to *slightly more rapid movement into parenthood after marriage,* a tendency that was common to whites and blacks, and across socioeconomic levels.[144] The trend was not matched, however, by similar increases in the years following the first one or two after marriage, a pattern that is congruent with the overall decline in fertility during the decade. First parenthood, then, following a marriage that often was earlier than in preceding decades was relatively often attained relatively early in the marriage: a substantial subset of couples was taking advantage of a period of relative economic promise by moving quickly through the steps of family formation. Other couples—notably those who had already resisted parenthood for the first phase of marriage—were more often than previously postponing parenthood for several more years, many presumably having chosen the temporary childless marriage as desirable for a while and having been in command of the technology that enabled this. After mid-decade, however, this pattern ceased and was replaced by one in which more couples than in the first half of the decade delayed parenthood longer after marriage. It is apparent from the data that it was not lifetime childlessness that took the place of the trend toward early parenthood within early marriage but rather a somewhat delayed parenthood within marriages that themselves continued to be contracted earlier in the American life course.

Birth control was rather widely but by no means universally diffused even in the late 1920s. Clinic data collected in the 1920s and 1930s indicate that the proportion using some method of fertility limitation had nearly doubled since the early years of the century, condoms being the method accounting for much of this increase.[145] At the time of the late 1920s marriages of the native white Protestants who were to be studied by the first major survey of such matters, the Indianapolis Fertility Study,[146] about two in three of these couples employed some method of birth control (not necessarily a contraceptive method, of course). The proportion doing so was only slightly in excess of half for wives who had ended their schooling before attending any high school but exceeded seven in eight among wives who had attended college.[147]

A retabulation of Kinsey data indicates that there were at this time sharp changes in marital contraceptive use (at least among Kinsey's relatively sophisticated respondents).[148] Coitus interruptus and the douche gave way to the diaphragm, while condom use remained constant. Retrospective data from relatively sophisticated New York City couples showed, likewise, a reduction by about half in dependence on withdrawal, but the condom, rather than the diaphragm, was becoming the contraceptive method of choice.[149] Women who used diaphragms were not only in a sense taking control of their own bodies; they were also taking a part in a revolution of sexual attitudes, in which the formerly unspeakable was necessarily now spoken.

Contraceptive information was not yet so widespread as it would be in subsequent decades. The Lynds described contraception in Middletown as publicly condemned but gradually tolerated as inevitable, couples of advantaged backgrounds being the quickest to embrace the practice. The Lynds were struck by a conflict between individual beliefs and behaviors and far more restrictive official group norms about birth control (as about much else) that suggested "an underlying bewilderment considerably . . . widespread and more pervasive of the rest of their lives." [150] The Kinsey data indicate that perhaps one in four women who had sexual intercourse before marriage conceived premaritally—a proportion that gave no signs of declining in the 1920s, even as the proportion of young women placing themselves at risk increased. [151] Only 6 percent of Indianapolis wives who were to practice some form of fertility control before their first births had known any contraceptive practices so much as a year before their marriages; another 35 percent learned shortly before their wedding day. The largest category of brides who practiced fertility control before their pregnancies *learned about contraception on their wedding night.* Indeed, almost 6 percent practiced fertility control in some form without *ever* learning about contraception. When wives knew of a method before their marriage, quite routinely that method was douching, a method that was under their own control, if not especially effective from a strictly contraceptive standpoint. [152] About half as many knew of the condom at this point; almost none of the Indianapolis wives knew of the medically controlled diaphragm.

The organized movement arguing the virtues of birth control and making an effort to diffuse contraceptive information reached few women, having elected a physician-and-patient model rather than a public-health model and promoting the highly effective but highly cumbersome and intricate diaphragm. [153]

In Indianapolis, only half of those couples marrying in the late 1920s who tried to postpone their first birth succeeded. [154] The risks of pregnancy were considerable even among those who approached coitus planfully, which suggests how extreme they must have been among neophytes, many of whom, even at marriageable age, were ignorant of all but the absolute rudiments of sexual matters. [155] Such uncertainty helped sustain the general understanding that premarital coitus was on balance not to be entered into with anyone whom one was not prepared to marry.

Within marriage, almost six in ten of the Indianapolis women who had not finished high school used contraceptives of some kind or other between their marriage at the end of the 1920s and their first childbirth. Three in ten postponed childbirth to beyond their second wedding anniversary. The comparable figures for high school graduates were four in five contraceptors and 45 percent with their first births so late. In Indianapolis, some means of fertility control was employed after marriage and before first conception by only half of those who, not finishing high school, married before 19. But two-thirds of their educational peers who delayed marriage somewhat more practiced family limitation in some form. Among high school graduates, 77 percent of those who married young employed a method of birth control, and no less than 85 percent of those who married at 23 or older, with the intermediate group middlingly prone to limit fertility.[156] The results are visible in the way these different groups of married couples structured the transition to parenthood. Fewer than one-quarter of the early-marrying non-high-school-graduates were childless on their third wedding anniversary (most of those with children having had them within the first year of marriage), but 35 percent were if they had delayed marriage until after 23. Among high school graduates, the proportions ranged from 36 percent of the young marriers childless at three years, and 51 percent childless among those who married late.

Girls' access to contraceptive information at this time, in fact, was closely related to their backgrounds and the kinds of lives they were moving toward. The clearest indication of this is probably the relationship of the timing of contraceptive education to level of formal education they eventually achieved, as shown in table 10.

We see at the end of the 1920s a diffusion of a morally significant piece of technological information. For those girls who were advancing the most markedly toward "modernity," contraceptive information was beginning to become something learned in adolescence, in advance of marriage, potentially able to structure boy-girl relationships, potentially able to affect the way marriage and family building were approached. Still modal, however, was for contraceptive knowledge to enter only

Table 10. Timing of Contraceptive Information, by Own
         Eventual Educational Attainment, Indianapolis Wives
         Who Contracept

	Grade School	High School		College	
		Some	*Graduate*	*Some*	*Graduate*
As girl	4.2%	3.2%	8.1%	3.7%	6.1%
Premarital	26.3	30.0	32.6	36.6	47.9
At marriage	40.7	39.6	42.2	43.9	47.8
After marriage	28.8	27.2	17.1	15.9	8.2
	100.0%	100.0%	100.0%	100.0%	100.0%

SOURCE: Computed from Indianapolis Fertility Study data, unweighted.

as an element of explicit premarital instruction rather than
as a part of the common wisdom of adolescence. (Girls of the
most straitened socioeconomic background—and many of these
must have seemed "bad" girls by the standards of the day—were
the most likely to have learned about contraceptive methods in
their girlhoods.)

CONCLUSION

Dating, petting, birth control, and an increase in the sexualization of life generally can be seen as having their roots as elements of the youthful life course well before World War I. That
these new arrangements ramified through the experience of
family life is apparent in contemporaneous revisions of divorce.
The decade saw a rapid increase in the numbers of divorces
which greatly alarmed contemporaries. In terms of crude divorce rates, however, the entire decade of the 1920s seems far
more like an accommodation to patterns rather suddenly introduced during the war period and its immediate aftermath.[157]
More precisely, divorce trends in the 1920s can be here seen in
good part as a response to impermanencies structured into
marriages *at their inception.* When one examines rates based on
cohorts of marriages begun at different dates, the second half
of the 1920s was a time when divorce *did* seem to pick up mo-

mentum.[158] Divorces characteristically occurred progressively earlier within 1920s marriages, although the most substantial enlargement of the deterioration of marriage occurred around the modal point for divorce, three to seven years into marriage. Accompanying the increase in the number of divorces was a parallel growth in the proportion of all divorces in which the stated grounds were "cruelty," rather than "desertion," the previous modal category. "Cruelty" was as close as the legal rules of most states at the time came to permitting divorce on the consensual grounds that the marriage just did not work out.[159] It was as though the visible challenge to lifetime marriage suggested by changing attitudes as the 1920s advanced led, in turn, to an increased willingness to contract marriages that were less and less seen as permanent at their inceptions. Elaine May's reading of divorce actions leads her to conclude that while "most divorcing urbanites were not in the vanguard of a moral revolution" at this time, they *were* subject to a new "confusion surrounding domestic aspirations" and the nature of marital happiness.

> The pursuit of happiness took couples . . . into wedlock, and then out again. Along with marriage, divorce was another step in this quest. . . . But, . . . rather than a triumph, it often seemed like a personal failure. In the divorce court, unhappily married individuals blamed their spouses. But away from the Court, they often blamed themselves.[160]

The 1920s promoted the emergence of our modern youthful life course, normatively sanctioned for the middle class, spreading among other urbanites: extended schooling combined with an early and gradual peer-structured courtship system, while promoting an early and often romantic marriage, in which the romance was in effect prolonged by the modest postponement of parenthood. The value change so often remarked in the 1920s was the sound that the middle class made in recording its somewhat ambivalent approval of what had increasingly become its own behavior and in proposing these values to the rest of the population as the right way to live. Where these values seemed morally vulnerable and also felt bad, as in the case of easier divorce, there breast-beating occurred, along with a tendency to try to excise that portion of the evolving family-formation process and define it as the product of individual error, capable of being reformed out of existence.

In the largest sense, we are dealing with a change in the way families organized their behavior over their life cycles and understood the ways they were doing so, thus influencing the way that individuals, in structuring their own life courses, anticipated coming into their own. This reorganization was considerably influenced by more general aspects of the outlook of Americans in the 1920s, an outlook in which proximate gratification of the self was more highly prized (or less commonly condemned) than before and in which optimism about the material possibilities of the future was at a new high. At the same time, such values—and the material circumstances that underlay them—were not uniformly shared throughout the population. They were, however, held particularly commonly by young people, thus creating a modest but challenging rift between generations and thereby setting newly formed families off on their own somewhat more than otherwise would have been the case.

Shortly, the Great Depression was to alter the economic organization of the family—and, to an extent, its moral organization. The impact of the extended economic downturn on the way young people came of age and sought to form their own families was ramified and was the more dramatic because of the contrast it posed to the 1920s. The life course had changed in the 1920s, when individuals gained new options. In the 1930s, fresh reminders of external constraint on the individual would modify once again the youthful life course.

4

IN THE GREAT DEPRESSION

YOUTH AND WORK

If the 1920s did not bring prosperity to all, times had been good for the families of most urban entrepreneurs, professionals, and salaried persons, and during most of the decade, urban manufacturing and service workers enjoyed rising wages and rather steady employment. White-collar jobs for both men and women had proliferated, and postprimary schooling had expanded concomitantly. A motif common to persons of both genders from these backgrounds was the assumption of fuller control over the construction of their own life courses, even if the families they founded were not particularly innovatory. The Great Depression was to cut bitterly into these newly developed life course patterns, even before the first cohort to enjoy them as adolescents had had their own children, even before youth could expect parents directly familiar with the new patterns to help in their implementation. Only one in twenty-five early-Depression teenagers and only about one in four of the late-Depression cohort of 'teens had mothers whose own teenage years had followed World War I.[1] The effects of the Depression on the structuring of the youthful life course were to be felt for at least two decades thereafter. And in the case of its effects on engagement, an institution with particular implications for the structuring of this part of the life course, the effects were to last at least through the mid-1970s.

Unemployment offers us a vivid clue to the severity with which the Depression hit young people. Children were still counted on as emergency economic assets in times of family economic hardship. However much they may have *wished* to do so, this was *not* what happened to young people in the depths of the Depression, for reductions in employment opportunities were greatest among young people, of both sexes. Seniority, quite understandably, often determined who would and who would not survive work force cutbacks. Initial entry to the labor force was exceedingly trying.[2] Partly because of the decline in competition by remunerative jobs, formal education continued its rapid expansion in the 1930s. Proportions of young people completing high school thus grew markedly during the Depression decade,even though the immediate economic rationale of extended schooling was weakened by the abysmal job market for new graduates. Especially prominent were the increases in the proportions of high school entrants who persisted to graduation.[3] The decade of the 1930s slowed but did not halt the long-term trend among youth away from gainful employment and toward school, while at the same time slightly hastening the more gradual long-term trend toward labor force participation by married women. Organized labor, and others not previously allied with the "progressive" coalition that had worked to reduce child labor, now had become more concerned that youth be as much as possible withdrawn from the already-too-large labor pool, that is, they should be retained in school or drawn into a National Youth Act group or other government-sponsored age-segregated youth setting.[4]

Massive numbers of young people sought work. The most detailed set of figures available are for a large group of varied urban places in 1935, a middling economic year by Great Depression standards. These patterns are displayed in figures 10 and 11, for young men and young women, respectively. Neither part-time work nor the combination of school and work cushioned youth's emergence onto the labor market: until their early 20s for both young men and young women, *complete idleness was the modal experience* at any given movement. Through age 18, more emerged to nonemployment than to employment, if we exclude those who were placed directly on the emergency-work rolls. A 1935 Michigan census showed that more adolescent youth were simply not looking for a job than were actively seeking a first job. Only at age 19 were more unemployed young men looking for their second jobs than for their first, despite their emergence from school some years earlier. And only at 18 were more of the employed youth working for

Percent

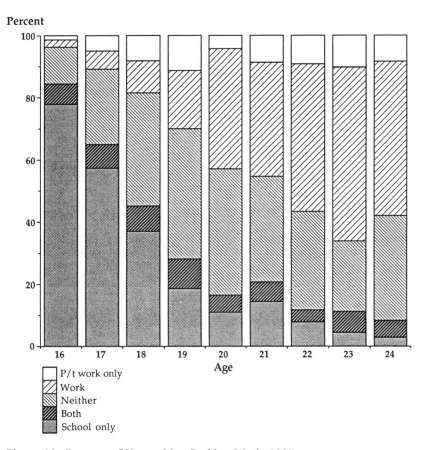

Figure 10. Patterns of Young Men Seeking Work, 1935

wage labor outside their family establishments. Dependence extended long for these young men.[5] In Massachusetts in 1934, a hard year in a hard-hit state, no fewer than 29 percent of all 19-year-old males in the labor force had been out of work for over a year, and 22 percent of the young women of that age. This was the peak for both, but even at ages 21 to 24, 22 percent of young men and 13 percent of young women in the labor force had been looking for jobs for no less than a year.[6]

More young women than young men, of course, did not offer themselves for gainful employment—and relatively often avoided distress in this sphere. There is some indication that given the occupational distributions of the two genders, young

Percent

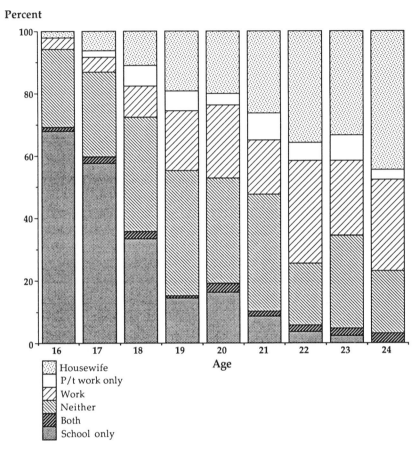

Figure 11. Patterns of Young Women Seeking Work, 1935

women's unemployment was exaggerated somewhat less by the Depression than was men's.[7] Even so, the proportion of young women unable to find full-time work was terrible—12 percent unemployed and another 21 percent not employed but seeking work at age 18, or considerably more than those actually employed at this age. By their nineteenth year, more young women were entering marriage than were leaving school, but despite this and despite the fact that many sought no job, unemployment was a common experience, even among those who had had a job before. Inexperience was a terrible disadvantage to young people entering the Depression job market, with graduation a highly anxious rather than a proud and optimistic moment.[8]

Many young people did not have the luxury of holding themselves out of a labor market they knew to be especially hard on them, because the pressing need felt by their families outweighed the trepidation they must have felt. Young men left school and became available for employment far, far more quickly than the clogged labor market could extend jobs to them. Six months after leaving school in 1936, over one in four male high school graduates in New York State were still unemployed, and one in seven was employed only part-time or seasonally. Of the employed male graduates, fully one-third had found jobs only as messengers, laborers, or assembly-line workers. Even though the quality of their jobs was somewhat better, graduation from high school had not much improved these boys' likelihood of finding any kind of a job at all, as compared with those who left school before finishing high school.[9] Those who found work, because of "their weak bargaining position, because of their inadequate knowledge of the labor market and the oversupply of young workers in relation to the available jobs," were forced into physically harsh, ill-paid, insecure positions with "little opportunity for advancement or training for more desirable work." This was hardly calculated to provide a sense of control over present or future.[10] A Massachusetts study of urban twenty-year-olds carried out in 1935 showed that unemployed boys were twice as likely as employed boys to "strongly agree" that the Depression had "retarded the prospects of youth" and one-and-one-half times as likely to disagree strongly that opportunities "to get ahead" were as good now as in the mid-1920s. Unemployed young women were even more discouraged—relatively and absolutely—than were young men. The attitudes of those still at school—evidently still somewhat protected from harsh realities—were approximately equivalent to those who actually had jobs.[11]

Youth's earning position by comparison with that of their elders had so deteriorated that, at the end of the Depression, the $629 median wage and salary income of young men 20–24 earning any income was less than half that of men their fathers' age. Even incorporating a wife's wage income, they summed to less than 90 percent of father's income, and the measured young-family wage and salary income was less than 60 percent of that for families whose heads were one generation older. We might contrast these figures to those of prosperous times a decade later: total family incomes of families headed by persons under 25 were 68 percent that of a generation older. Nonheads at 20–24 had incomes that were 63 percent those of men of their fathers' generation.[12]

For such reasons, children remained longer than before as members of their families of origin. In 1940, it was only at age 23 that half of the males had left off living as "children" in their parents' households, and only at 25 were fewer than half living either as children or other relatives, generally dependent. Although women married younger, only at 22 had half of them left their parents' homes.[13] Sometimes, however, children lived at home to help support the family. At the end of the Depression decade, if we except total family unemployment, more families had secondary workers than a decade earlier.[14] Among Maryland youth in mid-Depression, proportions who said that their parents were at all dependent on them financially varied from 15 percent among those whose fathers worked in professional or technical occupations to no fewer than 57 percent among those with fathers in unskilled labor and 64 percent for children of farm laborers.[15] A 1936 study of youth in agricultural villages revealed that even here, where family labor was quite underpaid, by the late teens a quarter of boys and 14 percent of girls shared expenses with parents when they lived at home, and another sprinkling paid board. By age 22–24, 24 percent of sons and 11 percent of the daughters paid board, and 43 percent of the sons and 36 percent of the daughters shared expenses, despite the obvious difficulty of locating paid employment there.[16]

Of course, while part of these differentials can be accounted for by class variations in unemployment and insecurity during the Depression, part can be explained by different needs for supplementary income even in the best of times. The class system as it affected growing up was no creation of the Depression. But the Depression in various ways exacerbated its workings.[17] Thus, it was the least-educated youth who were drawn into the labor force in the greatest proportion and who, with the greatest need to supplement family income, found that they were in the worst labor-force position.[18] They had to compete for unskilled jobs not only with one another but also with adult males who had been laid off from better jobs. The pathos of these differentials is recognizable close to the surface of the figures themselves. In two-worker families in Philadelphia in 1933, for instance, 25 percent of second workers were out of work when the first earner was himself employed. *But where the first worker was himself out of work, no fewer than 58 percent of the supplementary workers were also out of work.* This ironic syndrome had existed before the Depression, too, but now became considerably more acute.[19]

Even when husbands were out of work, wives were able to compensate by their own gainful employment only rarely. Wives of unemployed men found it especially difficult to find jobs when they presented themselves in the labor market, although it helped somewhat to be a bit older. But relatively few wives of unemployed workers were.[20] At this point, fully *nine in ten* men believed that married women should work only if their husbands are not "capable of supporting them." By comparison, nine in ten *favored* women working before marriage. At this time, 88 percent of women said wives should bow to their husbands' preferences in these matters. Another poll revealed that only 12 percent of the male respondents and 18 percent of the females said that they "believe[d] that married women should have a full-time job outside of the home," while an additional 31 percent of the men and 38 percent of the women would accept such employment by wives in time of duress.[21] The Depression thus helped create patterns of growing up that differed markedly from class to class just at a point when prosperity and social legislation, the cessation of immigration, and the development of a peer-conscious youth culture had seemed to be moderating such differentials. One tabulation in particular indicates the extent of this generalization and is presented in table 11 below. Based on a large and carefully conducted national urban survey taken in 1935–1936 aimed at eliciting socioeconomic variations in health conditions and services, the survey subdivided youth into five socioeconomic categories

Table 11. School or Labor Force Status of White Urban Youth, by Age, Sex, and Family Income, 1935–36

	Relief	<$1,000	$1,000-1,999	$2,000-2,999	$3,000-3,999
Males 16–17					
In school	63.8%	73.9%	80.7%	87.8%	91.7%
Employed*	10.7	8.6	8.1	6.1	5.2
Seeking work	23.2	15.1	9.8	5.3	2.3
Males 18–19					
In school	20.9%	33.9%	37.4%	45.0%	45.8%
Employed	33.6	30.3	35.1	36.6	31.2
Seeking work	43.2	33.6	25.9	17.0	9.1
Males 20–24					
In school	2.6%	10.5%	9.9%	12.7%	21.1%
Employed	58.5	62.6	69.6	71.8	68.7
Seeking work	37.2	25.9	19.8	14.7	9.6
Females 16–17					
In school	58.5%	65.4%	74.7%	80.5%	85.0%
Employed	8.3	7.6	8.0	9.2	8.5
Seeking work	17.6	11.5	8.8	5.1	2.4
Housewives	5.8	7.1	2.7	1.3	0.8
Females 18–19					
In school	14.0%	24.0%	26.3%	33.6%	39.9%
Employed	25.5	25.7	33.7	38.1	39.6
Seeking work	30.9	21.3	20.7	14.5	8.0
Housewives	18.9	21.3	10.5	4.8	3.2
Females 20–24					
In school	1.4%	5.3%	4.4%	7.1%	11.3%
Employed	25.6	33.9	43.1	57.1	59.9
Seeking work	17.9	11.6	10.2	9.7	7.1
Housewives	47.6	44.2	36.1	17.8	10.4

*For families on relief only, this category includes youth enjoying work relief, 3.9%, 14.5% and 26.4%, respectively, of all males of the indicated ages and 1.8%, 5.9%, and 5.4% of all females. "Colored" youth (N = 38, 523) were tabulated for only three socioeconomic levels and two age groups.

Source: Calculated from National Health Survey data tabulated in U.S. Federal Security Agency, Social Security Board, Bureau of Research and Statistics, *Statistics of Family Composition, vol. 11: The Urban Sample* (Bureau Memorandum No. 45 [Washington, n.p., 1942]), 165–167.

Note: Between 0.5% and 3.3% of boys, varying from category to category, and between 0.8% and 11.3% of girls were "at home," generally living with their parents but not at school, at work, or looking for work.

based on family income and included a distinction between on-relief and other low-income families. The table demonstrates how profound a difference family income made in how one grew up. Poor youth—reliefers somewhat more than families who were off the rolls at the time of the survey—enjoyed less schooling but experienced *less* gainful employment. By age 18–19, when a quarter to a third of youth were gainfully employed, the proportion at work had equalized between poor and better-off youth, and with increased age it was the better-off who found jobs. This differential was, if anything, even clearer among young women. The experience that was characteristic of poor children was "seeking work"—unemployment.[22]

GROWING UP WITH STRINGENCY

Families that suffered no direct economic deprivation seem, on the whole, to have maintained their prior consumption habits. But when families had to cut back, the realms in which they were most able to economize were precisely those areas that had become in the last decade so important to the new adolescent styles of life: recreation, automobiles, and clothing.[23] The Depression affected different categories of persons in different ways, even within individual families. Detailed expenditure data, presented in capsule form in table 12, offer a clue to how changes occurred. The table indicates how much a family with an income $10 greater than that of the next family would typically allocate to certain categories of clothing expenditures.[24] It shows, for instance, that in the expansive economy of 1918–19, a family that had $10 more annual income than the next family would probably allocate about 14 cents to more or better trousers and shirts for the male household head but fully 30 cents to more or better skirts, waists, and blouses for the late-adolescent daughter or daughters. In the straitened 1930s, fathers' pants would receive the same honor as before, while this aspect of daughters' clothing would receive only one-third the increment as before, less now than her father's.

During World War I, families had seemingly favored their adolescent children, especially their daughters. Daughters' increments had exceeded those for all other family members.[25]

Table 12. Average Increase in Expenditures on Given Family Members
for Selected Items of Clothing per $10 Increase in Family
Income, 1918–19 and 1935–36* (Increases in cents)

	Trousers, etc.**		Hats, Caps		Shoes	
	1918–19	1935–36	1918–19	1935–36	1918–19	1935–36
Husband	13.8	14.1	1.8	1.8	3.5	3.1
Wife	13.7	9.7	3.4	2.3	3.3	3.5
Son (15+)	22.0	8.7	3.2	0.8	7.4	2.3
Daughter (15+)	30.2	10.0	6.4	1.3	10.5	4.3
Son (12–15)	8.2	6.2	1.0	0.3	7.4	2.3
Daughter (12–15)	5.0	5.6	1.6	0.9	2.9	2.1

*Average for New England, West Central, East Central, and Rocky Mountain states.
**Includes also suits, shirts, skirts, waists, blouses, etc.
Sources: Estimated from U.S. Bureau of Labor Statistics, *Cost of Living in the United States* (Bulletin No. 357 [Washington, D.C.: USGPO, 1924]), Table C; and U.S. Bureau of Labor Statistics, *Study of Consumer Purchases: Urban Technical Series. Family Expenditures in Selected Cities, 1935–36: Vol. III, Clothing and Personal Care* (Bulletin No. 648 [Washington: USGPO, 1941]), table 5.
Note: Based on families with such members with comparable range of family incomes for each year and excluding open categories. The sequencing of items in the two surveys indicates that the researchers sought comparable categories of expenditure. The 1918–19 set includes five income categories over the range $900–2,500, while the 1935–36 includes four over the range $500–3,000, because the latter set is not limited to workingmen. I have excluded higher income categories included in this latter study so as to approximate the same socioeconomic range of families. The consumer price index was just slightly higher in 1918–19 than in 1935–36, so deflation does not much confuse these reckonings.

The comparison with somewhat younger children—girls especially—is most instructive. These children were apparently seen as simply too young to need much more than utilitarian clothing, and family budget patterns reflected this. And although wives' increments for hats slightly exceeded that of their adolescent and young-adult sons, sons received more for shoes and for outer wear than did their mothers or fathers. In this generally prosperous period, families were using a relatively substantial portion of their prosperity to adorn their late-adolescent sons and daughters, as these children neared marriageable age in the new marriage market that was beginning to incorporate dating.

The Depression intervened in this development, and the new regime fits with a particular frustration felt by youth of these ages, as we shall see.[26] On a per-capita basis, even after correcting for deflation, sons in two of the three measured categories of clothing and daughters in all three had *absolutely lower expenditures* on these kinds of clothes. There was, too, a general decline in the proportion of incremental income spent on clothing of all sorts for all family members except the male breadwinner, for whom expenditure patterns remained just about as they had been before the Depression. Wives and younger children lost out somewhat, but the really precipitous declines hit late-adolescent sons and daughters. The rearrangements of the budget is understandable: the father was still ideally and most often in fact the main breadwinner, and his appearance at work, or in applying for work, might be crucial in determining whether he could hold a job. Less important now was the sharp appearance an older son or daughter might make among his or her peers. *Fortune*'s acute mid-decade study, "Youth in College," discussed young women's tweeds, sweaters, and striking restraint in self-adornment. "With no make-up and little lipstick, she presents a casual, even an untidy, appearance while on the campus. And the casualness is carried over into the girl's surface air of self-possession, which is unstudied."[27]

Dating, which placed a premium on up-to-date dress and the material capacity for purchasing commercial entertainment for "a good date," was a system that had spread throughout the country only in the preceding decade. The parents of the children of the Depression had themselves generally not dated and thus had not experienced the particular strains on consumption capacities built into dating. While, as Glen Elder has cogently argued, in most families the need to pull together during hard times was obvious to all family members and no doubt generally acquiesced in, nevertheless, exactly how families might economize was by no means self-evident: each family had to make and did make its own decision. Who would pay the price of Depression stringencies and uncertainties had to be thrashed out again and again. This is exactly what Mirra Komorovsky remarked in her examination of family strain in the Depression. The extent of adolescent-parent breakdown in unemployed Depression families, she argued, depended considerably on the degree to which the child saw his or her own personal interests thwarted by the Depression. The example

Komorovsky used to illustrate this point had to do with expenditures on a girl's clothes.[28]

Depression stringencies and insecurities modified residence patterns, income composition, and family expenditure budgets. These modifications, in turn, affected the allocation of family members' time. The straitened circumstances described by Ethel Beer as pertaining to the single "business girl" living at home pertained far more widely. Families simply did not have the secure wherewithal to create the circumstances under which a young woman could move easily through courtship. She lacked the clothes. No less, she lacked the leisure. "She may not have any conscious antagonism towards her family. Nevertheless, she feels constrained in this environment." Marriage, for her

> is an escape, the only escape she can conceive of from her family. The husband as the rescuer from this tedious, restricted household is the only possible hero of her dreams. . . . How can she compensate for her social lack unless she breaks bonds and reaches freedom? Since to her the wedding ring represents this freedom, it is quite understandable that she should bend every effort towards procuring it.[29]

POSTPONED MARRIAGE

Knowing what we do about the operations of mate selection processes in American society at the time, it is fair to say that those who married young often married into chronic economic insecurity. The Depression in this sense served to exacerbate the impact of social class on family formation and, in effect, to segregate the young families of this time into two unusually sharply distinguished categories: those formed by people who could see a clear personal route through the uncertainties of the Depression, who married prudently and could generally hope to take advantage of a steady income and declining prices; and those formed only under some other, more generalized confidence of the ability to sustain their family in the future, by those who had but little to hope for economically in the immediate situation. In the Depression, marriages were postponed prudently by families of particular backgrounds and entered into with less prudence by others of other backgrounds. Sociologist James Bossard explained these kinds of differential marriage patterns in terms of the differing criteria that "older, more established groups" and "newer, less established groups" entertained for the conferral of status. Both classes were challenged by Depression stringencies. But the more established groups postponed marriage to maintain their "plane of living," while for the others, simply to marry was more honorific and important.[30]

It was difficult for young people when they wanted to do so to gain independence from their parents as reflected in neolocality and nuclearity. In the Depression, the ratio of household heads to currently married men of ages 15–24 declined from 79:100 in 1930 to 76:100 in 1940, although catching up to parity by ages 25–34.[31] Among whites, the more education, the more difference age meant to the circumstances of marriage: accumulation started slower among the more educated, making independent residence at marriage relatively rare, but given a few years, it had progressed faster, so that by their mid-twenties young married men with more education were considerably more likely to have their own households. Theirs was the greater "Depression penalty" if they married when young but the greater reward for patience.[32] Blacks married earlier, regardless of educational attainment, but for all educational levels and at all ages were far less able to afford independent households. At all levels of education, those who married later more typically settled into their own homes, independent of relatives and others. *For blacks*, whose generally precarious life courses were rendered all the more so by the Depression, it was *invariably* the more educated whose presumed wish for independent nuclear families was the more often denied—at least through their mid-twenties. The reason is eloquently simple: blacks in the Depression simply could not translate schooling into jobs that allowed a reasonably rapid accumulation for an independent residence at an appropriate standard of living.

The price paid for extended prudence under uncertainty was a challenge to the normative moorings that had governed the delicate timing of family-building transitions involved in prudence of this kind. How to maintain the nice degree of reserve required to commit oneself to a "steady" or fiancée but not foreclose other options, in view of the extended waiting time that prudence required in the Depression? How to postpone childbearing longer than the couple of years formerly characteristic for prudent but not downright emancipated couples, without falling into the selfishness that extended childlessness was thought to encourage? How to preserve the emotional tenor of such relationships over a different course than that worked out by the couples who had, within limits, redefined tradition just a decade before? Asked in a 1934 survey what irritated her about her extended engagement, a twenty-six-year-old secretary put it thus: "People asking when we are going to get married—giving us advice and making our plans and arrangements for us."[33] Much was now problematic: not the rules themselves as in the 1920s, but how these rules could work themselves out in particular lives.

It is eloquent testimony to the importance men and women attributed to marriage that although marriage rates were indeed affected by the Great Depression, they were only affected somewhat. The economic downturn far exceeded the nuptial downturn, a drop of 18 percent in gross national product between 1926–1929 and 1930–1934 for instance, was associated with only about a 9 percent drop in the number of marriages between the same dates. Marriages could be postponed only so long in hopes of happier economic circumstances without wholly disrupting the existing mechanisms of the marriage market. Eventually most would be celebrated, under modified economic expectations. Even during the course of the Depression, Jessie Bernard noted that young marriages that were postponed when the Depression first struck resulted in a bumper crop of marriages to somewhat older people only a few years later.[34] When we examine proportions ever married in the 1950 census, we find *no lasting deficits whatever* in the cohorts that might ordinarily have expected to marry during the Depression, those who might have found that they had postponed too long ever to marry.[35] Most did marry, even if many of these marriages were long delayed. Their taste for matrimony was not permanently or even long affected. Tastes for rather young marriage were still in place when war mobilization produced circumstances that promoted a speedy transition. And, as we will shortly see, the Depression had by then weakened the moral—and chronological—effect of engagement.

The Depression even had an impact on the ceremonial context of those marriages that were contracted in the face of its hardships and uncertainties. The scant data point to a tendency for Depression marriages to be undertaken with less ritual than before and, arguably, with somewhat less ritual oversight than was the norm. A subsequent poll that asked the setting of respondents' marriages shows a distinct dip in church weddings among persons whose age suggests they married in the early Depression years. Weddings in both city hall and in the home of one of the couple's parents increased correspondingly.[36] In Philadelphia, weddings at city hall (only the tip of the iceberg of marriages with reduced ceremony) rose from about 7 percent just before the Depression to 11 percent in 1932, 12 percent in 1933, then back down to 11 percent in 1934, and dropping to an ordinary level in 1936. Jacobson notes declines in New York City and Milwaukee and comments that "some of the couples, who would have had a church wedding, postpone their marriage[s] until better times; others are wed by a civil officiant."[37]

On the aggregate, marriage age edged somewhat upward during the early Depression, as relatively young and average-age couples postponed matrimony. The initial cluster of marriage delays came disproportionately from persons living in socioeconomically less well-off areas, but these residents adjusted to lowered material standards at marriage relatively more quickly than those living in more prosperous areas.[38] Detailed New York State figures on first-marriage age by single year and single year of age reveal also a change in preferred or prescribed marriage ages. In the late 1920s in New York State (outside of New York City), the age distribution at first marriage had been bimodal for women, with the primary mode at 21 but a pronounced secondary mode at 18. For men, the lone mode was 21, and it was sharply peaked. When the Depression hit, the numbers of young women's marriages at 18 and young men's at 21 dropped markedly, while marriages at older ages gained. Even as the Depression was ending, the 18-year second-

ary mode was not reestablished among women, and 21 remained in eclipse among men. For men and women, especially
women, the marriage ages, both the expected and the presumably preferred, had shifted later.[39] Whatever moral or emotional premium had been achieved by men and women who
married *precisely* at 18 or 21 was evidently foregone in the face
of sterner exigencies. But the marriage market continued to
run smoothly.

Both the New York State data and Massachusetts annual
data[40] reveal two interrelated patterns occurring over the Depression years. Numbers of first marriages varied from year to
year, following business conditions, *but not to an equal extent for
all age groups*. Both younger and older marriages—the latter
trending somewhat upward, the former downward over the period—varied less than did marriages at about the modal ages.
Younger marriages, it seems, were in a sense insulated from
economic cycle by the fact that many were contracted under
duress of pregnancy and in any case were rarely prudent. Many
of the marriages of older people, in contrast, were insulated by
the economic reserves many such people had accumulated.

Brides' marriage ages shifted toward grooms'. The point is
of more than only demographic significance, as can be seen by
contemplating the probable explanation for the phenomenon:
women's gainful employment before marriage. Quite likely, material accumulation before marriage was seen widely as more
crucial than before, if also more difficult. Women's contribution
was proportionately emphasized in the enterprise, and this was
surely consequential to the roles they could claim within marriage. And this new effort was most prominent among women
with the training to take up clerical occupations, which fared
rather better than manufacturing employment during the Depression, even drawing new kinds of entrants to the labor
force.[41] The tensions of marriage postponement, and certainly
the sexual ones, were mostly ascribed to the man, a pattern especially true in the late-marrying middle class.

Table 13 takes advantage of a special census carried out in
Cincinnati at the middle of the Great Depression. It reveals that
the downward trend in age at marriage that had characterized
the 1920s experience of both males and females, for native

Table 13. Proportion Ever Married in Cincinnati, 1920–1935, by Sex and Age, for Native Whites and Blacks (in percentages)

	Males			Females		
	1920	*1930*	*1935*	*1920*	*1930*	*1935*
Native white						
15–19	1.3	1.6	1.3	8.2	11.2	5.0
20–24	22.9	28.1	22.3	40.9	46.8	33.4
25–34	61.8	68.8	68.0	67.7	74.6	73.9
Black						
15–19	4.7	3.5	3.1	25.4	26.3	17.4
20–24	42.9	43.5	38.6	69.7	72.9	66.5
25–34	69.4	74.4	71.8	85.4	89.6	86.4

Sources: Calculated from Census 1920–1, 474; Census 1930–1, 977; Cincinnati Employment Center, Ohio State Employment Service, *The Population of Hamilton County, Ohio, in 1935* (Studies in Economic Security: II [Cincinnati: Cincinnati Employment Center, 1937]), 52–53.

whites and blacks alike, was sharply reversed in the first half of the 1930s. Proportions married by age 24 were invariably reduced to lower levels even than in 1920. But *for those above age 25, the Depression effect was almost invisible* in Cincinnati. As we have gathered from the national data, Cincinnati men and women were already catching up on their marriages, after a delay, by mid-Depression.

Small-area data for 1935—107 census tracts in the city of Cincinnati—allow us to explore the factors that influenced marriage timing as of 1935, examining the characteristics of census tracts that contained relatively high proportions married there for native white young men and women at 20–24 and 25–29.[42] Because we can compare correlates of marriage timing for different ages, we can infer from the *differences* the way various relevant factors impinged on marriage decisions made by those who may have felt themselves at a relatively comfortable age to delay and those who, a bit older, perhaps were more likely to be strongly propelled into marriage now rather than later. A common set of factors influenced marriage timing across genders and ages but with certain telling differences. For all age categories we are examining, a neighborhood sex ratio approximating equality with the opposite sex conduced to marriage, as did whatever circumstances had promoted population growth in that tract during the preceding five years. The presence of large numbers of foreign-born whites, for all groups, was associated with lower proportions married, probably because where there were many foreign born, there were also many of the young native white men and women who were second-generation Americans, long quite slow to marry. High-rent districts were characterized by late marriages. Finally, where high proportions of all adults—and thus of marriageable-age women—in the census tract were engaged in gainful occupations, marriage was considerably inhibited. The population growth variable (which may mainly have indicated suburbanization) was associated with enhanced marriage propensities of older more than of younger people. This relationship, however, was powerfully reversed for the economic variables, which were far more strongly associated with variation in younger people's marriage propensity. The impact of proportions at work, finally, differed for men and women: whereas for both sexes, high proportions of the tract's population at work inhibited marriage propensities, it did so more for *younger* men and for *older* women. But for neither was this factor anywhere near so powerful as the apparent tendency for those living in higher-priced areas to postpone marriage considerably more than those living in cheaper venues, *especially young people.* Put another way, whereas young people in relatively prosperous circumstances were much more likely than people of like age living elsewhere to put off their marriages in the middle of the Depression, by the time one was between the ages of 25 and 29, this differential caution no longer obtained. Normative considerations, and the possibility that people so well circumstanced had put aside an adequate nest egg to sustain a marriage even in uncertain times, now took over.

Numbers of marriages contracted from 1929 to 1935 by men in different occupational categories is shown in figure 12, indexed with pre-Depression numbers of marriages set equal to 100.0.[43] The graph shows that young men pursuing certain occupations in the early Depression—notably skilled workers (in part because of their sensitivity to the highly cyclical building

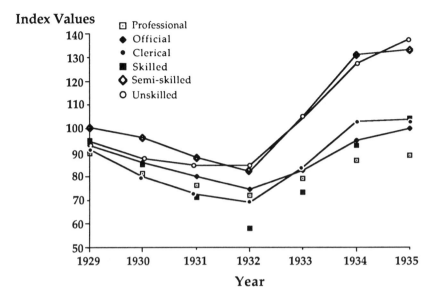

Figure 12. Marriage Rates for Men, by Occupation, 1929–1935

trades) and proprietors—characteristically followed the economic trends closely. But the semiskilled—factory employees— were slow to defer marriage and quick to resume it. Unskilled laborers, who no doubt were thrown out of work quicker than the others, showed a variant of this pattern. One suspects that for those with skills nowhere demonstrable outside the particular work situation, long-term prudence was not particularly called for, only good sense enough not to marry just at the moment one was oneself unemployed. Clerical workers were particularly quick to delay marriage but quite responsive as well to early signs of recovery. The professionals showed a distinctive pattern, promptly postponing their marriages and hardly letting up on their restrained nuptial tendencies, even as the Depression moderated, no doubt in response to the continuing need to establish a firm. Retrospective census materials on marriage age by educational attainment for native white women in 1940 show that as the Depression years passed, less-educated women seemed to countenance younger marriages, while the more educated essentially maintained their initial hesitancy. The kinds of cautions that the Depression imposed on young couples seemingly affected primarily those whose educational backgrounds suggested middle-class aspirations and a relatively high target of material sufficiency for marriage.[44]

Current and prospective unemployment, too, inhibited marriage more for those in some occupations than in others. The dividing line was not socioeconomic status, it seems, but job-related outlook on the future. Among higher-status males, young professionals and low-status white-collar employees, *but not proprietors*, were rarely married, for their human capital investment in the future was wholly dependent on the right employment opportunity. Among manual workers, too, it was those with valued, hard-gained skills who apparently held off marriage until reemployment. But for those who, like miners or masons, had skills their industries all too frequently underused, marriage postponement during unemployment was rarer.[45]

THE SUBTLE ALTERATION OF NORMATIVE PATTERNS: ENGAGEMENT

The dominant interpretation of the impact of the Depression on the American family is one in which the stress served in effect to weed out the less resilient families, emphasizing thus the considerable vigor of the family institution.[46] Elder's powerful work has especially had the effect of emphasizing this general conclusion.[47] There is, however, another way we can turn the family-in-the-Depression question around to suggest a somewhat different conclusion. For if the institution of the family emerged from the Depression strengthened, so also subtle changes were introduced. We will here turn attention to a single aspect of family building—engagement—that was subjected to a kind of pressure by the Depression which palpably modified its content. Thus modified, but still a common constituent of institutionalized family-building patterns, engagement made its contribution to post-Depression and particularly postwar marriages that looked much the same as what had come before but felt rather different.

One of eighteen "charges" brought against "Society" in 1935 during a well-publicized mock trial staged by the Council of Social Agencies was "allowing conditions to exist under which

young people are unable to marry due to lack of employment."
After a reported eighty thousand words of testimony and due
deliberation by a jury of twelve (adults) drawn from "all known
organizations" in the community, "Society" was held guilty on
six counts. Negligence to create material conditions conducive
to marriage was one of the six.[48] To be sure, the connection with
legislative action is strictly speculative, the item highly hypothetical and out of context in the brief questionnaire. However,
for all the caveats it properly calls forth, it is suggestive of the
terms in which large numbers of Americans contemplated the
specter of delayed marriage in the middle of the Great Depression. The eighth of "Ten Modern Commandments" of love
propounded in the same year by *True Confessions* was "Thou
shalt make use of thy emotional energy through sublimation."
It followed that "society's job just now is to make it economically
possible for young folks of marriageable age, who are in love, to
find fulfillment within marriage."[49] Roy Dickerson, the YMCA
marriage counselor, held that when "the natural hopes of a [en-
gaged] couple are frustrated, . . . they are likely to feel rebel-
lious against a social system that they hold responsible for their
disappointment."[50]

The idea of social action was cheerful fantasy. Perhaps instead, couples' "natural hopes" were redirected and the institutions channeling their hopes changed. At least one restrained
scholarly study argued that Depression age norms were so vio-
lated by delayed marriage that either economic or moral restructuring must "certainly" soon come.[51] A 1935 survey of
New York City youth found that one-fifth of young women
aged 18 to 24 and one-third of young men aged 21 to 24 believed "the Depression had interfered with their marrying."
The survey analysts noted "a sameness to the reasons [i.e., eco-
nomic] that is monotonous until one tries to visualize something
of the unique sense of misery" the youths were expressing.
They concluded that "the effect on mental well-being . . . is far-
reaching."[52] The engaged couples in the late-1930s study by
Burgess and Wallin repeatedly expressed frustration because
economic conditions prolonged their engagements unduly. Engagement, which had evolved into a time for testing true love,
had become a trying time in a different sense.[53]

Such respected experts on adolescence as Carolyn Zachry reflected on the marital-scheduling difficulties of the Depression as an opportunity to intermingle subsidy and socialization for marriage.

> To many an adolescent, a job is also the prime factor in determining whether or not he can get married. For those thousands of young people joblessness means frustration, not only of their ambitions in the business and professional world, but frustration of their psycho-sexual desires as well. Of course, in many boys and girls the desire for marriage is confused with their desire for status and prestige. . . . We—parents and educators and miscellaneous adults alike—[should] recognize that our task is much more than that of enabling young people to get married by helping them to become financially self-sufficient. We must also help them to achieve more mature attitudes toward marriage.[54]

Birth control advocate Robert Latou Dickenson, evolving a new notion of family formation that took fuller notice of the urgent drives of the parties involved, argued in 1936 that "early marriage and [a] shorter period of engagement are necessary; yet they are impractical unless contraception may be employed."[55]

Addressing frustrated youth directly, schlock publisher Bernarr MacFadden spoke less of maturity but trumpeted the same theme of the threat posed by frustration to the very institution of marriage.

> Young people are afraid to marry these days unless they can begin, materially, where their parents left off. They want all material comforts ready to hand, and an assurance that they will not have to give up one small thing for the added gift of love. . . . They get *things*, but miss the fine edge of marriage. That fine edge belongs to youth. It is *youth*, the joy of struggling together, of building together. . . . Security is no gift from the outside. . . . Why not marry while young?[56]

And eugenic marriage counselor and popular writer Paul Popenoe likewise urged direct action lest the road to marriage stretch so long that disastrous tensions develop. "In heaven's name, why wait? . . . If you are sincerely in love, old enough to know what you are doing, understand what marriage means and are free to enter into it, you have no right to let anything, least of all money, bar you from happiness. . . . I've never known of a home broken up by lack of money," exhorted the marriage counselor, noting that money worries were a special "ogre" to engaged people, so much so that it is sometimes "so frightening that they wish they weren't engaged."[57]

In 1937, the Roper Organization posed a remarkable question to a representative sample of the American population : "Should the government give financial aid to young people to help them get married and establish homes?" Remote as this was from the nation's highly private conception of the circumstances and basis of marriage, no fewer than 38 percent of all respondents answered "Yes." Just 54 percent rejected it.[58] Women were slightly more enthusiastic about Roper's government-subsidy proposition than were men: 41 percent to 37 percent. This difference showed up not among the younger respondents but among the older ones. Older women were almost as favorable to the proposition as were younger women: their vote was, in a sense, an assent to the critical importance of marriage to women generally rather than to their own immediate needs. For men, however, age mattered. Forty-three percent of both men and women under 24 supported the hypothetical proposition, but by gradual steps, assent among the male respondents declined to 29 percent among men 55 or older. Independent of age, socioeconomic status was negatively related to assent to the government subsidy.

Many contemplated a change in some of the rules surrounding the marriage process, a reorganization of some elements to preserve the essence. An institutionalized pattern that was located at a life course phase of deep frustration was engagement. Among Kinsey's respondents married during the Depression, between two-thirds and three-fourths had been engaged prior to marriage, with engagement just slightly more common among the college-educated than among those who never went to college. Kinsey's data also point to a slight but temporary decline of the incidence of engagement during the Depression.[59]

Too amorphous to be altered in any formal way, engagement was subtly—but lastingly—modified in its meaning, particularly with regard to the constraint the institution placed on sexual expression. The 1938 *Good Housekeeping Marriage Book* maintained that "an engaged couple who are sure of their hearts and minds should be helped to marry as soon as the plans for the marriage can be wisely worked out." Since "this usually involves financing, . . . wise parents today cooperate so that the young couple do not have to wait too long."[60] Family sociologists at Cornell University reported that as the Depression wore on, parental subsidy was in fact offered more often than before and accepted (even expected) more often, although the students were still wary of the possible strings that might be attached to such support. Their campus survey suggested that in 1940–1941, more than one-third favored parental support for college marriages and support while couples "get on their feet," and an additional one-fifth favored emergency aid.[61] A student poll at the University of Colorado in mid-decade reported that six in ten male and female students believed that financial aid from parents was acceptable to permit marriage; almost as many also said they would accept a "dowry" system.[62] Parental aid to prompt middle-class marriage was in the early stages of being institutionalized. But this was not yet common enough to take the pressure off engagement. "I was engaged for a long time, but I couldn't get a job." "We broke off—no money."[63]

In the Depression, engagement became an especially ambiguous institution. "About four months ago I met the man that I have chosen for my husband. He proposed about a month ago, but has not as yet given me an engagement ring. Should I consider myself engaged before I have the ring?"[64] Neither an element of peer culture, as was dating, nor a step of unquestioned legal significance, as was marriage, engagement was nevertheless held by numbers of advisors and commentators to be either or both. In law, engagement was equivalent to a contract to marry—but a contract that was open to highly discrepant construction. The engagement ring was legally interpreted as a "consideration" that made a promise to marry contractual, but both legal texts and advice texts indicate that many couples instead saw the ring as a gift. Presumably, they also viewed engagement as less than a formal contract.[65]

According to Burgess and Wallin, "the proportion of broken engagements is on the increase" in the mid-1930s, because "even engagement has become a trial relationship during which love is assessed."[66] Etiquette books of the day became distressed at the dyadic, negotiated quality of recent engagement, which, unlike betrothal, no longer required the suitor to have gained prior permission from his prospective father-in-law.[67] Burgess and Wallin chose to interpret engagement as an institution in transit from a less to a more important function. "In the past three decades [i.e., since about World War I] there has been a marked change in attitude toward engagement. It is now considered as the last stage in the selection process, . . . its preeminent function the final opportunity for the couple to find out if they are fitted for each other."[68] Engagement thus linked dating to marriage, enlarging the sphere of young people's volition. All writers agreed with Ernest Groves that "the engagement can have little value as a preliminary testing of the relationship before marriage unless with it goes the possibility of breaking off the relationship."[69] An etiquette for breaking an engagement was developed which was more completely elaborated than that for establishing one. And Burgess and Wallin found that 30 percent of their engaged respondents in the mid-1930s had been previously engaged.[70]

Engagement was now supposed to serve to help a couple navigate a safe course to lasting marriage where tradition had largely ceased to offer explicit rules for behavior. By the 1930s, dating couples might form and reform without great social or emotional costs, enabling young women and men to learn the range of personalities to be found among socially acceptable partners. Dating, however, depended so much on the partners exchanging the material and physical wherewithal of "a good time" that dating seemed too brittle, too brief, perhaps too exploitative, to contain the more tender phases of courtship.[71] For some, but not all, "going steady" constituted an intermediate step in this direction.[72] The question of sexual compatibility was something else again. "The social attitude toward betrothal should not be too rigid," wrote Popenoe, but should allow for a gradual, cautious, loosening of the inhibitions that govern dating. "Where betrothal is regarded as equally sacred and binding with marriage," that is, governed by social controls rather than the situational application of internalized values regarding intimacy, on the one hand, and the double standard, on the other, "this [exploratory] function is largely lost. Equal loss results from taking the betrothal too lightly—where it is merely regarded as a convenient cover for intimacies that would not otherwise be approved socially."[73]

The critical distinction between engagement and dating lay in the way that the extent of physical intimacy was settled on. When dating, boys proposed and girls disposed, this being one element of a culturally defined and peer-overseen negotiation. In engagement, the couple was now publicly recognized as a unit, the constancy between the partners reinforced by the social recognition of the "opalescent mist of gossamer delicacy" that convention enjoined between the couple.[74]

> When courtship prospers it leads to the mutual fixing of affection and this in turn creates need of a public recognition of a special relationship. The betrothal expresses the wish of both the man and the woman for a sense of security and exclusiveness in their love. From the point of view of its function as related to marriage, the engagement, by removing uncertainty in their relationship, provides favorable conditions for each person to become well acquainted with the other before making a commitment which is presumed to be a life union.[75]

The assumption was that the period of asymmetrical bargaining ended with engagement and that a wholly mutual period of "exploration and discovery of personalities, a period of adventuring in adjustments," ensued.[76] Engaged, one no longer simply accepted or rejected what one was offered. Instead, one sought to discern and perhaps to undertake those changes one should and could make in oneself in order to enrich the unity of the couple.

> An engagement period of about six months is not too long . . . to be sure that upon the instinctive basis of sex attraction a truly personal love has been founded. For sex must be built upon to create love. . . . These ideals of sex relationships and love relationships should form part of that great bulk of questions that must be talked over between a betrothed couple.[77]

A suitable degree of physical intimacy short of coitus, which would lead inevitably to "an anti-climax of relationship,"[78] was exactly one of the things a couple was supposed to discover in engagement. Margaret Sanger laid out the situation with unusual precision in 1926, and on entirely conventional premises.

> The fiancé's breath, odor, touch, embrace and kiss must be pleasing to her. If they are not . . . then under no circumstances should the engagement be prolonged. . . . The intimacies permitted during the engagement, the legitimate intimacies of kisses and caresses, in the protecting atmosphere of poetic romance, thus fulfill a distinct and all-important function—the deepening of desire and the commingling of the spiritual and the physical. The engagement with its growing emotional bond is thus not merely a social convenience; it is the fulfillment of a necessary and vital process.[79]

The sexual tensions of engagement were entirely congruent with the "frankness" appropriate to personality exploration. "Frankness means that whenever either one becomes aware of a rising surge of sexual desire, it will be possible to say, 'I think we had better be doing something else. . . . Engagement may be still further enriched by the development of the spiritual resources of personality."[80] An author in *The Good Housekeeping Marriage Book* reflected the ambiguity engendered by engagement in a time of general social stress and change when he reassured his readers both that, on the one hand, "if they have . . . decided to wait, they need have no fear that this indicates a lack of sex feeling," and that, on the other, if they find waiting hard, "they should be glad that they do have 'sex hunger.' "[81]

Some sense of the variability of engagement as an institution can be inferred from the great difference among instances of how long engagements lasted before marriage. Engagements might at their outset incorporate considerable certainty about a marriage date, or they might imply nothing more than an intention to marry at some point. Half a year to something over a year was generally held to be the optimal length for an engagement, but about one in three of Burgess's 1930s couples was engaged less than half a year before they married; Terman's findings were similar.[82] A slightly greater proportion of the entire Kinsey sample had short engagements.[83] However, these same sources indicate that almost two in ten engagements that eventually led to marriage were at least two years long. The Burgess couples reinterviewed after their eventual marriages on average scored higher "marital adjustment" scores the longer they had been engaged, although the evidence presented suggests that this was perhaps a function of duration of acquaintance rather than a result of engagement *per se*.[84] In an engagement lasting indefinitely, could one sustain such a subtle interpenetration of egos without at the same time according one's partner other intimacies? The institution was vulnerable. Timing and content could not be separated where couples were expected to pet heavily but to refrain from coitus, but the duration of this period was subject to unpredictable upward revision. "I am 20 years old and am engaged to a fine boy who is 21. Unlike most boys, he realizes that it is not right to monopolize me and keep me from going with other boys, because he is not working seriously and cannot afford to take me everywhere or to marry just now."[85] What was to be the content of engagement that was thrown off schedule, where mutual exploration would lead perilously close to forbidden sexuality, where even day-to-day pleasures were either riskily domestic or prohibitively costly?

Engagement was exactly that point in the family-formation process at which young people were supposed to experience, and weather, their acute doubts about subsequent steps in the process. The opalescent mist was also almost invariably a period of episodic tension. Longer engagements may or may not have promoted such doubts, but surely they were the occasion for many of them, especially in view of how hard the economic uncertainties of the period bore down on those in the family-formation years. The Depression induced a particularly focused eagerness to be done with one's engagement. The war would soon provide an occasion for this—and the prosperity that followed—so that the family-formation process came to be permanently modified through an eagerness to change it at its weakest, least defined, least normatively satisfying element: engagement.

A 1935 *True Confessions* story, "Love Hazards," purports to be parallel interviews with an engaged pair, Dorothy, 20, and Bill, 22, who have realized, after two years of waiting in the engaged state, that another two years wait will be required.[86] The editorial presence asks, "What is Society going to do about them—all these young people who want to get married and can't?" The editor says that the Depression is immediately to blame for this tension but that really it is built into the mores and the economy more generally. The whole is a mythic explanation for, and thereby justification of, change in the normative structuring of the youthful life course.

"But gosh," exclaims Bill in his text, "nature never meant the preliminaries to last two years! Nature never intended the courtship to be dragged out forever. . . . I can't think that it's anything but natural for a chap who's in love to want his girl. I can't think he'd be much of a lover or much of a man if he didn't." Bill worries that if unsatisfied, his "urgent physical need of her" would so structure their engagement that all her other attentions would cease to please him. "Our engagement and my disposition are being ruined." Bill contemplates having recourse to Jenny, "an easy girl, a good-natured, cheap little girl," to slake his immediate cravings but tentatively rejects this solution, out of respect for Dorothy (not Jenny). He also looks forward to heightened sublimation through his studies. Yet he cannot believe that the institution of engagement is binding enough to prevent jealousy from creeping in, given a long delay: "Can I expect a gay, pretty girl to stay home and hold her hands evening after evening for me?" Bill proposes, as the only half-satisfactory solution to this dilemma, immediate sexual consummation with his fiancée, an emotionally appropriate if morally mediocre expression of intimacy in engagement dragged out too long. "Suppose I knew she was all mine— really mine. Do you suppose I'd be jealous of any chap then? Not I. And do you suppose I'd ever look at another girl?" He quiets his moral qualms in classic fashion: "It's not us that's wrong, but Society."

Dorothy says no, and the matter is in limbo as of the narrative present. Dorothy protests that her physical needs are every bit as urgent as Bill's. "Girls aren't different. I do want you. . . .

But don't you see, don't you see, you're so worth waiting for." Where Bill evokes nature, Dorothy evokes "a sentimental little picture in my mind of our wedding night—mine and Bill's, myself in white satin and lace, shy and yet eager, Bill ardent and glowing." Under proper restraint, Bill's fancied animality suits Dorothy's conception of things, but much of the time, now, it seems all too much like Bill's lusting after cheap, easy Jenny. Dorothy knows that sex is not a sufficient basis for lasting marriage. Dorothy protests that "much as I want to belong to Bill, I can be happy just being engaged to him." But Bill puts it thus: "She'll someday be my wife, legally as well as actually." Mapped on the somewhat shaky double standard of the day, the idea that sexuality is the touchstone of possession together with the enlightened, volitional definition of engagement as a period of growing mutual commitment had made the institution itself a murky battleground between the sexes.

We are offered an unresolved mythic struggle between nature and culture, following the then-polite convention of man as natural, woman as cultural. The context, however, is distinctly historical. In their different ways, both Bill and Dorothy deny the operating assumptions of the double standard of sexual conduct. Yet circumstances prevent a symmetrically structured family-formation process. Even if the sexual and moral natures of male and female were no longer assumed to be at opposite poles, nevertheless Dorothy's sense of the strength of their love is only enhanced by the challenge the economic pinch poses to their shared timetable. But for Bill, "Society" proved bankrupt when it failed to provide the couple in timely fashion the promised marriage that was to be their reward for noncoital courtship.

Contemporary students of mores recognized the difficulties of the situation. McGill and Matthews noted that even dating was difficult because so few had their accustomed pocket money. Even worse was a decline in the quality of friendships between boys and girls because of "what happens to friendship between the sexes when this important possibility [marriage] is ruled out." Cavan and Ranck note that employed girls had the advantage that income brought in their dating lives, noting such forlorn expressions among girls of marriageable age but not employed as "has boy friends but no clothes to wear when she goes out" and "the boys do not have jobs."[87]

From a narrowly behavioral perspective, engagement timing seems to have changed only slightly during the period we are considering. We have already noted a slight reduction during the Depression among Kinsey's married respondents in the proportions who had been engaged. The same cohort seems to have had on the average only somewhat shorter engagements, perhaps only an extension of a trend established during the previous decade. The data, however, do point to a considerably more rapid decline in the average length of engagements as World War II approached and through the war, although the total period of acquaintanceship preceding engagement remained roughly unchanged.

Might not an institution, no longer restraining but now expressing a highly sexualized intimacy, shorter, and arising as marriage ages became younger now begin to lose the special, tentative, exploratory quality that many applauded, perhaps passing some of these on to the marriage itself? Might not the slippage of the institution, reflected in the notes of a young person's discussion group, be general? "Is it all right," the 18-to-25-year-olds asked the minister who led the discussion, "for engaged couples to have sexual relations and if not, why not? Suppose they can't afford to be married? What about couples who are not engaged? It's natural, isn't it?"[88] The unraveling of the one tie seemingly threatened the next. Nearly two in three University of Colorado students—with no difference by gender—told an interviewer that at least some "sex liberties" might be taken during the engagement period.[89] Hints of what happened can be found in the Kinsey sex-history data. These show that those who had not been engaged before marriage had for decades been those whose premarital sexuality had evidently been the less constrained by social conventions. This relationship held true in the Depression, at higher levels of premarital intercourse. In the Depression, too, long engagements *led more often than before or subsequently to marriages in which the couples had bedded before marriage.* In the Depression, long engagement came to mean something special to those who, like Dorothy and Bill, enacted it. We must at least entertain the idea that a part of the Depression concern about delayed marriage responded to a real change in the ways engaged couples understood their relationship—in the resolution, coyly omitted from the text, of the struggle of Dorothy and Bill.

On the whole, Kinsey's respondents who had married without previously having had coitus with their intended expressed higher assessments of their marital happiness. This relationship, however, was related to engagement and, interactively, with date of marriage. Those who had never been engaged were the least affected by premarital intercourse in their assessment of their own marital happiness; those who had had quite long engagements spoke commonly of unfortunate consequences of their transgression. This relationship makes perfect sense in view of the ambiguous test of restraint and intimacy that engagement still posed until the Depression: those couples who took the test most seriously, and passed it, celebrated their joint triumph in the day-to-day context of their marriages. But those who yielded to their frustration had failed, and this failure promoted a sense of weakness in their marriages. This was true up to those cohorts marrying in the Depression. But *the relationship began to be effaced in the Depression cohort.* No overt revolution overthrew engagement. But it changed within, and with this, one more small social restraint on individual (or dyadic) volition began to vanish.

The exemplary demographic investigation by Preston and McDonald has shown us that, followed for long enough, marriages contracted in the Depression were relatively prone to divorce, as though subject to particular strain at the outset.[90] Their analysis contradicts the common perception—based on *current numbers* of divorces—that the Depression, if anything, had a moderating influence on the divorce trend, as families pulled together and as divorce came to be seen as simply too expensive. Two material aspects of the Depression had impact on marital durability: reduced material means in the crucial years immediately following the marriage and unemployment and uncertain employment. Marriages contracted young appear to have been *relatively* even more susceptible than they previously had been to eventual divorce during the Depression, as compared to those contracted at older ages at the same time.[91] The *largest* effect of the Depression on marriage, however, may well have been on the cultural level, affecting in a widespread way people's senses of the importance of planning and self-reliance, of cooperation within intimacy. We may assume that these motifs were most prominent among the young, especially those whose imprudently conducted or terminated engagements broke loose from acceptable standards under Depression strains.

THE SURPRISING END OF THE BABY BUST

If the Depression weakened engagement by calling into question too many engaged couples' capacity for right behavior, it in a sense strengthened the dyadic component of marriage. One common response of families when the Depression hit, thus, was to limit fertility, a development of which contemporaries were quite aware. A national survey of women in 1937 discovered that three in four said "no" to the proposition that "young married people should have a child in the first year of marriage." No fewer than 84 percent of women under thirty answered this way, as did about the same proportion of single women.[92]

A variety of means existed by which fertility might be reduced, including a number of means of mechanical and chemical contraception that had begun to diffuse rapidly in the 1920s and seem to have done so even more rapidly in the 1930s.[93] Four in five American women (nine in ten of those under 30 years of age) told a representative survey in 1938 that they were "in favor of birth control."[94] Abortion, too, seems to have played a role.[95] For all this, though, the effect of the Depression on fertility was by no means uniformly and invariably to reduce it. In fact, in the middle of the decade, the direction of the birth rate turned around altogether, after a good century of steady decline. This surprising reversal—which began a two-decade rise that came to be recognized as the "baby boom"—coincided with the point at which young people who had postponed their marriages because of the Depression began to "catch up" with the family-building plans that we may presume they (or the culture in which they grew up) had had. The family had evidently retained—more than retained—its salience in hard times, and such a period now proved more conducive to the reassertion of older ways than had the assertive consumerism of the 1920s.

Some components of total fertility were more elevated as the Depression faded before the war economy than they had been at its beginning. Careful empirical investigations of the differential impact of the Depression on urban fertility rates indicate a common initial reaction of fertility reduction, across socioeconomic classes and holding for blacks as well as for whites. After about 1933, the more prosperous classes began to relax their cautions somewhat, while those poorer (but not blacks, at any economic level!) continued to restrict their childbearing. In a New York study, the reduction in differential fertility among whites was so great that the 67 percent separating the fertility rates of white women living in the poorest and richest fifths of the city's areas in 1929 dropped to 19 percent in 1941. The author of a Chicago study speculated that when combined with the generally earlier marriage schedule that emerged during World War II, the middle-class upsurge in fertility during the latter part of the Depression foreshadowed the less-class-differentiated family commitment so typical of the postwar baby boom.[96]

The differential fertility patterns, however, contrast sharply with those we have earlier seen with regard to marriage. Poorer people relatively quickly resumed their pace of marriage but returned only slowly to their earlier, relatively expansive fertility patterns. We may infer, accordingly, that the Depression systematically reordered the timing of childbirth and its relationship to the timing of marriage, and that it did so differentially by social class. Overall, just as the Depression made marriage timing more a decision that segregated the prudent from those whose circumstances did not encourage (or permit) prudence, so entry into parenthood came to constitute a second segregation point where once again the question of prudence was rather explicitly raised. At this point, those whose prudence in marrying had encouraged delay in marriage yet again postponed their transitions to parenthood. But as prosperity showed signs of returning, fertility patterns reversed themselves sharply, and the prudent moved briskly to complete their

Table 14. Average Annual Change during Selected Periods of Total
Fertility Rate and Age-Specific First-Parity Fertility Rates, by
Race (in percentages)

| | Whites 1st Children | | | | | Nonwhites 1st Children | | | | |
	All Fert.	All	15–19	20–24	25–29	All Fert.	All	15–19	20–24	25–29
1925–1930	−3	−1	−2	−3	−2	−4	−3	−3	−5	−6
1930–1933	−5	−3	−4	−6	−6	−3	−3	−3	−4	−7
1933–1937	0	3	1	4	3	0	2	4	0	−1
1937–1941	2	4	1	4	8	1	1	0	1	3

SOURCE: Calculated from Robert L. Heuser, *Fertility Tables for Birth Cohorts by Color* (Rockville, Md.: National Center for Health Statistics, 1976), 23–25, 30–32, 362–364, 369–371.

strongly held commitment to parenthood. The cumulative effects of postponing intimacy, marriage, and parenthood had brought the segments of the youthful population ordinarily the most prone to waiting prudently to the point where they were eager to grasp at the hopeful indications of future prosperity by the end of the decade to press toward early family formation.

A compressed account of selected birthrates is offered in table 14. First births—certainly among whites—had declined less sharply in the years preceding the Depression than did the fertility rate based on all birth orders. But in the first four years of the Depression, initial parenthood was if anything more inhibited than was the enlargement of families in being. The increase of first-birth rates after the Depression's initial impact is striking when compared with the trend for all births. So is its race- and age-specific pattern, the upturn affecting older childless white women from 1933, without a parallel tendency for black women. Postponing the transition to parenthood, then, was an early Depression strategy for coping with the uncertainty to which the disordered economy exposed young Americans, a way of permitting marriage while limiting sacrifice of material standards, a strategy that was consistent with already existing trends, which had by now begun to affect almost all segments of the American population similarly. The return to parenthood expressed by white women by about the middle of the Depression, however, reached black women only in a far more meager way.[97]

It was not primarily deprivation *per se*, but an *environment* of widespread deprivation that encouraged prudent behavior. One study of fertility between 1929 and 1932 showed that the age-adjusted birthrate for those who had become "poor" after having had a "moderate" income before the Depression was 39 percent *higher* than those who had maintained their moderate incomes, while those who once "comfortable" but poor in 1932 had a birthrate 26 percent *above* that of those who started comfortable and remained comfortable or at least "moderate."[98] In Indianapolis, the proportion of long-term family planners among couples marrying just before the Depression ranged from 38 percent among those with low income in the first years of their marriages to 58 percent among those whose incomes were high. But whatever aspects of personal organization promoted family planning, they were so strongly associated with those qualities conducing to husbands' material success in the work world that among those of low initial income who were to achieve medium or high incomes by the late Depression, family planning was *just as prevalent* as among those whose initial incomes were high.[99]

The Indianapolis research found that a sense of "economic security" characterized middle-class families to a markedly greater degree than those whose husbands enjoyed less-favored occupations and that these same people were less likely to feel "economic tension"—a sense of a gulf between desired material well-being and attained well-being. But these were also the very people who had married later and were also more likely to be more planful generally and specifically with regard to fertility. The most planful, when asked to sum up whether they believed that the Depression had caused them to have fewer children than they might otherwise have wished to have or had intended to have, were *the least likely to answer "yes."* For many but not all Indianapolis couples by the late 1930s, self-conscious family planning was an element of their ambient cul-

Table 15. Proportions Still Childless in 1940, for Urban Native White Women Still Living with Their First Husbands, by Age at Marriage and Successive Marriage Cohort (in percentages)

Approximate Date of Marriage	Age at Marriage				Older Minus Younger
	20–21	*25–26*	*22–24*	*27–29*	
1921–26	13.1	24.0			10.9
1923–29			18.8	28.6	9.8
1926–31	15.7	29.7			14.0
1928–34			24.4	26.7	12.3
1931–36	24.9	38.4			13.5
1933–39			44.5	51.6	7.1
1936–40	57.5	61.4			3.9

SOURCE: Calculated from Census 1940–4, 37–40.

ture, which they comfortably appropriated. And it served them in good stead in the trying decade. Planfulness in general, family planning in particular, a sense of economic security, feelings of personal adequacy, and a reportedly happy marriage were all correlated with one another. They were also all correlated positively to income.[100]

Retrospective questions about fertility and marital timing asked in the 1940 census enable us to sketch in more detail how the Depression family-building process altered the prudent considerations of families. Table 15 compares two sets of urban native white women, each still living in 1940 with her first husband, for a number of marriage cohorts, asking which of these sets—those who had married on the young side and those who married on the old side—still had not become mothers.[101] The women being compared, then, had been married just as long as one another but had married at different ages.

The rising absolute proportion of the childless, of course, is to a large degree simply a product of the briefer time those married more recently have had to give birth by the census date. The differences by age among those married for the same amount of time, however, is significant. Invariably, those who married younger were quicker to have a first child, were less prone to remain childless for the intermediate or long run. And *there is a marked increase in this differential between early- and mid-Depression marriages.* For *late Depression marriages, however, this differential declined,* rather more than could be explained by the truncation effect produced by the 1940 census date. Those, that is, who for reasons of prudence or normative conformity to socioeconomic-group values were late to marry were *also* more leisurely about moving into parenthood. But this was truest in the middle of the Depression—at which time, as we have seen, the marriage-timing considerations of the socioeconomic groups were diverging from one another rather sharply. The 1941 Indianapolis Fertility Study of native white Protestant couples who had married just before the Depression looked closely into attitudes of this sort, and found that even among their restricted sample, class background made an enormous difference to planfulness, generally and with specific reference to fertility behavior. The Depression brought about an immediate slowing-down of childbearing *among working-class families,* which in some cases led to a repeated postponement that led to lifetime childlessness. For couples marrying in 1927, the pace of entry into parenthood was fairly evenly distributed across classes. By 1929, it was working-class couples who, initially postponing their childbearing, continued to postpone their fertility into and beyond the third, fourth, and fifth year of marriage, with substantial proportions in fact remaining childless throughout their lives.[102]

The kind of prudence implied by relatively late marriage nevertheless had its most substantial impact among those of lower socioeconomic status who held off marriage, as table 16 shows. For them, considerably delayed marriage was somewhat unusual at this socioeconomic level, perhaps reflecting an especially self-conscious calculation of the *kind* of family life they considered fitting in light of their values. Such "prudent" behaviors were considerably more common among the middle classes, and on the whole, it is likely that the Depression did as much to reawaken these attitudes among them as it did to dif-

Table 16. Proportion Still Childless in 1940, for Urban Native White Women Marrying in 1930–1937 and Still Living with Their First Husbands, by Age at Marriage and Husband's Occupation (in percentages)

	Age at Marriage		
	16–21	*21–26*	*26–31*
Professional	39.2	47.5	47.6
Prop., Mgr.	38.0	44.5	49.6
Cler., Sales	37.7	48.2	56.5
Crafts	30.6	43.9	54.2
Operative	27.5	42.1	53.8
Service	35.3	45.2	54.7
Laborer	24.4	42.4	52.7
Unemployed	20.1	40.3	48.1

SOURCE: Calculated from Census 1940–4, 37–38.

fuse them to the working class. Marriage with white-collar workers, almost in and of itself, was associated with a slow move into parenthood in the mid-Depression. Equal prudence was not rare among the working class, but it was less uniformly distributed: only those who had also married at an older age than was ordinary in this class were so cautious about entering parenthood.

Planful attitudes toward family building was one among a complex of values and attitudes, most commonly found among the middle classes, according to which individuals felt more in control of their own destinies and, so feeling, successfully employed tools like effective contraception to that end. Even apart from their common relationship with socioeconomic status, there was also a separate, independent relationship between fertility planning and planfulness in affairs more generally, the very essence of a "modern" attitude toward the disposal of life's means to one's own end.[103] Fertility control made sense to planful people because children were too important to be left to chance and because children's economic well-being could be seen to only if there were not too many of them. Fertility planners were no less child-centered than those who considered children a gift of God, although planners expressed more *specific* pleasure in *specific* children and less in *parenthood per se.* The Indianapolis researchers found that fertility planners were *not* motivated by a sense that the Depression (or anything else) had made it impossible for them to carry out their chosen procreative roles.[104]

LOOKING TOWARD THE FUTURE

The 1920s had intimated to the middle class, and to those increasing numbers aspiring to a middle-class style of life, the possibility of an affluent, predictable world. In this spirit, many of the 1920s youth generation had set themselves off from the parental generation and successfully demanded the right to develop a modified pattern of family formation, incorporating enlarged volitional elements. Tendencies toward a lessening of the asymmetries of the double standard, toward a more overt acceptance of pleasure—and especially sexual pleasure—as a motive for behavior, and toward a more jointly planful attitude to family building characterized the patterns that spread during the decade.

The sharp age-specific reversals of the Great Depression undercut the material basis on which this new arrangement of affairs had rested. Youth were now needed as workers or money-earners with their parental families, and their income, when they had some, was less available for dating and for moving from engagement to marriage. Schooling was extended and with it, the setting in which the newly evolved dating system had developed, but the comfortable translation to adult roles that 1920s youth had anticipated was disquietingly uncertain for their immediate successors. There is evidence that an attitudinal set emphasizing planfulness surrounded and perhaps was furthered among many young people by the caution encouraged by the Depression. Others, however, their means of livelihood rendered regularly uncertain, were moved altogether to abandon planfulness and providence and to hope to find in their newly formed families a semblance of the content and satisfaction they had grown up to anticipate would be theirs as young adults.

The two ends of the family-formation process as I have treated it here were affected by this age-specific impact of the Depression in simple enough ways. Dating, although some boys were priced out of entry into the pool and some girls were unable to dress up to the levels they felt dating required, was not seriously affected but continued to spread with the high school and into the working class. Cheaper dates were not all that difficult to accomplish, and one might just date less frequently.

Upon first childbirth, the Depression seems to have had a basically temporary demographic effect, with attitudes we have called "prudent" leading to delayed childbirth with marriage, but most typically only for a few years. Couples, even the most prudent among them, rarely decided to wait out the entire unsettled economic period before having children; rather, they merely awaited enough of an upturn that they could execute their prior plans. In a 1936 poll, less than one-half percent of white Americans said that their ideal number of children was none at all.[105] The proportion who in fact were to have none rose sharply—a price, perhaps, of prudence—but for most groups, this was not a common outcome.

Correspondingly, the strains on marriages formed during the Depression showed in their slightly elevated propensity to end in eventual divorce, perhaps no less because of the fading normative structure of engagement and attendant tensions in the couples as they approached the altar. Under challenge, the marital institution stood up very successfully indeed and would soon prove a most attractive beacon to young men and women whose lives were caught up by the demands of a nation at war. But the modest plasticity of the life course surrounding marriage pointed to circumstances less under the control of the contracting partners than the innovative cultural prescriptions which their immediate predecessors had invoked. The marital institution, however, emerged from the Depression in a healthy state. To it, the war that ended the Depression was to prove a surprising tonic, providing it both material wherewithal and a fresh cultural sanction.

5

WAR AND ITS AFTERMATH

PROSPERITY AND OPTIMISM

Conventional wisdom holds that the frustrations built up during World War II gave rise to pent-up "familistic" motives whose eventual product was the baby boom. And there is some truth to the story. The war surely impinged in multifarious ways on the family-formation process. Yet, in the aggregate, it is hard to detect this. In fact, the dominant *lasting* effect of the war seems to have been that the economic forces it unleashed, and the personal optimism and sense of efficacy that it engendered, combined with prior preferences to set into being a post-war family-formation schedule that was at once more relaxed about what was seen to constitute adequate prudence, more flexible about both the sources and timing of economic wherewithal, and (perhaps consequently) more insistently early and modal in its timing. The impact of the war on various aspects of the life course was not uniform, sometimes surprisingly great, sometimes surprisingly slight, sometimes long-lasting, sometimes transitory. This chapter will show, for instance, that young people, briefly, reassessed the transition from school to work; that marriage rates fluctuated widely during the war and the years immediately preceding and following it, modifying the *immediate context* of marriage without modifying the rules of the marriage market; and that, seemingly, the new mechanisms and attitudes permitted over one-tenth of the American population to be called to arms and then returned to and reincorporated in the civilian population with life courses smoothly resumed.

Only when the nation entered World War II had economic optimism fully dissipated the cruel uncertainty that the seemingly endless Depression had engendered. Just months before America entered the war, a national survey found that six in ten of its citizens believed that "after the present war is over," people would receive lower wages than before the war, and a like proportion believed that there would be considerable unemployment. Only 11 percent thought that there would "be jobs for everybody," and fully seven in ten responded that "after the present war is over . . . people will have to work harder . . . [than] before it started."[1] But only a few months into the war, 46 percent believed that "the average young man will have more opportunity . . . to get ahead than a young man had after the last war," and only 17 percent thought they would have less opportunity. One year further into the war, the proportion expecting young men's postwar opportunities to exceed those at the end of the last war had risen again, to six in ten.[2]

Between 1935–36 and 1941, incomes had on average increased by a quarter, basically overcoming the effects of the Depression. The distribution of that income shifted somewhat to the advantage of Americans of lower income. The war years exaggerated these trends. For families as a whole, average income increased by 28 percent between 1941 and 1944, with a redistribution that sharply favored those of relatively low income. The mean income of the poorest one-fifth of all families grew by no less than 73 percent in these three years. The next-poorest fifth saw average increases of 52 percent.[3] Jerome S. Bruner concluded in 1944 that an important feature of the home front during the war was "the almost unconquerable faith of Americans in their own personal futures." Seventy-nine percent of employed men and women queried in March 1943 believed that their present job would continue after the war. Even 50 percent of *war workers* in eight large cities gave this response. Asked if they would have enough money to tide them over until they found another job, should they lose theirs in reconversion, two-thirds thought that they did. People evidently now believed that the economy was meaningfully changed, and for the better.[4] Perhaps, too, the war's uniquely widespread sense of economic well-being was amplified by the postponement of spending caused by war shortages and re-

Table 17. Approximate Age Structure of U.S. Armed Services during
World War II, Males Surviving to 1947

Born:	Number of Survivors 1947	Proportion of All Survivors	% of Birth Cohort Served	Disability Compensation	
				Number	% of Served
To 1902	333,000	2.4%	2.4	42,980	13.0
1903–12	2,035,000	14.8	22.8	343,412	16.9
1913–17	2,507,000	18.2	46.8	384,825	15.4
1918–22	4,344,000	31.6	78.4	606,343	14.0
1923–27	4,218,000	30.6	74.6	378,226	9.0
1928–29	328,000	2.4	17.9	2,881	0.9
	13,765,000	100.0%		1,758,667	

SOURCES: Calculated from Census CPS P20-15, 15; U.S. Administrator of Veterans Affairs, *Annual Report 1947* (Washington: USGPO, 1948), 160.
NOTE: War fatalities might have had an age bias, which would lead to an undercount of the proportions of age groups who served. Civilian mortality was highest in the oldest cohorts, but civilian mortality before 1942 would not much distort these figures.

flected in war-bond purchases that included perhaps 40 percent of all families and single consumers in the first three months of 1942 alone.[5]

Economic well-being, of course, could coexist with a profound sense of being balked in one's most important personal projects, surely during a war that was, predictably but to an unpredictable extent, to draw heavily on the nation's youth. As the leaders and populace of the United States began to contemplate what belligerency was going to demand of just whom, it was not clear whether young men might continue their schooling, whether young women might be in effect drafted into the labor force, whether lovers might be separated by national manpower needs, whether conscientious parenthood might prove difficult in view of competing time commitments and the kind of widespread challenge to morality that wars commonly pose.[6]

The military effort was to be an enormous one, calling to arms some fifteen million American men, as shown in table 17.

Of these, constituting more than one-tenth the total American population at the beginning of the war, six in ten were provided by the birth cohorts 1918–1927, requiring military service by three in four of all living American men born in these years. Overall, more than one in eight suffered a disability of some sort—generally small—and received monetary compensation from the government.[7]

MOBILIZING ADOLESCENTS

No segment of the population felt the war's impact more acutely than did youth, just as they had that of the Depression. For years a problem because unemployed and almost without hope of regular employment, young people were suddenly in heavy demand. This was to have an enormous impact on their life courses. Young people in the Depression had often extended their schooling so as to fill time usefully, but in the early 1940s, the vast enlargement of production began to draw young people from schools. Many of those remaining in school pressed for additional vocational training—echoing an argument made by some educators even before the war—that led in some cases to a reassignment of academic instructors to vocational courses. The national need came to be focused on the here-and-now, and schooling that led to use only through leisurely, indirect pathways caused distress.[8]

Shortly after Pearl Harbor, state legislatures were approached with proposals to relax child labor standards, but they generally resisted. Soon, however, legislators responded to the state of emergency. In 1943, "sixty-two acts affecting the employment of minors were passed in twenty-seven states. Of these, fifty-four included some backward steps. . . . Most of these statutes apply only for the duration of the war." Already in 1942 the pool of young people eager to enter the labor market was showing signs of wearing thin, so that by 1943, large numbers of young workers at 16 and 17 were taking full-time jobs, leaving part-time employment to those younger.[9] In industrial Franklin County, Ohio, increases in first-time work permits amounted to 52 percent in 1941, 184 percent in the following year, and 32 percent before they peaked in 1943.[10] A Census Bureau sample survey in April 1944 indicated that over one in five of school-boys 14 to 15 were gainfully employed, and over two in five at 16 to 17. By this time, 35 percent had left school altogether and were working. Teenage girls were less prone to both full-time and part-time work, but fully a third had jobs by 16 to 18.[11] The twentieth-century trend toward an extended period of economic dependency, based on school extension and exclusion from the full-time labor force, had been reversed momentarily.

The expansion of manufacturing production explains a fair amount of youth's enlarged work opportunity. In 1940, only one in five employed youths 14 to 19 worked in manufacturing. But by 1944, more than one in four working boys and more than one in three working girls were in manufacturing. In Franklin County, Ohio, this was true even of first-time work permit applicants, previously more likely to find work only in ill-paid (if somehow age-appropriate) service jobs. Manufacturing employment had important implications for the way these children grew up, because the kinds of demands the coordination of manufacturing work made on children's time were different from those in other sectors of the economy, making academic training difficult to maintain.[12] Even when the United States Employment Service asked local manufacturers to employ part-timers if at all possible so as not to disrupt schooling, the manufacturers, straining to meet defense contract deadlines, gave the request only lip service.[13]

In the industrial and port city of Duluth, Minnesota, there were signs among boys of increased dropping out of school as early as 1942–43, at ages as young as 14 and 15. Perhaps as many as a quarter more boys than before the war dropped out at 15, a third more at 16. The change in the life course of girls was not so massive, but it too was substantial, especially by age 17. As with boys, changes were apparent from 1942–43. In 1943, the typical grade level of young workers receiving their first regular employment certificates began to drop nationally, as labor demand exceeded available sources of child workers at the higher grades.[14]

The hours were often demanding by any standard, sometimes illegally so, and even when legal, the combined hours of employment and school of many schoolchildren were excessive.[15] Young people, however, compared their options with those their older brothers and sisters had enjoyed and responded enthusiastically. During the war, families that had more workers were generally unusually prosperous—more so than had been the case before Pearl Harbor.[16] A survey of young people in three Michigan high schools in spring 1944 found that the students reported that they found their jobs both educational and enjoyable and that they did not interfere with school.[17] In fact, boys (but not girls) who had gainful employment received *higher* grades on average than those who had no jobs. School absences, contrary to prediction, did not increase.[18] Curricula were massively given over to the perceived needs of wartime morale, and to preparing boys more speedily for military service, favoring especially vocational and civics training.[19] There was no marked increase in school absences. The usual determinants of educational attainment were somewhat scrambled but in the long run, not the average *level* of attainment.[20] The war drew many young people's attention from the schools, but in no long-term way.

As the eventual military outcome became a certainty, educators began to worry that in conceding so much to war exigencies, they had sacrificed the long-standing trend toward increased schooling. The Director of Pupil Personnel and Counseling for the Philadelphia Board of Public Education expressed his anxieties eloquently in 1944, as he looked forward to the postwar. "We can't very well blame children for succumbing to the lure of easy money [during the war]. They have half a notion that it can't last, but it's quite another thing to expect youngsters undergoing all of the uncertainties of adolescence to suddenly and quietly settle down after having known such bonanza days."[21] Given the go-ahead for a "National Go-to-School Drive" as academic year 1944 began, educators rallied the community to their side.[22]

> Hats off to American boys and girls! They have shown superb
> readiness and eagerness to share in the work of the war. . . . Mil-

lions of youngsters have taken full-time jobs. Others have added jobs on top of school work. Now the time has come when all of us must scrutinize far more carefully than we have in the first 3 years of the war the use that is being made of the capacities, energies, and time of our teen-age young people. . . . Some work experience may have significant educational value for some young people. For the vast majority of them, however, school provides the greatest opportunity for development, and adults should help them to give school PRIORITY NUMBER ONE now.

Pearlman and Eskin, however, writing at the end of the war, delineated acutely what the lasting impact of the wartime expansion of youthful employment would be. "The number of in-school workers . . . will vary with the level of economic activity. If a high level of employment is maintained, the number of students who take advantage of the opportunities for part time and summer work will probably exceed the number who were in the pre-war labor market."[23] One of the important schooling reforms of the past generation had been the reduction of the proportion of students who were straggling far behind their fellows, by a combination of exhortation, pressure, and easier promotion. Among boys, the war undid some of this, standard deviations of boys' grades at a given age increasing markedly at all ages during the war. In the years following the war, the trend toward increasing age standardization in school seems to have quickly reasserted itself. As of October 1945, however, the proportion of girls and, even more so, boys in their upper teens who were enrolled in school was still below that in 1940, and the older the youngster, the more pronounced this was.[24]

A common adult response to the reformulation of aspects of the adolescent life course is to decry "juvenile delinquency," and in this regard, the World War II period was no exception. The conventional wartime view asserted a substantial increase in juvenile delinquency and most particularly in the sexual delinquency of alarmingly young girls who were thought all too often to have "made the mistake of confusing sex with patriotism."[25] "'A guy ought to have something to remember when he's facing submarines and death', he said huskily. 'Something more than a few hugs and kisses.'"[26] The scare reflected the accurate perception adults had that the war had placed young people in control of aspects of their own lives formerly over-seen by parents.[27]

Some maintained that apparent wartime increases in juvenile delinquency were substantially to be understood not in terms of anything particularly related to moral change or to particu-larly important shifts in the circumstances of young people but simply to prosperity and to the temptations for forbidden plea-sures and objects that were all of a sudden placed before young people.[28] A U.S. Office of Education pamphlet addressed to counselors considered it "obvious" that there was an "unfortu-nate effect" of young people's sudden prosperity: their "oppor-tunity to have a good time; to enjoy elaborate food, clothing, automobiles." Counselors were urged to encourage suddenly prosperous youth to buy war bonds or to make other savings, lest they develop tastes the future would not be able to meet.[29]

The formidably upright Children's Bureau itself pooh-poohed those who thought they detected major moral trends. They did note "a sharp rise in the number of girls' cases [in juvenile courts]," but explained this by enhanced legal vigi-lance. The police were now raiding places where promiscuity was said to be practiced.[30] The juvenile court data that are avail-able in comparable form through the early war years give some support to the less alarmed view and certainly argue against signs of an unbridling of youthful sexuality.[31] Acute youth observers emphasized the "channeling of emotions into one burning feeling of patriotism," which often had no legitimate immediate channel. Because of conventional gender expecta-tions, adolescent girls in particular suffered from this problem. They were permitted, for instance, to join the women's military branches only at age 20, although in adolescence their physical and emotional maturity was farther advanced than boys', and boys could join up at 18. Boys, too, with more money in their pockets and more responsibility by far than they had ever faced, were agitated. "Reports from schools and other sources indicate clearly that restlessness, turbulence, and emotional in-stability are increasing among adolescents everywhere. There are evidences also of increasing hostility toward adult authority."[32] But in "Prairie City," the intensively studied adolescent was described by Havighurst and Taba as "down-to-earth and unimaginative," the peer group culture oriented to social participation, group loyalty, and individual achievement and responsibility.[33]

ACCOMMODATING WAR

At minimum, parents were beginning to *feel* differently about their children. War anxieties on the part of adults helped crystallize the notion of the age-stratified society, a formulation that was after the war to see full fruition in the functionalist concepts of—and partial concession to—a distinctive youth culture, notions that were reflected in youth policy during the war and afterward.[34] Although the government supported the war effort by exhorting married women to enter the wartime labor force, at the same time it supported the conventional role structure of the family (and, by intent, soldier morale) by providing dependency allocations for wives of servicemen. D'Ann Campbell points out that although the number of "new" adult women workers recruited to the labor force during the war years was only 2.7 million as compared with 12 million men drawn into military service, "wives continued to switch into and out of paid employment, only going into the job market a little more often than before the war," so that "the number of women with work experience" increased considerably more than would be gleaned from examining numbers at work at any given time.[35]

The best quantitative data on the relationship of women's labor-force behavior during the war to their family-formation patterns is contained in the 1944 Current Population Survey commissioned by the Women's Bureau. Retabulated slightly, table 18 indicates that whatever the pressures, whatever the opportunities for attractive or rewarding gainful employment during the war, marriage and particularly parenthood still militated heavily against employment. Women who were single in 1944 and had already been employed in December 1941, as had most single women not in school, usually remained in the labor force. But among women single and employed in 1941 who had married by 1944, large numbers had left the work

Table 18. Proportion of Women in the Labor Force in 1944, by 1941 Labor Force Status and Age and Marital Status in 1944 (in percentages)

	Not in the Labor Force in 1941		
	<20	*20–44*	*45+*
Single	29.4	59.2	10.1
Married, husband present	16.2	11.9	6.7
Married, husband in service	38.1	39.2	26.0
Married, other	23.9	32.7	13.9
Widowed or divorced	20.3	46.1	7.5
	In the Labor Force in 1941		
	<20	*20–44*	*45+*
Single	89.8	94.6	93.3
Married, husband present	26.0	65.2	81.9
Married, husband in service	56.0	71.8	87.6
Married, other	29.6	87.5	88.6
Widowed or divorced	43.7	93.2	86.0

SOURCE: Calculated from Mary Elizabeth Pidgeon, *Changes in Women's Employment During the War* (U.S. Women's Bureau, Special Bulletin no. 20 [Washington: USGPO, 1944]), tables 11 and 12. (The Pidgeon study was based on a special Current Population Survey.)

force during the war, even when they had worked for a period of time to get the marriage soundly on foot. Wives in 1944 whose husbands were at home were, however, fairly likely to be gainfully employed if they had been before the war—and this was only slightly truer for wives whose husbands were away in the military. *A considerably greater difference in 1944 labor-force participation rates was the product of women's 1941 work pattern rather than the stage of family formation.* Only a small proportion of wives whose husbands were at home and who were not already in the labor force as of Pearl Harbor were induced into gainful employment by 1944. This proportion was considerably higher when these wives' husbands were off fighting the war. But in a sense the most striking finding here is the fact that only about a third of wives with husbands away in the armed forces were in the labor force as of March 1944. (One in five of these had a child under 10, a proportion considerably lower than the proportion of working wives whose husbands were not under arms who had young children.)[36] The rest—surprisingly many of whom had already entered parenthood—were supported by their husbands' military allotments or in other ways.

As of May 1945, armed forces pay and allotments amounted to about one-third of the total family income among all families who received any such income, and because pay was higher for non-commissioned and especially commissioned officers, this proportion was roughly constant from relatively poor to relatively well-off families.[37] Military compensation amounted to approximately $900, almost identical to the average annual income at that time for gainfully employed women and about half the average annual income of all families headed by women, which often included military and dependency pay. The average income of these female-headed families, in turn, was about three-quarters that of families headed by men, a ratio that exceeded the comparable figure for 1939 and would not be equaled by the regularly declining ratios after the war ended.[38] To be sure, the proportion of single women who entered gainful employment during the war was not much higher, although these women did not have soldier's allotments as a source of income. It was preeminently the working wives of soldiers who did *not* share in the widespread wish of wartime women workers to continue work after the war was over.[39]

WAR AND MARRIAGE

As it turned out, the approach of war, and even much of the war period itself, actually promoted marriage. As the wartime marriage boom peaked, a family sociologist remarked, quite correctly, that "the function of war marriages is wider than that of marriages consummated in normal times" and cautioned marriage counselors that the basis for "success" in war marriages had become no less various.[40] An index of this is offered by a tabulation for the period 1940 to 1946 of the monthly totals of marriage licenses (which reflect impulse more directly than actual marriages) issued in thirty-four cities with popula-

Number

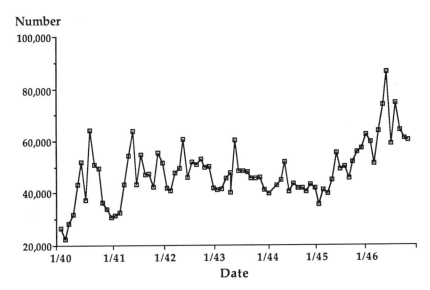

Figure 13. Marriage Licenses Issued Monthly, 1940–1946

tions of over 100,000.[41] These are shown in figure 13. As international rearmament brought increasing prosperity to the nation, the impulse to marry trended upward. Pearl Harbor, in December 1941, considerably changed matters, with a deluge of marriage licenses being taken out. If some of these represented snap decisions on marriage partners, most were probably decisions between persons long embarked on courtship and fearful of the war's interruption of their plans. After a settling-in period, the pace of marriage picked up again by 1943. By mid-1945, the war in Europe and then in the Pacific was won, and the pace of marriage began to pick up once again. The real outburst of marriages awaited November and December 1945. This pace continued into mid-1946, reaching a peak in June.

So successful had young people been in marrying during the war that *a higher proportion* of women under age 20 was actually married in February 1944 than in 1940, fully three in four of them married to men away in the armed forces. For women 20 to 24 years of age, marriage probabilities also increased during the war: 58 percent were married in 1944 as compared to 51 percent in 1940. Almost one in three of their husbands were living away from home because of military service. For wives

New Families

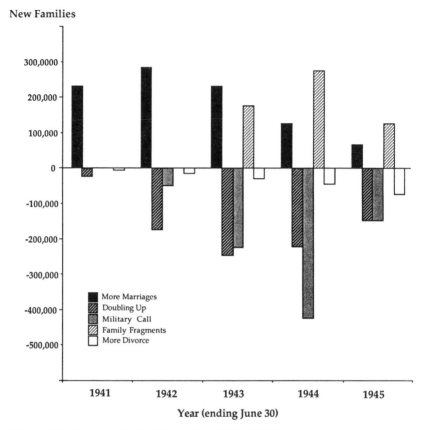

Figure 14. Wartime Family Formation, 1941–1945

aged 25 to 34, 13 percent of whose husbands were away serving their country, however, marriage patterns had fallen behind the 1940 pace.[42] Some fascinating estimates by Paul C. Glick of the special factors that contributed one way or another to the wartime household-formation rate provide an initial view of how the family fared in World War II. A condensation of these is presented in figure 14, where the source-specific contributions to the rate are shown as percentages of the approximate rate of household formation that would likely have occurred had there been no war. Aggregating Glick's estimates for the five years during which the nation was at war, we can say that overall a mere 400,000 or so fewer households came into existence than perhaps might have had the nation not been at war—a tiny number compared with the millions of new households that actually did form over the period.

Fundamentally, the wartime household-formation rate during the rearmament year and the first year of American involvement was a composite of the early and huge increase in the marriage rate and the inability of many of these new couples to find separate housing for themselves, or their reluctance to do so in view of impending induction. By 1943 (the dates in the estimates are for activity from July 1 of the preceding year through June 30 of the named year), actual draft calls were accounting for about as much delay in household formation as was postponement of uncoupling by newly married couples, and these each were weighing about as heavily as the now-declining marriage rate. Adding to the overall decline in household formation by this time was a growing number of divorces, products of wartime stresses, but more than offsetting this in a statistical sense was a rapidly growing number of what Glick calls "wartime families," couples or fragments of couples who in ordinary times would still be living with parents or otherwise nonindependently but who had found independent housing because of the recoupling of soldier families or who had found so much prosperity on account of war employment that they uncoupled early, or actually maintained two households, one of them in a city to which temporary labor opportunities called them.

In 1944, military requirements peaked and moved deeply into the ranks of the married, uncoupling many families, a number no longer even remotely offset by war marriages. By this time, the number of war dead who had been household heads came to be large enough to be registered in these estimates— but its impact was small. And in 1945, as the war wound down, family formation startlingly resembled the ordinary.

Many contemporary observers did not see wartime marriage as benign. Sociologist Constantine Panunzio remarked that

> the very movement of a considerable number of young people from the country districts and small centers to the large cities, the stimulation of city life, their being suddenly thrown together with persons of the opposite sex in boarding houses, shops, and restau-

rants, their need for intimate companionship to compensate for ordinary 'homesickness' and . . . [the] sudden possession of ready money in fairly good quantity—all of these no doubt contributed to the great increase of marriage in the larger cities.[43]

A religiously oriented marriage counselor wrote in 1945 that the war had powerfully exacerbated the tendency already in the American marriage system to elevate romance above other considerations in marriage. "Romantic marriage was society's attempt to recognize and protect the right to personal satisfaction and romantic happiness in marriage and its resulting parenthood." In wartime, personal satisfaction can hardly be had other than by lightning courtships and marriages.[44] Some contemporaries—including some marriage counselors seeking to enhance the felt need for their services—saw the rush as being led by women who feared that military casualties would spoil their chances of ever marrying.[45] The several phases of war-induced marriage patterns affected different age groups differently. That the impact of the war on marriage was extremely age specific is hardly surprising in view of the age specificity of military service. Prewar economic recovery most potently improved marriage chances at the more modal marriage ages, for both men and women. The beginnings of the draft, in contrast, produced a marriage rush that was quite focused in age among younger men (many of whom no doubt hoped to avoid military service through family deferment) but not quite so focused among women. War itself produced a dramatic surge of relatively young marriage—again more so for men than for women—followed by a dearth most apparent in the ages of army service. When the war began to stop moving young men about, they once again started to marry. Again, it was especially those in the very cohort—otherwise modally situated for marriage—that had been the most often denied timely marriages during the war who were the most affected. The women they married were characteristically of the ages deemed appropriate for such men, and this forced some younger men out of the marriage market—but not very many. As the impact of the wartime marriage deficit let up—and this occurred rather quickly—relatively young men and women seemed prone to try to keep up the marriage boom, but this could not be sustained on such slim residues of marriageable people. Nevertheless, marriage timing was becoming more modal, and younger, as a result of the new patterns of marriage developed with the postwar stabilization of the wartime marriage market.

New York State data are deployed in table 19, showing for the years 1939–1946 the trends in numbers of men and women marrying for the first time at ages that were relatively young (20 for men, 17 for women), roughly modal (24 for men, 21 for women), and on the old side (27 for men, 24 for women). Among males, a deformation of the age structure of marriage was adumbrated already by 1941, as younger marriage became especially common. By 1942, the tendency had become more pronounced, as many men somewhat older were already in uniform. The overall deficit of marriages in 1943 and, to a lesser extent, 1944, yet again shifted the age structure of marriage downward. By the last year of the war, older men, undoubtedly including large numbers of returned veterans, were marrying. For older people, the enormous postwar marriage boom began promptly. By 1946, all age groups were participating heavily, postponed marriages in part accounting for the excess of the

Table 19. Annual Increase or Decrease of Numbers of First Marriages in New York State (apart from New York City), by Sex and Age, 1940–1946 (in percentages)

	Males			*Females*		
	20	*24*	*28*	*17*	*21*	*25*
1939 to 1940	39.7	21.0	24.8	25.9	17.7	31.1
1940 to 1941	56.5	12.0	2.1	18.4	24.7	4.9
1941 to 1942	26.8	−17.5	−13.9	8.9	−7.4	−16.0
1942 to 1943	−40.7	−29.2	−26.4	−31.0	−61.8	−61.9
1943 to 1944	−6.3	−12.1	−19.3	−11.0	63.5	53.2
1944 to 1945	7.6	22.0	41.5	−52.4	15.1	75.5
1945 to 1946	56.3	87.9	77.0	43.1	71.0	74.9

SOURCE: Calculated from New York State, Department of Health, Division of Vital Statistics, *Annual Report*, annual.

modal-age marriage increase over the quite huge one for the young men and women. But just as apparently, the postwar marriage boom affected all ages.

Whites and blacks differed somewhat in their nuptial responses to the rapidly changing circumstances of World War II. Blacks apparently were a bit slower in intensifying their pace of marriage as the Depression faded—and the Depression really did not fade for blacks quite so rapidly.[46] By 1941–42, at any rate, blacks were moving even more smartly into marriage than were whites. Thereafter, blacks were somewhat more reluctant than whites to reduce their nuptiality in the mid-war period and, correspondingly, a little less explosive in their late-war and postwar marriage booms. Subject to severe constraints in their family-formation patterns during the especially long economic depression they suffered, blacks seemed to be even more reluctant than whites to hold back from transforming their new-found prosperity into marriage during the war.

Given the immensity of the personal upheavals promoted by the war and the tremendous annual variations in the *raw number* of persons marrying, the marriage market continued to function astonishingly smoothly, the widespread economic wherewithal proving able to conquer all in the presence of love.[47] The highly detailed New York data show that the age distribution of those in the marriage market varied greatly from year to year, as one would assume in view of the changing, age-specific nature of the draft call. One might anticipate that because the numbers of men who had access to the marriage market varied in an age-specific fashion, as that of women did not, the women theoretically available for men of different ages to marry would change over the war years.[48] Courtship patterns are structured by ascriptive characteristics, of which in the American system age is a most important one, as is also prior marital status. If there were a restructuring of the timing of marriage, a shuffling of age-related courtship patterns would be a likely concomitant. If younger women were most highly prized, for instance, one might anticipate that in a year like 1943, when relatively few men were present for marriage and in which the numbers of marriages was reduced accordingly, those men who did marry would marry relatively younger women. But this did not happen. Massachusetts registration data on age at first marriage of *both* partners in new unions indicate that the marriage booms, both during and immediately after the war, were achieved without much altering the *relationships* of age of bride and groom.[49] That is, the data suggest that young men and women sought—and found—mates whose age bore roughly the same relationship to their own age as in the late Depression. First-time grooms *were* over time just a little more prone to marry young in the wartime marriage market than they had been before the war, but somewhat surprisingly, the same shift was apparent among first-time brides.[50]

There was, however, a tendency during the war for first-time grooms to marry previously married persons more readily than they had previously. But, on closer inspection, this too represents not a shift in market patterns but simply the fact that there were increasing proportions of once-married people in the marriage market during these years, as there were to be subsequently. Indeed, separate examination of the previously married shows that when one takes the number and proportion of all marrying people into consideration, they became just slightly *less* likely than before the war to join in marriages with persons who had never before married. The marriage market held remarkably firm: cultural preferences were being maintained through the war, despite circumstances that led to the shifts in the *timing* of many marriages. Youthful marriage was youthful for both partners. Even the marriage of veterans would be accomplished without any particular upsetting of the age structure of marriage, despite the dramatic "time out" that had seemingly been introduced into their search for a mate. Youthful girls were not snapped up by the returning heroes. Rather, the veterans apparently picked up where and with much the same age group as they had left off.

The marriage market itself held up in a surprisingly orderly fashion through the war, in the face of the remarkable bursts of nuptial energy documented earlier in this chapter. In figure 15, we shift our angle to a longitudinal one, examining the single-year marriage probabilities at given ages of three birth cohorts of men, those born about 1916, 1920, and 1924, tracking each cohort through the war years. The retrospective data

Percent
Marrying

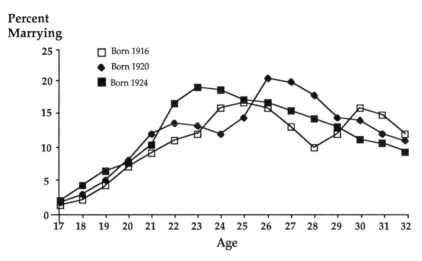

Figure 15. Percent of Single Men Marrying, for Three Birth Cohorts

used to construct the graph indicate that Americans only advanced or suspended marriage schedules during the war; they did not abandon them. And much of the change that took place was incorporated into a longer-term tendency to earlier marriage. Easily the largest part of the proportion of eligibles marrying at any given age as always was a reflection of the *ordinary* age curve of marriage. The 1924 birth cohort provides a nice example. The 4 percent of the single men of this cohort who married at 18 in the first full year of the war was *way* above the 2.7 percent of like eligibles who, four years before, had married at 18 but for all that, *only 4 percent married*, less than the proportion who married three years earlier at 19 at the end of the Depression, and less also than the single 19-year-old men in the very midst of the Depression.

The dominant pattern among the three birth cohorts of men in fact was not that induced immediately by the war but rather the secular trend toward increasingly earlier marriage. For all the distortions of the war, subsequent cohorts did not abandon under strain of war the "gains" in more rapid wedlock that previous cohorts had adopted. And shortfalls were made up quickly by those cohorts whose marriages had been temporarily postponed. In fact, among men, the retrospective data indicate that the most dramatic single-year shifts occurred in the huge marriage boom after the war. And yet, these shifts were general enough that they too were considerably outweighed in their effect on the age structure of marriage by the secular trend downward in marriage age.

When a mid-1946 survey asked a representative sample of Americans what they thought was the ideal age for men and women to marry, it found that the then-current youthful patterns were closely embraced by the majority.[51] In fact, ideal ages produced a high degree of consensus—a considerably higher degree of consensus than the actual behavior at the time. The norms, moreover, were more uniformly held than they would be even at the height of the baby boom. As a result, the war-time-marriage cohort—despite the distortions in detail produced by the war—was *more* likely than either the marriage cohort of the Depression or those preceding cohorts to endorse their own marriage timing as roughly the ideal, and this was so for both men and women. In the war-marriage cohort, neither veterans of World War II nor working wives nor husbands of working wives—those respondents whose own marriage timing had most likely been affected in the complex development of the preceding half decade—differed significantly from others in their ideals of marriage timing.

Burgess, concerned about the predictably fragile quality of wartime marriages, set up for his students an extensive interview protocol and in about 1945 directed them each to interview a handful of married women who had been separated from their husbands by the latter's wartime duty. The questions probed into the circumstances of the marriage, the strains of the separation and modes of handling strains by both partners, sexual jealousies and concerns, letter-writing, and plans, hopes, and anxieties about the reunion that would soon take place. The sample was inevitably weighted toward the kinds of women who would be acquaintances of University of Chicago students, but many of the novice interviewers were at pains to contact a variety of respondents. Selected quotations provide a sense of the *riskiness* of life course formation in wartime, combined with a shared belief in the *inevitability* of the sequencing that made sense of these events for the women.

Rare were interviewees who worried that their marriages had been contracted in haste, or too young.

> Although we liked the same things, and we were very much in love with each other, I can't really say that we had a chance to know each other too well. Our marriage was a continuation of our relationship except for the sexual aspect: we lead a transitory life.[52]

More commonly than not, those who were troubled by the unusual circumstances under which they had married still expressed satisfaction. Marriages thus contracted nevertheless met what the war so clearly had already revealed to be the basic American standard: love.

> There are going to be lots of cases like this. You get married and you don't have enough time to really learn to know each other. . . . But I'm not sorry I married him, and I wouldn't tell other girls not to marry like I did. I loved him and we were happy while we were together. It seems it was just meant to be like this. . . . Bill and I talked and laughed a lot, but when I stop to think of it, I guess mostly what we talked about was sort of superficial.[53]

Some even expressed a sense of a challenge met (even before postwar reunion with their husbands).

> We decided to get married when he was alerted for overseas duty. We hadn't thought he'd leave so soon. We hadn't talked about getting married until we decided to. . . . We didn't know each other very well, but I'm a good judge of character. It was clear to us both that we were going to be married sooner or later and thought it had better be now, as he was going overseas and we wouldn't get another change for perhaps two or three years. . . . There was some difficulty in not knowing each other too well—it's hard catching up on two whole lifetimes in two weeks. It was the best two weeks of my life, and he writes that we'll always be glad we made such a sudden decision.[54]

Separation, of course, was typically discussed in negative terms, but most commonly the interviewees spoke of *initial* difficulties, inevitable but manageable with time.

> I don't think of myself as something separate from him anymore. If there is any important decision to be made I always think of the two of us doing it, instead of something apart from him.[55]

I felt sort of numb after Bernie left for service, but I kept busy and that helped. . . . The lonesomeness hits the hardest when you see other couples go out having a good time. My closest friends all have their husbands here.[56]

My adjustment, on the whole is all right. I'm lonesome, of course, but it would have been foolish not to adjust myself because there's nothing I can do about the situation.[57]

One of the questions that propelled Burgess's inquiry, and about which he seemed to receive exclusively comforting replies, was whether war wives were dating other men while their husbands were away. Several of his respondents remarked that they missed male companionship, and handled this (often with their husbands' explicit approval) by going out in mixed groups or in settings defined in such a way that they did not threaten the faithfulness of the wives. Strong social pressures upheld propriety. When a Roper poll asked men and women in August 1945 whether "a woman whose husband is overseas should accept dates with other men" and whether "servicemen's wives" whose husbands were overseas should accept dates, it recorded an overwhelming consensus: 83 percent of the men and 87 percent of the wives said that they should not accept dates. One "Midwest" wife spoke eloquently of her circumstance and that of other servicemen's wives: "You can't go dancing, because in a town like this it would cause too much comment. And I do love to dance."[58] Without exception, respondents denied that their own sexual desires constituted a problem that could not be handled. In the early 1940s, sexual longing was in a sense a *fitting* way for young women to feel, without submitting to it.

There has been some difficulty in suppressing sexual inclinations but we sublimated them in several ways.[59]

I miss my husband. I'm a very affectionate person and I miss having someone caress me and kiss me and make love to me. You get used to not having this after a while, but sometimes I have terrific dreams my husband is making love to me.[60]

The dominant theme in the interviews is neither fear nor anxiety nor exhilaration but a sense of relief at the nearing of the end of a surprisingly undramatic challenge.

> Now after being away, he realizes how much home and family
> mean to a man and considers his financial problems insignificant in
> comparison. He knows it would be possible to manage somehow.[61]

The wives did not portray theirs as a heroic challenge but instead as an intensification of the kinds of problems that young
men and women in love characteristically faced: probably the
most commonly mentioned affect (loneliness apart) was irri-
tation at parents or parents-in-law for poorly managed co-
residence or other cooperative response to the absence of the
husband. And many women reported a pleasing growth of autonomy in their husbands' absence, although contemporary
ideology did not lead them to trumpet this.

> I think I am more domestic than I was, take more of an interest
> in the home as a center of our life—more than I had expected or
> done before. I also feel that I have become more independent and
> dominating than when he was here.[62]

Most conflicts were dealt with by a variety of compromises
that reinforced conventional role definitions within the family
institution.[63] Havighurst's study of returning veterans noted
that because of this situation, "the husband's return very often
precipitated confusion if not outright conflict."[64] On the whole,
domesticity had triumphed over frustration, just as the urge to
marry had triumphed over the threat to the marriage market
posed by the military effort. Reuben Hill's detailed study of
the adjustment to wartime separation (among families with
children) showed powerfully that while neither circumstances
of marriage nor particular military experience much affected
the family's ability to weather separation and then reunion
smoothly, the preexisting smooth functioning of the family unit
as well as an adequate material basis did.[65] Karen Anderson
concludes correctly that "despite the temporary changes of the
war period, the war did not promote a long-term revision of
sexual values or conduct." The revised double standard of post-
Victorian America persisted despite superficial strains caused
by war-created circumstances.[66] Partly, Anderson argues, this
reflected the "considerable anxiety" one can detect in contemporary documents "over the continuation of a marriage

and family system predicated on the willingness of women to subordinate their needs and aspirations to those of others."[67] Thus, James H. Bossard, one of the preeminent contemporary sociological students of the family, writing primarily for women, declared in 1945 that "it is vitally important to bring to American womanhood a white glow of appreciation of the role of the homemaker in our rapidly changing society."[68]

MILITARY SERVICE AND MARRIAGE

American family formation appears to have been remarkably undisturbed by the military effort of World War II; indeed, it was given a boost. While many of the nation's youngest and healthiest men were called into military service during the period, both government policy and public sentiment reflected the desire to protect the American family. This meant both the preservation of existing families and the encouragement of unmarried servicemen to act much as they might have in the absence of war—namely, to enter into marriage and subsequent parenthood. The continuity of preferred nuptiality patterns into the war, an implicit component of national policy on manpower and morale, was achieved with tonic effectiveness.

The draft had begun (before Pearl Harbor) with exclusions for married men. When military calls pressed on manpower pools, the draft age for the unmarried was first extended downward, and efforts were made to enlist physically and educationally less well qualified men, who had previously been rejected by the services. General Lewis B. Hershey, director of Selective Service, argued several months into the war that "it is in the interest of the government to maintain, if possible, the family as the basic social unit" by retaining a deferment for fathers. Although, gradually, occupational deferment became predominant in the minds of the more powerful planners of the war, public pressure to relieve fathers from the draft was not without effect, achieving first a Selective Service directive to local boards and then a Congressional enactment stating that each hold back fathers from service wherever possible.[69]

Because it proved impossible to defer married men, the U.S. government materially underlined its concern for the stability

of servicemen's family lives by providing in early 1942 a family allotment, prorated according to family size and structure.
"The effectiveness of war operations depends in large part
upon civilian and military morale. A vital factor in upholding
this morale is some reasonable maintenance of families of men
engaged in military service."[70] The sum paid was in part con-
tributory and in part a flat government allowance. The soldier's
contribution was fixed at $22, the government's share expand-
ing according to a schedule of needs based on family composition. No distinction was made between family obligations contracted before the military's call and since.[71] Since allotments
were not needs-tested, they must have provided a rather substantial incentive for marriage during the war: not only were
servicemen's wives able when they wished to find jobs that often
paid substantial semiskilled wages and not only were they applauded for doing thereby their patriotic duties in the absence
of their husbands, but on top of this they received a hearty
bonus, more than half of which was provided by the government. Indeed, the creation of a folk category, the "Allotment
Annie," expressed a concern that some unscrupulous women
would marry lonely soldiers for mercenary reasons, perhaps
even hoping for widow's benefits before long. As early as 1943,
a guide to wartime marriage noted that the fresh material resources provided to young couples in the war had put together
what the Depression had rent asunder. "Men were everywhere
and able to get married, subsidized by a government with a nest
egg of pay. And because work for women was everywhere available and the girl could add to the man's government allowance,
the couple was able to marry when they wanted to, young and
ardent."[72] Just before America entered the war, *True Romances*
had proclaimed that "Love Is Worth Waiting For,"[73] ennobling
self by denying both the intense drive of lust and the deep
emotional needs to which immediate marriage would speak—
upbuilding thus the usual sense of the relationship among marriage, passion, and long-term mutual knowledge. But headier
expressions carried the day, essentially concluding that being in
love was—as it had long been—the prime basis for a good marriage, that even in war lust was a poor but recognizable counterfeit, and that most marriages would survive, even if many

failed. Evelyn Duvall at nearly this same time counseled Doris and Fred, who had already been engaged for a year and a half, when Fred's draft status introduced a note of doubt into their movement toward the altar. They decided to postpone setting a marriage date until Fred's assignment became definite, but the military was typically oracular. Three months later, his training and subsequent assignment still not set and the couple no longer sure that they could wait with appropriate ennobling self-restraint, they decided to marry immediately, just as soon as the military's whim set a date and place for Fred's training. "The biggest mistake I've ever made," Fred wrote Duvall, "was not to get married before I left for [temporary training] here. It would have been much simpler to arrange everything." [74]

Others learned from examples like Fred's. The usually staid *Saturday Evening Post* published a passionate story of wartime marriage that proposed that the nature of love and life was actually clarified by the intensity of the times.

> Everything grows very simple. Big things are big, and little things are little, and presently the shape of everything comes clear—life and sorrow and happiness and fear and faith—and peace. We'll be married in the morning, Mary Jo. For two months we shall be happy. We shall be unhappy afterwards. But we shall hold the shape of peace whole between us. [75]

For its part, *True Love and Romance* set out a debate between conventional sentiment—beautiful but unfortunately inappropriate to the moment—and the deeper love that war sometimes promoted. A girl in love resents war's intrusion.

> I don't want all the beauty and wonder that should be spread out through the years to be crowded into a few hours, as it must be for my friends who are rushing into marriage. . . . I want as nearly normal a life as a girl can hope for, in these troubled times. I want love to come to me, breathlessly, but tiptoeing out of a dream. I don't want it to sweep down on me and carry me off to Paradise for a few hours, a few days of rapture—to be followed by endless waiting, praying, hoping.

But she is persuaded by her soldier-lover, who reasons that "we'll . . . crowd all the times we *can't* do into that one time; then tomorrow evening, we'll be about—let's see, ten months deep in our romance. Our wartime, can't-be-ordinary romance."[76] A mid-1942 poll of *Woman's Home Companion* "reader-reporters" gave a 63 percent endorsement to prompt marriage when asked "Is it right or wrong for men in the armed forces to marry," even if not optimal. *Companion* readers were concerned about too-hasty marriages—that is, marriages contracted on too-short acquaintance, but the quotation the article used as a lead was said by the author to have "leaped into our eager fingers all by itself": "What in the world would be the use of fighting a war if people are not to be allowed to decide whether or not they should marry or have a child?"[77] An advice book for prospective brides captured another aspect of the central position marriage assumed in time of war:

> The man is going off to war, and the only thing that is real and eternal to him is the present moment. The girl he loves becomes the symbol of all life, the life that he is fighting for and expects to come back to. . . . She represents the home he will forego for the present, the security he will dream of, the children he will hope for. She is everything to him, and he cannot wait to marry her. . . . Any consideration that might have influenced a young couple to delay in peacetime . . . is submerged in the great tide of emotions that sweeps over the youth of a nation in wartime.[78]

Those of age 20 to 26 were most prone to induction into the military, following Selective Service policy during much of the war. The proportion of inductees who were single at induction was to a great extent a simple function of age rather than being related to their age-group's draft-proneness. Thus, the proportion of young men still single when inducted into the army at 18 through 20 was still well over nine in ten, but this proportion dropped to three in four by age 23 and to one in three by age 27.[79] In contrast to the general population in 1940, single army inductees were only slightly more likely to have been chosen from among the single population when at the younger ages—when relatively fewer had children. But among older inductees, a far greater proportion was single than in the general population; this ratio was roughly double at 25 to 29 and even higher for men in their thirties.

One of the reasons that nuptiality prospered in wartime was that in surprisingly large numbers men entered the army and *then* married. Data exist which allow us to develop this surprising story in some detail.[80] The surveys I primarily employ here include white and black soldiers (surveyed separately, as befits a racially segregated army) who at the time were stationed in the United States.[81] Respondents were asked their ages, how long they had been in the army, whether they were married and had children, and whether their marriages had preceded or followed their induction. For each, information on branch of the army, rank, and whether conscript or volunteer was recorded, along with a variety of questions about attitudes toward the army and plans for after the war.

Did being in the army slow down the movement of young men into marriage? We can translate this question by asking whether years elapsed since induction "counted" as much as did years elapsed before induction. Would a 21-year-old unmarried inductee who then served for two years be as likely to be married at age 23 as would a soldier inducted single at 20, who then served three years in the army? The data offer an unequivocal answer, a schematic presentation of which is offered in figure 16.[82] The figure models separately the progress into the married state of white and black members of the 1944 army samples who were inducted at relatively young and at somewhat older ages. Annually after induction, an additional approximately 15 percent of single soldiers, whether white or black, married. Soldiers older at induction were more likely to be married at any term of service, but the difference a year of age attained *outside* the army made was less than a year passed in the army, especially for younger black soldiers. The search for a mate either became more urgent on induction or could be pursued then with greater success, so that at age 23, as the graph shows, soldiers who had served for several years were more commonly married than those who had entered more recently, having spent the years between 1941 to 1943 as civilians. Of course, it might be the case that almost all young men, as they approached induction, married their girls, if they had girls. In that case, in a sense, age at induction would be essentially irrelevant to marriage timing. Were this so, the search for

**Percent
Married**

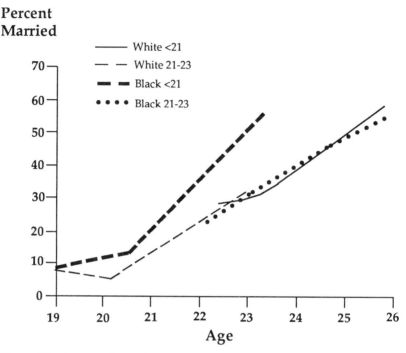

Figure 16. Percent of American Soldiers Who Married, 1944

a mate by soldiers would have been among a subset of young people who were on equal footing with one another; and the age of the vast majority of soldiers was neither so young nor so old that marriage in a year or two was out of the question for reasons of age.

Considerations of timing alone did not explain the differing propensity of civilian men to marry, and neither were various other factors irrelevant to the course to marriage of soldiers during World War II. Civilian men of higher socioeconomic status and extended formal education had long tended to marry older. The set of factors explaining these peacetime patterns involves the longer time required to attain favored occupational positions and the direct and opportunity costs of extended education and, possibly, subcultural values. But among World War II soldiers, the pattern was more complex. The survey shows that those whose civilian jobs were either white collar or skilled were *more* marriage prone than others, all else held equal statistically, while by contrast, soldiers with more favored educational backgrounds were *less* likely to marry between induction and 1944, all else held equal statistically.

Treating the 1940 proportions married as a reference point, we see that in the most general terms, even in 1944, well into the war, the fact of almost universal military induction did not actually deter marriage by these young men. Up to about age 25, the proportions married *at induction* were just about as great as one would anticipate in the white male population as a whole, although somewhat lower for blacks. This must have represented two countervailing tendencies—the deferment from military service of some proportion of those already married, particularly fathers, and the speeding up of marriages as induction approached. And if we consider both those married before induction and those married since induction, once again the age pattern of nuptiality of soldiers considerably resembles that for the population as a whole in 1940, all the way into the late twenties. Economic conditions were so much better in the period 1942–1944 when these soldiers entered the army than they had been a few years earlier that these young men were able to marry when they wanted to. Although military service was no doubt considered an awful job, it was a certain one, and soldiers' allotments, while not princely, were an appropriate basis on which to begin a family. Service may also have promoted a kind of reaching out for adult security in a world about to be rendered personally quite fearsome. The men who married during their time in the army acted out of a deeply felt optimism. Among the army sample, younger soldiers were more likely than others to answer that they thought that "things will be better . . . for you personally after the war than they were before the war."[83] This optimistic position was considerably more common among black soldiers than whites, especially among black soldiers from the rural South. Among whites, it was somewhat more common among younger soldiers. At every age, white soldiers who had *married since induction* were one-third again as likely as single soldiers to expect that things would get better after the war. Conversely, at almost every age, white men—but not black men—who had entered the army *already married* were even less optimistic about their postwar prospects than the singles.

The American Soldier observes that along a number of dimensions of morale, married soldiers tended to be more displeased with their situation than were unmarried soldiers. Stouffer and his associates, for instance, comment that "the very fact that draft boards were more liberal with married than single men provided numerous examples to the drafted married man of others in his shoes who got relatively better breaks than he did. Comparing himself with his unmarried associates in the army, he could feel that induction demanded greater sacrifice from him than from them."[84] Reanalysis indicates that *when* the soldier married—whether before or after induction—mattered very greatly, which fits with certain other insights scattered through but not developed systematically in *The American Soldier*.

The proportion of soldiers drafted, by race, age, and marital status as of the 1944 survey, is shown in table 20. Blacks, we note, relatively rarely volunteered—understandably, in view of their unequal treatment in the military as outside it. At virtually every age, while a majority of all soldiers were conscripted, the proportion of volunteers was much the lowest among those married before their entry into the army. More intriguing, it is much the highest among those who were to marry *after* their induction, even among blacks. Among white 21-year-olds, to give an example, while 15 percent of those who had been drafted when single had married since entering the army, 32 percent of those who had enlisted single had done so.

Attitude toward service obviously influenced and was influenced by marriage. So also with promotion. Each step up in rank increased by about 10 percent the proportion of whites subsequently married among those entering the army single, even taking into consideration age at entry to army and years since entry, prior occupation and educational background, and type of assignment within the army. Table 21 shows how well soldiers who married since entering the army prospered there.[85] Whites and blacks, it will appear, experienced quite the same process here, although blacks, as usual, paid a "price" for being black in terms of slower promotion at every level and age.

Soldiers who had married *since* entering the army were clearly *advantaged* in promotion, and those who had married prior to entering were just as clearly *disadvantaged*. In part, this can be seen as the product of other, common correlates of early

Table 20. Proportion Drafted among All in Army Sample, by Race, Age at Induction, and Marital Status at Induction and Subsequently (in percentages)

	Whites			*Blacks*		
	Single Always	*Became Married*	*Inducted Married*	*Single Always*	*Became Married*	*Inducted Married*
Under 18	66	80	53	88	89	67
18	66	83	46	82	100	56
19	60	79	52	79	90	42
20	65	71	50	82	93	67
21	71	72	65	79	86	66
22	80	81	76	84	89	84
23	48	81	27	85	88	68
24	53	75	51	86	85	68
25–27.5	82	82	79	90	95	89
27.5–32.5	82	87	68	89	94	83
32.5+	81	87	64	93	91	80

SOURCE: Computed from 1944 army surveys.

marriage, especially lesser educational attainment. But at the same time, we suspect an attitudinal difference, a different kind of integration into army life, between those who married before entering and those who were to marry afterward. This attitudinal difference was a mirror of the way that those responsible for granting promotions saw things. There had been something of a rush toward marriage prior to induction, especially for the younger inductees. Entry into the army constituted something of an event that in effect segregated the population into those who already had reasonably well-advanced courtships and those essentially nowhere on the path to matrimony. But perhaps it was also the case that those who married before entry and those who married afterward were quite different kinds of people.

The army itself was divided into different branches (and of course the army was different from the navy, itself subdivided), in which careers—both military and personal—

Table 21. Proportions Attaining Selected Ranks by Given Ages, by Race and Marital Status at Induction and Subsequent to Induction (in percentages)

	Whites			Blacks		
	Single Always	*Became Married*	*Inducted Married*	*Single Always*	*Became Married*	*Inducted Married*
PFC						
by 18	22.4	33.3	5.6	18.2	31.3	NA
by 19	51.1	5.5	35.5	38.7	43.8	NA
by 20	54.2	4.6	57.7	49.8	35.0	36.0
by 21	60.2	3.3	57.5	54.4	44.2	46.2
Corporal						
by 20	21.4	43.6	23.1	17.3	16.0	10.0
by 21	26.1	0.0	23.5	21.5	23.1	15.4
by 22	31.3	8.5	28.7	24.9	30.8	20.5
by 23	33.4	8.5	28.6	30.8	49.1	21.2
by 24	57.1	6.9	31.7	35.5	55.7	19.3
Sergeant						
by 23	14.8	32.3	9.6	14.9	33.3	12.4
by 24	32.3	9.6	12.9	16.3	36.7	9.6
by 25	39.2	5.6	18.2	26.7	46.0	14.7
by 26	33.0	0.7	15.3	22.5	43.4	14.6

NA: Too few cases in cell to compute stable percentage.
SOURCE: Computed from 1944 army surveys.

diverged sharply and were related significantly to prior background.[86] I limit my discussion here to the two branches that were by far the most heavily represented in the 1944 survey: the infantry and the U.S. Army Air Forces (AAF; subsequently an independent service). As we shall see, the latter was a particularly favored branch, while the former was, simply, the infantry.

Over time, the army developed a series of mechanisms to place new men—new white men, anyhow—more nearly rationally within the service, attempting to fill a shifting series of military purposes. This would tie the nature of military service strikingly to marriage. The superb account by Palmer, Wiley, and Keast[87] shows how on average these mechanisms tended to distribute the men most likely to succeed—in the military or out of it—to the air forces and those least likely to succeed to the infantry. The initial mechanism—assignment by prior occupation—produced this tendency. So did assignment by general-aptitude tests, the next approach the army tried. An attempt to upgrade the infantry by assigning according to physical capacity, with the ground combat arms receiving the best-qualified men, failed to accomplish its end, partly because it came too late to make much difference but also because adequate physical examinations could not be conducted.[88] Thus, the infantry drew heavily on draftees, often relatively uneducated. The AAF, by contrast, was staffed to an unusual degree by volunteers and by the well educated.[89] The infantrymen characteristically said that their army jobs were less interesting than did most others in the sample, and air corpsmen thought that their jobs were more interesting. Those in the AAF had considerably higher than average rank; those in the infantry somewhat lower than average rank. In the AAF, 61 percent who had served between 1 1/2 years and 2 1/2 years had made corporal. In the rest of the army, 46 percent had.[90] And AAF men, after the usual initial hesitation, married more readily than infantrymen of comparable age and length of service, as table 22 shows. A like pattern, however, did not obtain for black soldiers, as table 22 also demonstrates.[91]

A component of "success" for whites, then, was getting into the right branch, where the job was interesting and prospects for advancement great. How are we to explain the linkage of all this to high morale and to marriage? We can do this only speculatively. The army, as an institution, did not simply *enlist* such enthusiasm (including but not exclusively for the military task at hand) but *channeled* it as well, by providing superior and inferior vehicles for the reward of the right stuff. Immediately, the superior branch was more interesting and generally safer. In the longer run, the job skills in the superior branch transferred more readily to the peacetime economy, for whites. A veteran of the infantry—everything else being equal—might well see minimal continuity between his military career and peacetime pursuits. The opposite would likely have been true

Table 22. Proportions Subsequently Married among Those Single at
Induction into Army, by Branch, Age at Induction, and Years
since Induction (in percentages)

	Infantry				*Air Forces*			
	<1 yr.	*1–2 yrs.*	*2–3 yrs.*	*3+ yrs.*	*<1 yr.*	*1–2 yrs.*	*2–3 yrs.*	*3+ yrs.*
White Soldiers								
To 19	2.6	5.5	16.7	26.7	0.8	5.3	12.5	35.7
19–20	6.3	10.1	9.8	52.0	4.4	17.2	27.4	55.8
21–22	33.3	13.7	33.3	47.6	3.4	15.5	41.3	46.4
23–24	25.0	30.0	NA	46.2	0.0	40.0	NA	66.1
25–27	0.0	11.9	24.4	NA	0.0	22.1	35.0	NA
27.5+	0.0	26.1	17.5	31.6	0.0	26.2	31.3	60.7
Black Soldiers								
To 19	7.7	NA	NA	NA	2.4	3.2	NA	NA
19–20	NA	13.3	NA	NA	7.7	10.7	19.0	NA
21–22	NA	29.2	22.2	45.5	10.5	21.4	32.1	42.9
23–24	NA	25.0	NA	45.7	5.9	15.9	40.9	48.1
25–27	NA	NA	30.8	NA	NA	16.1	27.8	NA
27.5+	NA	NA	36.4	42.9	NA	44.4	33.3	NA

NA: Not enough cases in cell to calculate stable percentage.
SOURCE: Computed from 1944 army surveys.

of white AAF veterans—when those veterans could realistically
hope for a career in which the achievements of a prior phase
could be counted on to have weight at a next phase.[92] Blacks
could not count on this in their transitions from military to civilian role, as in other aspects of their life courses.

Marriage was very much on the minds of most soldiers. Another *American Soldier* survey, gathered in Italy in August 1945,
asked those not yet married: "Before you left for overseas, was
there any girl back in the states that you expected to marry
after the war?" Those who had a girl were asked how sure they
were that she had "stayed loyal" while they were away.[93] Neither
age nor length of military service deterred the soldiers from

maintaining such liaisons with girls back home: roughly six in ten whites and roughly four in five blacks did, at all ages and durations of military service. Most men believed that their girls were loyal to them—but this varied by both race and time since induction, intriguingly so. For white soldiers, the proportion of girls back home who seemed entirely to be trusted varied inversely with their men's time in service, declining from about six in ten to slightly under half for men who had been in the army for more than three years. For black soldiers, by contrast, the motive to have a girl to look forward to—stronger than among whites in the first place, to judge from the higher proportion overall who were in this sense "engaged"—seemingly influenced their beliefs about the loyalty of their girls, for the proportion thought to be loyal actually *increased* with time in service from four in ten to slightly over half.[94] Clearly, to judge from the patterns by branch, there was a compensatory element in the attachments some of the men claimed. Thus, among younger soldiers (where the differences were the strongest), almost three in four of the still-unmarried men serving in the ground combat arms (most prominently the infantry) had girls back home (of which almost four in five were thought loyal). By comparison, only six in ten of their AAF counterparts had girls they thought of marrying, and of these, three in ten seemed to be of uncertain loyalty. The branch most conducive to wartime marriage was, then, the least conducive to dreaming about marriage. And yet, most AAF men dreamed, too, and felt generally secure in doing so.

Among younger soldiers, those of lower rank were somewhat more likely to claim girls back home they planned to marry. Rank did not command more (or less) loyalty among the girls to whom the men aspired to return. Nor did combat discourage men from making some kind of an emotional commitment for the postwar. If anything, soldiers who had seen combat were somewhat more likely to give thought to marrying and were slightly less likely to worry that their girls were unfaithful to them while they were away. Overall, and most clearly for the youngest unmarried soldiers, those with more education were less prone to commit themselves emotionally to particular girls back home. The pattern, like the related pattern for branch, is complementary to the greater marriage-proneness among more-educated soldiers seen in the 1944 survey. The survey showed no particular differences in perceived loyalty by educational level.

The near-fiancée waiting back home—or the thought of one—mattered a good deal to the men. In most of the morale-related items on the 1945 survey, the soldiers who had a girl back home *of whose loyalty they were sure* were the most pleased with their current situations, a pattern true for both whites and blacks. Among whites, those with a loyal girl back home were more likely to think their war job both important and satisfying than either those with a girl of uncertain loyalty or no girl at all. The latter were somewhat more likely to find their job important than were the married. Among blacks, the married were by far the most disillusioned, and those claiming a loyal girl back home who they intended to marry were the most persuaded that what they were doing in the war was important. Those who looked forward to marrying a particular girl were both most likely to believe that they were well liked by their fellow soldiers and to enjoy working with them. For the soldiers, the anticipation of marriage was an element of continuity that fit the men for their current distasteful duty.

One reason that military duty interfered so little with courtship and marriage was that a double standard of sexual conduct allowed the men to slake their sexual drives on prostitutes and loose or distressed women without particular qualms and without a sense that this rendered them less appropriate marriage partners and at the same time protected the interests that most of them no doubt had in the virginity of their girls back home. This position was reinforced by literature that "stressed that wartime circumstances had made servicemen's infidelity understandable and forgivable."[95] The double standard, in effect, was reinforced. The 1945 survey asked the soldiers about their wartime sexual experiences. Results are shown in table 23, which presents the proportions of those who reported differing amounts of sexual intercourse during the past three months by marital status and self-assessed "engagement" status. Wartime virgins were *considerably less likely* to have had girls back home whom they expected to marry. At the other end of the scale, at

Table 23. Heterosexual Intercourse during Last Three Months while
in Army, by Race and Marital and Engagement Status
(by percentage)

	White Soldiers				Black Soldiers			
		Engaged				Engaged		
	Married	*Sure*	*Doubt-ing*	*Not Engaged*	*Married*	*Sure*	*Doubt-ing*	*Not Engaged*
None	47.5	37.1	27.0	33.7	12.7	7.5	6.5	7.1
Rare	26.9	33.5	32.8	30.1	35.7	32.2	24.9	23.0
4+ times	25.6	29.4	40.2	36.2	51.6	60.3	68.6	69.9
	100.0	100.0	100.0	100.0	100.0	100.0	100.0	100.0

SOURCE: Computed from 1945 army survey.

least among the youngest soldiers, the most frequent copula-
tors were *the most likely to be quasi-engaged.* It is strong testimony
to the definition given by the men to wartime sex that there was
no negative correlation between their perceived faithfulness of
their girls back home and their copulatory behavior while in
Italy.

Over six in ten black soldiers told the interviewers (perhaps
they were less guarded about admitting such things) they had
had sexual intercourse more than monthly over the past three
months while in the service; fewer than one in ten said they had
had no intercourse at all during this period. Roughly four times
as many whites said they had been entirely sexually continent
over this period, and only about half as many were regular co-
pulators. While the data for whites indicate they were more
likely to lose a bit of their restraint the longer they were in the
service, the black soldiers showed no such pattern.

From one perspective, apart from the race differential in overall propensities to sexual experience of this sort, the strongest
finding here may be the relative *lack* of additional inhibition to
extramarital sex that marriage promoted. The majority of this
sexual experience was casual in the extreme, of course, most of
it commercial. But so strongly was casual sex understood to be

within the realm of a soldier's experience that the sexual behavior of white troops who were married rather nearly resembled that of the men who had "sure" girls back home whom they expected to marry. The randiest solders were those with girls whose own faithfulness they doubted, their own sexual adventuresomeness perhaps part product of frustration at their girls' disloyalty, the disloyalty—or its claim—no doubt in part product of the men's sexual adventures. Blacks' wartime sex lives differed less among themselves along this dimension.

WARTIME PARENTHOOD

War, then, fit marriage, although the modest information on children in the army surveys confirms that if wartime marriage made sense to these men, wartime parenthood more often than not did not. At one level, the war scarcely disturbed the passage from marriage into parenthood. The reasons were more often practical than sentimental. The proportion of all families living in independent households who were childless was at first slightly below the 1940 census figure in May 1945, but most of this was more the result of the considerably enlarged number of separated families than of reduced parenthood among co-resident couples.[96] Before the war, the ratio of first births in a year had tended roughly to be equal to 60 percent of the number of marriages in the previous year. This ratio rose briefly to 65 percent in 1942, then declined to its usual level throughout the war.

In 1946, however, there was a genuine baby boom, and the ratio rose to 74 percent.[97] Three factors accounted for the postwar boom: a general exuberance affecting couples generally, at least those with no more than one or two children; a special exuberance and eagerness to get on with married life among new couples formed at war's end; and an amount of "catch-up" parenthood among veterans' families, who in number, perhaps, roughly equaled the number of newly married couples who had been postponing parenthood at the tail end of the Depression. The boom, however, proved not to be a mere interlude in which uncharacteristic behavior promoted by the war was expressed. In fact, it proved to be formative of the

Table 24. Annual Increase or Decrease in Numbers of First Births, by Race and Age of Mother, 1940–1947 (in percentages)

	White First Births				Nonwhite First Births			
	<19	*20–24*	*25–29*	*30–34*	*<19*	*20–24*	*25–29*	*30–34*
1939–40	−2.8	2.6	5.8	6.1	−5.6	−0.4	−0.7	4.9
1940–41	7.3	15.2	13.6	11.4	5.9	7.3	8.3	15.8
1941–42	11.0	21.9	21.0	19.1	4.3	8.8	10.5	7.1
1942–43	−0.9	−9.0	−11.1	−3.1	0.2	−0.1	6.0	17.7
1943–44	−14.7	−9.8	−17.9	−13.1	−9.4	−3.5	1.7	8.4
1944–45	−6.7	−4.8	−4.1	−1.5	−1.8	−1.3	1.5	9.9
1945–46	20.1	42.1	51.5	35.0	3.1	24.6	28.4	8.3
1946–47	42.8	22.3	15.3	12.4	29.2	30.8	27.1	24.0

SOURCE: Calculated from USNCHS, *Vital Statistics, Vol. II: Data by Place of Residence,* annual.

longer-lasting and quite general baby boom that was shortly to appear. The careful study by Rindfuss and Sweet shows that "during the 2 years following World War II, the mean age of fertility declined by approximately one year for each education group except the highest. Similar large shifts were recorded for other parameters of the fertility distribution." They show further that not only frequent and early childbearing were characteristic of this sudden transitional era but that more of that childbearing than before was concentrated in a short number of years early in marriage.[98]

Initial fertility was much more labile than subsequent fertility, especially for whites. Table 24 displays annual changes in numbers of women becoming mothers for the first time, divided by age and by race. The decision to become a parent, hinged as it was on the decision to get married, clearly was related in a large way to external events. It is immediately apparent, and striking, however, how much more dramatic an effect the war had on the fertility behavior of whites than of nonwhites, presumably a function of the more widespread ability of whites to control their marital fertility but also of the less close engagement of the life courses of blacks with the presumptively national events that so affected whites, as we have earlier seen to have been to some extent the case with regard to the transition to marriage. We find, thus, that the "ending" of the Depression in 1940–41 did far more to promote increased numbers of whites than of blacks entering parenthood. Correspondingly, the war years saw less of the up-and-down in parenthood patterns for blacks than for whites. Only in 1947 was there a distinctively strong response by blacks.

Among whites, it was obviously the initial fertility of women in their twenties which was most directly influenced by the war; this was, of course, the product of the fact that these were the women who were married to soldiers, or potential soldiers. Parenthood for women of these ages increased very sharply through 1940 and 1941, then became markedly less common year after year through the end of the war. If 1945 saw the beginning of the outburst of postwar marriages, 1946 saw a baby boom among wives in this age group which was a boom indeed. And although the proportionate increase declined after 1946, the numbers continued to rise, and to rise sharply through 1947. To a less dramatic extent, like patterns were present among older and younger whites and among blacks. This was at last a thoroughly universal postwar *parenthood* boom. In fact, families were not so much universally *enlarging* as were young men and women making the transition to the challenging, normatively enjoined status of parent. They were young, indeed younger, and more uniformly so than before the war.

As soon as the war appeared to be finished and the troops began to be demobilized, a remarkable burst of family formation ensued. Detailed data from the annual *Vital Statistics*, reported in table 25, show that almost all the boom was the product of parenthood on the part of young people of military age. The data for fathers' ages show that there was almost no increase in numbers of births to fathers under 20, even between 1945 and 1946, or between 1946 and 1947, but a very sharp increase in both these years for fathers 20 to 24. The commitment of this group to family building was strong indeed. The difference between the showing of this group and those 25 to 29 is instructive: whereas the younger men increased the number of children they fathered by almost one-third in both years,

Table 25. Annual Increase or Decrease in Numbers of Births, by Age of
Father and by Age of Mother, 1945–1948 (in percentages)

	Fathers' Ages					*Mothers' Ages*				
	20–24	*25–29*	*30–34*	*35–39*	*40–44*	*14–19*	*20–24*	*25–29*	*30–34*	*35–39*
1945–46	32.3	36.3	16.2	9.4	0.1	14.7	31.9	23.9	10.6	5.6
1946–47	30.3	16.2	7.2	2.2	1.8	32.0	15.7	11.1	4.6	2.9
1947–48	−3.0	−5.2	−5.9	−5.5	−3.1	1.4	−4.7	−5.8	−5.9	−5.2

SOURCE: Calculated from USNCHS, *Vital Statistics, Vol. II: Data by Place of Residence*, annual. No
data for fathers on births by birth order is available.

the rate of increase of children to men 25 to 29 tailed off after
the first postwar year. Births to still older men showed the same
pattern as those 25 to 29 but at a lower level. By 1948, virtually
all age groups were tailing off in their fathering, by roughly the
same amount. The immediate postwar baby boom was over.

VETERANS RESUME A CIVILIAN LIFE COURSE

Partly in recognition of the highly structured life course of
American young men, serious thought was early given to ways
in which veterans would be reincorporated into the national
life, their lives put back into right sequence. Remembering vividly the sad experience of the World War I veterans' bonus, the
nation devoted considerable wartime planning and postwar
programmatic energy to the situation of veterans when peace
arrived.[99] A 1943 poll revealed that provision of immediate
postwar income support by the government was overwhelmingly approved by the American people, with the modal period
of support envisioned being "about six months." But many
favored a year or even more.[100] The remarkable successes
achieved in reincorporating thirteen million veterans into the
civilian population bespoke no less the motivation of most of
the veterans themselves to resume their life courses than the
enormous vibrancy of the economy in supplying normatively
appropriate roles to the returnees. Havighurst's study of "Mid-

west's" returned soldiers acutely portrayed the gradual sorting
of these men over time into those who threw themselves with
striking urgency into peacetime activities—like getting a "real"
job—and those who delayed this now-unfamiliar challenge.
Some of the latter took advantage of the long-term nonemployment benefits for veterans to form the "52–20 Club," those
who through choice or necessity took advantage of part or all
of the one-year government-sponsored subsistence-level unemployment at $20 a week. For some, it proved a psychologi-
cally difficult transition from army life to a peacetime economy,
from a situation in which one's job sought one to a situation in
which one had to go out and seek a job in a competitive
economy of still-untrusted resilience.[101]

Most prominent among the policies designed to help the veterans reestablish themselves in American society was the "G.I.
Bill of Rights," especially its provision of extended educational
benefits.[102] While many G.I. Bill programs had but occasional
takers, such as the policies designed to help soldiers become
own-account farmers or small businessmen, the educational
benefits were widely used. In no small measure the educational
plan fit soldiers' view of the postwar world and seemingly, too,
their view of themselves. The strong support of the educational
industry contemplating its own conversion to peacetime helped.
The number of veterans in school reached its peak of 1.2 million in January 1947, constituting 8.9 percent of all demobilized
male World War II veterans. By 1952, 58 percent of the veterans now 25 to 34 years old and 51 percent of those 35 to 44 had
achieved a high school graduation, compared with 38 percent
among nonveterans of both age groups and of high school
graduates. A slightly larger percentage of the veterans went on
to college. Proportions taking advantage of G.I. Bill educational benefits included 60 percent of those under 25 at separation from the military, 39 percent of those ten years older,
and 21 percent in the oldest category as well as 55 percent of
all disabled veterans.[103]

A superb comparative study of veterans and nonveterans in
college in 1946–47 offers insight into the mood of many of the
veterans as they found their way back into American society,
reconstructing their postponed progress into ordinary adult

roles.[104] The study of Fredericksen and Schrader sought explicitly to discover what, if anything, the military experience contributed to veterans' well-reported success in college by controlling carefully for socioeconomic selectivity, local conditions, and the initial aptitude that students brought into college with them. Only 13 percent were married at the time they responded to this survey; of the married veterans, three in four were childless. The student-veterans had in fact been less privileged: slightly over one in three came from families where the head's income was over $4,000, as compared with one in two for nonveterans attending the same colleges. Nineteen percent of veterans' fathers, but 29 percent of nonveterans' fathers, were college graduates. Yet although the overwhelming majority of veterans at school had taken advantage of G.I. Bill benefits, perhaps no more than 20 percent of the veterans who attended would definitely not have even had they received no aid. Veterans spent less, not more, time on schoolwork. They were more seriously vocational minded, but this was not closely enough tied to success in college to explain veterans' success there. A number of attitudinal items that were posed to the veterans and the nonveteran comparison groups proved not to be correlated with veterans' superiority in college. Nevertheless, "overachievement" was consistently more common among the veterans than among those who had not served.

The study made some very striking discoveries from a life course perspective. They found, thus, that a standardized test *better predicted veterans' performance in college* than it did that of the nonveterans. By contrast, *high school grades* predicted markedly better among the nonveterans than for the veterans. The military experience, that is, had effaced part of those high school attitudes and behaviors that commonly led to achievement at lower levels than capacity would suggest was possible. These were replaced by a set of attitudes *that brought attainment closer to potential.*[105]

Both age and recency of separation from the army affected veterans' emergence into the ordinary civilian life. In 1946, for instance, table 26 shows that over one quarter of the very young veterans 18 or 19 years of age—who evidently had been only briefly in the army before demobilization—were still neither in

Table 26. Labor Force and School Status by Age and Veteran
Status, October 1946–1948 (by percentage)

	WW II Veterans			Nonveterans		
	1946	*1947*	*1948*	*1946*	*1947*	*1948*
18–19 years						
School and LF	4.1	4.9	5.0	7.9	8.0	9.6
School, No LF	28.2	18.2	15.1	19.6	24.7	26.1
LF, No School	40.0	55.1	68.2	62.1	60.0	57.0
Neither	27.6	21.9	11.7	10.5	7.3	7.2
	99.9	100.1	100.0	100.1	100.0	99.9
20–24 years						
School and LF	3.4	4.7	4.7	2.4	1.7	2.9
School, No LF	16.9	15.1	14.3	5.5	5.2	8.1
LF, No School	64.2	72.0	74.7	84.0	85.8	82.1
Neither	15.6	8.2	6.4	8.1	7.3	6.9
	100.1	100.0	100.1	100.0	100.0	100.0

SOURCE: Census CPS P50-14, 7.

school nor in the labor force: they were biding their time until they had reoriented themselves to civilian life. This was well above the 10 percent figure for those who had not served in the army. Over time, the young veterans worked their way back into civilian roles. The 18- and 19-year-old veterans were, by 1948, only about as often without clear adult roles as were those of like age who had not served in the armed forces, two years earlier. For older veterans, 1947 was already "normal" in this regard. By 1948, for neither age group did the proportion of veterans who were unemployed *exceed* that for nonveteran counterparts who shared a school status. In the aggregate, 41 percent of male World War II veterans were not employed in November 1945. By June 1946, this number was down to 21 percent. By June, 1947, it was all the way down to 13 percent.[106] It was obvious that although some former soldiers were in school, and while some had difficulties entering civilian employment, the great bulk of them found their way into the labor force promptly and surely. Quickly, wartime anxieties on

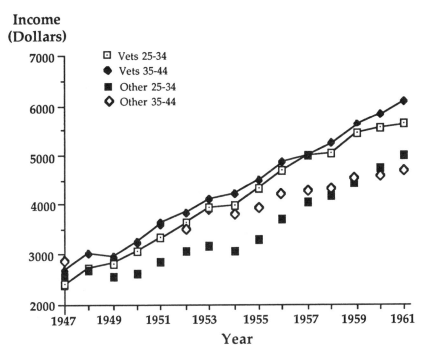

Figure 17. Annual Income for Men, by Age and Veteran Status, 1947–1961

the part of planners and men alike of widespread unemployment were overcome both by the success of the government's plans to incorporate the returnees more smoothly than had been the case in the past and by the magnitude of the postwar prosperity—and by the demonstrable competence of most veterans themselves to handle assignments in the peacetime economy.

Veterans suffered an initial income deficit by comparison with nonveterans in the same age groups—but quickly made it up, and then some. Figure 17 examines patterns of annual income for age groups (unfortunately, not age cohorts) of veterans in the decade and a half following the war. The initial deficit for both the younger and the older veterans was rapidly converted to parity and then to an increasing superiority in income, until the mid-1950s, when it leveled off. Fifty-seven percent of spending units with veteran members in them increased their income "much" or "somewhat" in 1946, the same percentage again in 1947, and 63 percent in the following year. Comparable figures for other spending units were far lower: 37 percent, 46 percent, and 47 percent, respectively.[107] The ex-soldiers did not long suffer economically for their having served: if anything, their experience helped to put them on a surer path to economic success, as veterans who attended college similarly succeeded there. Veterans moved smartly toward higher incomes, as newly acquired education and perhaps employer preferment brought them superior jobs, and as the continued prosperity of the postwar period kept employment high enough for them to overcome deficiencies in seniority.

Veterans' ability to marry and to establish families was closely linked to earning capacity—far more so than to such circumstantial considerations as the availability or price of housing in the locality. In a large group of nonsouthern urban areas, only about four in ten employed veterans whose weekly incomes were under $40 were married by 1946, as compared with two in three veterans whose incomes were in the $40 to $60 weekly bracket and five in six of those with higher incomes.[108] In April 1947, all but 3 percent of male veterans who headed couples were in the labor force. Yet fully 21 percent were living in another family's home. This figure, three times as great as for nonveteran-headed couples, pointed to the only slight ability of physical shortfalls to interrupt the life course of men who were, released from the military and itching to resume their chosen paths as well as to the strongly normative tie of the status of young husband and breadwinner.[109] Wives, to be sure, continued to work: no doubt, what determined the wife's labor force participation for many veteran families, and what ultimately timed the setting up of a new household, was the arrival of a first child. This explains why the proportion of women above age 35 who were in the labor force in early 1947 was well above the figure for 1940—and almost equal to that for the wartime period—but that women in the prime age for childbirth were markedly *less* likely to be gainfully employed than before the war.[110]

The 1950 census recorded that men of the cohort of prime military age during World War II—25 to 29 in 1950—were far more likely to have married than had men of that age a decade

Table 27. Proportions of Males Single in 1945 Who Married by Subsequent Years, by Age in 1945 and Service in World War II (in percentages)

		By 1945	By 1946	By 1947	By 1948	By 1949	By 1950
17–18	Veteran	1.9	5.3	13.8	30.1	40.3	47.8
	Nonveteran	2.9	6.6	15.4	21.2	28.0	34.4
19–20	Veteran	7.0	17.0	32.5	47.7	55.2	64.4
	Nonveteran	7.4	14.5	27.0	36.3	41.8	45.7
21–22	Veteran	12.6	26.9	44.8	56.2	62.9	70.2
	Nonveteran	13.1	21.9	31.7	43.7	49.2	53.0
23–24	Veteran	16.1	37.0	50.2	62.5	68.2	72.0
	Nonveteran	15.2	24.5	35.8	45.0	47.7	51.7
25–26	Veteran	15.9	34.3	49.8	59.0	64.8	67.3
	Nonveteran	15.4	26.5	41.9	48.5	52.2	55.1
27–29	Veteran	18.1	36.8	50.0	60.2	65.8	68.1
	Nonveteran	21.5	31.3	42.3	48.5	51.5	54.6
30–34	Veteran	16.4	31.0	41.6	48.9	53.6	56.2
	Nonveteran	9.8	18.8	25.6	31.6	36.3	39.3

SOURCE: Computed from 1950 Census Public Use Sample.

earlier: 76 percent as compared with 64 percent. Examining the nuptiality patterns of men who had not married prior to 1945, presented in table 27, allows us to examine the American veteran "catching up" to his civilian counterpart.[111] Of the nonveterans in our sample who were unmarried in 1945, 58.5 percent remained single in 1950, whereas only 38.1 percent of the veterans had not married within five years of the war's end. Even at given ages, veterans married in greater proportions than nonveterans in the years following the end of the war.[112]

The youngest veterans were overall more prone to marry but tended to lag behind more than nonveterans of the same age in the first year or two immediately following the war, catching up shortly, as table 27 indicates. Younger veterans caught up only gradually, in part, because they often had other matters to attend to which generally had to precede marriage, like finishing school and finding a job. Most of the initial difference in overall proportions married was the far greater proportion of veterans still at school or jobless. In the year following the war, veterans who were in school included a considerably smaller proportion of their numbers at work than did nonveterans who were in school. There was a startling difference, too, between the proportions of veterans who were not in school (at a given age) who had found jobs and like proportions for their civilian counterparts. In 1946, over 85 percent of out-of-school non-veterans had jobs at 18 to 19 years of age, but less than 60 percent of veterans not in school at these ages did. For those 20 to 24, the proportions were 91 percent as compared with 81 percent. In 1947, these disparities began to be reduced, as did also the discrepancy for those in school. By 1948, the veterans had quite caught up to their nonveteran counterparts.[113] Veterans who were slightly older and had reached their peak marrying years during the war did not exhibit any lag in catching up. Military service had little effect on marriage patterns among the oldest veterans, those in their late thirties and early forties during the war. Black and white veterans fared exactly alike in the advantages in postwar marriage that they enjoyed relative to nonveterans of their own race.

Table 28 shows that both white- and blue-collar veterans, as well as veterans who were farmers, had higher marriage rates than their co-workers who had not served. Veterans at all income levels (as of 1949) had married in greater proportions than their nonveteran counterparts, although the increase in proportion of marriages varied with income level. Those with relatively high incomes ($4,000 and above by 1949) apparently began to catch up almost immediately at war's end, while those with lower incomes seem to have taken about a year before they began to marry in significantly greater proportions. One might argue that these men were waiting to improve their economic situations before marrying, but this may be a spurious association inasmuch as income tended to increase with age.

Veterans were able to marry as promptly as they did in part because the women they married were prepared to accept somewhat nontraditional household arrangements on a temporary basis. The flexibility within marriage that the war had

Table 28. Proportions of Men 22 to 47 and Single in 1945 Who Married in Subsequent Years, by Service in World War II and Occupational Type (in percentages)

Married:	By 1945	By 1946	By 1947	By 1948	By 1949	By 1950
White collar						
Veteran	12.9	25.8	40.3	53.2	60.8	67.6
Nonveteran	11.0	18.9	28.6	37.5	43.7	47.9
Blue collar						
Veteran	10.4	24.0	39.7	53.6	60.3	65.4
Nonveteran	8.6	18.0	29.1	37.4	42.5	47.1
Farm						
Veteran	9.7	28.1	37.8	48.5	53.6	58.2
Nonveteran	10.1	16.6	27.0	32.8	36.1	41.2

SOURCE: Computed from 1950 Census Public Use Sample.

produced thus continued into the postwar period. The Census Bureau reported that as of June 1946, the proportion of married co-resident couples who were "doubled up" had increased by 100 percent since V-J Day, to a level that was 40 percent above that in 1940.[114] Such practices were highly concentrated in the veteran population—16 percent compared with 2 percent living *as* subfamilies, 15 percent compared with 2 percent living *with* subfamilies in Los Angeles County, 19 percent as subfamilies, 18 percent with subfamilies in Cleveland as compared to 3 percent each for nonveteran couples.[115]

The deficits in family-building that were so quickly made up by the smooth operation of the marriage market were shortly made up in parenthood too. The data do not bear on *first* child *per se*, but the differences between the veterans and the nonveterans are nevertheless so strong that we can have no doubt about what was happening in parenthood. As of June 1946, veterans of any given age who were married and living with their wives had on average only about half as many children under five as their nonveteran age peers had.[116] The patterns of family-size increase between 1946 and the following year are most instructive: younger married veterans were prompt to enlarge their families, and older married veterans seemed to be downright assiduous in doing so.[117]

World War II and its aftermath were, in a sense, paradoxical in their impact on the youthful life course. In some ways—as in luring young people out of the schools and into the labor force—the results seemed retrograde. So, too, did the reinforcement that military service provided for aspects of traditional gender roles. Yet by creating a setting in which marriage might be acceptably (and suitably to institutional context) contracted on a basis that was surely not prudent in the sense ordinarily understood before the war—marriages that moreover were intensely sentimentalized and linked as soon as possible to parenthood as part of their promised fulfillment—the war promoted the emergence of a new organization of the life course. It looked, indeed, to a postwar life course for young Americans that—far better than that of the 1920s and much of the Depression decade—freed the volitions, fulfilled the imperatives, invited the general assent of an increasingly homogeneous, prosperous, and individuated population. The fulfillment of these directions would await the new, but as it developed, oddly impermanent structures that individuals constructed in the baby boom.

6

THE BABY BOOM

"COKE FOR BREAKFAST"

The prosperity that World War II brought to young people continued into the 1950s, if on somewhat changed terms. The rebuilding of residential America after fifteen years of neglect—often but not exclusively in the form of suburbs—provided them with congenial settings to enjoy their personal prosperity. So, too, did the large consolidated high schools that rapidly appeared in the period. The success of the nation's young men and women in establishing marriages during the war or immediately following its conclusion—if relatively many failed, most succeeded—and of the returning veterans in picking up and improving on the life courses they had left off was apparent. Young people in the postwar were led to a cool assertiveness about their ability to make their own choices, which, challenging no moral precepts, their elders were in no position to deny. As one trashy but perceptive piece of short fiction had it, they could have, "Coke for Breakfast" and still come into their own, in their own time. This chapter explores the rather shallow limits of adult resistance to the modest youth innovation of this period and the operation of the dating system, the classic locus of American youth culture at its most elaborate. Dating, in turn, will be seen in its relationship to marriage and, in particular, to the way that baby boom families organized themselves, temporally and ideologically.

"Coke for Breakfast," published in *True Love* in 1959, places in mythic high relief the cultural motives that accompanied the baby boom's downward revision of the timetable for family-building.[1] The story recounts the challenged but ultimately successful efforts of a very young couple to assert the right to be married *and* still drink Coke for breakfast rather than coffee, as convention prescribed. "I know. Married couples don't drink Coke for breakfast. They don't stay in bed till noon and they don't party till dawn. . . . That is, *other* married couples don't. *We* do."

The marriage of Jill and Pete in "Coke for Breakfast" began a bit too soon but much too impetuously. After the fall Bunny Hop, four long-standing high school couples, on a mutual dare, drove to a Gretna Green to get married. "Buzzy jumped up on the bed, waving his cup and shouting, 'Teenagers of the world—unite!' And we all began throwing rice at each other." Parents shortly intervened and brought about the annulment of two of the marriages, the third couple, refusing, was disowned by their parents. Although skeptical, neither Jill's nor Pete's parents forced the issue. Their school allowed them to remain enrolled but expelled them from extracurricular activities.

And Jill and Pete truly loved one another, as sixteen-year-olds sometimes did in the 1950s. Being married seemed to suit them and, of course, it demonstrated a further assumption by adolescents of prerogatives formerly their parents'. "Just think—no one telling us what time we have to come home, no one nagging we see each other too much. . . . And best of all, no more saying no to each other." The marriage was a fulfillment that Jill and Pete had long expected, although not so early.

> It seemed like the whole sixteen years of my life had been building to this moment—being Pete Tempest's wife. We'd been steadies since the end of my freshman year and his sophomore year in high, and we hadn't made any secret of how we wanted to be married. Our folks didn't mind—the Tempests liked me and my folks were flipped over Pete—but we got the usual 'wait-till-you-finish-school' routine. And that meant two whole years because I was only a junior. But maybe we'd have stuck it out, if it hadn't been for tonight.

On the whole, marriage proved to agree with the young couple, who worked out home routines that resembled a continuation of going steady, and suited them both—although they were a little unconventional by adult standards.

The problematic aspect of the story was not conflict within the marriage but the adult world's insistence that if they wish to be accepted as actually married, they must abandon Coke for breakfast, and like childish practices. Pete's young married cousins visit, at parental behest, to instruct Pete and Jill in proper married behavior.

> I wondered, too, if maybe our folks weren't right in a way. We didn't act married; we acted like kids on a spree. And the more I looked around at married people I knew, the more different Pete and I seemed. . . . When you got married you followed a different set of rules and you had different friends—not a bunch of high school friends. It didn't matter that we were still in school. Getting married had changed all that; we'd stepped over the line into another world. And as far as I could see Pete and I didn't belong to either world. We were no longer kids and we hadn't become real marrieds yet.

Jill is more torn than Pete, who, naively, defies adult definition of the necessary grimness of their situation by buying a lovable puppy. This act, perhaps because of its blatant family-formation symbolism, irks the Tempests into cutting off all allowance. Pete responds by switching to night school and finding a day job adequate to keep them in Coke and the moderate squalor they choose.

> "If not getting their ten dollars a week means not having to listen to their lectures, I can spare it. We can manage without them, and believe me, it'll be good living our own lives!" "That's right—Coke for breakfast!" I said hotly. . . . "Look, if the English eat smoked fish for breakfast, why can't we drink Coke? We're married, for crying out loud!" "Then why don't you act married?" I yelled. "What married people live like we do—always partying, living in a pigsty?"

They "try it," but near-adult sobriety predictably does not suit the marriage. And then, the trial that Jill had most feared: signs (later to be disconfirmed) of pregnancy. To her utter surprise, Pete is delighted. His love is true and of an order to sustain the full baby boom model of the home, indeed, to form and sustain the ideal-type baby boom life course. To Jill's even greater surprise, Pete self-assuredly reasserts his values even as he declares himself comfortable with postponing graduation so that he can

work to support the baby, self-consciously pouring the breakfast coffee down the drain and opening a Coke.

> The anger began to rise in me again. 'Pete, how could you be a
> father and—and drink that for breakfast? How can you run things
> when you act like a kid?' He sighed. 'I don't know why I married
> such a thick woman! Look, have we fallen on our faces yet? Have
> we had to ask your folks to help us out of a jam? Have I ever not
> gone to work or not done my homework? We're getting along
> fine—at least where it counts. So what if we want to act crazy the
> rest of the time? Who's to say how married people act?' . . . So that's
> what I learned. Maybe Pete and I are just goofy because we're
> young; maybe we'll settle down, . . . maybe we'll drink Coke for
> breakfast all our lives. But whatever we do, I know now we're not
> irresponsible and we're not immature. We have a good marriage—
> and if we have a ball too—well, like I said in the beginning, some
> people are born lucky.

They were lucky indeed. Their insistent cultural innovative-
ness did not drive their parents away—really, they liked their
goofy kids quite well, however baffling their choices. Nor did
their imprudent timing preclude economic survival. Their surroundings were remarkably kind to them. And so it was in the
baby boom.

In the mid-1950s, David Riesman remarked that teen culture, with its focus on the stylish date and proper appearance,
especially for girls, was highly materialistic, engaged in consumption patterns that constituted anticipatory socialization for
a nice house in the suburbs.[2] In 1961, a local probability sample
of adolescents, 16 to 19, both boys and girls, was asked whose
tastes they used to "size up" their own prospective purchases of
such items as personal clothing, toiletry, sports equipment,
small appliances, insurance policies, and cars and related transportation. For virtually all items, parents provided the "buying
frame of reference" more often than did friends, salesclerks,
print media, and television.[3]

That advertisers could now pitch their copy to young people
in terms of credit purchases had a cultural significance that
pushed beyond the merely economic and spoke to the self-
image of the whole generation. Riesman and Howard Rose-

borough argue that "marriage itself, so to speak, is now bought on the installment plan, following the 'anticipatory socialization' of going steady from the seventh grade on. . . . [A child like this] will as a young married person assume as a right many of the items that for his parents were delayed and planned-for luxuries." They characterized these as part of "the capital equipment for domesticity."[4] The "youth market" discussions found in marketing journals during these years looked at adolescents as more and more numerous, more and more prosperous, and thus able to command the respectful attention of conventional merchandisers, who, if shrewd, would sell to the adolescent a junior version of the kind of thing they soon would be buying as adults, adjusted to their essentially anticipatory life course stage.[5] Teenage girls, wrote one shrewd student of advertising, "will be interested in knowing things that will help them make a better, happier marriage . . . They respond to appeals that take their problems seriously—that are stated in intense emotional terms."[6] With self-fulfilling prophesy, advertisers assumed that girls and boys of the middle class (or aspiring thereto) were caught up in the baby boom idealization of the family—"the home"—as the source of affirmation as a competent, independent individual.

AFFORDING COKE FOR BREAKFAST

Young people's belief that they could structure their lives *ad lib* derived significantly from a sense of economic well-being that spread rapidly after an initial period of uncertainty. When World War II ended, doubts—but not gloom—had temporarily replaced the buoyant optimism that had been engendered by the war economy. Seven in ten Americans in February 1946 thought it was "likely" that "we will have a widespread depression within the next ten years." Particularly diagnostic of the momentary mood of the respondents was a pair of questions that asked whether they thought their own "opportunities to succeed" exceeded those of their fathers and whether their sons' opportunities to succeed would exceed their own. Seven in ten thought their own chances were superior to their fathers', and even more believed that their sons' chances were better than their own. But the trends since 1940 reinforced the point: while the item about *own* trends showed an upward trend, Americans were no more optimistic than they had been at the end of the Depression about their *sons'* opportunities to succeed.[7]

Evidently, Americans knew how good the war economy had been to them but had serious concerns about whether their sons would find an economy no more reliably vibrant than the one that had followed World War I.[8] The war's gains, in short, were initially seen as having been highly significant to their own lives, as wiping out the Depression's legacy of personal setback, but as possibly superficial, not structural. In the 1946 poll and to an even greater extent in another similar poll in mid-1947, the overwhelming majority—between eight and nine in ten—of Americans believed that "the prices of most things you buy" had increased in the past six months and a substantial majority—between six and seven in ten—that "compared with six months ago" they were "finding it harder . . . to make both ends meet."[9] Inflation worry was widespread, even as the public successfully demanded the cessation of price control so as to make the consumer goods after which they lusted the more rapidly available. The kind of individualistic economic and consumption motif that Marshall B. Clinard so acutely recognized in the widely condemned but never-eradicated wartime black market, however, soon found its voice, carrying the people along with a fervor that, rather than being sated, turned into personal optimism, especially among younger couples.[10] Periodic inquiry into consumer finances (by the Institute of Survey Research at the University of Michigan) shows that in 1946, 41 percent of households headed by persons 20 to 29 years of age anticipated higher income that year than the last. Only 21 percent in the same age group anticipated declines in income. These figures contrast with 19 percent optimists and 26 percent pessimists among those 40 to 49. In 1947, the comparable figures for those 18 to 24 (the age categories had changed) were 38 percent expecting increases compared to just 11 percent anticipating declines. By the next year, anticipated gainers were more common than anticipated losers in every age category under age 65, by three to one among those 25 to 34 and by more than two to one among those 35 to 44.[11]

Benjamin Caplan has argued that, paradoxically, it was the safe passage through a mild recession in 1948–49 that finally overcame the underlying doubts of Americans about the robustness of their economy.[12] The early postwar period, consisting in long upswings, short downturns, and gradually rising prices, was as a whole experienced as unique in American history, despite or even because of its cyclicality.

> Postwar psychological attitudes also fostered prosperity. Successful prosecution of the war, and the production feats which contributed so much to that success, had swept away the prewar pessimism about the viability of the economy. . . . [With short-term gains repeated over time] the foundation for continuing prosperity was strengthened by focusing attention on the underlying real prospects for expansion instead of the latent potential for depression.[13]

The government's basically Keynesian behavior, coupled with an astonishingly rapid growth of installment credit throughout the latter half of the 1940s, kept the economy moving rapidly enough that even if inflation—initially fearsome—was present, it became an expected part of the economic environment, and not a cause for individual economic actors to be alarmed. "A principal reason for the continued inflation of the postwar years, then, is that depression has been avoided. . . . To a large extent, the inflationary bias exhibited by the postwar economy has been merely another aspect of its expansionary bias."[14] Spending patterns changed.

Not irrelevant to Americans' expanding expression of material well-being was the huge savings that had been accumulated during the war, while the government held down consumer purchases so as to enlarge war production and hold back inflation.[15] The contrast of this situation with the shattered economic resources of the Depression spoke eloquently. Most consumers in early 1946 did not expect to use much of their liquid assets in the coming year, but numbers who actually did so grew remarkably from 1945 to 1946, with particularly rapid increases seen in the youngest groups, *even where these households had high incomes.*[16] But for a majority of American families in 1946, a certain amount of dissaving was pursued even to meet "general living expenses," as Americans became accustomed to living higher, in a material sense, than they had before. War bonds were held widely, and Americans commonly allowed these to mature without renewing them: they were, after all, *war* bonds. Some even cashed them in before they matured.[17] Not without some reversals, acute fears of inflation abated in the later 1940s, the sense of "good times" spread, and Americans began regularly to define themselves as better off than they had been in the previous year. In the minds of Americans, regularly increased wages outweighed the regularly increased prices: "making more money seems to be associated with the feeling that one is better off."[18] One year into the Korean War, somewhat more people believed that the economic effect of the war would on balance be bad for the civilian economy, but by the end of 1952, almost three times as many thought that the war was *good* for domestic business.[19] Commitment to the cold war paid off domestically. In 1953, consumers expected that prices would shortly decline again but that their incomes would continue to climb, so the war's end was accompanied by a *decline* in consumer confidence. But when the inflation fear proved nugatory, consumer confidence soared to a new high by mid-1955.[20] From 1956 through the end of the decade, about one-third of consumers expected their economic situation to improve during the next year, and at all points except mid-1958 (where it reached 10 percent) fewer than one in ten expected that their economic situation might worsen.[21] Not only had consumers developed a robust faith in the beneficence of the American economy but their *personal* economic optimism had come to depend less on their assessment of short-term trends.[22] Between 1950 and 1960, optimistic and acquisitive consumers nearly doubled the ratio of outstanding credit to disposable income—a rise from 7 to 12 percent. As the future came to seem more certain in its material attributes, one could—and families and their creditors did—increasingly make advances on it: during the period, the mean length of installment-credit contracts increased by 40 percent for automobile loans and 18 percent for other durables. By 1956, consumer debt (apart from mortgages) was a part of the financial situation of two-thirds of American households in which the head was under 35. Between 1951 and 1956, the proportion of families with some consumer debt increased for all life-cycle stages, but it increased the most often, both absolutely and relatively, *among young families.* The highest increase was *among young married couples with children.*[23]

The suburbs burgeoned, making available relatively excellent, spacious, inviting housing prices that young couples could afford. Mortgage lending, aided by government guarantees, gave young people of the middle classes and sometimes the stable working class the credit they needed. To be sure, the suburbs were not the exclusive habitat of young married couples, but the popular association of the phenomena had an empirical basis. No less than 18 percent of the owner-occupied housing added to the stock between 1950 and 1956 went to families in which the husband was under 35 years of age. Sixty-three percent of metropolitan housing occupied by the young families between 1945 and 1950 was in the suburbs, 69 percent of that occupied in the first half of the 1950s, and 76 percent of that occupied between 1954 and 1956. Fully 44 percent of the houses owned by those under 35 were in the suburbs. The under-35 families had the 50 percent ownership mark in sight by 1956, and even the absolute number of renters under 35 decreased.[24]

The increase in women's labor force participation in the 1950s was large and foretold major social change. By 1960, the overall rate of female labor-force participation exceeded its World War II maximum, and thoughtful bureaucrats, labor union officials, and women's advocates began to sense a new social trend.[25] Young women just out of school and presumably in most cases ready for marriage did *not* increase their propensity to work for pay. But young wives and even young mothers *did.* The availability of part-time and, even more important, part-year work contributed to this trend, especially among wives with young children. Between 1948 and 1960, the proportion of wives with no children under 18 who were at work rose only from 28 percent to 31 percent. Over the same period, the proportion of wives with children between 6 and 18 who worked rose from 21 percent to 36 percent, and those with children under 6 rose from 11 percent to 23 percent.[26] These patterns ran contrary to the initial response at the end of the temporary World War II demand for women's labor, when "family-building" ideology clashed sharply with gainful employment.[27] Almost three in eight wives at the height of the baby boom were working at about two years into their marriages—a great proportion of all those who had not yet borne children. The pattern was most prevalent among wives of white-collar husbands (a product of the higher earning capacity of many women who married such men, complementing their relatively delayed fertility) and most prevalent among women married to men working in sales, whose toehold in the middle classes was the least secure.[28] The integration of marriage, fertility, and gainful employment was already in the 1950s taking on a startling new tenor. At the same time as the 1950s stressed domesticity, and the unique role of mothers in the care of their children, more and more young mothers were working. Growing proportions of teens, correspondingly, were less closely supervised.

THE PERVERSITY OF YOUTH

In a world like this, however, money in the pocket sometimes seemed to threaten destructive temptations as much as to offer positive options. The family as well as the school and other social institutions often seemed to be weakened, age and gender roles to be in flux. Inevitably, many children must grow up too fast, and bad. Concern over the sexual delinquency of girls with soldiers had ended with the war, but in about 1953 "juvenile delinquency" once again became a hot topic, with a new focus.[29] In 1954, F.B.I. Director J. Edgar Hoover listed no fewer than nine major causes of juvenile delinquency, including a lack of religion and growing permissiveness. His list also included subcategories, four variants of failure within the school system and ten within the family.[30] Converging surprisingly with this ideological theme was another that stressed the importance of "loyalty" to a solidary if pluralist school body. In furtherance of this theme, school officials pressed hard against such blunt instances of teenage particularism as high school fraternities and sororities, ethnic- and neighborhood-based groupings whose exclusionary behavior toward other students goaded officials who sought loyalty to the democratic whole.[31]

A generalized concern over juvenile delinquency evokes the sense of ill-chosen innovation such as Coke for breakfast which haunted the period. Not very deep below the surface lay the fear of a youth culture with distinctive values—about the restraint of impulse and sexuality more particularly—and a deep resentment of that portion of adult commercial culture that pandered directly to the developing distinctive tastes of youth. Once before, commercial entertainment had been brought to heel—in the depth of the Depression, the Breen Office had an effect on the overt content of motion pictures. In the 1950s, the danger seemed everywhere. Feeding on this concern was a continuing three-year Senate hearing on aspects of juvenile delinquency. Senator Estes Kefauver here mixed together a somewhat forced view of children as innocents and revulsion at the culturally revolutionary possibilities of commercial culture, and young people's tendency to respond to the winds of change far faster than did public educational agencies. The star witness of these hearings was a psychiatrist, Frederic Wertham, who feared the disaffiliation of a whole generation.

> There is a school in a town in New York State where there has been a great deal of stealing. Some time ago some boys attacked another boy and they twisted his arm so viciously that it broke in two places, and, just like in a comic book, the bone came through the skin. . . . In this same high school in 1 year 26 girls became pregnant. The score this year, I think, is eight. Maybe it is nine by now. . . . Here is a general moral confusion and I think that these girls are seduced mentally long before they are seduced physically, and, of course, all those people there are very, very great—not all of them, but most of them, are very great comic book readers, have been and are. As a remedy they have suggested a formal course of sex instruction in this school.[32]

Even adolescents recognized these tensions, as, for example, in the realm of sexual expressiveness. Thus, in 1949, a national sample of high schoolers was asked whether they considered it "all right for young people to pet or 'neck' when they are out on dates," and whether their mother and their father thought so. Only 10 percent of boys thought it was always wrong to do so, but 39 percent thought their mother thought so, and 26 percent thought their father thought so. Among girls, considerably more—26 percent—thought it was never right to pet or neck, but even more—59 percent—thought their mothers believed this. And, consistent with gender-differentiated parental roles, 65 percent thought their fathers would prohibit all petting, if they could. Between 1950 and 1961, the plurality of comparable national samples of high school students who agreed that "intimate petting should be delayed until after marriage" grew slightly.[33]

The subtle interpenetration of adult and nonadult criteria is neatly reflected in two lesser institutions identified with the period: teen magazines and parent-teen codes. The former, first produced in the 1950s, have had the reputation of being empty froth. The parent-teen codes, an older notion that grew to fleeting prominence in response to the juvenile delinquency scare of the 1950s, seemed to be merely joint communiqués of no binding force whatever. Both the magazines and the codes were adult inventions that depended on taking seriously teenagers' definitions of their own situations, each attempting to set limits to the scope of the youth culture's moral innovations, especially in the realms of sex and courtship. Each conceded seriousness to teenagers' self-supervised courtship institutions, while seeking to co-opt the youth culture to draw physically safe and morally unexceptionable lines around these and other practices.

Charles H. Brown's perspicuous analysis lays out the content and function of such texts as *Teen World, Modern Teen,* and *Teen Parade.* "The basic format is double-barreled: it has a confessional aspect and a cultic aspect. . . . The articles deal with the most intimate of matters. . . . The world of the teen-type magazine is the world as it looks to the teen-ager, and it often has a threatening or sinister aspect to the mothers of its readers."[34] Throughout, the teen magazines "are edited in a way to protect the girl who is not ready for the advances of boys while at the same time not alienating the girl who is."[35] The message, repeatedly, is autonomy of the individual, the need for each girl (or boy) to know herself and not to be ruled by exaggerated perceptions of the requirements for meeting peer pressure, particularly in the realm of sex. "The teenage magazines recognize that the absence of fixed and rigorously enforced codes puts a terrible burden on the unawakened girl. . . . The magazines' insistence on autonomy, therefore, is meant to furnish the same kind of protection to girls as that once supplied by the mores."[36]

The movement to produce written voluntary compacts between groups of teenagers (typically presenting themselves as the whole teenage community) and parents (also presenting themselves corporatively) had its origins in the breakdown of the chaperonage system a generation before, but it spread widely only after World War II, particularly in the mid-1950s. Codes were typically drafted by committees of well-qualified, responsible youth and modified and ratified by parents. They characteristically addressed themselves to adolescents' responsibilities to their own parents, delineated proper and improper social behavior at parties and in dating, and established definite parental responsibilities for supporting legitimate adolescent activities. Allowances, transportation, and, most critically although most diffusely, a properly respectful attitude toward the self-conscious age group were offered.[37]

As in earlier decades, the high school provided the main context for the evolution of adolescent perspectives on their own development. Large numbers of new students posed a challenge to educators. New facilities were required, and, especially in suburban jurisdictions demographically most nearly exclusively given over to childbearing, these were provided by taxpayers with an exceptional openhandedness. The comprehensive high school, offering a choice of both vocational training and college preparatory courses to virtually an entire age cohort, was viewed as a source of pride and provided a curricular goal to focus the consolidation of rural districts.[38] Twenty-eight thousand high schools held the nation's high school students in 1950; but by 1960, only 2,000 new schools had been added—on net—to accommodate all the new students.[39] The average number of students per public secondary school increased by nearly one-half between 1946 and 1960.

Part of the reason for the greatly accelerated flow through secondary education was its increased articulation with a much enlarged higher education system. The pace of change here was especially impressive: around 1950, 41 percent of high school graduates went on to college, but a decade later, the percentage was up to 53 percent. Grade retardation was once again reduced. Where 25 percent of 14-year-old school enrollees were "too old" for their grade according to the figures in the 1950 census, by 1960, only 14 percent of 14-year-olds were "too old." In 1950, 77 percent of high schoolers were 14 to 17; in 1960, 82 percent were.[40] The early postwar period was characterized by one particularly dramatic effort on the part of adults to segregate adolescents from younger children—the junior high school, an institution begun decades before to cater to the particular needs of the pre-adolescents, as that stage of development came to be defined. In the first session after the end of World War II, only 35 percent of secondary school students were attending a school that was a separate junior *or* senior high school, neither combining them nor lumping them with the elementary grades. Within six years, this proportion had climbed to 40 percent, and by the end of the 1950s, the proportion was up to 56 percent.[41]

The schools came to provide virtually all adolescents with several years in a setting where, insulated from children of other ages and divided from the adults present by the formal and increasingly bureaucratic authority wielded by the latter, adolescents set powerful local norms, and devised polynucleated social structures that would enforce these on the children.[42] The system, from one perspective, was better cut to the needs of the children within it, but at the same time, the children subjected to an institution so structured surely became more acutely aware of the normatively created need to keep up with the standard pace. The impact of the markedly increased age homogenization of the setting in which adolescents found themselves surely was substantial in itself, quite apart from explicit goals of educators, which, as Graebner argues, included the inculcation of a "vision of a democratic and therefore homogeneous student body."[43]

Talcott Parsons, describing "the school class" of the late 1950s, saw the large, variegated high school as a field in which youth sorted themselves out according to a pattern fitted to adult role requirements but with the details of the patterns overseen by the youth themselves. Large comprehensive high schools mixed many more categories of student than had the neighborhood-based schools that preceded them; and by the 1950s, high schools were replete with extracurricular activities. Students might distinguish themselves favorably either according to the intellectual criteria indicated by marks or according to criteria erected by the students themselves, like "personality." For Parsons, talents along the former lines suggested "specific-function" careers, "more or less technical ones."[44] By contrast, students who were socially outstanding—"popular"— and prospered in semi-autonomous youth culture headed toward expressive "human relations" careers. Since reputation was assigned within the youth culture according to diverse criteria, cliques promoting particular variants and particular individuals were perhaps even more prominent in the 1950s than in earlier decades.

THE ELABORATION OF THE DATING SYSTEM

The emotionally charged atmosphere of World War II, the lessened supervision of adolescents by their parents entailed by war absences and war work, and the much increased amounts of money available to adolescents had persuaded virtually the last shy boy to give dating a try and had spread the teen institution into every nook and cranny. A statewide Minnesota Juvenile Poll asked teenagers in 1946, "At what age do you think boys and girls should start having dates?" Less than one percent of both boys and girls said that they should not start having dates at all, and only 22 percent of boys and 6 percent of girls named an age as old as 17. A Minnesota State poll in the following year asked young people whether they "believe[d] that a boy or girl should consult his or her parents before making or accepting dates." On the whole, about two-thirds of the adolescents (12 to 17 years old) who expressed an opinion thought they should, girls to a considerably greater degree than boys. Neither socioeconomic variables nor religiosity nor rurality explained the variation within gender; what *did*, was a highly generalized compliance with authority, whether national or intrafamilial.[45] By the late 1940s, to judge from Lowrie's several high-school samples, dating was virtually universal by the end of high school.[46]

From the perspective of the youth themselves, and, as it developed, from a life course perspective as well, dating was a key chore and opportunity.[47] Some sense of how well understood and well accepted dating had become by the baby boom period can be derived by comparing girls' replies to a 1939 youth poll with a 1956 poll of adolescent girls, both asking about sources of conflict with parents. Disagreements over boy friends had afflicted 30 percent of the girls in 1939; only 7 percent so reported two decades later. How often to date, or appropriate places to go, brought half of the girls into disagreement with their parents before the war; but in 1956, only one in nine reported such conflict. And whereas almost three in four girls and their parents had struggled over how late it was appropriate to stay out on a date in 1939, only one-sixth of the girls in the baby boom period had not achieved a smooth entente with their parents on this touchy point. Perhaps these numbers overstate the change, but they do not belie the fact that what less than a generation earlier had been a common matter of contention between parents and daughters no longer was, now that parents had themselves grown up under the dating system.[48] If dating in the 1920s had represented an aggrandizement of authority on the part of adolescents, parents by the 1950s agreed that dating constituted an arena within which adolescents learned values and even behaviors that were thoroughly, conventionally adult.[49]

In his closely reasoned empirical analysis of 1950s high schools, James S. Coleman denies that the baby boom high school career constituted a moratorium phase during which adult-world criteria were suspended; nor was it the point at which a new generation remade its status system *de novo.* Rather, these were part of a social order in which mixed criteria were used to locate, evaluate, and pair up with one another for diverse enterprises. When Coleman inquired into the bases of regard among high schoolers, he found that the athletic stars were the most universally admired boys but that for girls, the single attribute that best explained prestige was popularity with boys. The valued characteristic was in each case significantly dependent on personal, individual achievement, influenced only slightly by family background. Each was overseen by the adolescents themselves.[50]

Not everybody in high school was outstanding in any particular characteristic, achieved or ascribed, youth dictated or adult prescribed. Because high schools were typically so large that some kind of categorization was necessary so that students could comfortably understand the social constellation that related directly to themselves, cliques were even more the order of the day in the 1950s than earlier—formations directed to not necessarily clearly formed special interest or talent but overtly to assigning and maintaining clear social positions within the school. In Coleman's schools, clique structure was founded on the very important dimension of grade level, plus two variably interrelated elements: socioeconomic background and (in essence) attitude toward the officially sanctioned activities of the school as opposed to one or another way of having a good time in ways designated by the teenagers themselves.[51]

Cliques generally defined both the proper range of partners and the proper behavior on dates, and through gossip and other means of practical mutual regulation, cliques facilitated dating by reducing the very considerable uncertainty the practitioners might hold. And while *frequency* of dating was not in a simple way a function of clique membership, nothing made more difference to a girl's popularity with boys (that standard of value on the dating market) than being known as a member of "the leading crowd," composed of students who dressed well and knew it, who could project that self-confidence so rare among adolescents, who excelled in the organized social life of their schools.[52] Insofar as dating and thus "popularity" had become a proximate step on the way to marriage, then, neither ascriptive criteria nor adult-defined criteria of achievement now dominated this part of the courtship process. Instead, what dominated were *social structures endemic to the high school itself.* A follow-up examination of marriage timing of the students whom Coleman studied in 1957–58 shows that for both girls and boys high school experiences contributed more to the explanation of marriage timing than did measured IQ, family socioeconomic background, educational expectations, or enrollment in a college-preparatory curriculum. Dating frequency was *strongly* associated with prompt marriage. Higher grades were associated with later marriage.[53]

Arthur Stinchcombe's acute study of the uneasy accommodation to adulthoods of only modest prospects among students at a primarily working-class high school shows how dating could still play a role in "rebellion" but in a different sense from a generation before. Stinchcombe found that many of the students he studied were alienated from the formal expectations of the school and, in search of symbolic expression of their alienation, arrogated as many markers of adulthood to themselves as they could. Smoking and driving were among these markers, and *so was young marriage*. Girls and (especially) boys who spurned the officially defined right behaviors were markedly more likely to claim these rights. They were also considerably more likely to date frequently.[54]

The press toward marriage was particularly acute in the case of those girls who—unlike most—simply could not accommodate to school.

> The ascriptive symbols of adulthood for girls tend not to require active claims. Adolescence for girls is a period of waiting until someone asks them to get married. . . . The substitution of the marriage market for the labor market [as in the case of boys] reduces rebellion among girls by providing symbols of coming adulthood which are not compatible with current adolescent status.[55]

Havighurst discussed the same phenomenon in his 1950s investigation of a medium-sized midwestern city. There, some girls

> followed marriage rather than school as a pathway to adulthood. . . . As they felt their way toward adulthood, they found the school to be an obstacle, a confusing, baffling situation, while it seemed just natural for them to quit school and get married. . . . Marriage is the only constructive behavior of which this type of girl is capable. Too often, she cannot support this role effectively, and no one is there to help her. But it works frequently enough.[56]

Commonly enough, the respectable if somehow deviating early-marriage path to adulthood in fact turned out to provide young wives (and young husbands) with the structure they needed in which to build psychological strengths.[57] A life course could include Coke for breakfast when so many attendant structures led in just that direction and when Coke, in the end, was just another consumer product, ultimately assimilable to marriage and adulthood.

High school newspapers by the 1950s covered the dating scene assiduously. Under a variety of rubrics, the papers published lists of couples currently in being, clucked over the couples recently broken up, prodded more not-yet-formed couples into publishing their intentions, and built guessing games around such material. The *Saint Paul Central High School Times* even regularly published—evidently from official sources—a list of all the couples attending the climactic Junior-Senior Prom, until, in 1954, "since over 350 couples signed up for the Junior-Senior Prom, it is impossible for the Times to run the complete J.S. guest list."[58]

Responses to a more or less representative national sample of high school students indicate a slight movement toward consensus that fourteen or fifteen is "the approximate age at which you think teen-agers should have their first date." (There was a like tendency to agree on preferred age at marriage.) The sexual content of dates also became more uniformly understood: in 1950, a minority of 35 percent had rejected the idea of a dating couple kissing on their first date, but eleven years later this minority was reduced to 25 percent. At the same time, the decade saw a substantial shift toward gender asymmetry in the structure of the date. The minority who agreed that "it would be a good thing if girls could be as free as boys in asking for dates" declined from 37 percent to 26 percent, and the majority who considered it "a good thing if girls would pay half the expense of dates" declined from 25 percent to 18 percent.[59]

A national sample of high school youth, interviewed in 1960, indicates that by the freshman year in high school, a very considerable majority of girls and only slightly fewer boys had begun dating, at least occasionally. For both boys and girls, dating typically began in a sporadic fashion, after each had, according to self-perception, been "in love" and had had a "girlfriend" or "boy friend" but before they really had any clear notion of reproductive biology. (A year, on the average, would pass before

Table 29. Proportion Who Had Ever Dated, by Sex, Grade in
           High School, and Occupational Type of Father, 1960
           (in percentages)

	Boys			*Girls*		
Grade	*White-collar*	*Blue-collar*	*Farm*	*White-collar*	*Blue-collar*	*Farm*
9	64.5	66.3	71.4	86.0	71.4	70.3
10	89.7	85.9	77.6	91.3	72.5	77.8
11	96.4	91.7	92.7	95.9	93.0	89.3
12	98.8	95.7	89.5	100.0	97.5	97.4

SOURCE: Computed from Public Use Sample, Project Talent (N = 4000).

the first "special" kiss, to be sure.)[60] Table 29 indicates the proportions who had dated among members of each high school
class, categorized by the students' fathers' occupational type.
The results demonstrate the almost complete ubiquity of the
institution at this time, although there is a small reminder at
the early grades of the middle-class origins of dating.[61]

While the general outlines of the institution of dating were
by this time common to both whites and blacks, black boys seem
to have begun their engagement in the dating system somewhat
earlier and black girls at the same age. Broderick's study of children from 10 to 17 in a single Pennsylvania city revealed that
"Negro boys . . . showed none of the heterosexual reserve of
the white boys, . . . and, in fact, showed a higher level of heterosexual interaction at 12–13 than the girls did." Broderick
speculated that "the pattern of social-sexual development in the
Negro subculture may differ markedly from that of the dominant culture."[62] For present purposes, however, what is most
notable is the extent that dating among blacks resembled that
among whites by this time, in view of the very considerable racial differences in marriage patterns, and the slight development of the dating institution among black youth a generation
earlier.

The first date for both boys and girls was a moment of considerable anxiety, a real hurdle in growing up. About two-

thirds of a sample of seniors, both boys and girls, in a southern urban high school in 1954 agreed that on their first dates they "felt pretty scared that I'd say or do something wrong."[63] A large but nonrepresentative survey of high school students in the mid-1950s found that "dating" was an item of extremely widespread "interest" to freshmen and sophomores—boys slightly more than girls—outstripping among them even "normal sex relations" and "demands of the opposite sex." By junior and senior year, however, interest in dating *per se* had dropped slightly, so that the other two subjects exceeded them in breadth of interest, particularly among girls, for whom subjects relating directly to marriage were also highly salient.[64] A representative national survey in 1963 revealed that half of high school freshmen worried about how seldom they had dates, a proportion that gradually declined to one in three by senior year.[65]

Median dates per week grew rather steadily throughout high school, for both boys and girls, of white-collar, blue-collar, and farm backgrounds. The age that boys and girls had begun dating continued to matter throughout high school: those who had entered the dating market relatively early were the more frequent daters at subsequent ages. By the junior and senior years (even omitting those who had never dated), the differences in dating frequency between early daters and later daters amounted to almost double for boys.[66]

GOING STEADY

Going steady became the linchpin of the whole system of developing adolescent heterosexual relationships in the 1950s. The "steady" arrangement added a strong, institutionalized node in the career that led from early heterosexual sociability to early marriage and extended downward into the high school years some of the emotional comforts of marriage. Going steady was by no means a brand-new postwar phenomenon, as we have earlier seen, but was rather one whose prevalence and particularly importance in organizing the feelings and behaviors of adolescents grew markedly in the baby boom period.[67] The proportions of boys and girls whose dating included at least episodes of going steady advanced grade by grade, girls

Table 30. Median Weekly Dates for Those Who Had Gone
Steady in the Past Three Years and for Those Who
Had Not, High School Students in 1960, by Grade
(number of cases on which median is based in
parentheses)

	Boys				Girls			
	Has Gone				Has Gone			
Grade	Steady		Has Not		Steady		Has Not	
9	1.39	(135)	0.39	(198)	1.45	(161)	0.57	(218)
10	1.61	(221)	0.60	(238)	1.88	(248)	0.66	(219)
11	1.76	(236)	0.71	(218)	2.22	(291)	0.74	(176)
12	2.11	(253)	0.83	(180)	2.40	(331)	0.92	(161)

SOURCE: Public Use Sample, Project Talent.

always somewhat more prone to going steady than boys. Steady
dating was closely integrated with frequent dating; indeed, one
is almost tempted to say that only those who were prepared to
commit themselves at least sometimes to a steady relationship
were likely to prosper in the dating system, at least as it was
practiced in most places during the baby boom.[68] Even in the
early years of high school, serious daters went steady, as table
30 shows. Essentially, the trends visible there are as true for
boys as for girls, but not only were girls at any given grade level
more often experienced in steady dating than boys at the same
grade (one might characterize girls as just about one grade
ahead of boys in this regard) but girls enjoyed a greater "premium" in dates for going steady at given ages than did boys.
The reason that this was so, furthermore, was *not* that boys who
had not gone steady were especially penalized in dates but
rather that girls who had had steadies dated *much* more than
others.

While dating was comfortably accepted by parents in the
1950s, going steady was considerably more alarming. In 1955
and again in 1963, over two-thirds of adults queried by the
Roper Organization said that they thought that "boys and girls
in high school" should not be permitted to go steady but should

instead date different boys and girls.[69] To adult observers, going steady seemed—as had dating itself a generation earlier—to propose an unfathomable developmental sequence, to offer youth premature liberties, dominated by a code of alien design. "Teenagers were trying to do the unthinkable—to factor competition out of the equation. Adults were appalled. To them, going steady, with its extreme rejection of competition in favor of temporary security," so characteristic of prewar dating, "represented all the faults of the new generation."[70] Writers in *Parents* urged their readers to recognize that "going steady is here to stay" but that it no longer had the meaning it once had: "to the boys and girls who are engaged in it, going steady doesn't mean anything like being engaged. . . . Where we read marital implications, they read popularity and security."[71] Young people expected to go steady a good deal, but they also expected to change "steadies" quite frequently, seeking not dangerous intimacy but a calm friendship of a sort that the more competitive dating setting precluded.

But to other adult observers—and they were the more correct—going steady was rather an early stage in a courtship sequence that youth had begun to form out of the inchoate independence left from the war period. A study conducted in an Iowa high school in 1958 suggested that middle-class youth, perhaps because they usually did not anticipate marriage soon, had a considerably cooler view of going steady than did working-class adolescents: they changed steadies more often and were less likely to define any given steady as an "in love" relationship.[72] One observer noted no fewer than three additional steps after going steady but before formal engagement: lavaliering, pinning, and (wrist-)watching. A more raffish step was proposed in *Personal Romances* in 1959: "Macel said, 'Dickie and I are changing pillows tonight.' 'Changing pillows. . . . ?' I still didn't understand. 'You see,' Macel explained, 'when steadies exchange pillows that is the next thing to actually sleeping with each other.' "[73] Analytically, pillow-exchange differs from, say, lavaliering only in its open reference to sexuality, the exercise of which, however, is in theory no less postponed. Each proposes a youth-controlled, ritually solemnized sequence of stages of commitment, ideally eventuating in marriage, but with a discontinuity at the engagement stage. At varying points in the sequence, but in the spirit of the era quite early, would come a (private or public) commitment of love, the expression that "in our culture implies one is thinking about a commitment to marry."[74]

Going steady did often seem to incorporate a sexual progression along with the more overt components, although usually not coitus. Young people in the baby boom era often felt as uncertain about this as did their parents. Crist found that a majority of the high schoolers he talked to in 1950 who were going steady "said that they did not think it was a good idea. They said they believed those who went steady 'too much' became moony and sappy, that they might become too emotionally involved."[75] A high school senior, speaking to another investigator in 1950, was even more explicit about the too-close tie of going steady and sexual-emotional commitment.

> When a boy goes steady with a girl, you automatically are letting yourself in for a lot of troubles that will come up. If you both have good strong morals, I think you can sort of get through everything. . . . Some kids think that they're in love. Leaves a lot of hard feelings, and there's a lot of resentment, and there's a lot of 'Why did I do this?' . . . I don't think that there's very many people in high school that are really sure that they're in love.[76]

A national survey of adolescent girls in 1956 found that many more girls were negative about going steady than were positive, and the negative responses rose sharply with age.[77]

But socially—despite considerable instance-to-instance variation of just what the practice involved—going steady made sense to youth, although boys and girls disagreed sharply about how much petting going steady should entail.[78] Ira Reiss argued that going steady in high school pushed toward—as behavior and as norm—"heavy petting with affection." Neither abandoned nor simply sensual, heavy petting with affection was mutual, expressive, and moral at core: "high school couples who are going steady . . . feel it is proper to engage in heavy petting, . . . the justification being that they are in love or at least extremely fond of each other."[79] The importance and meaning of a boyfriend or girlfriend shifted decisively from the highly externalized rating marker described by Waller in the

1930s to a surprisingly deeper inner meaning, attached to the search for one's self.[80] *The Times* of St. Paul Central High was "glad to see that Mary Jane Witt and Ray Nelson have patched things up," three months later reporting of Mary Jane and Ray that "after a date, you'll find them in their favorite restaurant listening to 'Anytime' and eating another favorite, spare ribs."[81] The breezy tone is exactly to the point. The same treatment was accorded students briefly profiled in the context of particular achievements or honors. Going steady was a characteristic event in the life that the high school newspaper chronicled and helped to diffuse. "I imagine that most of you have noticed some of the girls in Junior High are wearing dog collars on their ankles. Let's get together on which ankle to wear them. If you have a guy please wear it on the left ankle and if you don't, buckle it on the right. Okay?"[82]

The classical dating relationship, as devised a generation before, employed girl solidarity to put safe bounds to the bargaining between boys and girls. For boys, the arrangement had clear advantages over the prior regime, but by the 1950s the power of girls' gossip irked boys, who no longer could see its compensating advantages. Boys had to propose; girls who said no could also tell their friends. The fear of being told no— especially for younger boys at the beginning of their dating careers—was a specter many dreaded, since girl gossip might record the concurrent loss of face for all the school to see.

> A boy feels like a sap if he asks a girl and she says, "I'm busy tonight." And the next time he calls her up and she says, "I'm busy tonight." And it's the girl's place to show that—I don't know, that—I don't know—just how she feels. A fellow depends on a girl all his life, and he's not used to making up his own mind.[83]

To this, a perspicuous girl answered, "I know that's one reason why a whole lot of people do go steady. At least, you're sure a fellow doesn't have to get his courage up to ask for a date. When a dance comes along, he just says, 'Let's go.' "[84] Surveys revealed that in the 1950s, boys more than girls worried about being clumsy with the opposite sex generally and about their inability to be comfortable dating. They also worried a good deal more about sex.

For boys, going steady was more comfortable, often far more

comfortable, than dating. If dating had been the innovation of girls, going steady responded to the special exigencies in boys' life courses. It was a haven from anxiety for boys who were insecure of their reputations: "when it is well-known and advertised, there is definitely prestige in it." It was less expensive, and it promoted heightened but safe sexuality. "Lots of the fellows won't go out with a girl unless they can go steady."[85] Girls more than boys worried about whether to go steady, their focal concern of marriage rendering that institution especially portentous.[86] From the girls' standpoint, the loss in circulation among pleasing partners and the added risk of sexual transgression was compensated by the added emotional intimacy available in steady dates, for masculine swagger and bravado were minimized in such a relationship. "It doesn't mean a steady date at all. It's just liking someone and it's better going out with him than anyone else. I don't know, it's a feeling, I guess, that someone's always there and you always have someone to turn to."[87]

> You have a period in adolescence in which there is a terrific confusion or something. No one seems to know exactly where he is going. The girl begins worrying about boys. The boy has a hard time getting up his nerve to ask the girl out, and the girl is wondering if he is going to ask her out. When you pass that stage, and a boy and girl can like each other and can head toward each other and would like to be with each other, they have achieved a maturity.[88]

Many, varied dates were important when adolescents had counted on dating to signify in a very public way one's participation in the recently emerged youth culture. But now, a generation later, such participation was taken for granted.[89] The pursuit of warmth and intimacy, always present, now emerged.

The sharp downward shift in the marriage age drew girls into going steady, despite their reasons for ambivalence. Among girls 16 to 18 in 1955, those who were going steady more than those merely dating and even more than those not dating at all believed that popularity depended on one's sensitivity and understanding and that popularity with boys depended on the same inner qualities. Merely external social skills seemed notably less important to girls who were going steady; so, too, was appearance. Going steady was evidently congruent with a view of the adolescent social world that emphasized the qualities of persons commonly thought central to modern marriage.[90] Going steady was no trial marriage, but it was a trial on relatively familiar ground of some of the sentiments and qualities one sought in marriage. The "home" found a junior counterpart in the steady couple.

The external signs of these kinds of relationships fit nicely the requirements of a socially coherent high school student body and were, accordingly, celebrated not only in the halls but in more official quarters. Thus, when the *St. Paul Central High School Times* published their lists of those in attendance at the junior-senior proms, the names were not segregated by gender but were published by couple, alphabetically by boys' family name. The publication of such lists of affiliation served to reinforce the strength of going steady as an institution and perhaps encouraged longer relationships. To lay two successive lists side by side is to discover that where boys (juniors, evidently) returned for a second prom, about half returned with the same girl, and half with another. Private, and to a degree *ad hoc* in its behavioral aspects, the steady relationship became in a sense the property of the mainstream of the high school community, an enactment of the capacity of that community to promote and protect an area of privacy for mutual support in growing up amid a highly institutionalized and sometimes troubling social environment.

A late 1950s Connecticut study examined the "courtship progress" of high school students. Going steady was very widespread, as table 31 suggests. Boys and girls were about equally likely to have gone steady at some time, with less ambitious and less accomplished students somewhat more likely than scholars to have steadies. Engagement (among steadies) had a more differentiated distribution than did going steady *per se*, for its prevalence was more closely related to just where the students were in their life course. But the two patterns also showed obvious parallels. Seniors who had gone steady were three times more likely than freshmen who had also gone steady to have become engaged. Girls were twice as prone to engagement than

Table 31. Going Steady and Progress toward Marriage, by
Selected Characteristics, Connecticut High School
Students, Late 1950s

	Percentage Who Have Gone Steady	Of Those Who Have Gone Steady, Percent Privately or Publicly Committed to Marriage with Steady
Males	59.2	16.2
Females	63.2	36.7
Freshmen	54.7	13.9
Sophomore	54.8	27.6
Juniors	66.1	25.6
Seniors	73.9	42.6
Grade point 90+	50.0	17.0
80–88.9	58.2	28.9
70–79.9	67.6	26.3
Less than 70	61.9	34.6
Sure of college	56.8	20.4
Probably college	58.6	24.6
Probably no college	69.2	29.3
Surely no college	68.9	35.0
Believes could marry as soon as finished with high school	67.8	41.5
Does not so believe	58.3	19.5

SOURCE: Recalculated from Jerold S. Heiss, "Variations in Courtship Progress among High School Students," *Marriage and Family Living* 22 (1960), Tables I and II.

were boys, and they married younger. Particularly striking is the very substantial increase in overt commitment to marrying one's steady among those who had definitely ruled college out.[91]

By strong contrast, with surprisingly little variation from category to category, an additional six in ten of those who had at some time gone steady but had made no commitment to marry had given thought to marrying their steady.[92] Not only was going steady a ubiquitous form of social relationship in 1950s high schools but it was a relationship that in the minds of the participants had some resonance with thoughts of marriage. "He was in my class in high school, and we went together to practically everything. He wrote, too, while he was in the Army. . . . Of course, I thought that someday we'd be married. Oh, I didn't tell anyone that—least of all, Bernie—but I thought about it a lot."[93] The likely explanation is also the one that fearful parents of the day expressed: the kind of comfortable intimacy going steady provided also encouraged thoughts of extending this intimacy into a marriage, soon, although its relationship to marriage was ambiguous rather than explicit.[94] Going steady was not a functional substitute for engagement; it looked outward to the youth peer group rather than to the older members of the family, and the relationship of steady to steady's parents was casual. A popular boy at Roosevelt High in Minneapolis "has dark brown hair and blue eyes and rates Mrs. Lampstad's chocolate cake and beef tenderloin steaks as his favorite food. [He] works at Vic's Drive-In as a cook and spends most of his spare time with Ann Lampstad."[95] It nevertheless now served as the transition point at which the level and nature of premarital physical intimacy was defined.

How closely dating and going steady were tied to the transition to marriage during the baby boom is revealed by an analysis of data from Project Talent. Students were asked, "How old do you expect to be when you get married?" Their responses indicate that those who were more deeply entwined in the dating-and-steady system had already adjusted their expectations to earlier marriage, were prepared emotionally for interpersonal intimacy but also believed that their "search" for a desirable mate had already accomplished something. In table 32, boys who expected to marry before age 23 and girls who expected to marry before age 21 will be considered "early" in this regard. For girls, their success or lack of success in the dating system inevitably served as a gauge to them of their progress toward marriage. For boys, this relationship was revealed only gradually, over the course of high school, but by their senior years, boys' anticipation of marriage hinged almost as much on dating frequency and going steady as did girls'. For boys, a his-

Table 32. Proportion Expecting to Marry "Early," by Current Dating Frequency and History of Going Steady, by Sex and Grade, 1960 (in percentages)

| | Boys (Marry before 23) | | | | | Girls (Marry before 21) | | | | |
| | Dating Frequency | | | Steady | | Dating Frequency | | | Steady | |
Grade	Two+/ week	One/ week	None	Yes	No	Two+/ week	One/ week	None	Yes	No
9	52.8	50.0	48.0	53.7	47.1	54.7	38.1	27.7	45.1	27.3
10	54.0	47.6	40.8	56.9	37.2	58.0	32.8	15.5	49.2	22.0
11	44.4	41.1	32.0	43.0	36.1	47.2	35.0	26.3	43.4	31.9
12	51.6	24.4	25.0	47.2	21.7	55.8	34.4	21.9	55.8	28.4

SOURCE: Computed from Public Use Sample, Project Talent.

tory of having gone steady was from an early age more closely tied to marriage expectations than was mere dating frequency, although its relevance, too, emerged over the course of high school. For girls, going steady, as with dating, mattered consistently throughout high school, and it mattered a lot.[96]

Nor were these anticipations off the mark, in part, as Bayer has shown, because the anticipations themselves predisposed the young people toward subsequent lines of action that fulfilled the prophecies they embodied.[97] The high school students whose late-1950s dating behavior we are discussing were reinterviewed eleven years later, by which time most of them had married. Table 33 demonstrates that in the baby boom success in the dating system very distinctly did in fact *predict prompt marriage* and, whatever their prior thoughts on the matter, no less so for boys than for girls. Dating and going steady, then, constituted parts of a system that was consequential *not only in that it altered expectations but also in that it set up thereby long-lasting patterns of behavior.* An openness to sexual exploration, too, seems to have hinged in part on the early readiness for the *social* exploration that dating represented.[98]

MARRYING

In the counseling idiom then current, one married a mate who supplied those particular kinds of supports one felt one required and who needed of one just what one could, in turn, give; that is, there was "need complementarity." Robert F. Winch's classic formulation of this notion tells us much about the ideology of marriage in the 1950s. His 1958 treatise seeks to express "in concise, naturalistic terms what is meant by love," for in America "we marry for love," drawing attention to the sometimes mysterious attraction of opposites remarked at length by Plato.[99] The centrality of this contemporary formulation can be gauged from the breadth of its popularization. *Personal Romances* thus advised its readers that "in the perfect marriage one mate supplies the talents or virtues the other lacks, and vice versa. . . . There is no greater declaration of enduring love than the three simple words, 'I need you.' "[100]

The essence of Winch's work is the psychological rating of

Table 33. Percentage Who Actually Married "Early," by Participation in Dating System, Grade When Interviewed in 1960, and Sex (in percentages)

Grade at 1st Interview	Boys					Girls				
	Dating Frequency			Steady		Dating Frequency			Steady	
	Two+/ week	One/ week	None	Yes	No	Two+/ week	One/ week	None	Yes	No
9	77.5	63.5	49.5	65.5	51.6	72.1	58.6	54.9	66.7	53.3
10	73.9	67.1	41.7	69.4	50.0	77.8	58.2	53.0	71.1	38.1
11	63.5	46.1	38.1	57.3	39.3	62.3	40.0	58.1	60.3	35.9
12	67.5	35.3	21.1	64.6	25.0	59.7	33.3	38.1	59.2	27.1

SOURCE: Computed from Public Use Sample, Project Talent.
NOTE: Percentage shown is of those marrying within eleven years of interview in high school, the great majority of all who would ever marry. Based on only those who had married by 1971.

both partners on such qualities as assertiveness, receptivity, and self-deprecation and an empirical inquiry into what kind of a person, thus defined, marries what kind of person. There was a right mate to be found but not a universal best mate. One finds one's best mate by being oneself, and thereby one discovers "the personality contours of a prospective mate. . . . not in general but rather with specific reference to" one's own traits. Submissive people made dominant ones feel good and, in turn, were gratified by the opportunity to submit. "We love those persons. . . . who provide gratification of our needs and thereby bring us pleasure."[101] Life course decisions in the 1950s were psychologically relativistic, even when not following Winch's formula. "Maturity," psychologically defined, was a common criterion. "If you're crazy in love with a man, you may not stop to consider if he's emotionally mature enough to make a good husband and father. After all, isn't love all that really matters?"[102] *True Love Stories'* hortation follows up with a list of ten practical indicators of maturity, which amount to moderation, considerateness, and commitment to the marriage, qualities that, like those supplying complementary needs, could be found—indeed *were* found—among relatively young people.

Figures 18 and 19 show actual first-marriage rates for the period 1945 to 1959 for white and nonwhite single women for small age groups. These rates were paralleled by men's rates, except where draft age influenced men's marriage probabilities. We may take 1949, a relatively low point following the accomplishment of most of the marriages "postponed" by World War II, yet before the impact of Korea, as our starting point. The very youngest group shown—14 to 17—and the oldest—30 to 34—both had markedly parallel histories of marriage rates during this period, each tending on the whole downward. Those 18 to 19 and 22 to 24 also show quite parallel trends, but these two age groups both show a gradual increase after the midpoint of the Korean War until 1955 and a marked increase for the next two years, followed by a slight decline. The most popular ages for young women to marry were 20 and 21, and these ages, increasingly popular during the period, peaked at 1957. Whites and nonwhites basically shared the same temporal patterns, although the two had different age schedules of mar-

Percent
Probability
of Marriage

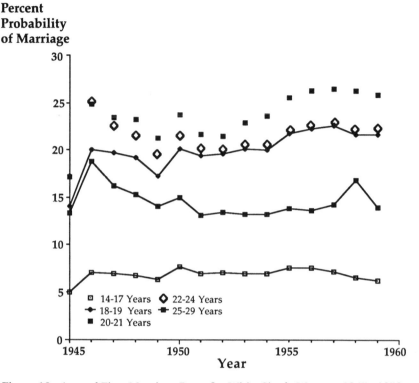

Figure 18. Annual First-Marriage Rates for White Single Women, 1945–1959

riage, with nonwhites' timing throughout the era less uniform than whites'.[103] Black age patterns shifted slightly during the decade, perhaps as the result of rural-to-urban migrations. A smaller proportion of black women came to marry very young, while, contrariwise, the likelihood of marriage by relatively old single black women grew.

Korea seems to have marked a decisive change in the relationship between the way men as compared with women experienced the age structure of the marriage market. Prior to Korea, men's and women's marriages for a given "pair" of ages pretty much paralleled each other, year by year. But in the 1950s, what amounted to devaluation of older women in the marriage market came to operate more effectively, year after year. Women, thus, experienced the 1950s shift in the marriage-timing schedule more abruptly than did men. The pres-

**Percent
Probability
of Marriage**

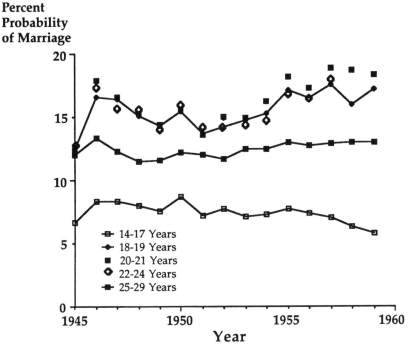

Figure 19. Annual First-Marriage Rates for Nonwhite Single Women, 1945–1959

sure to marry felt by young unmarried women was to play a part in subsequent developments.

A particularly acute form of sanctioning occurred in a common phrase, "old maid." Old maids were not figures of abhorrence so much as they were objects of condescending pity.[104] The pity depended on the secure, unquestioned knowledge that such a position was not seen by any but deviants as a valid alternative to marriage and motherhood. An even more central belief was that the satisfactions of the " home" would be denied old maids, who would be lonely, bored, unloved, joyless. "Well, you want to marry like other girls do. You can't look forward to being an old maid. It's a woman's place to marry and have a family."[105]

Over the 1950s, average income levels increased, permitting a higher proportion of young people to marry and then to have children. Income levels grew over this decade at a pace that kept the standard of living of newly formed families in a very steady relationship to that of older families at the same time, and also to people of the same age who had not yet married or not yet had children.[106] Subjective material minimal requirements for *becoming parents* enlarged along with incomes. A repeated question on Gallup polls indicates a basically constant ratio of "the smallest amount of money *a family of four* (husband, wife, and two children) needs each week to get along on in this community" to actual average income. Prosperity was shared by the young couples contemplating marriage or parenthood, but they took out only a portion of their "dividend" directly in family formation, the balance going to increased home ownership and a variety of related appurtenances. Thus, in this era of devotion to the family, family life became, in a material sense, richer.[107]

Tastes for *marriage*, however, moved with income in a somewhat different way in the decades after World War II. We have, first, a comparison of prewar and postwar poll data on economic sufficiency targets for marriage. In 1938, women's median targets of adequate incomes on which to marry—no doubt these included cushions against future unemployment not considered so necessary after the war—were about 2.6 times median current disposable income per capita. By 1946, however, the ratio had fallen to 1.8 times: immediate marriage was, on the average, much more feasible.[108] Peter Lindert's elaborate state-level regression analysis of American age at marriage shows that in 1930 and 1940, aspects of population composition—percentage foreign born and sex ratio in particular—were the major variables that statistically explained why women married younger in some states than in others. Insofar as average current income from employment played a role (as it did in 1930 and 1940), it was a negative role: states with higher average incomes were states where women married older. In 1950 and even more so in 1960, however, the positive relationship of income and marriage timing was strong enough to suggest that sufficiency targets were regularly exceeded by burgeoning current income. Young people now responded *positively* to high local average income.[109] As has been argued elsewhere, after World War II "the basis for 'decision' about marriage timing has changed, then, from involuntary to preferential, from a structurally constrained to an individually determined basis."[110]

Overall, then, the 1950s not only saw earlier marriage but a falling off of marriage probabilities for those who did not marry as promptly as current standards proposed they should. In a behavioral sense, marriage between about 18 and 24 became highly normative during the baby boom, aided by a widespread diffusion after World War II of parentally subsidized marriage and even subsidized parenthood.[111] Women had to get on the with the task of getting married at a rather brisk pace or see their chances to marry at all actually decline—in a period of heightened nuptiality and marriage-consciousness. The tensions built into this new scheduling eventually came to affect the way that women, traditionally younger at marriage than men, understood their ability to achieve emotionally satisfying marriages, even to contract the marriage with the feeling of certainty called for by the folk knowledge that governed behavior.

> Out of it all I faced the fact that I didn't love George at all. I didn't love George any more than Gracie loved her husband or Penny loved Bill. . . . How would I end up? Loving a split level and a car, or simply loving the idea of marriage? How? Not happy certainly? . . . What was I settling for? Marriage before I was nineteen, with my picture in the paper[?] . . .[112]

She splits with George. "For the first time since I'd known George, I felt like me—Florence Mackenzie. . . . Now I will wait for a man to love who will love me—until I am twenty-seven if necessary—until I am forty, if it has to be." But, statistically, Florence was making a mistake, if she was really determined to marry. Florence's divorce occurred in the year that Betty Friedan published *The Feminine Mystique*.

There is evidence that initial postwar ideals of marriage timing more or less resembled those that preceded it.[113] But they did not survive long thereafter, as the prosperity and evolving courtship mechanisms of the baby boom era made early marriage more attainable. As more individuals were enabled to marry according to or ahead of their schedules, normative age schedules shifted toward younger marriage. Ideal marriage age closely paralleled behavioral trends. Table 34 documents this,

Table 34. Comparison of Median, Mean, and Standard Deviation of Ideal Marriage Ages with Actual Ages at First Marriage, 1946 and 1957

	Ideal			*Behavior*		
	Median	*Mean*	*S.D.*	*Median*	*Mean*	*S.D.*
1946						
Male	24.4	25.0	2.9	23.7	25.3	6.4
Female	21.0	21.9	2.4	20.5	22.3	5.9
1957						
Male	23.9	24.0	3.5	22.6	24.3	6.0
Female	20.4	21.3	3.1	20.3	21.3	6.1

SOURCES: Computed from APIO 377 and AIPO 578. See Appendix 4. The behavior medians are inferred from marital-status-by-age data from the contemporaneous *Current Population Surveys,* while the means and standard deviations are from the 1960 and 1970 first-marriage retrospects in the population censuses of that year.

comparing ideals derived from representative national polls taken in 1946 and 1957 with actual marriage timing for those same dates.

At both dates and for both sexes, the median of the ideal marriage age was somewhat above that for contemporaneous behavior.[114] At the same time, the means of marriage behavior generally were above the means of ideal age at marriage. The distribution of *ideal* ages of marriage at any given time has consistently been more uniform than that of *actual* marriage. Unintended pregnancy, of course, explains many younger-than-ideal marriages, and lack of timely opportunity many that were older than ideal. Ideals of marriage age were subject to periodic revision and the 1950s were a period of noteworthy downward revision. This was no less true for older married people than for young people still contemplating their own transitions to the married state. Baby boom youth were eager to get on with "family-building" and drew from their elders a set of values that situated this earnest desire squarely within their common notion of the good life. Ideals and behavior had different distributions, but they also *changed together*, moving up to the peak of the baby boom. They shortly were to reverse together.

Hogan shows that median age at leaving school increased by over a year among young men from the 1937 birth cohort as compared with those born a decade earlier. In the 1927 birth cohort, the average young man completed his education at age 17.8 and married at age 23.3—five and a half years later. The cohort born in 1937, on average, married at 23.0, after having finished school at 19.0, their wait having shrunk on average a year and a half in a decade. Among those who did not serve in the military, the decline was especially sharp, but even among those who served, the average hiatus between leaving school and marrying was reduced. The transition time to adulthood was thus compressed sharply in the baby boom decade. Yet despite the difficulties inevitably posed often by the exacting new scheduling, Hogan is able to show that atypically sequenced transitions occurred only somewhat more often in the baby boom, rising from about 20 percent for the 1927 birth cohort to a peak of about 25 percent for the 1932 cohort (marrying, on average, about 1955) and settling back to a level of 23 percent for the 1937 cohort. This increase is distinctly less than one would expect if—in view of the way average school-leaving and marriage ages were moving toward one another—young men and women were not making an increasingly strenuous effort to keep their life courses "normative."[115]

An important component in the new nuptiality regime was the large peacetime army to which the nation was committed. Even though young men who served married a little later, in those years when the military made particularly severe demands on the manpower pool, *overall age at marriage declined*. In Hogan's calculations, based on single-year time-series analysis, variations in military demand had about as much effect on nuptiality as did variations in unemployment rates but, of course, in the opposite direction. In the aggregate, military demand encouraged single men, especially those relatively older, to take the plunge. The effect of military demand was in fact strikingly direct and prompt. Stanley Lebergott puts it nicely: "The brassy brilliant call of country leads young people to marry not only until—but *before* death do them part. Perhaps in more halcyon times, or climes, the rate of time discount might not be so formidable." Rate of first inductions explained

about half the quarter-year-to-quarter-year variation in marriage rates.[116]

Proximate reminders of the possibility of the interruption of
one's course to adulthood by a stint in the army, for the most
part, seems to have occasioned the wish to be on with it, to hasten marriage.

> We were sophomores in high school when we started to go
> steady, and by the time we were seniors, we knew we wanted to get
> married. . . . Ted's draft notice came in May and instead of giving
> me my engagement ring for Christmas like he'd planned, I got it
> that July before he left.[117]

Fathers were not drafted at this time, and husbands were
drafted only rarely. Student deferments declined fairly steadily
after 1952, and from this same date, Type IIIA deferrals (registrant with a child or children and registrant deferred by
reason of dependents) increased regularly as a ratio to inductees and enlistees.[118] For young men, the existence of conscription nevertheless legitimated youthful marriage—old enough
to fight, old enough to be responsible for a wife—and also provided a practical reason for quickly achieving it as well as a
potential backup job in case of unemployment. As "juvenile
delinquency" stereotyped the younger part of male youth as
threatening and disorganized, the army stereotyped the older
part as manly and responsible.

For those who served in peacetime, the military offered a
sharply age-graded experience, of limited duration, during
which both emotional and human capital were accumulated,
and sometimes tangible capital. In the baby boom period, one
anticipating being drafted did not necessarily do himself a dis-
service by marrying and indeed may have thereby mitigated
some of the rigors of army life. Many postings during this period were domestic; other men, stationed in Europe, could with
the aid of the PX provide a level of family living not inimical to
most wives. For the men, marriage posed a way of escaping
group quarters and the constant military superintendence that
implied. As peacetime military service became more institutionalized during the decade, the proportions of those in service

who were married increased, despite increasing dependency deferral. Indeed, the shift to young marriage during the decade was sharper among those in the military than among civilians. By 1960, more of those age 18 or 19 in service were actually married than were civilians at the same ages; and only a ten-percentage-point difference (it had been nineteen points in 1950) separated civilians from soldiers in proportions married at ages 20 to 24. Much as was college and even high school education, so also army life was accommodated to the enhanced drive toward youthful marriage so apparent during the decade.[119]

PARENTHOOD AND FULFILLMENT

The baby boom ideology of "family-building" understood the family to a surprising degree in terms of parenthood as the cement to marriage, as goal for marriage, as link with God, or destiny, or prescribed gender role. What exactly to make of marriage without the goal of proximate childbearing was a foreign notion to young people in the 1950s. The transition into parenthood during the baby boom in fact followed much the same path as that into marriage, except among those who, in defiance of the trend of the times, married on the late side. For women closer to the modal first-birth ages, however, just as for those marrying at the peak marriage ages, the baby boom was extremely pronounced. The marriage boom of 1950, a product of the Korean War, led to a very marked jump in first births in 1951, and for those of typical marriage age *the trend to prompt parenthood did not cease but continued.* The strongest and most pronounced first-birth surge was among women at 23 to 25, a few years older than the peak first-marriage group, and for them the end of the Korean conflict sparked an even more dramatic rise in first-birth probabilities. The birth schedule became more focused as it moved downward, with the marriage schedule. Women who had not yet had their first child by the time they approached their mid-twenties hastened to do so.

Demographer Norman B. Ryder decomposes completed fertility into a number of analytically separable decisions, of which completed fertility is the result. In twentieth-century America, according to Ryder, how early women began childbearing is as predictive of overall childbearing as is how effectively they prevented those births they wished to prevent. The baby boom, in his account, was produced by a group eager and able to begin marriage and childbearing in a rush and, *in addition*, rather careless about preventing fertility in excess of the rather modest targets they had established. In a powerful piece of analysis based on birth registration data, Ryder argues that "most of the baby boom would have occurred without any change whatsoever in the numbers of births per woman. . . . Of the two components of those changes [that did occur, in the tempo of childbearing], the dominant element has been changes in ages at first birth." [120] And in a highly technical and rather speculative analysis of retrospective survey data, the quickening of the fertility tempo in the baby boom is further analyzed into a number of contributing factors.

> During the phase of rising fertility, commonly known as the baby boom, it is approximately correct to say that there was no change in the mean number of intended births. There was, however, a deterioration in the effectiveness with which unintended fertility was prevented . . . [amounting to]a substantial decline in the length of intended delay [before the first child] accompanied by substantial decline in the ability to achieve that intended delay.[121]

The complicated patterns of the parenthood transition in the baby boom are displayed in table 35. The rates shown are *monthly* probabilities of becoming a parent for those married but as yet childless, for specified periods within their marriages. In the aggregate, initial-fertility probabilities declined substantially the more remote from marriage one was, for those who married younger and those who married older, for the less educated and for the more educated. But in the years 1945 to 1949, this was truer for the less educated and for those who married younger, whereas by 1955 to 1959 *it was truer for those who married older and who were more educated.* This means that the baby boom was a period in which the groups that were once known for moving relatively slowly and cautiously from marriage to parenthood reversed their pattern of behavior. Nor-

Table 35. Average Monthly Probabilities (per 1,000) of First Childbirth within Specified Terms after Marriage, by Age at Marriage and Educational Attainment, Married Childless Women in Three Marriage Cohorts

	Married during Years			Percentage Change 1945–49 to 1955–59
	1945–49	1950–54	1955–59	
Married <22				
9th–12th month	68	68	77	13
12th–16th month	49	55	55	12
16th–20th month	49	54	51	4
20th–24th month	46	41	40	−13
Married >21				
9th–12th month	47	44	63	34
12th–16th month	34	40	48	41
16th–20th month	38	33	33	−13
20th–24th month	28	27	32	14
Not high school graduate				
9th–12th month	63	71	86	37
12th–16th month	41	49	56	37
16th–20th month	50	45	59	18
20th–24th month	37	37	41	11
High school graduate				
9th–12th month	47	59	72	53
12th–16th month	45	52	55	22
16th–20th month	47	46	40	−15
20th–24th month	35	35	33	− 6
Attended college				
9th–12th month	47	35	55	17
12th–16th month	36	35	42	17
16th–20th month	26	46	42	62
20th–24th month	29	39	33	14

SOURCE: Calculated from Census CPS P20-186, 41–44, 17–48, 50–51.

mative structures—a certain regard for what was once considered prudence—that had governed the parenthood transition
for the middle class had changed. What was now normative was
to have a child promptly once marriage was contracted, to have
a family, a *home*.

Parenthood probabilities generally increased during this period but by no means uniformly so. Table 35 makes clear that
changes in the parenthood transition in the first part of the
1950s barely foreshadowed what was to come in the height of
the baby boom. The first part of the decade seemingly was a
period of overall modest increase over the postwar half-decade,
itself the composite of postponed "family-building" and the
slow emergence of the new patterns that were to characterize
the baby boom. These modest increases were very varied in the
points of the family histories that they showed up, from group
to group. In the second half of the decade, the focus of initial-
fertility increase shifted toward the early months of marriage,
quite generally. Over the whole decade, the most pronounced
rearrangement of the path from marriage to parenthood was
among the kind of women, themselves becoming less common,
who postponed marriage.[122]

Marriage, emotionally the climax of the life course as recently as World War II, was less climactic in the 1950s. We can
discern this in the decline of marital childlessness to near the
biological minimum, in a corresponding decline among those
for whom childlessness was seen as desirable,[123] and, correspondingly, in an increase in the number of adoptions.[124] In a
curious fashion, the very ease—and earliness—of marriage
now marked it out as less the moment of entry to the status of
adult than as a continuation of the prior stages along that road.
In "Coke for Breakfast," Pete proves himself a real (adult) husband by responding eagerly and "maturely" to the idea of becoming a parent. An emergent norm of parental underwriting
of young marriage may even have somewhat undercut the independence formerly announced by the marriage transition.
What women came to focus on at any rate was the establishment of the "home"; and that meant children.[125] For young
women in the mid-1950s, this word expressed the natural and
unquestioningly desired location of family life, and, indeed, the
affective life more generally. Young men's beliefs, less well

documented, seem to have resembled young women's but to have been less vivid. In a 1953 survey, it was women considerably more often than men who looked to the *experience* of marriage, and presumably parenthood, as something not to be missed.[126] With very few exceptions, the home was seen as the central point of the life of young wives, from which they would emerge to take part in occasional entertainment, in voluntary association and religion, and, perhaps at a later age, in gainful employment but to which all these activities must conduce. "It's the whole purpose of marriage. There wouldn't be any children if people didn't marry, life wouldn't exist if people didn't have children. If I couldn't have children, I'd go crazy. Home isn't a home without children."[127] The master symbol of the "home" often expressed the affective as well as the locational side of the family institution. In many cases, it connoted also "woman's sphere."

The young woman who established a home was fulfilling a very high purpose, although home was sometimes seen as instinct, sometimes duty, sometimes joy, and sometimes simply an assumed part of the world. That children "bind together" a family was a notion offered again and again by single women, reflecting often the overarching ideology of the "home." In the 1953 survey, when asked to explain what was important to them about marriage, both single and married women mentioned specific child-rearing goals more commonly than anything else, by a good bit. For men, this goal was fairly common but less so than were several others. In numbers of the texts gathered in the 1955 single women's survey, marriage itself is portrayed as either a fragile affair or one of relatively low salience. "It [child rearing] is the thing that holds the family together. Because a home is not complete without children. Children are the center of any family and the reason for marriage."[128] Children bind it together by giving the parents something in common to care for but, even more, something to look forward to. "Work together" was a common phrase, suggesting that for at least some of these women the substantial role segregation of 1950s marriage suggested a weak marriage could in some cases be overcome by the common effort wife and husband would expend on their children.

Children benefited marriages, too, because husband and

wife "can grow up with" their children. The ideology is consistent with the brief periods preceding "maturity" and "adjustment": one did one's own growing up with the developing home if one was a young woman in the 1950s. Because other aspects of personal growth were often considered selfish, to build one's family early so that one would be young enough to "grow up" with one's children made sense.

Table 36 offers the detailed breakdown of the proportion of all the 1955 single women respondents who volunteered given marriage and parenthood ideologies in the course of their interviews. The difference between the two columns is instructive, as is the common emphases of the two. Children were much more salient to these young women than was marriage. The average young woman offered 1.41 different justifications for marriage (excluding demurrers); she gave 2.16 in behalf of children. The young women often expressed "ontological" justifications—that marriage or childbearing was simply *in the nature of things*. No sanctions, material or moral, were mentioned, for none was needed, since to be a wife or parent was simply "natural." The 1953 survey reveals that this kind of answer was almost exclusive to women, hardly ever shared by men. Closely related were a variety of de-ontological or *should* answers. These were more common and came in several varieties.

Although "should" still might be a part of the sense conveyed, the largest number of these were those respondents for whom wifehood or motherhood meant *self-fulfillment.* That one owed it to oneself was the dominant tone among the replies arguing self-fulfillment, as distinct from replies in which one owed it to the proper fulfillment of one's role: one acted out of a wish, not out of an obligation. Distinct once again were a large set of bases that proposed some specific pleasure or reward in return for being wife or mother. In citing love (or some variant of it), these young women were ideologically locating the reason for their future demographic choices in a reward to be pleasurably experienced by themselves. Formally, ontological ideologies treated the woman as though will and feeling were irrelevant. De-ontological ideologies implied that the woman acted out of will but (here) without regard to feeling. "Self-

Table 36. Proportion of Single Women 18–24 in 1955 Volunteering Specific Marriage and Parenthood Ideologies (in percentages)

	Marriage	*Parenthood*
Ontological	28.7	17.3
Deontological: God	4.3	4.3
Deontological: Society/role	8.7	16.9
Deontological: Self	7.9	9.4
Goal: Society or role	1.6	5.1
Goal: Self	31.5	75.9
Fun	0.8	4.7
Enjoyment	9.8	29.1
Pleasure	2.8	9.4
Love	6.7	13.8
Companionship	11.8	9.1
Keep busy	0.4	2.3
Other hedonistic	2.8	1.2
Security	6.3	3.1
Lineage	0	1.2
Understanding	0.4	0.4
Avoid selfishness	0.4	6.7
Not important	4.8	2.3
Conditionally important	5.9	2.8

SOURCE: Computed from Growth of American Families Single Women Study. See Appendix 4. Coding by the author.

NOTE: Respondents could offer as many as four ideologies pertaining to marriage and four pertaining to parenthood.

development" ideologies emphasized will and feeling but did not distinguish pleasure in particular. And "hedonistic" ideologies focused on pleasurable return to the woman herself.

Hedonistic ideologies, surprisingly rarely appealed to on the whole, were remarkably rarely used to explain why marriage in particular was important. The importance of children, however, was sometimes said to rest in the "fun" or pleasure they offered their parents. Love, a bit more common (though surprisingly rare in view of our expectations), was likewise conspicuously rarer with respect to marriage than to childbearing. The related notion of companionship outweighed love as applied to marriage, while the reverse was the case when respondents were talking about parenthood; the two summed were 30 percent more common in explaining childbearing than in explaining marriage. In the 1953 study, companionship was the most common reason for marriage nominated by single men and one of the most common among married men, but it was rather rare among women, both single and married. Almost nobody proposed love as an explanation for the importance of marriage. Enjoyment, midway between the least and the most emotionally freighted of the more hedonistic responses, was also the most common. Three times the proportion of young women explained the importance of childbirth in these terms as spoke this way of marriage. Was marriage no pleasure to these baby boom women?

Childbearing, in contrast, was deeply linked into these young women's sense of self-fulfillment—an ideological justification that was much the most common. The line separating self-fulfillment from the obligation to become all one can or, alternatively, the goal or obligation of becoming what one should be is no doubt a fine one to make in just a few words, depending no doubt on linguistic quirks or verbal clichés of the day. And yet the evidence in table 36 does surely seem to indicate a predominance of an expansive sense of goal-seeking self-fulfillment at the very heart of the baby boom ideology, achieved through becoming a mother. Such a sense of expansive voluntary self-fulfillment, too, most often justified marriage ideologically, but the gap between its application to the two aspects of family formation is large and eloquent.

Noteworthy also is the far higher component of obligation when the young women came to explain why they felt that marriage was important. Thus, two and one-half times as many of the young women said that voluntary self-development was the reason for childbearing as said this about marriage. But only one and one-third as many said the duty of self-development explained childbearing as explained marriage in this way. Relatively few respondents justified family formation in terms of voluntary assumption of women's roles. Of these, however, more were found among the ideologies of parenthood than of wifehood, and this was truest among those women who said they thought these roles were important to take on for reasons of obligation. God's duty was only occasionally invoked here, but when it was, it was as likely to refer to marriage as to child-bearing. And the unexplored assumption that family formation was in the nature of things far more often referred to marriage than to parenthood. To be a mother was very much more vivid, important, thought-about, and valued at the height of the baby boom than to be a wife.

As early marriage came to be in some tension with a declin-ing romantic motive, and childbearing became correspondingly more focal to marriages, a contradiction developed between the felt economic needs of the young couple and the wish to be-come parents. A fair amount of the growing consumer pros-perity of the postwar had been premised on the capacity of young wives to earn second incomes. Young wives were encour-aged to work, but they were culturally expected to be full-time mothers when children came. Blood and Wolfe present data showing a drop from 62 to 16 percent in the labor force par-ticipation of wives with husbands' incomes below $5,000 when children entered the family, and from 43 to 3 percent for wives whose husbands earned more than this.[129] When children came quickly, they often pressed parents into a very trying phase in the marriage, as wives' roles shifted rapidly and family incomes were slowly constricted by the loss of wives' earnings and the demands of the new baby. Both in families with husbands bringing in a relatively large amount of money and those less fortunate in this regard, "satisfaction with the standard of liv-ing declines with the onslaught of children, ebbing still further as they acquire school-age appetites and wardrobes."[130] The trend in the 1950s was toward heavier participation in the paid labor force for wives with young children (11.9 percent of those with children under six in 1950), growing rapidly during the Korean conflict but continuing to climb in the latter part of the decade, attaining 18.7 percent in 1959.[131] The trend ran steadily against the very definitions of parenthood according to which childbirth was the climactic, confirmatory, central event of the youth-to-adult portion of the life course. The drama of young people's family formation sequence in the baby boom thus often ended with a most ambiguous curtain.

The youthful life course of the baby boom embodied a paradox: highly "traditional" satisfactions were dependent on highly asymmetrical gender roles, accomplished through an unprecedented translation into young individuals' hands of the material resources they required to accomplish their volition. The baby boom era was ushered in by a cresting wave of economic optimism, especially prominent along a cohort of young people that was relatively small and thus relatively favored. It could not last, and it did not. By the late 1960s, the national economy was in the throes of a gnawing inflation, and the first children of the much-enlarged postwar birth cohorts were coming of age, no longer confronting rapidly or surely growing material resources.[132] At the same time, ideological critique found pervasive flaws in the gender asymmetries and individualistic materialism that underlay the baby boom life course. In the era that was to follow, such characteristic baby boom institutions as dating, early marriage, and parenthood promptly after marriage were to fall into disuse.

7
MODERN IN A NEW WAY

QUESTIONING MARRIAGE

When a national survey of a representative sample of American adults in 1976 asked how marriage changes people's lives, answers differed characteristically from the way people had answered an identical open-ended question at the height of the baby boom. Marriage, to start with, was now simply less *interesting* to Americans, or, at least, they talked less about it.[1] In 1957, female respondents had offered an average of about three answers, while men had on average offered about two answers apiece. In the middle of the 1970s, women suggested fewer than two ways in which marriage changed life, while men saw fit to mention only about one and a quarter, on average. More telling, both men and women changed most in the number of *positive* ways in which they thought marriage changed life. Negative comments declined less, almost approaching positive ones in frequency. The feeling-tone with which people contemplated the marriage transition was much more removed, less engaged, and, where engaged, absolutely far less positive, and relatively far more nearly centered near neutrality.[2] Already, as we have seen, marriage in the baby boom had seemed to young women an institution not complete except as complemented by parenthood. By the mid-1970s, certainties about parenthood had faded, too, and marriage had to face scrutiny unclothed in the glow of "the home." The post-baby boom decade, too, offered mainly problematic and self-conscious life course choices on the way to marriage, as to adulthood generally. The focus of youth culture ceased to be on popularity and the social graces on which popularity had rested; and a peer group hesitant to render judgment ceased to oversee heterosexual rela-

Table 37. Average Number of Responses to Questions about How Life Changes at Marriage and Proportions Offering Selected Responses, by Sex, 1957 and 1976

	Males		Females	
	1957	*1976*	*1957*	*1976*
Distinct Responses per Respondent				
Positive	0.93	0.39	1.11	0.53
Neutral	0.89	0.65	1.45	0.96
Negative	0.30	0.25	0.52	0.40
1976 Less than 1957				
Positive Emotional Changes				
Any exaggerated response	1.6%	0.6%	1.2%	0.4%
Other emotional benefits				
n.e.c.	2.7%	1.3%	2.5%	0.9%
Positive Changes in Personal Characteristics				
Settles you down	9.1%	5.0%	3.0%	0.7%
Become less self-centered	3.2%	2.5%	6.1%	3.2%
Gives you a goal	5.8%	2.7%	2.2%	0.5%
Gives you ambition	5.3%	1.3%	0.7%	0.1%
Other personal characteristics n.e.c.	4.5%	2.6%	2.5%	1.8%
Positive Changes in Situation Entered				
Have your own home	5.8%	0.8%	4.6%	1.2%
Have family and children	3.0%	1.3%	3.8%	1.9%
Neutral Changes in Relationship				
Settles you down	15.1%	7.2%	5.7%	2.5%
Other	3.7%	2.4%	4.4%	1.3%
Neutral Changes in Situation Entered				
New things to be done	15.3%	12.4%	18.1%	13.7%
You stay home	7.2%	2.8%	4.0%	0.9%
1976 More than 1957				
Neutral Changes in Relationship				
Must learn to get along with spouse	6.1%	10.2%	13.7%	16.8%
Do something for someone else	9.3%	17.2%	18.5%	28.8%

Table 37. (*continued*)

	Males		Females	
	1957	*1976*	*1957*	*1976*
Neutral Changes in Situation Entered				
New responsibility in situation	21.1%	34.1%	15.4%	17.5%
Negative Changes in Situation Entered				
Less freedom	13.6%	21.1%	15.0%	19.9%

SOURCE: Computed from data set, "Americans View Their Mental Health, 1957 and 1976: Selected Variables." See Appendix 4.

NOTES: Numbers of cases were 1957 males–1,077; 1957 females–1,383; 1976 males–960; 1976 females–1,304. The questions read: "First, thinking about a (man's/woman's—SAME SEX AS RESPONDENT) life. How is a (man's/woman's) life changed by being married?"

tionships, robbing dating of its mechanism and meaning, which had depended on, and promoted, imminent marriage.

Table 37 shows the proportion of men and women in each year who expressed particular versions of what happens in the transition to marriage. The table includes a large number of categories of response that became markedly less common and a smaller number of responses that became more common. The latter are grouped at the bottom. Attention to *emotional* aspects of the marriage transition was never common and became only somewhat less so. More common in both years but considerably reduced in the intervening two decades were changes that marriage brought to *one's self*, conceived as benefits. In 1957, nearly one in ten men had thought it a positive aspect of the marriage transition that men then began to "settle down." Only half this many men saw marriage in that light in 1976. In 1957, even more men had remarked "settling down" negatively, and *this* response, too, lost half its currency, as did the neutrally evaluated "you stay home" response. The marriage transition, that is, simply implied less about men's other roles. Similarly, women in 1957 commonly saw themselves as too selfish before marriage, but by 1976 this motive had also declined by half. In 1957, men who lacked goals and ambitions had commonly found them when they married; this was no longer the case in 1976. The powerful symbol of "home," which we found prevalent among unmarried young women in 1955, was also common among men in the 1957 sample. Yet for both men and women, the symbol of home lost some of its valence over the period.

There were some things about marriage that 1970s respondents remarked more commonly than had been remarked in the baby boom. There is a common thread in the way marriage came to affect life over these years. What previously had often had a *positive* affect attached to it, when dealing with how marriage makes one a better person by giving one various responsibilities, now was presented neutrally: one must learn to get along with someone else (not having done so quite so prominently before in one's life); one must learn to do something for someone else (rather than for oneself, as previously was typically the case); and the situation contained new responsibilities (responsibility no longer being so commonly as before something to be sought for one's justification in the world but merely as a neutral fact of life). Moreover, while negative evaluations, as we have seen, were not very common in either year, one was—that one *lost freedom* on marriage. The loss of autonomy that accompanies marriage came to be considerably more frequently remarked, expressed by one in five men *and* women in 1976.

By the mid-1970s, men and women entered marriage with changed timing, following a somewhat altered process that itself was evaluated differently, transformed that relationship into parenthood more reluctantly, and, startlingly more commonly, terminated it. What recently seemed natural no longer seemed so.

Even by the end of the 1950s, signs had appeared that the baby boom had reached its limits. Overall fertility rates peaked in 1957. For childless women at age 21, the probability of becoming a parent within the year reached its peak that same year. Annual marriage probabilities for single girls under 21 peaked, too. Young men, however, continued to marry younger well into the next decade. Through the 1960s, men's marriage

**Annual Rate
(Percent)**

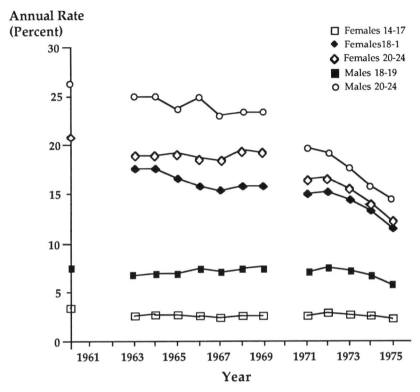

Figure 20. Annual Rate of First Marriage, by Age and Sex, 1961–1975

probabilities at the modal ages held steady, but for women, that decade represented a retreat in marriage probabilities at virtually all ages. National data permit us to portray the story with precision, in figure 20. For the very youngest brides (and grooms), many of whom married under the duress of pregnancy, rates remained roughly stable. Among women, the once-prime marriage age of 18 to 19 saw fewer and fewer marriages through the first half of the 1960s, leveled momentarily, and then became less common once again in the first half of the 1970s. Much of this pattern also characterized women at 20 to 24, although somewhat less emphatically. For young men, young marriages actually increased in the mid-1960s, and held fairly strong into the early 1970s. The rate that truly collapsed in the 1970s was for marriage at the most typical ages.

MARRIAGE BY CHOICE

Women who enjoyed a relatively broad range of roles, alternative to marriage, had long been likely to marry later, everything
else being equal.[3] Of these roles, one—gainful employment—
had grown considerably in prevalence over the past few decades and in the 1960s and 1970s grew especially rapidly
in acceptance as a thoroughly appropriate role for women,
whether married or single, mother or childless. From 1968 to
1972, as Waite and Spitze found, both enrollment in school and
a positive evaluation of gainful employment (although not momentary employment *per se*) contributed substantially to marital
postponement. The authors conclude that in this period, "the
chances of [single women] marrying appear to decrease with
increases in the availability and attractiveness of alternatives to
the wife role and in the costs of assuming" that role.[4]

The late 1960s and early 1970s were characterized by a widespread cultural politics regarding the nature of gender, marital, and familial roles, which was made possible by a generation
of economic growth, increased education, and emancipation
from parental oversight and given force by an ultimately feminist perception that marriage had a differential impact on
the lives of women and men. As economic sufficiency and the
propriety for which it was the metaphor became a less salient
aspect of marital timing, the relationship of love to marriage—
and even love's signs—came into question. As Mason and Bumpass found in a close analysis of a 1970 national survey of
women, a reasonably clearly defined cluster of attitudinal items
cohered by this date, amounting to a "sex-role ideology" among
women.[5] These items, strongly correlated with education and
religiosity, included a generalized item regarding gender-role
symmetry, several regarding potential conflict between work
and motherhood, and one involving the degree of happiness
associated with the homemaker role. Understandably, one's position on this increasingly salient dimension was closely connected both with how one had arrived at that position and how
one intended to build one's family thereafter. The life course
was being debated, piecemeal.

Two aspects of marital ideology that might be expected to

have had a bearing on life course timing concerned gender roles within marriage and premarital sexuality. (1) Couples favoring "segregated" marital roles, with the domestic sphere and the world of work clearly demarcated and assigned to wife and husband, respectively, would in theory anticipate delay in marriage mainly to be sure of true love and to attain a material sufficiency. The latter problem might be alleviated for those contemplating a two-career "nonsegregated" marriage, but the uncertainties about residence, coordinating extended education, and other matters would seem to be considerably enlarged, and the success of the marriage to rest on their proper working out. (2) More permissive views regarding premarital sex would seem to challenge the baby boom outlook on marital timing, according to which true love is unique, closely identified with marriage and parenthood, and sanctified by avoidance of extramarital sex if at all possible. Under newer, more permissive interpretations that separated marriage from sexual expression, we should expect that people would contemplate delayed marriage, for the decision to marry would now involve many considerations besides locating one's true love. And with freer sexual expression outside of marriage, one pressure to early marriage would be removed. Even as expressed in conventionalized love sequences of popular music in the late 1960s, one finds in contrast to the 1950s courtship sequences the emergence of a more openly sexual definition of love and a marked loosening of the classic love-and-marriage sequence.[6]

Two questions on a representative national survey carried out in 1974 which treated premarital sexuality and two questions that dealt with marital roles give us quantitative evidence of the strength of these theoretical ties.[7] Slightly fewer than half the respondents said that they could "find acceptable" an arrangement in which a hypothetical daughter of theirs, just out of school, lived unmarried with a man. Six in ten agreed that "premarital sexual intercourse is immoral." About one in three women respondents, asked whether they preferred "to have a job outside the home" rather than "stay home and take care of a house and family," chose the job alternative. Slightly fewer women said that they thought that "a traditional marriage with the husband assuming the responsibility for providing for the family and the wife running the house to take care of the children would give them personally the most satisfying and interesting life." These four ideological variables were allowed to enter a multiple regression after numerous background items (including respondent's ideal number of children) had been entered. In predicting ideal age at marriage proposed by both male and female respondents, all four ideological items made significant contributions. Even after accounting for the effects of numerous other items, the more contemporary ideologies a respondent asserted, the later the ideal marriage age he or she was likely to hold out—about a quarter to half a year later *per ideology.*

By 1974, then, ideals of marital timing were part of a structure of values and attitudes then actively under contest within the population at large. Never strictly a product of position within the social structure, never strictly a product of the rationalization of prior behavior, ideals of the timing of marriage had always been subject to "period" shifts. And the generation that approached "family-building" in the late 1960s and early 1970s was, increasingly, a *large* generation, competing sharply (or anticipating a sharp competition) for a set of economic niches that was growing only at a moderate pace. It was, moreover, as Richard Easterlin has argued forcefully, a generation whose tastes for material well-being had been formed during the exhilarating economic optimism of the baby boom period, when they were growing up in their parents' homes. "An important factor affecting a young couple's willingness to marry and to have children is their outlook for supporting their material aspirations. If the couple's potential earning power is high in relation to aspirations, they will have an optimistic outlook and will feel freer to marry and have children. If their outlook is poor relative to aspirations, the couple will feel pessimistic and, consequently, will be hesitant to marry and have children."[8]

Changes in gender-role behavior and ideology, in attitudes toward divorce, and in the privileging of private feeling as the ideological basis for marriage point to the emergence of a new structure for American marriages, one that left standing much of the formal institutional significance of marriage. Insofar as women's lack of adequate material and emotional alternatives to marriage formerly kept them from protesting or leaving unions that were in substantial ways distasteful to them, recent labor market trends have been causally related to the increase in divorce. Wives' and mothers' increasing labor-force participation more and more has incorporated the notion of *career* and the belief that engagement and success in the job arena is an important, positively sanctioned, and fulfilling task. For unprecedented numbers of Americans, the family-formation process has involved a more or less brief first marriage, an ironically—or embarrassingly—recapitulative second courtship, and a remarriage, often with different expectations from the first time around. No less, most Americans do not assume as they once had the enduring quality of marriage, much as they also no longer so easily assume its unique sway over sexuality and its capacity to make one whole.

We have, then, a two-phased phenomenon: first, a retreat from the baby boom in the early 1960s, and, second, the establishment of a new "marriage-bust" schedule in the early 1970s. The former may perhaps be understood as the *restoration* of the previous normal. But the latter raised questions in many observers' minds that the nation's youth had turned decisively away from the family. By traveling a bit afield we can find some intriguing clues. These clues, understood rightly, however, challenge the argument that family formation *per se* had lost ground as a vital step in the lives of young people.

The timing of marriages *during the year*, for instance, offers indirect evidence of a tendency toward *increased selectiveness* in marriage in the late 1960s and 1970s. It is no news that more marriages are contracted in some months than in others. June marriages, for instance, have for some time been particularly favored by Americans, offering sentimental connotations that are valued by many. The most "selective" marriers (in terms of a preferential choice of months) are typically those who marry at the modal age—just as modal-age marriages typically are the most often celebrated religiously. Although June's popularity was perennial between 1960 and 1975, ever-larger proportions of the year's marriages were celebrated during the half-year that extended from March through August. And the shift was most dramatic at the modal marriage ages.[9] Thus, in 1960, only the slightest of majorities of marriages of men at age 20 to 24 had been celebrated during the March-August period—51.0 percent. (September was then a more popular month for marriages than it was to become.) By 1975, this proportion had risen to 59.8 percent. For those marrying very young, there was essentially *no trend*. But for those marrying at the modal age, or a little on the old side, there was a decided trend toward *increased selectivity*. For men marrying at 20 to 24, the increase was from an average coefficient of variation of 0.275 in 1960–61 and an identical reading in 1964–65 (before the change in men's marriage patterns toward more delayed marriages had really begun) to an average of 0.325 in 1969–70 to an average of 0.350 in 1974–75.[10] The change in selectivity in just fifteen years is not quite so great as the age-to-age difference in any given year, but they approach those differences.

Analogously, figure 21 shows that when young people married, they were increasingly likely to do so at home. Proportions of brides marrying away from their home states declined by half and more, especially when the bride was quite young. The postponement of marriage resulted in a *great reduction of elopements*, especially at the youngest age. As youthful marriages of girls and their marriages altogether become less common, marriage became a more deliberate matter, and elopement more frowned on. (Recall the trend to more elaborate weddings, reported in chap. 1.) Marriage, arguably, had become less romantic by comparison with the baby boom, but this surely does not mean that it mattered less to its participants. For brides at the acceptable but rather old age of 25, by contrast, the decrease in out-of-state marriages was not very striking. The changes in marriage, such as they were, *affected young marriages in particular*. Further reinforcing this conclusion is the fact that (for 1972 to 1975, when such data are available) the category of marriage that was declining in frequency the *most* rapidly during this period was usually the least considered kind of marriage: young, migratory, civil marriage.

Despite the turning away from early marriage, *eventual* marriage was nevertheless an important element in the plans of adolescents even in the mid-1970s. The 1976 National Study of

Percent

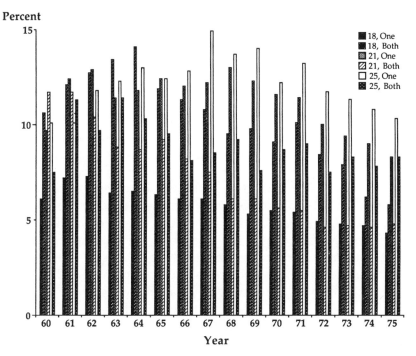

Figure 21. Percent of Nonresident Marriages, 1960–1975

Adolescent Female Sexuality, employing very sophisticated survey methodology,[11] yields some interesting insight into the subjective side of the marriage process. The survey asked about current marital status, and also whether "you ... are ... engaged or seriously considering getting married to someone you are now dating." The proportion already married at age 15 was close to 2 percent, rising slowly to 6 percent at age 17. At 18, the proportion was 16 percent, rising to 29 percent at 19. But already at age 15, 9 percent of those not already married had marriage plans, a proportion that rose regularly to 30 percent at 18 and 31 percent at 19. At each age, then, more girls had marriage plans than had yet been married. To judge from Monitoring the Future, a contemporaneous survey of high school seniors, about one out of three of these girls who were seriously contemplating marriage were formally engaged. Formal engagement, however, was at this point a fairly rare phenomenon among young people. As of 1976, a bit under 10 percent of senior girls were engaged and only 4 percent of the senior boys (not yet married).[12] Strikingly, socioeconomic status and size of town hardly affected engagement probabilities at all, net of their slight relationship to the age of the senior, which had a significant but not overpowering relationship in the expected direction.[13] Students for whom religion played a large role in their lives were significantly more likely to be engaged, but here, too, the relationship was not overpowering. Part of the reason was that by 1976, higher education seemed to foreclose, or at any rate push back, near-term marriage plans. Only rarely were those intending to go on to college currently engaged; the surer about college plans, the less likely was engagement. In the 1970s, quite unlike a half-generation earlier, plans to enter the armed services, albeit now rare, had the same effect. Having higher grades, net of their effect on college plans, led to a marginally *greater* likelihood of being engaged.

All these plans were caught up in patterns of the seniors' current social lives. Those who dated much were less likely to expect to graduate from college. And they were *very much more likely* to be engaged. Those who instead socialized with peers on a nondate basis were *less* likely to be engaged. The nature of seniors' current social lives exercised an effect on engagement far more prepotent than any of the background or near-term plan variables. Engagement seemed to represent a unique commitment that ran somewhat against involvement with nondate peer activities.

NONMARITAL COHABITATION

If engagement amounted to a presumably declining "traditional" path to marriage, nonmarital cohabitation surely became more common. Arguably, it even competed with marriage, at least for a phase in young people's lives. Cohabitation was once characteristic largely of lower-class persons; now, as it spread, it was increasingly acceptable within middle-class mores.[14] As of the 1970s, however, the pattern was far more common among blacks than among whites and, within each race, among less well educated persons.[15] Clayton and Voss, who also found that blacks cohabited more but that the propensity of young men to cohabit was not particularly closely related to their socioeconomic status, found instead a number of ideologically relevant indicators that were most closely related to the decision to cohabit. These included past use of marijuana, attendance at rock concerts, and political activism. Those who attended church frequently, by contrast, rarely engaged in this now common life course practice.[16] Of those young men who did not attend church services, for instance, 26 percent had cohabited, whereas only 7 percent of those who attended church weekly had; a quarter of the young men who had sometimes used marijuana had cohabited, but only 8 percent of those who never tried it cohabited. Strikingly, age at initiation of sexual intercourse was not particularly predictive of having cohabited. The initiation of coital sexuality no longer carried social meaning as cogently as it once had, certainly for young men. The kinds of "life-style" preferences to which premarital cohabitation was connected were ones that reflected relatively public stands. Beth L. Bailey suggests that in the 1960s and 1970s "metaphors of revolution" replaced "metaphors of economy" in the terms in which young Americans gave subculturally sanctioned meanings to their sexuality.[17]

The simple fact of easy access to appropriate housing facilitated cohabitation and probably contributed to assumptions about autonomy that fit this newly acceptable arrangement. By 1975, at a given moment, one in seven young people 20 to 24 years old were living solo, and many were obviously able at their convenience to arrange their private lives as suited themselves. Between 1970 and 1975, the proportion of young single men living by themselves more than doubled. Among young women, the gains in singles living alone were equally dramatic. Living apart gave individuals more ability than other arrangements would to set the terms of their own day-to-day existence, to discover a life-style that fit their "personality," to gain a sense of what might be wanted in a long-term partner, and in addition to have an arrangement consistent with a growing "segregation by age, both within and outside families."[18] By far the largest part of the increased propensity for living alone—not only in youth but at all ages—can be explained by a rise in disposable income that allowed unprecedented numbers to realize their wish for privacy.[19] Apparently, too, living outside of family contexts has had the effect of teaching young women "tastes and skills that are likely to reduce their orientation to family roles" in the future. Indeed, longitudinal data from the mid-1960s to the mid-1970s shows conclusively that *quite apart from initial predispositions*, those who spent relatively great proportions of their youths outside of family contexts were more likely to favor such characteristic post-baby boom innovations as working mothers and small families.[20]

Did "living together," one element of nonfamily living, constitute a phase in life that was an *alternative* to marriage or was it, instead, an emergent life course stage on the way to marriage? What were the implications of a widespread acceptance of a form of behavior recently considered scandalous, in view of the fact that its condemnation had been so closely associated for so long with both the immediate reasons for marrying and the deeper assumptions underlying marriage? Answers to these questions depend on whether nonmarital cohabitation tended to postpone marriage, to inhibit it, or actually to preclude it. When we have a grip on the life course implications of the arrangement in the 1970s, we can turn to an examination of the ideological correlates of affirmation of cohabitation to see whether it fit together with a set of values that might disparage, or at any rate discourage, conventional values about marriage and the family.

The empirical literature offers little data suggesting that cohabitation discouraged eventual marriage, even when it postponed it. Indeed, there is some suggestion in the literature that cohabitation did not even much postpone marriage.[21] In Clayton and Voss's sample of young men, cohabitation led to marriage in a bit over one in three cases; it was, that is, about half as likely to lead to marriage as had engagement a few decades earlier. The phase was one of experimentation, but it was usually a serious experiment about a long-term relationship, not one of mere convenience or of promiscuous sexual adventure. Cohabiting couples were somewhat more likely than other courting couples of like ages and who had known one another for about the same length of time to express love toward one another. They also tended to consider themselves especially open to a wide range of intimate sharing. Cohabiting young men also considered themselves, but did not prove themselves to be, more open to symmetrical gender-role structures.[22]

Two separate time series, based on large and carefully drawn samples of young people, indicate that sometime around the mid-1970s affirmation of cohabitation as a value reached a peak and declined thereafter, having fallen short of becoming normative. In the first, Astin *et al.* collected data on assent to an item asking college freshmen for their response to cohabitation as an experimental period, posed positively toward the notion that a couple *should* live together for some time before deciding to get married. These show peaks of support of 43 percent for girls in 1976 and 55 percent for boys in 1977.[23]

The second time series is based on the annual Monitoring the Future surveys of high school seniors. The first question posed cohabitation as a prior *supplement to marriage* ("it is usually a good idea"), while the second posed it as an arrangement rightly *precluded by marriage* ("fuller and happier lives" were based on legal marriage "rather than staying single or just living with someone"). Between 1976 and 1980, male students gradually withdrew their assent to cohabitation as a supplement to marriage; female students gradually enlarged their conviction that marriage ought to preclude prior cohabitation.[24] With these trends, the two genders moved toward more nearly shared responses to the two values.

The survey also proposed an item that hypothetically rejected monogamy, because "having a close intimate relationship is too restrictive for the average person." Fewer than a quarter of the high schoolers—more boys than girls—accepted this notion. Monogamy, at any rate serial monogamy, was not an issue that was a part of the distinctive set of attitudes young people contemplated in the mid-1970s. But cohabitation, as we have seen, was. The religious overwhelmingly rejected cohabitation. Even more strongly, those whose youth-oriented "radicalness" extended to approving of the legalization of marijuana use *favored* it. Youth who believed that the conventional family system seemed in crisis—with few marriages that worked—favored cohabitation, as did those whose general political views were to the left. Those who reported much conflict with their parents favored cohabitation, as did those who spent a lot of evenings out with the gang. *Frequent daters, however, were only marginally more prone than infrequent daters to favor cohabitation.*[25] These patterns should be contrasted with those regarding formal engagement, the "traditional" path.

MARRIAGE AND PARENTHOOD BY CHOICE

Table 38 examines for the period 1960 to 1975 the ages of brides and grooms each of whom were marrying for the first time in the year noted, *in relationship to one another.* We look here for indications in change in the cultural rules and individual expectations governing the way marriages were contracted. The table presents data on only the considerable majority of first marriages that, at these relatively modal ages, were with spouses who had not previously married. The decline in average groom's age relative to bride's is noticeable here at all brides' ages, following from women's earlier and more marked tendency to postponement after the end of the baby boom. For younger brides, we see, most of the decline was in the early 1960s, between 1960–1961 and 1964–1965. However, the standard deviations give evidence of the *selectivity* of their choice of spouse.[26] And what this portion of the table shows tells a very important but less obvious part of the story of the "marriage decline" of the 1960s and 1970s. Except for the youngest brides, selectivity on the basis of age *increased* in this period. For rather young brides, the increase in selectivity of age occurred in the early 1960s, when their grooms became younger. For brides from about age 21 and older, however, the period of most marked change was the late 1960s. Grooms' ages, that is, were increasingly likely to be *similar to one another*, as brides of a given age found husbands who (in this respect) more nearly resembled one another and, presumably, the "norm." Alternatively, the brides found grooms more alike, in this respect, because the *process* by which they found them was becoming more similar.

And this occurred *without* grooms at given ages (certainly beyond the quite young) themselves becoming less selective in their choice of spouse (with regard to age). The age selectivity

Table 38. Mean and Standard Deviation of Spouse's Age at Marriage for Brides and Grooms of Selected Ages, When Both Partners Are Marrying for First Time, Selected Dates, 1960–1975

	Means					
	Grooms, at age			*Brides, at age*		
	20	*23*	*26*	*18*	*21*	*24*
1960	18.7	20.4	22.0	21.0	23.4	26.3
1961	18.8	20.4	22.3	21.0	23.5	26.9
1964	18.8	20.6	22.1	20.8	23.0	26.0
1965	18.8	20.7	22.1	20.6	23.1	26.0
1969	19.0	20.9	22.6	20.5	22.7	25.8
1970	19.0	20.9	22.6	20.5	22.8	25.8
1974	19.0	21.0	22.7	20.4	22.8	25.5
1975	19.0	21.0	22.8	20.5	22.9	25.5

	Standard Deviations					
	Grooms, at age			*Brides, at age*		
	20	*23*	*26*	*18*	*21*	*24*
1960	1.65	2.35	3.52	2.74	3.47	4.41
1961	1.59	2.64	3.60	2.81	3.44	4.90
1964	1.62	2.28	3.10	2.56	3.14	4.19
1965	1.66	2.26	3.07	2.49	3.08	4.31
1969	1.69	2.34	3.34	2.54	2.88	3.91
1970	1.67	2.28	3.19	2.60	2.89	4.07
1974	1.73	2.40	3.32	2.67	2.90	3.76
1975	1.85	2.43	3.27	2.73	3.23	3.69

SOURCE: Calculated from USNCHS *Vital Statistics*, III, annual.

of marriage at given ages became more pronounced as young people turned away from early marriage toward a seemingly more deliberate model of this life course transition. There is, of course, nothing inherently excellent about homogeneity, but the fact that modality was more than preserved and, indeed, considerably accentuated in the post-baby boom regime indicates that marriages were not just contracted slowly but also carefully, according to rules or processes that were commonly recognized within the cohorts who married. The finding here corresponds to ones regarding month of marriage and elopement.

The predominant trend in fertility within marriage through most of this period was markedly downward, as "family building" lost prominence among the motives of American young people. But, as with marriage, a new perspective on the matter can be discovered by subjecting some of the detailed patterns to close scrutiny. One way of seeing what happened as the distinctive baby boom fertility patterns receded is to examine what kinds of couple were most likely to *recently* have had children. Ronald R. Rindfuss and James A. Sweet have done this, comparing the 1960 and 1970 censuses.[27] Table 39, extracted from an exceptionally comprehensive analysis they performed, compares the numbers of children born in 1957–1960 and 1967–1970 to women currently married and under 40 years of age at the census date. The table presents deviations in recent fertility according to age at marriage, years since marriage, and numbers of children already in the family, *net of* the impact of race, husband's occupation and income, wife's education, region, and type of place of residence.[28]

Table 39 indicates that by 1970, a marital fertility schedule was in place in which—in strong contrast to 1960—any completed family size of *over one* had on net an inhibitory effect on recent fertility. But childlessness, or having only a single child, was seemingly still a situation to be remedied through childbearing, *indeed, to a greater degree than in 1960.* At the end of the baby boom, too, fertility was considerably more likely to be crammed into the years immediately following marriage than was to be the case a decade later. Net of all other factors, late baby boom couples in the third to sixth years of their marriages would likely have had no fewer than 1.07 children under 3 years old, whereas in 1970, such couples would have only 0.73 children. The peakedness and sharpness of decline over the course of the marriage was markedly more pronounced at the end of the baby boom in a mother's late thirties. The reduced

Table 39. Net Impact of Selected Family-Building Characteristics on Deviations from Mean Number of Children under Three Years Old at Census Date, Born to Currently Married Women, 1960 and 1970

	1960	1970
Wife's Age at Marriage		
<18	.09	.04
18–19	.03	.04
20–21	.00	.00
22–24	−.05	−.06
25–29	−.15	−.12
30+	−.30	−.20
Years since Marriage		
<3 Years	.08	−.02
3–5.9 years	.53	.32
6–8.9 years	.24	.19
9–11.9 years	−.04	−.01
12–14.9 years	−.23	−.14
15–17.9 years	−.33	−.24
18–20.9 years	−.44	−.30
21–23.9 years	−.52	−.33
24+ years	−.48	−.32
Children Previously Born		
None	−.01	.11
1	.00	.05
2	−.06	−.10
3	.00	−.10
4	.15	−.04
Mean Number of Children under Three	0.55	0.41

SOURCE: Extracted from Ronald L. Rindfuss and James A. Sweet, *Postwar Fertility Trends* (New York: Academic Press, 1977), table 4-1. Based on multiple classification analysis model with the above variables plus race, husband's occupation, education, region, and type of place of residence in the model.

fertility of the late-1960s was a bit more *ad hoc* in this sense than in the baby boom. So, too, age at marriage, once a very pronounced factor in explaining fertility patterns had become less pronounced in the late 1960s, without the pattern itself becoming entirely vitiated. The early baby boom marriage schedule was prominent among the same kinds of women for whom the rapid conversion of the couple into the family—the making of the "home"—had been the most compelling. More than vestiges of this pattern remained, to be sure, but they were passing by 1967 to 1970.

Reliable, representative national data on contraceptive use (among women ever married) suggest rather slow growth from the 1940s until the 1960s. (Contraception, of course, is only one aspect of fertility limitation.) White and black women who married young were throughout far less frequently given to contraception than were women who married a few years later and perhaps were more deliberate in their approach to life course transitions generally. A radical change in *method* employed seems to explain a good deal of the rapid change in the 1960s. Withdrawal was practically gone from the repertory of fertility limitation by then, but a premonitory decline in favorability to douching foreshadowed the sharp moving away from both condom and diaphragm (and douche) brought by the technical advances in the anovulatory pill and then the intrauterine device.[29] In the 1960s, the nature of control in contraceptive activity shifted again, as the condom and diaphragm were replaced in general use by the pill and the IUD.[30]

An important part of the fertility decline was in the *pace* of entering parenthood.[31] Retrospective marital and fertility histories taken in 1975 indicate that for both whites and blacks, marriage and parenthood had faded considerably as a *joint* pattern, a pair of statuses chosen and entered in close sequence as part of a single package.[32] The change, preferences, or means that affected new families in the early 1970s focused particularly on *not becoming parents immediately on marriage*, on being married and childless for a period of time, much as increasing numbers of couples were electing a period of premarital cohabitation *as couples*. The tenth month of marriage, for example, was one-fourth less likely to be a fertile one for whites marrying in the second half of the 1960s than in the first half of the decade (but just about as likely for black women); it was almost half less likely to be fertile, again, for women whose marriages came in the first half of the 1970s as those in the previous half-decade (and this time, black wives reflected the new pattern of postponed parenthood even more strongly than did white wives). Only by about the end of the second year of marriage did these declines in monthly parenthood probabilities cease. It is obvious that the diffusion of legal abortion after 1973 had begun to play a role, but abortion was merely a means to an arrangement of one's life over time which already made sense to numbers of people, enlarging a pattern that had begun to be manifest. It can be seen as a further extension of the spread of contraceptive knowledge and practice, which, continuing into the 1970s, had become almost universal (within marriage) by middecade.[33]

Tsui's tabulations, based on raw data from the same 1975 retrospects, indicate that overall the average interval (for those who had children after marrying) from marriage to first childbirth remained roughly constant over this period but that *the standard deviation increased.*[34] Partly, this decreased concentration of childbearing followed from a *reduced impact of the timing of marriage on the balance of family formation,* a pattern also visible in table 39. In the baby boom, young women had found it uninspiring, or practically inconceivable, to think of marriage without parenthood. But now, a volitional phase of childless marriage was more than merely thinkable.[35]

In contrast to the heightened expectations and desires for intimacy between husband and wife, voluntary childless marriage became an acceptable and technically possible arrangement by the mid-1970s, and relatively more parents expressed neutral or even negative orientations to parenthood.[36] Parents seemed to anticipate many of the same good things from having children in 1976 that they had two decades earlier. By 1976, however, an apparent taboo in the earlier year against mentioning bad things about one's relationship to one's children had broken down. Between the mid-1950s and the mid-1970s,

Americans rated the importance in a marriage of understanding, love, and companionship increasingly high relative to the
importance of children to the marriage.[37]

Blake and del Pinal have looked closely at the way a representative sample of American adults in 1978 balanced in
their minds the costs and benefits of becoming parents.[38] They
found that only about one in seven men and women thought
that the benefits of having a child did not at least balance the
costs and that over half of both genders thought that the benefits predominated. They also found that although in the aggregate, younger respondents were less impressed by the advantages of having children, this by and large could be accounted
for by other characteristics jointly associated with relative youth
and less warm attitudes toward parenthood—such as being
currently single. The authors were particularly impressed by
the closeness of the relationship to attitudes toward parenthood
of a set of attitudinal items touching on attitudes toward female
roles, approximating the "women's sex-role ideology" discussed
above.[39] The authors conclude that "it is abundantly clear that
the variables of importance for women are all those measuring
actual and normative (or expected) social roles." With variations in degree according to context, these items each had influenced childbearing attitudes even when all background items
were statistically controlled, just as we have earlier seen was the
case for ideal marriage timing in 1974. Women (and to an extent men) were, by the late 1960s, sorting out family-formation
plans *in terms of contemporary ideological controversies about gender
role.*

Just as marriage had become a less engaging subject to
Americans during the late 1960s and early 1970s, so also had
parenthood, as table 40 indicates. But the change differed in
degree. In fact, a question about the meaning of the parenthood transition (akin to the marriage question discussed earlier) evoked many fewer distinct responses per respondent in
1957 than had the marriage question. But in 1976, it very
nearly did. The reason for the modesty of the decline in numbers of responses between 1957 and 1976 was that there were
by 1976 absolutely more neutral and negative responses than
there had been. In 1957, many of the same values that had

Table 40. Average Number of Responses to Question about How
Life Changes at Parenthood and Proportions Offering
Selected Responses, by Sex, 1957 and 1976

	Males		Females	
	1957	1976	1957	1976
Distinct Responses per Respondent				
Positive	1.10	0.88	1.04	0.86
Neutral	0.57	0.69	0.55	0.63
Negative	0.21	0.27	0.39	0.51
1976 Less than 1957				
General Positive Responses				
Happiness	13.2%	8.5%	13.5%	10.2%
Marriage is completed	4.0%	1.7%	3.6%	1.5%
Other general positive				
n.e.c.	3.7%	2.6%	3.9%	3.0%
Positive Affiliation-related				
Improves relationship				
with spouse	4.6%	2.0%	3.1%	1.0%
Positive Achievement-related				
Ambition	6.5%	2.7%	1.2%	0.2%
Other Positive Satisfaction or				
Interest				
Goal in life	8.4%	3.8%	8.5%	2.4%
Positive Respondent's Personal				
Characteristics				
Less selfish	4.5%	3.1%	8.3%	6.3%
Neutral				
Stability	5.8%	2.9%	3.8%	1.7%
1976 More than 1957				
General Positive Responses				
Fulfillment	2.1%	3.8%	3.7%	7.7%
Positive Influence-related				
Someone to teach	4.1%	5.7%	3.0%	3.4%
Neutral				
General responsibility	23.3%	38.6%	18.9%	32.4%
Negative				
Restrictions on freedom	8.0%	12.3%	18.9%	28.8%

SOURCE: Computed from data set, "Americans View Their Mental Health, 1957 and
1976: Selected Variables."
NOTE: The questions read: "First, thinking about a (man's/woman's—SAME SEX AS
RESPONDENT) life. How is a (man's/woman's) life changed by having children?"

explained what marriage was all about also explained parenthood. By the mid-1970s, as with marriage, Americans less readily espoused values of selflessness, ambition, stability, and the improvement or completion of marriages—*concerns lying outside of themselves as individuals.* Likewise, they were less likely than before to believe that parenthood brought happiness.

What people *did* mention with increasing frequency in 1976 were fulfillment and the value of having someone to teach; and they were now likely to remark, neutrally, that a child brings more responsibility. Growing even more quickly, especially among women, was what amounts to a negative evaluation of the same fact: children are demanding of one's time and energy. More than one in four women and about one in eight men responded negatively that what happens when one becomes a parent is that one loses one's freedom. The author of a study based on representative national surveys about hopes and fears in 1964, 1974, and 1981 described a decline in aspirations for one's children as "the most striking change" in a whole battery of questions about hopes. Noting the rise in children's autonomy and the corresponding decline in parental authority, the author speculated that withdrawal of this aspect of parental affect probably represented "an acceptance of the inevitable."[40] Undoubtedly, concerns of this sort had influenced many men and women in earlier decades. What was new is that these kinds of self-interested criteria not only (and more than before) influenced couples' decisions but they also found articulate form in the new ideologies that swept aside the assurances of the baby boom. Men and women now chose family much as they might choose any other important complement to their selves.

THE NEW ROLE OF DIVORCE

Coincident with the newly deliberate outlook on family formation was a marked upturn in divorce probabilities, backed by a newly accepting outlook on divorce as a legitimate if unfortunate outcome of marriage. The baby boom was a period of relatively stable and low divorce rates. But by 1962 or 1963, the rates began to rise, at a pace that seems too rapid to be explained by changes in the demographic supply and demand in the marriage market.[41] Survey evidence, discussed cogently by Andrew Cherlin, shows that as late as the mid-1960s (a few years after the beginning of the increase in actual divorce behavior) no more Americans than at the end of World War II were in favor of more lenient divorce legislation but that thereafter the proportions of respondents acceding increased sharply for a decade. Cherlin speculates that the increase in actual divorce behavior had actually preceded the change in attitudes. And "once attitudes toward divorce began to change markedly—probably at the start of the 1970s give or take a few years—then the shift in people's beliefs may have provided a new stimulus for further rises in divorce."[42] Before then, individual circumstances or preferences rather than coherent, articulated new value patterns may have propelled the upward trend in marital dissolution.

The rise in divorce affected all marriage cohorts, couples married long ago availing themselves of divorce at a rate that would have been shocking among long-established couples a decade before. In fact, if one looks very closely, one notes a slight tendency throughout the period for a relatively smaller proportion of marriages ending in any given year to have been ones of very brief duration.[43] There was apparently no change in the *seriousness* with which married individuals would contemplate the end of their marriages but rather *a widespread decline in the stigma attached to divorce as an outcome to a marriage, an increased acceptance of divorce as a part of a marriage system* in which the stakes—personal fulfillment—were thought to be very high. There were even signs of a view that divorce was healthy, often initiating a period of personal growth that made the divorced person more sophisticated and interesting.[44] Indicative of the generality of acceptance of divorce, too, is the increase in divorce relative to separation, a pattern consistent from age to age.[45]

The ideological touchstone of this normative trend was "no-fault" divorce, which removed the former adversary structure of divorce proceedings. Family law had previously defined marriage as a lifetime contract unless the flawed behavior of one spouse made such a contract destructive to the other party (the state having an interest in the continuance of marriages). But

Table 41. Proportion of Persons Married 1960–1964 and 1970–1974
Divorced before Next Decennial Census Date, by Age at Marriage, Sex, and Race
(in percentages)

	Whites			Blacks		
	(1) 1960–64 Cohort	(2) 1970–74 Cohort	(3) Ratio of (2) to (1)	(4) 1960–64 Cohort	(5) 1970–74 Cohort	(6) Ratio of (2) to (1)
Men						
14–19	14.7	19.7	1.3	8.9	12.4	1.4
20–24	7.7	11.9	1.6	6.8	12.9	1.9
25–29	4.9	9.6	2.0	5.6	9.4	1.7
30–34	4.6	11.7	2.5	4.7	11.0	2.3
Women						
14–19	17.1	18.2	1.1	7.8	8.5	1.1
20–24	10.7	9.0	0.8	6.6	6.6	1.0
25–29	5.0	7.9	1.6	5.2	7.0	1.4
30–34	3.9	11.3	2.9	4.9	8.7	1.8

SOURCES: Calculated from Census 1970–2, table 4; Census 1980–2, table 18.

under no-fault, marriages were formally assumed to be contracts entered for the length of time the parties jointly preferred to continue them. The state now had no moral interest in perpetuating the union, although it had a practical one insofar as a two-parent family was thought a superior context for raising children. Beginning with California in 1969, almost all states adopted no-fault divorce legislation, developing a number of variants, including the notion that conditions (like "marital breakdown," "incompatibility," or "separation") not necessarily the product of fault were appropriate reasons for granting divorce. Halem argues that despite wide differences in detail and practical circumstance, the new divorce proceedings shared the assumption that divorce might actually be a *therapeutic* process, not a pathological one, and that revised divorce legislation might bring into the marriage system a greater degree of egalitarianism and fairness between the genders.[46] The divorce reform movement of the late 1960s and early 1970s had at its core much of the substantially feminist and individualized (and psychologized) perfectionism that characterized so much of American social thought at the time.[47]

The durability of marriages declined sharply after the mid-1960s, but by no means uniformly according to the circumstance of their formation. Table 41 indicates the proportions of marriages, among those contracted in 1960–1964 and 1970–1974 by whites and blacks at selected ages, that had ended by divorce before the next census date.[48]

In the 1960s, young marriages had been exceptionally risky, certainly among whites. In the 1970s they became riskier but less exceptionally so. Both men's and women's marriages were more durable when contracted older, but this advantage declined sharply as the marriage regime changed during the decade. If marriages contracted older were more prudent, prudence did not so much promote durability as it once had, before divorce became such a regular, expected feature of marriage—not a fault but a miscalculation, not a stigma but a misstep. (We are reminded also of the lessened link between older marriage and slower entry into parenthood.) Correspondingly, the legitimization of divorce was linked with wives' still-increasing propensity to work and, notably, to *remain at their jobs* even as they entered the married state.[49] It was linked also to the tendency to enter marriage later and to include a lengthy phase of close physical intimacy within courtship. And it was linked to the widening propensity to postpone parenthood after marriage. In all, the sharp discontinuity that a wedding had long wrought in lives, especially women's, was replaced by a far smoother, more closely articulated, less consequential transition.

Divorce was now increasingly incorporated into the family system. Parenthood became less of a bar to divorce, both absolutely and relatively, divorce less of a bar to subsequent remarriage. Divorced people who remarried became less prone to marrying only one another and increasingly prone to marry nondivorced people. To be sure, there was even by the mid-1970s still a good deal of "endogamy" among divorced people at any age, produced in part by their relative inability to participate comfortably in the conventional courtship mechanisms set up by and for the never-married to promote their marrying.[50] Robert S. Weiss, in a challenging essay, proposes that "a new marital form: the marriage of uncertain duration" had emerged.[51] Individuation, self-realization, and a new way of interpreting marital conflict characterize this form of marriage, along with the acceptance at marriage (and at parenthood) of the real possibility of divorce.[52] The argument is given real cogency by a striking finding made in the 1976 replication of the 1957 study of well-being analyzed by Veroff, Douvan, and Kulka: Americans in 1976 continued to care a great deal about the quality of their marriages, perhaps more than in 1957, but that at the same time they were *increasingly critical of how their own marriage was going.* It was a very good thing to be married, too, but it was not necessary. Nor was it as stigmatizing as once to be either single or no longer married. In their broad survey of changes in *The Inner American*, they found in no other attitude "such a dramatic change from 1957 to 1976 as we have in . . . increased tolerance of people who reject marriage as a way of life, . . . [a] loosening of the normative necessity of being someone's wife or husband in order to be a valid adult. . . . Divorce has become more than a peripheral institution. It has come to be a much more viable alternative to marriages that are not successful."[53]

THE DECLINE OF THE DATING SYSTEM

Dating had been one of the more important adolescent inventions of the early twentieth century, and by World War II it had reached most teenagers throughout the country. It was the institutional matrix within which a degree of physical affection was legitimately incorporated into adolescent heterosexual relations but kept in check short of coitus. The preeminence of this adolescent institution was challenged in the mid-1960s. New patterns spread, similar to dating in that they were initiated by youth but far more individualized. A 17-year-old boy in 1973, for instance, declared the term "dating" to be "much too formal. "Dating" makes me think of calling up a girl a few days in advance and asking her to go out to dinner or something."[54] Even dating itself became a far less formalized affair. Boys and girls got together for "the intrinsic satisfaction the relationship provided rather than for prestige."[55] Continuing encroachments on the double standard seemed to render the mechanism of "classical" dating irrelevant, while enlarged sexual expressiveness, common to the society at large, made the language and customs of dating far less relevant in protecting unsteady beginners from strong emotions and drives. In classical dating, "a complex ideological system, based on historically and culturally produced understandings of male and female roles and systems of value and exchange, opposed the developing youth culture. It denied that the unity of youth could or should overcome the opposition of gender and insisted that sex could not be liberated from that opposition."[56] When exactly this happened in the 1960s and 1970s, dating ceased to embody crucial cultural categories and became merely one form of social contact among many.

Dating came to occupy a smaller and less important portion of the adolescent's social life. The rejection of an institution, even one that was largely of their own making, was characteristic of adolescents in the mid-1960s and early 1970s. Lueptow's careful empirical examination of trend data on youth attitudes in this period reveals "an increased emphasis on hedonistic, individualistic purposes and on interpersonal considerations that seemed to replace institutional arrangements."[57] Few teenagers abandoned dating altogether, but they began dating somewhat later. Between the late 1950s and the late 1960s, the proportion of boys dating by age 15 declined from 78 percent to 59 percent, the proportion of girls from 82 percent to 65 percent.[58] The 1976 Monitoring the Future survey of high school seniors indicates a palpable decline in the *amount* of dating since the classical period, particularly at the more typical quantities, although the proportion of both nondaters and heavy daters seems to have remained roughly unchanged.[59]

Many structural attributes of dating persisted but with lessened intensity. Thus, just as in the baby boom, boys in the late 1960s dated a little earlier than girls but dated somewhat less frequently once they began. (This continuing asymmetry may be a reflection of a relatively great number of boy "specialists" who dated many girls but of a relatively few girls who did so, or it may be a function of boys entering the date pool slightly younger and marrying out of it considerably older, leaving more of them to go around.) Girls' more frequent dating was connected with their greater likelihood of going steady at any given point and thus with their continuing to take the emotional side of dating somewhat more seriously than did boys.[60] In the late 1960s just as at the beginning of the decade, commitment to dating (as indicated by age at which dating had begun) for both boys and girls was associated on the individual level with children's income from their own work.[61] This may have provided a mechanism that to some extent offset ideological shifts that were rendering dating less important, that it made it materially easier for boys and girls to go out, thus reducing the decline in the frequency of dating.

What began to take the place of dating was a wider involvement with mixed-gender peer-group activities, often "parties" of amorphous composition and focus, on the one hand, and an unstructured but warm intimacy, on the other.[62] Boys and girls by the 1970s were assumed to get along with one another on less formalized terms than they once did, to be able to work out their relationships on an individual basis, without so much structured group oversight as in classical dating. Girls were more strikingly engaged than were boys in both of these trends: they became considerably more active (and thus more like boys) in their nondating "going out for fun and recreation," and they became slightly less active (and thus more like boys) in their dating. Girls' experience, as judged by these data, was becoming more varied, less modal, less dictated by convention. Where senior boys in 1960 had enjoyed a median of nearly a date a week, only half this much dating was at the median for senior boys in 1976.[63] Girls in 1960 had dated even more, their median approximating 1.2 dates a week. By 1976, the median senior girl dated only half this frequently. By contrast, the median senior boy went out for fun and recreation more than thrice a week in 1976, the time drawn from dating. Medians for girls, too, rose, from slightly over two and one-half times a week out for fun and recreation to slightly under three times a week.[64]

Race and sex were complexly related to trends in socializing among high school seniors, as table 42 illustrates. For both whites and blacks in 1976, boys went out for recreation with their peers other than on dates more often than did girls. This same pattern had held exactly in 1960, but the differentials had been considerably more marked. This pattern was far more marked in blacks than in whites. However, for both whites and blacks, girls dated more often than did boys, and *this* pattern was more marked in 1976 among whites than in blacks. By 1976, black boys went out for fun and recreation slightly more frequently than did white boys, but they dated a fair amount less. Black girls *both* went out with groups and dated considerably less frequently than did white girls. Heavy dating, then, was more thoroughly a white institution in 1976 than it was a black one. But at the height of the baby boom, heavy dating had especially characterized blacks, for whom a distinctive life course organization seemed to be in train by the mid-1970s.

The data indicate that dating and going out with peer groups may well have been competing for individuals' attention and that they surely were competing, over time, *on the level of youth culture as a whole.* It would seem that some factor—homework, parental pressure, or deficit of material resources—limited the total number of times young people could go out, so that to some extent those who chose to go out on dates had that much less time to go out with their friends in other contexts. One might have found a pattern, earlier in the century, where parental oversight was so close that there might well have been a

Table 42. Proportions of High School Seniors Who Dated Frequently and Who Went Out Frequently for Fun and
Recreation, by Sex and Race, 1960 and 1976
(in percentages)

	Date 2+ Times a Week		Go Out 4+ Times a Week for Fun and Recreation	
	1960	1976	1960	1976
Nonblack				
Boys	41.3	27.5	22.9	30.6
Girls	59.6	38.4	14.9	26.5
Black				
Boys	59.1	22.8	22.7	31.8
Girls	66.7	27.7	18.3	16.4

SOURCES: Computed from *Project Talent* and 1976 *Monitoring the Future* data sets. See Appendix 4.

positive correlation between going out on dates and going out at all (especially for girls, one would anticipate): in such a situation, the leniency of parents would presumably have been the dominant explanatory variable rather than, as in 1976, the adolescents' own selection of activity.

Table 43 explores changes in the dating institution between 1960 and 1976 by comparing several correlates of dating frequency among high school seniors in the two years. For boys and girls, blacks and whites, for each year, the table indicates the partial correlation coefficients with dating frequency for each of the independent variables *when all the other variables are held statistically constant.* Large *positive* partial correlation coefficients indicate that even apart from other aspects of this interrelated set of teenage characteristics, among those who were high on the attribute (e.g., those who had relatively demanding after-school jobs), relatively many were those who dated a lot. The reverse is the case for *negative* coefficients.

Table 43. Parital Correlation Coefficients (Pearsonian) of Selected High School Senior Behaviors with Number of Dates per Week, All Others Controlled, by Race and Sex, 1960 and 1976

	Nonblack				Black			
	Male		Female		Male		Female	
	1960	1976	1960	1976	1960	1976	1960	1976
Religious	-.055	.018	-.017	-.089	.013	.131	.082	-.019
Study	-.077	-.068	.006	-.017	-.133	.029	.107	.038
GPA	-.022	-.104	-.016	.032	.204	.032	.016	.093
School plans	-.021	.042	-.264	-.155	-.066	.060	-.018	-.078
Job	.189	.083	.038	.064	.103	-.121	.076	-.026

SOURCES: Computed from *Project Talent* and 1976 *Monitoring the Future* data sets.
NOTE: I have used for 1960 the black values for all four grades, with grade an additional control in the partial equation, because there are so few black seniors.

We look first at what kind of seniors dated relatively frequently in 1976, first comparing this across subgroups and only then comparing it to the comparable figures from the baby boom sample of 1960. We find, thus, that boys who received better grades were less likely to date frequently. Among whites, boys who studied a lot did not go out with girls a lot, but this negative relationship was not present in blacks. Both white and black boys who were confident about their college ambitions, moreover, were not less and perhaps were *even more likely* to be doing a lot of dating. Among whites, boys who had relatively demanding after-school jobs dated a great deal, but this was not the case among black boys.

The dominant pattern among girls in 1976 was that planning to attend college was associated with reduced dating, more so among whites than among blacks. Grades, however, had a slightly positive relationship to dating, especially for black girls. The relationship of college ambitions and dating differed tellingly between boys and girls: girls typically married younger and were thus thinking relatively more concretely of courtship in their senior years. In many cases they had had to reconcile their courtship behavior and their schooling behavior and plans. For boys, the educational ambitions were in no particular way in conflict with current dating. But school achievement was, and boys, as always, differed more among themselves than did girls in how thoroughly they gave themselves to school tasks. These quite conventional patterns, and the negative association of religious attendance and dating, all showed up in the mid-1970s seniors, even as dating was on the whole receding.

The boys' pattern, notably, the relationships between school and dating and jobs and dating, was not markedly changed since 1960: seriousness about school was associated with relatively slight engagement in dating, but earning money—and having it to spend on one's date—continued to matter in the mid-1970s as it had in classic dating. As in 1960, the competition would show up most strongly among girls in their *anticipations* for future education. For boys, the competition was especially apparent between time spent in dating and time spent doing homework. A part of the decline in the relevance of study time to dating by 1976 may be a function of the considerable decline in average weekly study time between the two periods, amounting to a median of nine hours in the 1960 study and a bit under four hours in 1976. In 1960, before that arrangement became as ubiquitous as it would be in the mid-1970s, there was a striking positive relationship between after-school jobs and dating, stronger for boys (who worked more and paid for the dates) than for girls.

The competition in 1976 between school and dating was, however, less sharp than that between schooling and the nondate group activities that proliferated in the late 1960s and early 1970s. As table 44 shows, a negative relationship between going out for fun and recreation and both hours of homework and achieved grade point average obtained for both boys and girls, among both whites and blacks. For girls, there was also a negative relationship of high educational ambitions and socializing, although it was not particularly strong—as, indeed, we should expect since there was no particularly compelling reason (other than generic life-styles that might somehow be in conflict) for such a relationship. Among whites, attendance at church was decidedly less common for those who went out a lot with the gang, but this was not so among blacks. A time-consuming after-school job in 1976 seems neither to have bank-rolled nondate social activities nor to have taken up much of the time that might be spent on them. Or perhaps in the aggregate, these two ties were offsetting.

This pattern was also not markedly different from that which had obtained at the end of the baby boom, if we focus on the big picture. At that date, study time and educational ambitions were similarly in competition with group activities, but grade point average was not so much related. The relationship between outside work and dating was, as it was to be in 1976, positive for whites, negative for blacks. So, whereas dating declined somewhat and became somewhat more closely associated with a lower commitment to formal education, group activities grew more frequent while retaining their only somewhat differently constituted negative relationship with school ties. That is, the *structure* of the institution of dating seems *basically un-*

Table 44. Partial Correlation Coefficients (Pearsonian) of Selected High School Senior Behaviors with Number of Nights per Week Out for Fun and Recreation, All Others Controlled, by Race and Sex, 1960 and 1976

	Nonblack				Black			
	Male		Female		Male		Female	
	1960	1976	1960	1976	1960	1976	1960	1976
Religious	.037	−.056	−.007	−.120	.125	.079	.050	−.033
Study	−.147	−.098	−.103	−.098	.046	−.073	.089	−.087
GPA	−.028	−.101	.031	−.065	.189	−.085	−.003	.097
School plans	−.096	−.009	−.154	.032	.130	.088	.013	−.297
Job	.126	.043	.023	.051	−.014	−.003	−.020	.009

SOURCES: Computed from *Project Talent* and 1976 *Monitoring the Future* data sets.

changed in its articulation with adult-sponsored institutions. But its *relationship to the adolescent life course* was changed, for the young people themselves were here taking a greater hand.

How adolescents spent their time outside the house was in part a function of the material resources they brought to those activities, for by the mid-1970s, the costs of transportation, refreshment, and entertainment had become rather substantial. For whites (among blacks, income did not matter much to the way they spent their time), dates *and dates only* were associated with the money that young people earned on their own jobs. Perhaps because date money was derived from jobs and because dates and other age-peer activities competed, money from own jobs was—albeit weakly—associated with *fewer* evenings out with nondate peers. (Or perhaps those who earned a good deal of money had less free time all told and cut back on their group socializing but did not much reduce their complement of dates.) The effect of earned income on socializing did not differ by gender among the white high school seniors. In 1960, own job income had been irrelevant to girls' dating patterns, as one might have guessed, but instead had contributed to more peer-group outings.

If the structures remained largely the same, we may ask whether known trends in the determinants of dating and peer-group socializing might in part explain the partial replacement of the former by the latter between the baby boom era and the mid-1970s. We know that hours of study declined markedly but college plans proliferated, although achievement in academic subjects declined. The employment of high schoolers increased markedly. Religious observation by young people probably declined.[65] Looking at whites,[66] we can see that the reduction of study time would have promoted more dating, as would also the rise in after-school employment; college plans would have been irrelevant; and the declines in academic achievement and religious observation would both have encouraged dating. The impact on the reduction of study on *peer-group outings* would also have been positive, as would the rise in employment and by 1976, the declines in religious observation and academic achievement, while by 1976, the increase in college-mindedness would have become irrelevant. On balance, then, we can deny

Table 45. Parital Correlation Coefficients (Pearsonian) of Selected High School Senior Behaviors with Age at Which Marriage Is Anticipated, All Others Controlled, by Race and Sex, 1960 and 1976

| | Nonblack | | | | Black | | | |
| | Male | | Female | | Male | | Female | |
	1960	1976	1960	1976	1960	1976	1960	1976
Religious	.055	-.069	-.007	-.091	-.027	.144	-.023	-.121
Study	.053	NA	.091	NA	-.005	NA	.093	NA
GPA	-.049	.103	.048	.048	.216	.186	.063	.228
School plans	.182	.190	.300	.380	.254	.125	.363	.188
Job	-.031	-.014	.061	.008	.026	-.032	-.083	-.094
Dates/week	-.243	-.183	-.346	-.133	.017	.290	-.137	-.039

SOURCES: Computed from *Project Talent* and 1976 *Monitoring the Future* data sets.
NA: Hours of study was not asked of the subset of Monitoring the Future respondents who were asked at what age they anticipated marriage.

that *structural* change directly led to the reduction of dating's role. Indirectly, we can at least propose that structural change had so strengthened the peer group that dating now often lost out in competition for scarce evenings out.

Dating's unsuccessful competition with peer-group socializing in fact occurred simultaneously with a change in a whole set of institutionalized expectations that had been associated with family formation. Table 45 presents the partial correlation coefficients for a number of independent variables (adding dating frequency to the five variables already discussed) in their relationship to anticipated age at marriage.[67] (How often one went out for fun and recreation had *not* been tied with marriage plans in 1960, nor was it in 1976.)

What determined high school seniors' ideal marriage timing in the 1970s? On the whole, those who attended church frequently were more likely to expect to marry soon: the correlation with age at marriage was negative. Quite the opposite was the case among those who were highly oriented to formal education: both high grade point average and (especially for girls) plans to attend college characterized those who did not expect to get married very soon. After-school jobs were essentially irrelevant here, but dating mattered a great deal, certainly to white boys and girls. Among these young people, in 1976, *a heavy commitment of time to dating was associated with a solid commitment also to their own prompt marriages.* When we look at the 1960 columns of table 45, we see that, if anything, *these close relationships of the dating system to the road to marriage had declined between 1960 and 1976,* even as dating itself had become less common. The relationships between school orientation and marriage plans seem on the whole to have held about steady over the decade and a half, with college plans mattering less in 1976, grade point average more. There are suggestions that religious involvement had become a more important determinant of expectations of early marriage. But, in any case, even in 1976, this consistently important indicator of ideological commitment was less significantly involved with marriage timing expectations than was dating.

For all the decline of dating, it was still connected to a firm engagement in the "family-building" process. Table 46, treating

Table 46. Partial Correlation Coefficients (Pearsonian) of Frequency of Dates and Group Recreation with High School Seniors' Attitudes toward Marriage and Rock Music with Controls for Selected Behaviors,* by Race and Sex, 1976

| | Nonblack | | | | Black | | | |
| | Male | | Female | | Male | | Female | |
	Date	Recreate	Date	Recreate	Date	Recreate	Date	Recreate
Sure about marriage	.176	.035	.178	.093	.113	.207	.275	.229
My marriage will last	.117	−.020	.114	.005	.158	−.141	.108	.048
Too much rock music now	−.085	−.145	−.099	−.242	−.197	−.047	−.182	−.155

SOURCE: Computed from 1976 *Monitoring the Future* data set.

only 1976, because the dependent variables were not present in the 1960 survey, differs also from tables 44 and 45 in that it does not display the values of the five control variables that nevertheless were entered in computing the displayed partial correlation coefficients between both dates and peer outings with three explicit *value* items. These are (1) the respondent's certainty that he or she wanted to marry; (2) his or her confidence in the durability of his or her own hypothetical marriage;[68] and (3) the respondent's affirmation of a statement that there was too much hard rock music on the radio—to shift the terms of analysis to outlook on the conventional youth culture of the day. Modest racial differentials appear. Within races, the findings for the two genders are essentially consistent. Among both whites and blacks in 1976, both those who dated a lot and those who went out often for fun and recreation were especially likely to be certain that they intended to marry eventually, that they would prefer to have a mate. But among the white boys and girls, *involvement in the dating system was considerably more likely to promote certainty that they wanted to marry.* Their own success in and involvement with close relations with a member of the opposite sex led to the not unreasonable conclusion that they would eventually intensify these relations and make them permanent, and this encouraged them to have a warm outlook on the receding institution that made this relationship possible. At the same time, there was surely also some hanging back from the dating institution by those who had their doubts about marriage.[69] This Janus-faced relationship of expectations and values is made the clearer by a second value that once again shows that those who dated were comfortable with the institution of marriage, had confidence that it "worked," and, in fact, that it would "work" for them. Frequent daters were significantly more likely, net of antecedent conditions, to *believe that their own marriages, once contracted, would endure.* Dating had moved from a "thrill"-based innovation half a century before to a somewhat fading bastion of essentially "traditional" marriage values.

The same relationships did *not* convincingly relate frequency of going out for fun and recreation to these marriage values. Among blacks, recreation seems to have been relevant to the certainty-of-marriage question, but it was not among white boys, and, among white girls, it mattered only to a considerably smaller extent than dating. And for no subgroup was fun and recreation related to confidence in the lasting quality of marriage. The two forms of evening recreation, to an extent competitive (over time), drawing in different ways on the current efforts and plans for the future of high school students, promoted different values.

Dating was still a part of youth culture but less so than before. The bottom row of table 46 indicates that dating was tied, but less than was group outings, to a reflexive defense of contemporary youth culture. The high school seniors were asked for their responses to a small battery of opinion items that included the commonplace adult assertion "There is too much hard rock music on the radio these days," to which nearly half disagreed strictly and another quarter disagreed "mostly." The strength of the dissent from this frumpy assertion is indicated by negative correlations in the table, where we see that for all subgroups of seniors in 1976, dating was negatively correlated with such an adult-oriented assertion.[70] Black boys and girls who dated a lot were not just rather opposed to this conclusion but *very* opposed. For white boys and girls, however, it was not so much dating as it was peer-group outings that mattered. In 1976, dating led out of the peer group toward a kind of life course that was not embraced by as many youth as it had been sixteen years earlier. But peer-group outings were of the essence of the age-group culture for white adolescents. We are dealing, then, with two differing orientations of young people, orientations that had begun to diverge in the late 1960s and early 1970s.[71] In 1976, deep embeddedness in the culture of dating was associated with a close concern with marriage—and indifferently to the adult institution of school—as well as to the youth culture. By contrast, deep embeddedness in the youth society of heterosexual partying (and rock) was negatively related to sanguine and alluring thoughts about marriage and negatively as well with those credentialing aspects of school that expressed adult authority's control over their autonomy.

Dating in the mid-1970s retained for whites some but not all of the patterns it had developed by its classic period. But it lost much of the function that had given it substance: the peer over-sight of sexual restraint and, specifically, over girls' virginity. And much as a palpable part of the change in marriage timing depended on changes in the way large numbers of young Americans had come to understand gender and family roles, so also gender-related changes in ideological evaluation of plea-sure and of the body were at the heart of changes in behavior. For blacks at the same time, dating was neither as opposed to schooling nor so indifferently integrated with support for rock music and the youth culture. Further, it was more positively related to religious observation and to familistic attitudes than among whites. The meaning of dating for black youth was ob-viously different from its meaning to their white contemporar-ies. The baby boom structure of dating had changed from the mid-1970s for black youth as for white, as a close examination of table 43 will confirm, and in the process the kinds of distinc-tion between the races became more pronounced. As table 42 has revealed, this occurred while the institution of dating re-ceded far more rapidly among black youth than among white.

SEXUALITY IN A NEW LIGHT

Most data on adolescent sexuality between 1945 and the mid-1960s point to no major enlargement during this period of the role of coitus or even heterosexual genital sex play more gen-erally—even though *attitudes* apparently shifted enough in an accepting direction to alarm many adults into inferring a real increase in adolescent sexual behavior.[72] At just about this point, however, as the double standard of sexual conduct fell out of ideological favor among adolescents (as among adults), sexual expression *did* increase, although without its ideological attachment to lasting affection being much challenged.[73] Atti-tudinal developments in the late 1960s and early 1970s add up to a near-revolution in received values regarding people's rela-tionships to one another, including the sexual.[74] The definitive national surveys of adolescent girls' sexual activity carried out by Zelnik and his associates show that the attitudinal change was accompanied by a change in behavior. They found a marked enlargement of the proportion of single girls having

Percent
Non-virgin

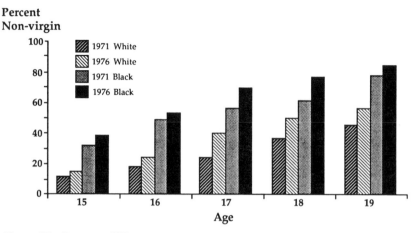

Figure 22. Percent of Young Women Having Had Premarital Intercourse, 1971 and 1976

had coitus from the early 1970s to the mid-1970s and again to the late 1970s.[75] The proportion of single girls no longer virgins through the teenage years is shown in figure 22. Sharp increases in nonvirginity took place at all ages by both white and black girls. For both, the sharpest increases were at around the ages at which virginity was no longer the modal state—18 for white girls in 1976, and 16 for black girls.

Quite generally, premarital coitus had become much more acceptable. When a Roper poll asked a national sample of adults in 1959 whether they thought "it is all right for either or both parties to a marriage to have had previous sexual experience," only 22 percent said that they thought it was all right, and an additional 8 percent said it was all right for the man but not the woman. By 1972, when another national sample was introduced to the idea that "there's been a lot of discussion about the way morals and attitudes about sex are changing in this country" and asked "If a man and a woman have [nonmarital] sex relations do you think it is always wrong, almost always wrong, wrong only sometimes, or not wrong at all," only 47 percent thought it was wrong more often than only sometimes. And by 1975, this proportion had dropped to 42 percent.[76]

Marriage in this sense, too, had become less special—sex outside of marriage and sex within marriage became technically and ideologically more similar. Sexual advice books ceased being written (as though) for married people, because the kind of advice that married people needed was no longer even said to be unique. Much of this evolution was also taking place in social scripts of a much more mundane sort—for instance the "rhetorical visions of interpersonal relations in popular magazines." In the mid-1960s the older vision—in which "characters . . . played roles in society rather than playing parts in a personal drama"—was shattered by feminists such as Betty Friedan. In the new vision, according to Kidd,

> growth was portrayed as the natural state of life and the ultimate legitimatizer for behavior . . . In such a world of growth and change, neither rules nor meanings could be absolute. . . . Meaning was negotiable, between the individuals involved. . . . In a dramatic scene which contained no predetermined meanings, the structure of relationships and roles was also negotiable. The dramatic scenarios included experiments in marriage and family life styles [and] freedom in sex behavior.

In the 1950s love had been defined in terms of meeting role expectations. Now it was "characterized by 'meeting the needs' of the other through interaction, commitment, affection, and nonpossessiveness."[77] Mutuality was no longer a theme of "coming together" in mystic sexual union but rather of each partner enhancing the other's happiness. Each couple represented a fresh negotiation of promising but uncertain potential that would endure while each partner gratified the openly pleasure-seeking *self* of the other.

Sexuality, in fact, was an important theme of the feminism of the period, and this entailed a revised interpretation of sex in which women's needs were seen as physiologically different from men's *but not because they were less urgent*. Masters and Johnson had taught women the importance of the clitoris in female sexual response. Now popular writers could argue that "the ease with which women [achieve] orgasm during masturbation certainly contradicts the general stereotypes about female sexuality. . . . The truth seems to be that female sexuality is thriving—but unfortunately underground."[78]

Murray S. Davis describes an ideological contest in this period among proponents of three value orientations: those who would sustain the old order by *repressing* sexuality, those who (like rebels of the 1960s) would overthrow the old order by *celebrating and inverting* sexuality, and those "Naturalists" who would treat sexuality as a *morally neutral phenomenon.*[79] These last, the children of Kinsey, exercised an increasingly powerful sway in the 1960s and 1970s, their most characteristic text Masters and Johnson's 1966 study, *Human Sexual Response.*[80] That pleasure itself was a good thing was taken for granted. So substantial was the repositioning of sexuality within American culture that theorists have suggested that its expression rather than its repression came to lie near the core of the energy that structures the society.[81] This fits with a broader drift away from values derived from an ethic of work toward an ethic based on the expansion and glorification of the self. The quantitative balance of work and leisure time has shifted nowhere near so much as the evaluative balance placed on the two. Leisure was no longer thought of so much as an opportunity for self-improvement as an occasion for enjoyable self-expression.[82]

Masters and Johnson's study, based in part on direct observation of couples engaging in sexual intercourse, was highly technical but sold extremely well on the trade market, inspiring both the Playboy Press and the New American Library to publish interpretations. The introduction to one of these characteristically explained to readers that Masters and Johnson talk more about female than about male orgasm, because "emphasis on female orgasm is warranted by the fact that its absence so frequently sets a limit to human experience. Once that limit is overcome, the whole transcendent experience with all its psychological and physiological overtones can follow."[83] Sexuality became a recognized, valued, worthy, even necessary component of the good life, a prime means of attaining self-discovery. David Reuben told Americans, very many of whom bought his book in 1970, that "an active and rewarding sexual life, at a mature level, is indispensable if one is to achieve his full potential as a member of the human race."[84] A broadened, thoroughly legitimized notion of sex education had become a vehicle for expanding the normalization of sex and the sexualization of life. Kahn, for instance, moves from her discussion of themes of sexual fantasy to a proposal for sex education within the family such that

> each reproductive part of the body has a dual function: physiological and pleasurable. What I am calling for is the acknowledgment of this very important second function so that children can begin to be comfortable associating their developing sexual body with their increasing sexual desires and needs. By providing specific recognition and approval of the pleasurable dimension of sexuality, the parent can help the child to develop a sense of achievement and growth that is directly related to the enhancement of the sexual self.[85]

The powerful ideology no less than the powerful instrumentation of medical science was now fully connected to a view that sexuality, indeed orgasm, was linked to "the whole transcendent experience." Davis describes an ironic outcome:

> Having reduced copulation to behavior and having permitted it in any way with anyone or even anything, Naturalists are often surprised to discover that they have succeeded in weakening sexual motivation itself. Those who no longer feel that their sexual behavior transgresses major taboos [i.e. ideological structures sustaining social structures] may find that their sexual desire is no longer reinforced by psychological, social, or cosmic overtones."[86]

Survey data point to the increasing breadth of acceptance of sexuality as a good thing, a view held by both women and men, young people *not* set off from their elders in this regard. Americans with increasing uniformity came to employ at least some method of birth control and approve of the dissemination of information about how to control births.[87] The development of tidy and efficient methods under the direct control of women has allowed a more nearly symmetrical approach to sexual enjoyment, an agenda of "choice," in this sense, achieving a dominant position in the public sphere.

Sexual intercourse seemed if anything to have become a positive part of the structure of dating in the mid-1970s. A 1973 replication of an excellent 1970 local study showed that even over this short period, coitus had increased in incidence for both boys and girls, now began younger, and was more closely

Table 47. Proportion of Girls Dating Sometime in Previous Four
          Weeks, by Past Coital Experience and by Attitude
          toward Premarital Sexual Intercourse, by Race and
          Age, 1976 (in percentages)

	Sexual Experience		*Premarital Intercourse Is OK*		
	Non-virgins	*Virgins*	*Always*	*Before marriage*	*Never*
White girls					
15	76.3	45.0	59.0	54.5	43.9
16	83.8	62.2	69.6	79.5	55.6
17	87.0	63.1	79.1	78.2	64.0
18	81.1	59.7	67.7	78.0	56.9
19	83.1	60.5	74.4	82.3	58.9
Black girls					
15	60.8	30.5	56.8	51.1	20.9
16–17	67.7	41.1	64.1	55.3	43.8
18–19	72.5	66.0	74.1	67.8	67.5

SOURCE: Computed from National Survey of Adolescent Female Sexual Behavior, 1976. See Appendix 4.
NOTE: Smallest numbers of cases in particular cells are for white girls of 15 who affirm that coitus is always OK (39) and who have themselves had coital experience (45), for black girls of 15 who affirm that coitus is always OK (44) and who have themselves had coitus (52). Most other cells exceed 100 cases.

integrated into the formerly conventional series of "stages" of sexual expression.[88] What had happened was, simply, that "going all the way" was increasingly "on the scale," not normatively out of bounds but rather integrated into the range of activities formerly carried out within but limited by the dating system. Table 47, based on Zelnik and Kanter's 1976 National Survey of Adolescent Female Sexual Behavior, indicates that even as young as age 15, sexually faster girls were also those girls who were actively engaged in dating.[89] And those girls who absolutely rejected premarital intercourse as necessarily a bad thing were also less likely to date than were girls who believed either that eventual marriage plans justified premarital intercourse or that no justification was needed.[90]

The detailed findings in table 47 deserve some exposition, partly because they point to changes with age, and differences between whites and blacks, within the generalizations just proposed. Thus, we find that for both races, dating as a system was still spreading between age 15 and age 16: some girls did not yet date who, obviously, shortly would. This was true both for those who had had intercourse (and for those who approved of it in theory) and for virgins. The point to be emphasized is that sexual behavior and dating to some extent spread, with age, independently of one another. This same pattern of a general proliferation of dating (from a lower point of initial spread) can be seen among blacks even at 18 and 19: apparently at, or by, this time, dating simply was just not what black girls did to the same extent as white girls. Among white girls, nonvirgins were about 20 percent more likely to have dated in the past four weeks than were virgins, regardless of the age. But among black girls, age made a great deal of difference in how much sexual status affected dating: among the youngest black girls, twice as many (a percentage difference of 30 percent) separated nonvirgins from virgins in their likelihood of having dated recently, but this difference declined gradually to barely perceptible. Why might whites and blacks differ in this regard? I suspect that the considerably lighter moral weight that blacks gave to premarital coitus—certainly by the late teens—meant that among them girls who had and girls who had not just were not so different as were white girls who had and who had not, even in 1976. This is borne out by the parallel significance of the attitudinal question by race. For young black girls, expressed attitudes toward premarital coitus was tied to their dating behavior as it was not for older black girls. But for whites, the significance of dating for attitudes toward premarital coitus was in no way diminished through the teen years. For whites and young blacks it was those girls "in circulation" as defined by the dating system who seemingly were more exposed to the values— and opportunities—that led to a reevaluation in more modern terms of the meaning of premarital sexuality.

But then there is the surprising fact that for blacks the attitude that marriage plans justified sexual intercourse was asso-

ciated with *almost as much* dating as a belief that sexual intercourse was always acceptable but that among white girls the
association of premarital sexual intercourse and eventual marriage to one's sex partner was associated with *more* frequent dating. What we see, apparently, is that although many things
contributed to the link between dating and premarital coitus,
among white girls but not among black girls the link between
dating and marriage was cemented by a positive evaluation of
the sexual link that led from dating to marriage. But in the
mid-1970s, as had not been the case in the classical dating system, this sexuality might be fully consummated before marriage: necking need not be enough.

Together, boys and girls embraced the idea that sex was, on
the whole, under the proper conditions, a good thing—which
did not necessarily exclude marriage. We can gain an idea of
what happened during this period by looking closely at the
main findings of two intensive studies of sexual attitudes, separated in period of observation by the experience of the 1960s.
Reiss's study of high school and college youth between 1959
and 1963 establishes a baseline that shows us the emergence but
not yet the preeminence at that juncture of what, with nice precision, he calls "permissiveness with affection."[91] Essentially, the
relevant part of Reiss's depiction of adolescent sexual attitudes
just at the end of the baby boom can be abstracted to three
dimensions, representing beliefs young people held about the
relationship of sexual behavior to marriage, on the one hand,
and to love, on the other, and about the relationship between
love and marriage. In essence, he found that each of these relationships varied with the *dating experience* of his respondents,
with their *sexual experience*, and with their *gender*. Thus, girl respondents who had dated more frequently were more likely to
have approved of the sexual expression of love; they were also
more likely to have seen a strong and vital link between love
and marriage. But those whose experience had included one or
several episodes of having fallen in love were *less* likely to have
linked love and marriage very closely. The pattern of relationships found by Reiss is fairly complex, but it shows that dating
in the late baby boom period was interrelated to beliefs about
the morality of premarital sexual expression in a complexly in-

terwoven pattern, on the whole more crystallized for girls than for boys. In this complex, "shoulds" tie the individual's status in the dating system to what he or she believes about sexuality, both through normative constraints on behavior and through ideologically governed notions concerning the relationship of feeling to the path toward marriage.

There were, of course, many young people who did not fit this pattern: it was a statistical pattern only, and one undergoing change at the time. But it is fair to say that as of 1959 to 1963, the young people Reiss interviewed by and large held a view of the right way to grow up, in which feelings and sexuality were tied together through dating, which in turn linked them to the marital institution. There was a path, and very many adolescents felt themselves on it and understood what they felt and what they did sexually in those terms. Reiss explicates this arrangement:

> The young person gains his basic set of values from his parents, his friends, and from the basic type of social groupings he is exposed to as he matures. As dating begins he comes increasingly under the influence of the more permissive peer values that dominate the courtship area. How quickly he responds to these permissive pressures depends on their strength as well as the type of basic values brought to the situation from his parental upbringing. These values in turn reflect his position in his own family, his race, sex, social class, city size, religious attitudes, [and] level of general liberalism. . . . Following marriage the individual comes more under the influence of the adult-run family institution and its relatively low premarital permissive values [i.e., values favoring premarital coitus].[92]

By the early 1970s, this sense of a normatively defined path had become obliterated. DeLamater and MacCorquodale's fine 1973 study of Wisconsin college students and high school graduates (aged 18 to 23), oriented in part by Reiss's earlier study, permits us to see how this had happened.[93] In that survey, belief in the "abstinence" standard—a standard proposed by a majority of the girls and over a quarter of the boys in Reiss's study a decade earlier—was now held by *less than one in ten*. Likewise, the double standard was gone. "Permissiveness with affection" had more than doubled, to become the majority position. Barely present as an articulated value in Reiss's study but attracting about a third of the 1973 respondents was *sex without affection if with mutual consent.*

SEXUALITY AND LIFE COURSE DEVELOPMENT

Reiss had found major differences by gender both in parameters and in patterns, but DeLamater and MacCorquodale found essential uniformity in 1973. In social standards, both young men and young women were permissive with affection, quite generally. Age at which dating had begun, although related to respondents' backgrounds, was now related to *nothing having to do with premarital sexuality*, whether behavior or attitude. The dating system no longer much structured the realm of sexuality.[94] What the analysts found to be quite closely tied to sexual behaviors and attitudes of both young men and young women was ideology—ideology regarding sex roles (then very much under discussion) and ideology regarding general sociopolitical issues. (An element that remained an important correlate in 1973 as in the period 1959 to 1963, however, was church attendance.)

The most important correlates of what young people did and thought they should do sexually were the particular characteristics of the dyadic relationship they happened to be in. Early-1970s young people were often in intense relationships, within which they found a level of sexual intimacy that commonly exceeded that of previous eras, which was certainly new in the sense of righteousness that accompanied it. This was not free sex without guilt, or reckless hedonism; but it was built on a set of specific, valued relationships. These relationships, however, were recognized as possibly transient and not so much institutionally structured as individually negotiated.[95]

Some of the terms of the new value structure are visible in the 1976 National Survey of Adolescent Female Sexual Behavior. Three components are tied together in a way that is especially revealing of its role in the life course of adolescent black and white girls, as table 48 shows: premarital sexual intercourse (here I measure separately behavior and the profession that

Table 48. Attitude of Single Girls toward the Relative Importance of Career and Parenthood and the Double Standard of Sexual Conduct by Race, Age, and Premarital Coital Behavior and Attitudes, 1976 (in percentages)

| | Proportion Denying that Career May Supersede Parenthood | | | | Proportion Denying Women Equal Premarital Sex Rights | | | |
| | Has had pre-marital coitus | | Coitus permissible without marriage | | Has had pre-marital coitus | | Coitus permissible without marriage | |
	Yes	No	Yes	No	Yes	No	Yes	No
White								
15	39.5	36.0	25.6	38.0	5.3	33.3	2.6	33.8
16	42.6	40.3	26.8	44.1	11.8	31.3	3.6	32.2
17	26.0	29.7	19.4	32.1	4.0	30.1	0.0	27.4
18	38.5	29.3	30.2	34.8	6.3	27.9	3.2	24.5
19	26.0	30.9	18.6	25.7	6.5	43.0	2.3	32.8
Black								
15	33.3	34.6	22.7	38.2	23.5	38.3	9.3	43.3
16–17	36.8	27.4	28.2	37.0	16.4	33.6	11.4	34.3
18–19	25.8	25.9	26.0	26.6	12.0	34.0	8.9	29.6

SOURCE: Computed from National Survey of Adolescent Female Sexual Behavior, 1976.
NOTE: The *career* item asks respondents to state whether they agree strongly, agree, disagree, or disagree strongly with the statement "A woman should not let bearing and rearing children stand in the way of a career if she wants it."
The *sexual-rights* item asks respondents to state whether they agree strongly, agree, disagree, or disagree strongly with the statement "Women have as much right to sex before marriage as men."

intercourse does not require the justification of marriage, present or future); the orientation on the part of the girls to the needs of a career even as against the value of parenthood; and the assertion that the double standard of sexual conduct, as applied to premarital intercourse, no longer has any bearing. (The table presents proportions who *rejected* the "modern" work-role and gender-role ideologies.) The simplest generalization to be drawn is that *all three values*—sexual freedom, gender symmetry, and the volitional nature of parenthood for women—are rather closely correlated for all subgroups, but that *for white girls only* actual premarital intercourse is unrelated to orientation to career rather than parenthood. But the finer-grained details call for a closer examination.

Before attending to these, however, we must ask how closely professed belief in the justifiability of premarital intercourse paralleled reported coital behavior. The relationship was, in fact, exceptionally strong for both white and black girls and can be summarized rather simply. The proportion of girls who maintained that premarital intercourse was acceptable behavior even in the absence of marriage plans was far greater among those who had had coitus than among those who had not (ever-married girls are excluded from all these tabulations), for instance, by a 42-percent-to-10-percent margin for white girls at age 15, and by a 57-percent-to-19-percent margin for black girls at age 15. Among whites, the proportion affirming premarital coitus increased slowly among the growing proportion who had had coitus, to 51 percent at age 19, while the proportion of adherents to this belief among the sexually inexperienced remained small and did not vary with age. Among black girls, the rise in affirmation of sex without marriage increased even more sharply, to 71 percent for girls 18 to 19, while the ideologically committed among those with no coitus remained level. The figures show that there was a certain amount of "play" between value and ideology, *especially in the direction of girls having had intercourse but rejecting its acceptability other than in the presence of marriage plans,* plans that for many could have barely been present, in view of their ages. But relatively few girls *who had not already themselves had coitus* professed belief in the acceptability of premarital intercourse in the absence of marriage plans. One infers the importance of circumstance and opportunity in promoting behavior that in turn drives particular adherence to ideology. But of course, the belief in the inherent goodness of sexuality and of the compatibility of sex and acceptable behavior was "in the air" by the mid-1970s.

None of these relationships depended on age. The value complex was nearly exactly as true for midteens, for whom marriage was considerably in the future and for many of whom sexual activity was just beginning or had not yet begun, as it was for young women of 19. As we have earlier seen, the amount of, and the attitudinal favorability toward, sexual intercourse rose through these years. This rise was wholly "responsible" for the parallel increases in values that traded off parenthood for career and that maintained that the double standard of sexual conduct did not apply. Within the subcategory of the coitally active, within the subcategory of those accepting premarital intercourse as quite acceptable behavior, as within their complements, there was essentially no change with age in the proportions favoring the "modern" value orientations. The exception to this was for black girls, with regard to the double standard. Sexual experience was not such a dividing point for young black girls as for young white ones with regard to adherence to the double standard, for its stern rejection was relatively common among all young black girls. But, increasingly with age, the dwindling category of black virgins became more and more different from nonvirgin blacks with regard to their gender ideology (and more like white nonvirgin girls of any age). Conversely, it was adherence to the ideology supporting premarital intercourse that especially clearly divided the gender-role beliefs for the youngest black girls, but decreasingly so. A belief in the acceptability of premarital intercourse with no reference to marriage was particularly common among black girls; those who rejected it at 15 were particularly outside the value complex on the gender-role issue, but decreasingly so, even as their numbers dwindled with age.

What we see, then, is that in many ways the acceptance of coital sexuality had by the mid-1970s come to be at or near the core of a new adolescent-girl outlook on the female life course. Circumstances, opportunity, inborn physical attractiveness, and artifice all contributed to the likelihood that a girl would have sexual intercourse before marriage. The outcome of this complex process would, as table 48 has indicated, markedly affect her outlook on herself as a woman and on women's role.

The old pattern was substantially broken, but no tight new sociological pattern had emerged. The genders were not identical but were not so different in experience or in belief as they once had been. The pronounced gender asymmetry that had structured dating was no more. By the same token, as De-Lamater and MacCorquodale point out, experience in heterosexual contexts made a lot of difference to what young people believed, but those contexts were no longer so structured as they once were. So what now emerged was in good part a matter of what the current partners felt about one another, which in good measure depended on personality. To be sure, it also depended in part on what they thought they *should* feel, and this was subject in part to current ideological debate. Surely they thought they should feel strongly and fondly,[96] but this feeling was not as attached as it had previously been either to clear-cut ideas about how it might be institutionalized in marriage or to actual early steps already taken on a generally recognized path toward marriage. Young people were evolving a pattern, but it was a pattern that was subject to very considerable couple-to-couple variation. And couples were transient. Early marriage would simply make no sense under these circumstances. The figures of Herzog and Bachman show clearly that young people by no means rejected marriage, nor did they strongly seek to redefine it (gender roles apart).[97] Rather, they wished to postpone its application to themselves. And in this, many succeeded.

The new sexuality was by no means wholly divorced from contemporary notions of "family-building." At the same time, contemporary sexual behaviors and beliefs for many girls chartered a sense of self-determination that was ambiguously related to the movement into family formation. Table 49, based once again on the 1976 National Survey of Adolescent Female Sexuality, relates coital experience and attitudes toward the propriety of such behavior to answers to a question about ideal age for marriage for young women. Once again, age and race

Table 49. Selected Responses of Single Girls to Question about
Ideal Age for Marriage, by Race, Age, and Premarital
Coital Behavior and Attitudes, 1976

| | "At Maturity" | | Of Those Offering a Specific Age, at 22+ | |
	Nonvirgins	Virgins	Nonvirgins	Virgins
White girls				
15	12.9%	2.7%	22.2%	35.8%
16	5.1%	4.9%	41.1%	45.1%
17	12.3%	2.5%	46.5%	58.1%
18	16.9%	7.5%	53.6%	63.6%
19	9.1%	8.3%	73.3%	63.6%
Black girls				
15	6.7%	4.0%	26.2%	54.2%
16–17	9.7%	3.1%	30.0%	50.5%
18–19	9.8%	6.1%	37.4%	54.3%

| | "At Maturity" | | | Of Those Offering a Specific Age, at 22+ | | |
| | Premarital Intercourse Is OK | | | Premarital Intercourse Is OK | | |
	Always	Before marry	Never	Always	Before marry	Never
White girls						
15	12.9%	1.2%	2.9%	55.6%	32.1%	31.3%
16	10.4%	4.1%	3.4%	47.6%	37.6%	47.8%
17	15.8%	3.9%	1.8%	58.3%	57.5%	50.0%
18	16.4%	10.1%	7.3%	71.7%	54.9%	54.9%
19	11.1%	12.3%	2.1%	87.5%	64.0%	60.9%
Black girls						
15	5.3%	2.3%	7.5%	31.6%	42.9%	56.8%
16–17	10.5%	4.3%	3.6%	36.3%	34.3%	48.1%
18–19	13.8%	3.8%	0.0%	42.5%	36.0%	45.9%

SOURCE: Computed from National Survey of Adolescent Sexual Behavior, 1976.

are complexly and revealingly related to the essentially strong relationship between these elements of teenage life and belief. Delayed marriage timing—ideal marriage ages of 22 or older among those expressing any particular ideal age—bore a strong relationship to the ages of white girls but at most a moderate relationship to sexual experience, with experienced girls preferring younger marriages. But among black girls, sexual experience mattered more, and age considerably less.

Essentially, among all categories of girls, the sexually inexperienced proposed *later* marriages than did girls who had already had coitus—a fact undoubtedly related to the lingering relationship between sexual intercourse and the kind of love that commonly, even if not by explicit plan, led to marriage. At the same time, girls who had had intercourse were markedly more likely than the sexually inexperienced to tell their interviewers that, in essence, "maturity" rather than simple chronological age was the appropriate determinant of when a girl should marry. *Attitudes* about premarital sexuality bore a markedly different relationship to ideal marriage timing, however. Although girls who believed in sex without marriage were those considerably more likely to tell interviewers that maturity should determine the timing of marriage, it was also those same girls who were more likely to hold out for *later marriage*. Or, at least, this was so among the white girls. "At Maturity" was a response that reflects a point of view, that looked to individualized rather than socialized characteristics, here quasi-psychological, as a basis for socially sanctioned role transitions like marriage. The relationship of this value to expressed *attitudes* toward adolescent sexuality was considerably greater than to the act of sexual intercourse, as the second panel of table 49 shows. White girls espousing maturity as a basis for deciding when to marry were especially concentrated at the lowest ages. With age, among white teenage girls, maturity as a value became increasingly common among those girls who would allow intercourse before marriage, if marriage was in mind—evidently as more girls with such beliefs contemplated actually having sexual intercourse themselves. For black girls, these patterns were different: those girls who espoused coitus without marriage plans were those whose commitment to maturity increased with age; the others never much favored this position. Indeed, there is the suggestion that the relatively few black girls who espoused virginity at marriage in 1976 were, with age, decreasingly prone to assert the individuated perspective that maturity should determine marriage timing.

Whites and blacks differed markedly in even the simple relationship of sexual attitudes to ideal marriage timing. Among white girls, it was those who espoused the modern, individuated perspective on sexual intercourse who were also the most likely to prefer postponed marriage. This is entirely consistent with the general argument here that sees delayed marriage as a response to a value cluster that developed around a growing preference for immediate, individuated gratification and the celebration of such an orientation as right and good. For blacks, however, it was *not the most sexually outgoing but the sexually most conservative* girls who held back from early marriage, preferring later marriage. Blacks, it seems, were by no means undergoing the same sexual-values reevaluation that whites were, and the split within their community on the premarital intercourse item was not one that indexed general ideological "modernity," as it did for many whites. Accordingly, it was the highly respectable, relatively reserved black girls who held out for sexual restraint until marriage and who saw too-early marriage in the same light as white people of middle-class status commonly did: somehow mildly scandalous, suggesting not just a preference for prompt family formation but undue haste under constraint.

The once-great gender differentials in sexual behavior and the meanings attached to these behaviors had declined. Casual sex had increased, but love and marriage had not disappeared. And these were still strongly associated with sexuality. Adult definitions had lost some of their legitimacy. Adolescents' sexual practices were, however, scarcely less ordered, for being under their own individual control. But at the same time, sexuality was given more play, and earlier, the energies derived from its repression less available than formerly to structure the youthful life course. From the perspective of adolescents, sexuality expressed well and rewardingly the individualized sense of assertion of self that was among the fruits of their recent social history. And yet, as we have earlier seen, the successful *accom-*

plishment of coital activity by girls was generally associated with
favorability toward earlier marriage, as was also the easy acceptance of premarital sexuality among white girls. The path to
marriage, as experienced, was now associated with the enjoyment of the very pleasures that had recently been uniquely con-
secrated to marriage itself.

In their very challenging exegesis of a survey of Illinois adolescents in 1971, Miller and Simon put a like trend in different
terms.[98] They discern there the convergence of girls' and boys'
figures for the coital activity and, at the same time as there was
a broadening of the number of girls engaged, a reduction in
the class differentials in this tendency. There was, as they put it,
a disappearance of the "bad girl" social category, a reduction in
the number of girl specialists who would—at the price of their
reputation and presumably the respect that the boys would
give them, and presumably at the cost of proper marriages—
give boys what they wanted. If all girls were now bad girls, then
there were no bad girls any more. And if there were no *especially* bad girls, girls could better insist on their terms—
emotional commitment—to boys who wanted them to go all the
way. Along with the rest of the population, boys' attitudes toward gender roles was increasingly one of denying difference
and, in the process, accepting emotionality (once decried as
girlish) as an appropriate part of life.

YOUTH

The late 1960s and early 1970s saw the simultaneous development of a number of related aspects of the youthful life course,
many of these having a common theme: the increased ability of
young people to craft their own life courses virtually *ad lib*, at
least in the immediate future. Relatedly, even as young people
earned absolutely more money than they had in the baby boom
period, they changed from being a group highly oriented to
saving to one of the most heroically committed to *dissaving*.[99]
We have earlier taken note of Easterlin's observations of the
increased difficulty young people were having in finding economically satisfying adult niches for themselves in an economy
that grew more slowly than did the cohort coming of age. Eas-

terlin documents this, among other ways, by citing youth income and unemployment rates *relative* to those of their elders.[100] At the same time, however, a wide variety of roles were emerging that left a great deal of room for young people to enlarge their economic activities—both as producers and as consumers—*as long as they did not seek to support full adult establishments.* We find, thus, over the course of this period, that gainful employment and school, once antagonistic or at any rate successive parts of adolescents' lives, had become increasingly intertwined. More adolescent students had jobs while they were attending school, and these jobs demanded more time than they used to.[101]

The reason that gainful employment could so much more often be integrated into the school life of adolescents was in part a change in the nature of the labor market and, no less, a reduction in the exclusive attention schools once demanded. In 1980, high school students, on average, spent a mere *four hours a week* at homework. "While schooling is designated by society as the primary adolescent activity, it is clear that work and secondary education are not [any longer] mutually exclusive. . . . Although high school students work [gainfully] less than older members of society, work isn't necessarily a marginal or peripheral activity for them. The time spent at work appears to be second only to the time spent in the classroom. . . . Work activity may well be an integral part of adolescence, even as schooling remains the focal activity at this age."[102] Between 1960 and 1970, the gainful workweek for in-school youth increased, along with the proportion of enrolled adolescents at work. For boys, this meant an increase in the proportions working 35-hour workweeks or longer; but the dramatic growth for both boys and girls occurred in the increasingly modal 15-to-34 hour category. Similar levels of work commitment were characteristic of most groups of high school students.

The peacetime draft was abolished in 1973, as young people withdrew their support for military activity in Southeast Asia. At first, with the Vietnamization of the war, and then with the all-volunteer army, the proportions of adolescents called on to serve in the military dropped to levels lower than at any time since World War II. With an all-volunteer army, the military ceased to interfere with young men's plans and, in fact, became just another option for them. Adolescent males, as we have earlier seen, had previously been kept "on schedule" by contemplation of the military service they might face. We thus find that the beginning of a decline in male first-marriage rates in the early 1960s was interrupted by a heightening with the Vietnam phase of military demand. By about 1970, the youthful service and the youthful marriage patterns began to collapse together. The prominence of military service in young men's plans through most of the postwar period can perhaps be indicated by a large national survey of high school seniors in 1960 that asked boys "What do you *expect* to do about military service?" and "What would you really *like* to do about military service?" Fully six in ten of those asked about their intentions and preferences had definite plans that incorporated military service and said they "liked" these plans. With Vietnam, things changed. Although fully 56 percent of a like sample in 1969 anticipated eventual service, only 14 percent said they would "be happy to serve," and about half as many said they would serve but would do so under duress, or would actually refuse service. After 1976, "the proportions of males who expected to serve declined steadily from 1976 through 1979," with proportions pleased with such an outcome declining in parallel.[103]

There are many different ways to understand the dramatic changes in American life in the 1960s and 1970s. Here I have explored changes in the way people entered into emotional relationships with one another and came to structure families. By way of tying these together into a different package, however, I would like to propose that many of these developments can be understood as congruent with—producing and in turn produced by—the emergence of a new phase of life for Americans, a phase bearing some intriguing similarities to the phase of unattached youth associated more with European societies than American. During the 1960s and 1970s, young people increasingly began to see themselves and came to be seen as a group unto itself, with distinctive activities, interests, and subculture. The aspects of this development under discussion in this chapter are obviously "personal" and not political in the sense of the young radicals in whom Kenneth Keniston saw, or foresaw, early traces of a *youth* phase emerging in the American life course.[104] And yet, as we have seen (and as was directly expressed by many young people of the "sixties generation"), the personal ideologies that structured the life course were in fact related to the more public ideologies under debate at the time.

Collective youth resistance became recognizable in the Vietnam crisis, at which time the often substantial military demand on youth, generally accepted calmly until then, focused—if only briefly—a distinct political interest for young people as a social category. The impact of these events on how the generations understood their relationships was considerable. In the postwar period and, basically, up to the early 1960s, adult writers on questions of youth had emphasized developmental problems, their notions being that parents and adult institutions, properly directed, were strong enough to lead their charges toward more reliable, sound, sturdy growth toward adulthood. "Juvenile delinquency" in the 1950s had been a characteristic, common scare, differences between the generations seen as individually based and eradicable by right effort on the part of parents and their agents. But after the late 1960s, adult anxiety and fascination about *a generation* replaced the concern for the individual development of adolescents. The characteristic precosity was no longer emotional but now, in a sense, moral or quasi-political. Development was less worrisome now, for these new adolescents seemed in ways preternaturally sophisticated, as though they had stepped outside of the developmental process itself. Adult institutions made major concessions to young people as a group. The strategic retreat of these institutions left young people more nearly to make what they wished of their own lives, to evolve for themselves the bases on which to organize their passage through their lifetime.

8

COMING INTO THEIR OWN

The varying size of successive age cohorts and the reordering of the allocation of public and private goods to the several age groups in recent years have made us wonder with new intensity about the structured ways individuals negotiate their biographies. The differentiation of society by age has become a focal concern of today's social science, and of social history, and a subject of considerable currency in policy debate and in culturally informed personal experience. In the United States, we sense that structural contrasts between one life course stage and the next have become greater, at the same time as we increasingly believe that individuals are responsible for crafting their own biographies, for discerning and nurturing their "selves" and presenting these to the world.

Young people, as this work evidences, have increasingly taken control of the construction of the youthful life course: adult-maintained convention has crumbled, and young people have been left the pieces and much of the mortar needed to construct it afresh. Young people, we have heard regularly over the half-century that this book documents, have become precocious. At the same time, however, revisions in tastes have outrun the capacity to satisfy them, and young people have often felt less able individually to control the circumstances that have permitted their early assumption of "mature" characteristics. The period of youth has been extended. Youth have purchased a commercial culture that erects cultural distinctions between themselves and the "adults" located on the far side of some chronological dividing line. Yet young people as individuals have become increasingly dependent on certification from formal institutions controlled by adults and find themselves entangled in bureaucratic career lines of frustratingly gradual ascent.

Such presentist concerns have in part motivated this volume. But in constructing an account of changes in the youthful life course of Americans in the period 1920 to 1975, I have tried resolutely to write in the past tense. In doing so, I have implicitly argued that 1975 is not "now." And in many ways it is not: for a decade there have been abroad many indications, quantified and otherwise, that in important ways the sharp move away from the now-"traditional" family-building sequence, described in chapter 7, was over. Were I to develop this perspective fully, I would seek to document ways in which a modest return of favor for solo dating was becoming integrated with a still-evolving trend toward premarital cohabitation, in which a rather leisurely schedule of marriage was somehow integrated with a seeming recovery of favor for parenthood.

But I wish instead to invoke the historian's privilege of leaving the present to others and merely to assert that 1975 is simply *not* now, enough so that I may treat the period following the baby boom and before 1975 as in a sense closed, its historical meaning now accessible to us in a way that "now" is not. Greater historical distance, which patience alone can offer, may reveal that this asserted inflection point in fact is not one. This concluding chapter, then, will look once again backward, not forward, and will venture commentary on what has happened in the youthful life course over the period covered in this volume, not prognosis of what will shortly happen.

Social history is typically written in one of two ways that treat time differently: either the account is drawn in broad-brush fashion, covering relatively long periods, in which directional change in one realm is interpreted in relation to directional change in others, or it is drawn with a fine brush, in which essentially coeval aspects of society are explicated in their interrelationship to one another. My account here attempts an intermediate approach, aiming to describe elements of change quite close up and in a nuanced way so as to be able to offer evidence more directly than is usually offered on the relationships among aspects of social change, cultural tranformation, and individual experience. The question of the extent to which 1975 is or is not "now" in 1989, given my approach, is just one version of a larger question: how "then" and "before then" differ, when they are not long-distant from one another. The periodization I have employed and my heavy reliance on behavioral evidence has, I hope, allowed me to indicate how the separate tiles in an often-modified mosaic have been moved, how these moves have been constrained by the tiles' relationships to one another, and how the *gestalt* of the mosaic has *appeared* to those whose aggregated behaviors at the same time constituted it. But since the tiles in fact have been in frequent, irregular motion and since no *gestalt* is definitively crystallized, it is admittedly arbitrary for the analyst to distinguish "then" from "before then," just as "now" from "then."

Perhaps no less arbitrary is the answer I will offer to the historian's perpetual question of whether there has been more continuity or more change. I hope that stating the question so baldly embarrasses it a bit: I have never found the question admitted of a definitive answer, on any subject. In the body of this book, I have emphasized change. In these concluding reflections, however, I will emphasize continuities, common themes drawn from a more-distanced look at the materials I have presented. These common themes, I hope, represent both useful generalizations about trends in the lives of youth people in twentieth-century America and contributions to the sociology of the life course at the height of the period of "chronologization," to recur to Martin Kohli's challenging macrohistorical argument.

Much of the discussion in the preceding chapters has had explicit or implicit reference to changes in gender roles. Put simply, in a variety of relevant ways—from labor-force participation to understandings of sexuality—American women have become more like men than they were, over much of the period we are discussing. And as this has happened, the paths they have chosen are under constraint and in ongoing negotiation with the previous generation.

On the whole, too, the paths taken by diverse socioeconomic groups have become more alike. Relatively poorer young people have become absolutely more wealthy, have gained relatively more control of their own labor power, have had relatively more human capital investment made in their own capacities and demeanor. Increasingly, they have been able to devise, and presumably have devised, youthful life courses not dissimilar to one another.

But the same cannot be said for blacks and whites. Here there are signs of life courses that have long been distinctive and have, if anything, been further diverging from one another. It is rather apparent that gender roles differ between whites and blacks (at least between most whites and a large subset of blacks) and that sexuality has differed in its expression within the life course. Unfortunately, the mosaic that I have been able to construct, indistinct enough when "American" young people in general are in question, is sketchy in the extreme when "black Americans" in general are in question.

The historical experience documented here indicates that in the twentieth century, changing material circumstances have frequently influenced the choices that individuals have made in constructing their life courses—but within apparent limits. The market demand for labor, on the one hand, and the needs of the family economy, on the other, have been among the external circumstances that have had the most impact on the temporarily varying shape of the life course and so also have been the quantity and nature of available housing and state provision of schooling services to young people. These factors have produced mainly irregular fluctuations in life course patterning, being themselves subject to considerable fluctuation over the short term in which life course decisions are made.

But at the same time, my examination of the Great Depression and World War II strongly suggests the ability of the normative component of the life course to outweigh enormous circumstantial difficulties. Such a young and fragile institution as dating, despite its initial dependence on commercial recreation, seems only to have continued its spread through the Great Depression, despite the hindrances that empty pockets caused to its adherents. Even engagement proved in a sense to be viable: its indefinition permitted the emptying-out by Depression circumstances of some of its content, without the practice disappearing or even losing nominal adherence. And the seemingly formidable incompatibility of marriage and military service during World War II seems to have been overcome quite directly, with service marriages even gaining a somewhat heroic aura that was borne out in the superior performance of soldiers partaking in the experiment. Postwar divorce rates rose briefly, representing clearing-away of the surprisingly modest debris of war marriage, and promptly returned to prewar levels. They rose again, very far, a decade and a half later, not under external challenge so much but as a central mechanism for the restructuring of the relation of affect to obligation and of men to women, within marriage. This point appears especially vividly when we consider the implications over the entire life course of marriage now being understood as possibly transitory rather than normatively for a lifetime.

Members of cohorts whose youth intersected massive external events were greatly affected in the construction of their life courses—but the effects were in every instance temporary. Virtually no case appeared of a cohort that was so distracted from marrying or parenthood that it did not eventually catch up. Nor was any cohort prompted by great external events to assume a more rapid schedule in a way that outlasted the immediate circumstances. In fact, there seems to have been no year-to-year "momentum" in the pace of transition. The momentum, rather, was produced not by circumstance but by normative redefinition, when such occurred. And normative structures could both outlast such massive external change as that from 1929 to 1945 and change as though autonomously, as in the middle 1960s. At such times, last year's enlarged crop of postponed marriage, or divorces, or whatever, probably had a "demonstration effect" on those who contemplated such actions the following year. But the immediate post-World War II marriage and baby boom was different in kind from the classic baby boom as well as separated from it by several years, and the postwar divorce boom was promptly reversed.

The year-to-year volatility of rates of life course transition seems to have increased over the twentieth century. This was not a product of increasing openness of young people to the vagaries of external circumstances; if anything, it has been the contrary. Young individuals have gained more control over the resources that allow them to choose timing of their own life course events and have come increasingly to value the expression of personal choice in this as in other aspects of their own lives. And, increasingly, these very events have come to be a subject of public discussion.

Underlying this debate has been an imperative—not unchallenged, to be sure, especially during the 1930s—to couch discussion of institutional arrangements in terms of their implications for the realization of selfhood. Conformity to (adult) expectations, certainly at no time irrelevant to life course decisions, has come to matter less. One's own identity has come to matter correspondingly more. Even by 1920, "love" was an almost acceptable ideological justification for the timing of marriage. Over time, perhaps more sophisticated but no less individuated and situational rationales have more and more justified physical intimacy, going steady, becoming a parent, divorcing.

The youthful life course has been an arena in which young people have throughout the twentieth century been innovators. A central theme in their innovation has been the injection of increasing volition into the youthful life course. Individuals have come to be in a position to hasten or postpone their transitions and to sequence them more *ad lib* than once. The aggregate of such decisions has become the basis for noticeable short-run alteration in life course patterns. Initially, as in the construction of dating as a courtship process, young people *qua* young people took control of and provided social oversight of a phase that made explicit room for sexuality, that understood individual physical gratification, as "thrills," now an appropriate part of growing up. The arrangements that young people constructed came shortly to be fully accepted and capable within a generation of sustaining even such marked modifications as going steady, an arrangement in which physical expressiveness began to move from the relatively externalized "thrill" to something more nearly approaching "intimacy" in our current sense of the word.

In the Great Depression, and then again during World War II, young people found that material circumstances interfered in individual cases with the volitional reconstruction of the youthful life course. The tension thus produced led to debates both over the appropriate social provision for on-time family-building and the appropriate extent of what was seen as essentially improvised patterns of courtship and marriage. Even at the height of the baby boom, young women contemplating careers—what now seem to have been "selfless" mothers—valued the transition to parenthood because it enabled their selves to grow.

The experience in improvisation was a surprisingly smooth one, and confidence in the ability of love (and volition) to structure the life course increased. Further encouraged by feminist and more general ideological currents in the 1960s and 1970s, peer-group oversight of youthful heterosexual relationships has retreated the more, leaving couples to do what seems right. With sexuality increasingly understood as an element of individual good rather than as a socially or divinely proscribed misjudgment, and with gender asymmetry considerably reduced, heterosexual dyads have become far more idiosyncratic in their dynamics.

None of this would have been possible had the twentieth century not been a period of markedly enlarged resources for young people. Income is the most obvious, young people benefiting here greatly from the generally enlarged disposable material resources over the twentieth century. We need not maintain that young people have achieved *relatively* greater material resources *vis-à-vis* their parents and other adults. It is sufficient rather that they have become more nearly able to sustain on their own the costs of the youthful life course transitions, and this has indeed been the case. We are talking (as it were) of a queuing process, with young people increasingly receiving an adequate residue to sponsor the portions of their growing up that interest us here. Especially important has been the steady freeing-up of young people's labor power from limitations imposed by the family and by institutions of the state. Increasingly, young people have been able to purchase commercial entertainment, transportation, and housing—the materials of occasional or frequent independence from the supervision of their elders—to innovate in the construction of immediate aspects of their own life course. At the same time, we must not overlook the consternation—and improvisation—engendered by interruptions in the long-term trend toward increased material resources in the hands of young people. Too, we must recall that the overall phase to a degree happened one gender at a time, with boys initially but decreasingly advantaged relative to girls.

Relevant also has been the great enlargement in human capital investment made in young people in the form of education. Such an investment, made by the state and by parents, among other things has transferred both potential material resources and immediate cultural resources (as I have argued in regard to the meaning of the high school, some of these of their own making) to young people. Both commercial and social motives have led to the diffusion of simple and inexpensive birth control technologies to young people. This has proved an important resource to those who wished to modify the life course to permit more choice.

A general tendency discussed in particular chapters has been the liberating of one transition from the next—the weakening (but not the overthrow) of determinate sequences and intervals. Once again, we can understand this in terms of resources in the hands of youthful innovators. If sanctioned social provision is made for work force entry succeeding, not preceding, school departure, if sanctioned social provision is made for parenthood succeeding, not preceding, marriage, the young actors can overlook the sanction if they can command the resources allowing "deviant" sequencing, just as a newly married couple can long or forever postpone parenthood if they know how and can "afford" the married-and-childless status.

Where alterations to the life course have proven at all lasting, they have shortly been enshrined as normative—even seen as the restoration of tradition. Exigencies in the adult world—the need for family income, for war workers, for soldiers in war and in peace, for full-bore consumers of material goods, for well-groomed minimum-wage employees—made it impossible for adults to speak in a single voice about the proper way for youth to construct their life courses. Broad-gauged cultural debates over the appropriateness of dating, petting, going steady, younger marriage, older marriage, earlier and later parenthood, and even divorce promptly gathered about them phalanxes of experts who sought to reassure those older than the innovators that rather than real innovation the new patterns merely refined the values inherent in the previous pattern. Repeatedly, those who sought to examine the "generation gap" with regard to elements of the construction of the life course found no fundamental disagreement, because adults espoused positions that looked like those of their seemingly dissident juniors.

In fact, the process by which young people's innovative behaviors emerged has itself worked to produce eventual consensus. Few families were riven along generational lines. What was at stake, in any case, was not a new organization of family structure but rather of the youthful life course, which at most modified but did not seriously challenge the *long-term* obligations children owed to their parents, or to adults. In twentieth-century America, parents never possessed enough of a monopoly of resources that they could plausibly enforce exactly their view of the right way to grow up. Children, adult and independent children just as adolescents, were in theory supposed to weigh parental injunctions along with other considerations and make their own choices. A built-in negotiation procedure, thus, promoted the emergence of commonalties between generations, even as change has taken place.

Young people in the twentieth century have come into their own in ways that regularly have baffled adults and have seemed to young people to be true to themselves. Family formation, accordingly, has been challenging and perilous, an arena worthy of receiving—and in fact gaining—the close attention of the actors and the many categories of interested bystanders. To a degree, the arena has changed auspices; and to a degree, its rules have evolved apace. But no less than before, young adults come into their own in due time and in due course.

APPENDIX 1
DATA UNDERLYING FIGURES

Figure 1: Census CPS P20–385, tables 7B and 7C.

Figures 2 through 5: Census 1960–4, table 2; Census 1970–2, table 2; Census 1980–1, table 16.

Figures 6 and 7: Census 1930–1, 1180–1181.

Figures 8 and 9: Census 1930–1, 846–47.

Figures 10 and 11: U.S. Office of Education, *Bulletin 1936, no. 18. VI: Community Surveys*, 3. These data are derived from thirteen cities surveyed by the Office of Education's Committee on Youth Problems. Total sample size was 48,801.

Figure 12: Melvin Schubert Brooks, "Wisconsin Birth and Marriage Rate Trends by Occupation, 1920–1936" (Ph.D. dissertation, University of Wisconsin, 1941), 82, 159.

Figure 13: U.S. Federal Security Agency, U.S. Public Health Service, National Office of Vital Statistics, *Monthly Marriage Report*, Series PM-4, no. 13 (April 21, 1947), table 2.

Figure 14: Census P46–4, 2, 3.

Figure 15: Census 1960–4, table 2.

Figure 16: Model based on ordinary least squares linear regression on the 1944 *American Soldier* white data set. See discussion in text and Appendix 4.

Figure 17: Census CPS P60, annual numbers dealing with income.

Figures 18 and 19: Census 1960–3, tables 1 and 2.

Figures 20 and 21: USNCHS, *Vital Statistics*, III, annual series (gaps in original).

Figure 22: Melvin Zelnik, John F. Kantner, and Kathleen Ford, *Sex and Pregnancy in Adolescence* (Beverly Hills: Sage Publications, 1981), 65.

APPENDIX 2
SHORT-FORM REFERENCES TO PUBLICATIONS OF THE UNITED STATES, DEPARTMENT OF COMMERCE, BUREAU OF THE CENSUS

DECENNIAL CENSUS REPORTS

Thirteenth Census of the United States, Population, General Report	*Census 1910-1*
Census of 1920, Population, General Report	*Census 1920-1*
Fifteenth Census of the United States: 1930, Vol. II, Population, II: General Report	*Census 1930-1*
Fifteenth Census of the United States: 1930. Vol. VI, Families	*Census 1930-2*
Sixteenth Census of the United States: 1940. Population: General Characteristics	*Census 1940-1*
Sixteenth Census of the United States: 1940. Population: Education, Occupation, and Household Relationship of Males 18 to 44 Years	*Census 1940-2*
Sixteenth Census of the United States: 1940. Population: Differential Fertility 1940 and 1910. Fertility by Duration of Marriage	*Census 1940-3*
Sixteenth Census of the United States: 1940. Population: Differential Fertility 1940 and 1910, Women by Number of Children Ever Born	*Census 1940-4*
Sixteenth Census of the United States: 1940. The Labor Force, Part 1: United States Summary	*Census 1940-5*
Sixteenth Census of the United States: 1940. Popu-	

*1970 Census of Population. Subject Report PC(2)-
6E. Veterans*   Census 1970-5
*1980 Census of Population. Subject Report PC80-
2-4C. Marital Characteristics*   Census 1980-1

CURRENT POPULATION SURVEY

*The Current Population Survey carries out several
concurrent series from which I have drawn here.
Many numbers have subject titles, and some have
stated authors. These all are referenced here
simply by series and number, however, as, for
instance, the short-form entry for Series P-20,*   Census CPS
Number 385 is: P20-385

OTHER SERIAL PUBLICATIONS

*Population—Special Reports, Series P-46, No. 4
(1946)*   Census P46-4
*Population—Special Reports, Series P-46, No. 8
(1946)*   Census P46-8
Population, Series P-S, No. 10 (1946)   Census P-S-10
Population, Series P-S, No. 16 (1947)   Census P-S-17
Population, Series P-S, No. 22 (1947)   Census P-S-22
*Current Population Reports, Housing Statistics,
Housing Characteristics in 108 Selected Areas,
Census Series HVet., No. 115 (1947). (Pub-   Census Hous-
lished in conjunction with the Housing and   ing 1947
Home Finance Agency)*

OCCASIONAL PUBLICATIONS

*Historical Statistics of the United States, Colonial   Census Histori-
Times to 1970. Bicentennial Edition*   cal Statistics
Marriage and Divorce 1930   Census Mar-
                                                          riage 1930
Marriage and Divorce 1931   Census Mar-
                                                          riage 1931

Marriage and Divorce 1932	*Census Marriage 1932*
1956 National Housing Inventory, III. Characteristics of the 1956 Inventory	*Census Housing 1956*
Population Trends in the United States 1900 to 1960 ("Technical Paper No. 10")	*Census Population Trends*
Trends in the Income of Families and Persons in the United States: 1947 to 1964 (Technical Paper No. 17)	*Census Trends in Income*

APPENDIX 3
SHORT-FORM REFERENCES TO FEDERAL *VITAL STATISTICS* PUBLICATIONS

U.S. Public Health Service, *Vital Statistics of the United States*	USNCHS *Vital Statistics*
U.S. Public Health Service, National Office of Vital Statistics, *Monthly Marriage Report*, Series PM-4, no. 13 (April 21, 1947)	USNCHS Monthly Marriage Report
U.S. National Center for Health Statistics, *Patterns of Aggregate and Individual Changes in Contraceptive Practice: United States 1965–1975* (USNCHS "Vital and Health Statistics," Series 3, no. 17, 1979)	USNCHS Series 3-17
James V. Scanlon, *Self-Reported Health Behavior and Attitudes of 12–17 Years* (USNCHS "Vital and Health Statistics," Series 11, no. 147, 1975)	USNCHS Series 11-147
Dorothee K. Vogt, *Health Attitudes and Behavior of Youths 12–17 Years* (USNCHS "Vital and Health Statistics," Series 11, no. 153, 1975)	USNCHS Series 11-153
Carl E. Ortmeyer, *Demographic Characteristics of Persons Married between January 1955 and June 1958*	

(USNCHS "Vital and Health Statistics," Series 21, no. 2, 1965)   USNCHS Series 21-2

Trends in Illegitimacy: United States 1940–1965
(USNCHS "Vital and Health Statistics," Series 21, no.15, 1968)   USNCHS Series 21-15

Robert H. Weller, *Wanted and Unwanted Childbearing in the United States*
(USNCHS "Vital and Health Statistics," Series 21, no. 32, 1979)   USNCHS Series 21-32

Alexander A. Plateris, *Divorces by Marriage Cohort*
(USNCHS, "Vital and Health Statistics," Series 21, no. 34, 1979)   USNCHS Series 21-34

Alexander A. Plateris, *Duration of Marriage, United States*
(USNCHS, "Vital and Health Statistics," Series 21, no. 38, 1981)   USNCHS Series 21-38

U.S. National Center for Health Statistics, Vital and Health Statistics, *Advancedata* 102
(December 4, 1984).   USNCHS, *Advancedata*

APPENDIX 4
CITATIONS TO MACHINE-
READABLE DATA SETS

An important set of sources for me as I have written this account has been machine-readable data sets of surveys or other investigations or of routinely generated materials. Many such data sets, including most of those that I have used here, are held at and made available by archives devoted to this kind of material; others have been provided by researchers who have gathered them. Those who have provided machine-readable materials to me and to whom I am indebted are:

- University of Wisconsin, Data and Program Library Service (Wisconsin)
- Georgetown University Center for Population Research (Georgetown)
- Institute for Sex Research, Indiana University (Kinsey Institute)
- Inter-University Consortium for Political and Social Research (ICPSR)
- Minnesota Political Data Archive, University of Minnesota (Minnesota)
- Philip Morris Corporation (PM Corp.)
- Roper Center Archives, University of Connecticut (Roper Center)

The machine-readable files that I have used here, together with their dates of publication, sample sizes, and archival location, follow on page 344. Except where noted, the data approximate random national samples. In some instances (described in text) I have used subsamples that are proportionately smaller than the total number of cases in the archived file.

ACKNOWLEDGMENTS

The Inter-University Consortium for Political and Social Research, University of Michigan, provides users with data supplied to it by the organizations who created it and does not vouch for their accuracy. All tabulations and interpretations presented in this volume are my own. I should particularly like to thank Jerome Clubb, Director, Erik Austin, Director of Archives, and Janet Vavra, Technical Director, for their devotion to scholarship, in addition to their particular assistance to me over the years.

The Roper Center Archives, University of Connecticut, likewise houses numerous data sets that I used in this study. Marilyn Potter, of User Services, has been unfailingly helpful and polite.

The Indianapolis Fertility Study data set has been recoded by Jeanne Clare Ridley of the Georgetown University Center for Population Research and her associates. Their purpose was to provide a methodological sample for comparision with a retrospective study of their own. Their providing me with a data tape even before they had published their own analysis is an exceptionally fine example of scholarly cooperation. I thank Dr. Ridley and her assistant, Deborah Dawson.

The coded Kinsey-study data are made available in machine-readable form by the Institute for Sex Research, Indiana University. I should like to thank Paul Gebhart, Director of the Institute, for his assistance to me in understanding and gaining access to these data.

William Flanigan of the Department of Political Science, University of Minnesota, a good friend to historians at and beyond the university, helped me indirectly to acquire various of the AIPO polls from the Roper Center and directly to acquire the Minnesota youth poll from the archive he himself directed.

Alice Robbin, Director of the University of Wisconsin Data and Program Library Service, was an enthusiastic supporter of my project of entering and encoding the rather open-ended materials gathered from single women in 1955 by the Growth of American Families Study and is curator of these data, which had been until I located them wisely preserved by Larry L. Bumpass, Department of Sociology.

Finally, the preservation and annotation of these data would have served me hardly at all had I not had the assistance, in sequence, of Phil Voxland and John Stuckey, then Director of the Social Sciences Research Facilities Center, University of Minnesota, and Director of Computing at the College of Humanities and Social Sciences, Carnegie Mellon University, respectively. Each of these fine people is seriously committed to the research endeavor and possesses the quick wit and sense of humor that makes a process that sometimes is infuriating usually a pleasure.

Study	Date	Cases	Location
AIPO 099	1937	1965	Roper
Kinsey Sex History Study (non-random sample, whites only)	1938-1963	10845	Kinsey
Roper Commercial Poll 15 (children 10–19 years old)	1939	3161	Roper
Indianapolis Fertility Study (native white Protestants married between 1927 and 1929 and living in Indianapolis)	1941	860	Georgetown
American Soldier S-106	1944	9892	Roper
American Soldier S-144	1944	4678	Roper
American Soldier S-233	1945	2685	Roper
AIPO 377	1946	2816	Roper
Minnesota Juvenile Poll 41 (Minnesota youth only)	1947	591	Minnesota
1950 Census of Population (1-in-100 public-use sample)	1950	461130	ICPSR
AIPO 516	1953	1547	Roper
Survey of Consumer Attitudes and Behavior (SRC613)	1953	970	ICPSR
1955 Growth of American Families Single Women Study (single women 18–24)	1955	254	Wisconsin
AIPO 563	1956	2000	Roper
AIPO 578	1957	1504	Roper
Americans View Their Mental Health	1957	5247	ICPSR
Project Talent (high school students; public-use sample)	1960	4000	ICPSR
Virginia Slims Women's Poll	1974	3800	PM Corp.
Current Population Survey	1975	108963	ICPSR
Americans View Their Mental Health	1976	4251	ICPSR
Monitoring the Future (high school seniors)	1976	16677	ICPSR
National Survey of Adolescent Female Sexual Behavior (girls 15–19, stratified to oversample blacks)	1976	2193	ICPSR

NOTES

1: Defining One's Own

1. Faith Baldwin, "Can She Bake a Cherry Pie?" *Ladies' Home Journal* (December 1941): 23.

2. Michael C. Keeley, "The Economics of Family Formation," *Economic Inquiry* 15 (1977): 238–250.

3. Frank F. Furstenberg, Jr., *et al.*, "The Life Course of Children of Divorce: Marital Disruption and Parental Contact," *American Sociological Review* 48 (1983): 656–668; Robert H. Mnookin *et al.*, *In the Interest of Children* (New York: W. H. Freeman and Company, 1985).

4. "Never Been Kissed," *True Confessions* 26 (March 1935): 16.

5. William J. Goode, "The Theoretical Importance of Love," *American Sociological Review* 24 (1959): 38–47; David M. Schneider and Raymond T. Smith, *Class Differences and Sex Roles in American Kinship and Family Structure* (Englewood Cliffs, N.J.: Prentice-Hall, 1973).

6. Helen Gurley Brown, *Sex and the Single Girl* (New York: Cardinal Books, 1963 [1962]); Betty Friedan, *The Feminine Mystique* (New York: Dell, 1977 [1963; excerpts were serialized in 1962]).

7. Brown, *Sex*, 2.

8. Friedan, *Feminine Mystique*, 351.

9. Brown, *Sex*, 5.

10. *Ibid.*, 73.

11. Friedan, *Feminine Mystique*, 40.

12. *Sex*, 246.

13. "Engagement Jitters," *True Love Stories* 67 (May 1957): 32.

14. Hannah M. Stone and Abraham Stone, *A Marriage Manual* (New York: Simon and Schuster, 1937), 278–281, and *A Marriage Manual*, completely rev. ed. (New York: Simon and Schuster, 1952), 228–229.

15. Not all intimacy is heterosexual, of course, nor all lasting unions. Nor do I wish to imply that heterosexuality is part of the biological program and homosexuality a perversion. I understand sexual preference to be part of the cultural script. And yet, partly for evidentiary reasons and partly because the choice of sexual preference typically occurs considerably earlier in the life course, I have elected to omit this theoretically relevant aspect of sequential self-definition.

16. Even less precise, but no less real, are the "institutionalized images of social and emotional maturity," expressed within peer groups,

that explain the timing and other circumstances of *dating*, developmentally the earliest of the life course transitions I treat in this book. In a fascinating study, the conclusion of which I quote, Dornbusch *et al.* have shown that stage in physiological sexual maturity (as of 1966–1970) had *no* impact on the inception of dating, apart from its correlation with the socially underlined *chronological age*. Sanford M. Dornbusch *et al.*, "Social Development, Age, and Dating: A Comparison of Biological and Social Influence upon One Set of Behaviors," *Child Development* 52 (1981), 179–185.

17. The editors of *Bride's Magazine, Bride's Book of Etiquette* (3d ed. revised and updated; New York: Grosset & Dunlap, 1973), 19. See also Marguerite Bentley, *Wedding Etiquette* (Philadelphia: John C. Winston Company, 1947), vii. And see Barbara Wilson, *The Brides' School Complete Book of Engagement and Wedding Etiquette* (New York: Hawthorn Books, 1959), and Flora Bryant and Kendall Bryant, *It's Your Wedding* (New York: Cowles Book Company, 1970).

18. One clergyman in the late 1930s neatly conflated the dimensions at work here: "Most people who have money, and can afford to, are bound by tradition to get married in church. If they are wealthy, they want to. As a matter of fact, they are expected to make a big splurge of it." Ruby Jo Reeves, "Marriages in New Haven Since 1870" (Ph.D. dissertation, Yale University, 1938), VII-7. See also B. F. Timmons, "The Cost of Weddings," *American Sociological Review* 4 (1939): 224–233. A national survey in 1953 asked respondents what type of wedding they had had and how much income a young couple needed to get along. There was a strong correlation, both between educational level and type of wedding and *within educational level*, between type of wedding and the amount of income a young couple was seen to require. Computed from survey AIPO 563, machine-readable data. See Appendix 4 for details on machine-readable data sets.

19. United States National Center for Health Statistics, *Vital Statistics of the United States*, III, annual, 1960–1975. The exact bibliographical data for these volumes have varied somewhat over this period. These and other references based on *Vital Statistics* are henceforth abbreviated as USNCHS *Vital Statistics*. Appendix 3 gives details on abbreviated references.

20. Reeves, "Marriages in New Haven," II-11.

21. *Philadelphia Mayor's Report*, Report of Division of Vital Statistics, annual.

22. Paul H. Jacobsen, *American Marriage and Divorce* (New York: Rinehart, 1959), 57.

23. A national survey in 1953 suggests an *increase* in church wed-

dings over the several decades preceding, interrupted perhaps by the Depression and surely by World War II. Home weddings was the category that became less frequent, as more elaborate religious weddings, at church, became more common. AIPO 563, tabulated by age to approximate trends over time.

24. To be sure, wedding notices in newspapers bear on only that subcategory of weddings for which there were newspaper reports, presumably biased toward better-off people and those who marry in conventional fashion.

25. The years for which I gathered articles have no special meaning, except in that they permit me to describe trends over time. For the last observation, the newspapers were not so readily available, at the Minnesota Historical Society, as they had been for earlier years. In addition, the St. Paul newspaper had ceased publishing wedding notices by this date, a more prestigious Minneapolis paper having assumed this function. The choice of data from Minnesota—as of many of the locality-based materials used in this book—was based largely on convenience; the ritual patterns, however, are surely essentially national.

26. *Bride's Book of Etiquette*, 28.

27. Goode, "The Theoretical Importance of Love," 38–47.

28. Automobile ownership registration systems do not compile their data by age, but drivers' licensing systems do and capture adequately the developmental pattern of *access* to automobiles and the mobility they make possible. These data are published annually in U.S. Department of Transportation, Federal Highway Administration, *Highway Statistics Summary to 1975* (Washington: USGPO, n.d.), 68–80.

29. Data on state drivers' licensing regulations are published annually in the *Information Please Almanac*.

30. Anne Foner and David Kertzer, "Transitions Over the Life Course: Lessons from Age-Set Societies," *American Journal of Sociology* 83 (1978): 1081–1104; Joseph F. Kett, *Rites of Passage: Adolescence in America, 1790 to the Present* (New York: Basic Books, 1977); Talcott Parsons, "Age and Sex in the Social Structure of the United States," *American Sociological Review* 7 (1942): 604–616; Michael B. Katz, Michael B. Doucet, and Mark J. Stern, *The Social Organization of Early Industrial Capitalism* (Cambridge: Harvard University Press, 1982); Harold L. Wilensky, "Orderly Careers and Social Participation in the Middle Mass," *American Sociological Review* 26 (1961): 521–539.

31. Leonard I. Pearlin, "Discontinuities in the Study of Aging," in Hareven, ed., *Aging and Life Course Transitions*, 55–74.

32. Richard B. Freeman and James L. Medoff, *The Youth Labor Market Problem: Its Nature, Causes and Consequences* (Chicago: University of Chicago Press, 1982), 47.

33. A careful empirical specification of several aspects of this phenomenon, dealing with the late 1950s and 1960s, is Margaret Mooney Marini and Peter J. Hodson, "Effects of the Timing of First Marriage and First Birth on the Timing and Spacing of Subsequent Births," *Demography* 18 (1981): 529–548. See also Glen H. Elder, Jr., "Role Orientation, Marital Age, and Life Patterns in Adulthood," *Merrill-Palmer Quarterly of Behavior and Development* 18 (1972): 3–24.

34. *Happiness in Marriage* (New York: Blue Ribbon Books, 1926), 199. For some modest contemporaneous empirical support, see Katherine Bement Davis, *Factors in the Sex Life of Twenty-Two Hundred Women* (New York: Harper & Brothers, 1929), 49.

35. New York: McGraw-Hill, 1938, 171–173.

36. Evelyn Millis Duvall and Reuben Hill, *When You Marry* (New York: Association Press, 1949), 302; Robert O. Blood, Jr., and Donald M. Wolfe, *Husbands and Wives* (New York: The Free Press, 1960), chaps. 5, 8.

37. Norval D. Glenn and Sara McLanahan, "Children and Marital Happiness: A Further Specification of the Relationship," *Journal of Marriage and the Family* 44 (1982): 71.

38. For a relevant discussion of the changing impact of the transition to parenthood on marital stability, see Elwood Carlson and Kandi Stinson, "Motherhood, Marriage Timing, and Marital Stability: A Research Note," *Social Forces* 61 (1982): 258–267.

39. John Modell and Tamara K. Hareven, "Transitions: Patterns of Timing," in Hareven, ed., *Transitions*, 245–270.

40. Alice S. Rossi, "Gender and Parenthood," in Rossi, ed., *Gender and the Life Course* (New York: Aldine Publishing Company, 1985), 162–169.

41. Marian B. Sussman and Lee Burchinal, "Parental Aid to Married Children: Implications for Family Functioning," *Marriage and Family Living* 24 (1962): 320–322; James A. Davis, *Stipends and Spouses* (Chicago: University of Chicago Press, 1962).

42. Gunhild O. Hagestad, "The Aging Society as a Context for Family Life," *Daedalus* 115 (Winter 1986): 126.

43. Norman B. Ryder, "The Cohort as a Concept in the Study of Social Change," *American Sociological Review* 30 (1965): 843–861.

44. Matilda W. Riley, "Age Strata in Social Systems," in R. H. Binstock and E. Shanas, eds., *Handbook of Aging and the Social Sciences* (New York: Van Nostrand Reinhold, 1976), 189–217; Bernice L.

Neugarten, J. W. Moore, and J. C. Lowe, "Age Norms, Age Constraints, and Adult Socialization," *American Journal of Sociology* 70 (1965): 710–717.

45. Paul B. Baltes and K. Warner Schaie, eds., *Life-Span Developmental Psychology: Personality and Socialization* (New York: Academic Press, 1973).

46. Glen H. Elder, Jr., "Family History and the Life Course," in Tamara K. Hareven, ed., *Transitions: The Family and the Life Course in Historical Perspective* (New York: Academic Press, 1978), 23.

47. David L. Featherman, "Biography, Society, and History: Individual Development as a Population Process," in Aage B. Sorensen, Franz E. Weinert, and Lonnie R. Sherrod, eds., *Human Development and the Life Course: Multidisciplinary Perspectives* (Hillsdale, N.J.: Lawrence Erlbaum Associates, 1986), 101.

48. Tamara K. Hareven, "The Life Course and Aging in Historical Perspective," in Hareven, ed., *Aging and Life Course Transitions: An Interdisciplinary Perspective* (New York: The Guilford Press, 1982), 8.

49. Glen H. Elder, Jr., *Children of the Great Depression* (Chicago: University of Chicago Press, 1974).

50. Glen H. Elder, Jr., "Perspectives on the Life Course," in Elder, ed., *Life Course Dynamics: Trajectories and Transitions, 1968–1980* (Ithaca: Cornell University Press, 1985), 23–27.

51. "The World We Forgot: A Historical Review of the Life Course," in Victor W. Marshall, ed., *Later Life: The Social Psychology of Aging* (Beverly Hills: Sage Publications, 1986).

52. Susan Littwin, *The Postponed Generation: Why America's Grown-up Kids Are Growing Up Later* (New York: Morrow, 1986).

53. *Ibid.*, 16–17.

54. Elder, "Perspectives on the Life Course," 29.

55. Deemed a highly encouraging trend by the President's Science Advisory Committee on Youth in 1973, gainful employment by schoolchildren is currently under fierce attack, explicitly because jobs of the fast-food variety are said not to promote the transition to adulthood as once hoped but, rather, "pseudomaturity." See Ellen Greenberger and Laurence Steinberg, *When Teenagers Work* (New York: Basic Books, 1987).

56. Sandra L. Hofferth, "Updating Children's Life Course," *Journal of Marriage and the Family* 47 (1985): 93–115.

57. Uhlenberg, "Cohort Variations in Family Life Cycle Experiences of U.S. Females," *Journal of Marriage and the Family* 36 (1974): 284–292; Uhlenberg, "Changing Configurations of the Life Course," in Hareven, *Transitions*, 65–97; Uhlenberg, "Death and the Family,"

Journal of Family History 5 (1980): 313–320. Uhlenberg's methodological and, to an extent, conceptual influence on my present study is evident in John Modell, Frank F. Furstenberg, Jr., and Theodore Hershberg, "Social Change and Transitions to Adulthood in Historical Perspective," *Journal of Family History* 1 (1976): 7–32.

58. Dennis Hogan, *Transitions and Social Change* (New York: Academic Press, 1981).

59. John Modell, "Levels of Change over Time," *Historical Methods Newsletter* 8 (1975): 116–127; see also John Modell, "Public Griefs and Personal Problems: An Empirical Inquiry into the Impact of the Great Depression," *Social Science History* 9 (1985): 399–428. On age-specific contextual effects in the Great Depression, see Howard M. Bell, *Youth Tell Their Story* (Washington, D.C.: American Council on Education, 1938); Nettie Pauline McGill and Ellen Nathalie Matthews, *The Youth of New York City* (New York: Macmillan, 1940); *Milwaukee Youth Report Their Status* (Milwaukee: Milwaukee Vocational School, 1942).

60. John Modell, "Changing Risks, Changing Adaptations: American Families in the Nineteenth and Twentieth Centuries," in Allan J. Lichtman and Joan R. Challinor, eds., *Kin and Communities* (Washington, D.C.: Smithsonian Institution Press, 1979), 119–144.

61. Modell, Furstenberg, and Hershberg, "Social Change and Transitions to Adulthood"; John Modell, "Normative Aspects of American Marriage Timing Since World War II," *Journal of Family History* 5 (1980): 210–234.

62. Logically, "aging" processes could have changed, too, but we may assume that they did not for people of the ages in question here.

63. Pascal K. Whelpton, *Cohort Fertility: Native White Women in the United States* (Princeton: Princeton University Press, 1954).

64. We are, to be sure, dealing with phenomena somewhat different from Whelpton's. By definition, *first* events (like becoming a parent) are unique in any person's life, whereas the whole of the "fertility schedule" is open-ended, continuing as long as 25 or 30 years beyond initiation. Basically, then, we cannot discuss tempo or quantity, only timing.

65. David Levine, *Family Formation in an Age of Nascent Capitalism* (New York: Academic Press, 1977).

66. Remarriage, the study of which is understandably a growth industry among demographers these days, is not treated here.

67. The most obvious "paydirt" on this question is the large empirical study by Ernest W. Burgess and Paul Wallin entitled *Engagement and Marriage* (Philadelphia: Lippincott, 1953). But despite this

book's title, engagement was largely uninteresting to the authors, except for the "predictive" information that could be collected by themselves during this phase on couples that would in many cases subsequently marry so that they might discern the characteristics associated with happy marriage. They were barely interested in what predicted longer or shorter engagements, or marriage *per se*. I also examined the questionnaires gathered by Burgess and Wallin in the Ernest W. Burgess Papers, Special Collections, Regenstein Library, University of Chicago, and found that they never had cared much about engagement as such.

68. An excellent example is Harvey J. Locke, *Predicting Adjustment in Marriage: A Comparison of a Divorced and a Happily Married Group* (New York: Henry Holt, 1951), 91–96.

69. Susan Cotts Watkins, "On Measuring Transitions and Turning Points," *Historical Methods* 13 (1980): 181–187.

70. Herbert H. Hyman, *Secondary Analysis of Survey Data* (New York: John Wiley & Sons, 1972).

71. Appendix 4 describes machine-readable materials used in my research and the mode of citation I employ.

72. Short-form references to national census materials are listed in Appendix 2. Like listings to national vital statistics materials are listed in Appendix 3.

2: The Changing Life Course of America's Youth

1. *Census—Historical Statistics* I, 379; *Census-CPS P20–390*.

2. On the changing relationship of educational attainment to socioeconomic background, see Robert D. Mare, "Change and Stability in Educational Stratification," *American Sociological Review* 46 (1981): 72–87.

3. The temporary parallelism of the trends was not coincidental. For an insightful historical overview of the evolution of the youth labor market, see Paul Osterman, *Getting Started: The Youth Labor Market* (Cambridge: MIT Press, 1980), chap. 4. Aggregating the experience of white and black young people conceals the fact that the extension of schooling may have affected the two differentially with regard to subsequent exclusive commitment to the labor force. A subtle analysis of how this has happened in the past two decades is Robert D. Mare and Christopher Winship, "The Paradox of Lessening Racial Inequality and Joblessness among Black Youth: Enrollment, Enlistment, and Employment, 1964–1981," *American Sociological Review* 49 (1984): 39–55.

4. These data depend on tabulations of service by age reported in the 1960, 1970, and 1980 censuses, which are broken down according to whether there was *any* wartime service or none at all. Service was up to the date of the census and, here, refers to people varying somewhat in age at time of the inquiry but typically only somewhat beyond ordinary military ages.

5. Catherine S. Chilman, *Adolescent Sexuality in a Changing American Society* (DHEW Publication No. [NIH] 79–1426, 1979), 115.

6. Alfred C. Kinsey, Wardell B. Pomeroy, and Clyde E. Martin, *Sexual Behavior in the Human Male* (Philadelphia: Saunders, 1948), 400; Alfred C. Kinsey *et al.*, *Sexual Behavior in the Human Female* (Philadelphia: Saunders, 1953), 339. In the Kinsey data, as one *should* find, premarital coitus was closely linked with approaching marriage (for women especially), but Kinsey's sample greatly oversampled men and women who had married late or had not married at all. For the reanalysis I employ here, I have therefore restandardized Kinsey's data by year of interview and educational level to reflect better than would the raw data, or the published tabulations, the marital-age and educational composition of the U.S. white population. This type of standardization, however, is devilishly difficult to carry out, in view of imprecisions of date and the wide range of years of interview. See Appendix 4. For the Kinsey data, see Paul H. Gebhard and Alan B. Johnson, *The Kinsey Data* (Philadelphia: W. B. Saunders Company, 1979).

7. There are simply no remotely reliable early data on the sexual behavior of nonwhite Americans. A small sample of retrospective data for white and black women in low-income areas in sixteen cities indicates that for the earliest cohort queried (born 1920–1929), the proportion of black women who had had premarital intercourse by age 17—about one in two—greatly exceeded that of whites. Some of this remarkable difference might be due to differential reporting, since in the 1970s, premarital coitus was considered far more shameful among whites than among blacks. Over succeeding cohorts, the reports by whites converged somewhat with those of blacks, which were roughly stable. J. Richard Udry, Karl E. Bauman, and Naomi M. Morris, "Changes in Premarital Coital Experience of Recent Decade-of-Birth Cohorts of Urban American Women," *Journal of Marriage and the Family* 37 (1975): 783–781. Carlfred Broderick's intriguing early 1960s single-city study comparing white and black children's reports of heterosexual relationships indicates that the preadolescent and adolescent peer culture of black *boys, but not black girls*, was considerably more "sexualized" than that of white counterparts, at least in the ritualized ways characteristic of young people of that era. Thus, at all

ages from 10 through 17, black boys were more likely than white boys to have played kissing games, to have kissed a girl seriously, to be going steady (but not simply to be dating), to identify a girlfriend, and to enjoy romantic movies. "Social Heterosexual Development among Urban Negroes and Whites," *Journal of Marriage and the Family* 27 (1965): 200–203.

8. Harold Christensen and Christina Gregg, "Changing Sex Norms in America and Scandinavia," *Journal of Marriage and the Family* 32 (1970): 616–627; on the 1950s, see Chilman, *Adolescent Sexuality*, 118, and Eleanore B. Luckey and Gilbert D. Nass, "A Comparison of Sexual Attitudes and Behavior in an International Sample," *Journal of Marriage and the Family* 31 (1967): 364–379.

9. Donald Carns, "Talking about Sex: Notes on First Coitus and the Double Standard," *Journal of Marriage and the Family* 35 (1973): 677–688; William Simon and John Gagnon, "Beyond Anxiety and Fantasy: The Coital Experience of College Youths," *Journal of Youth and Adolescence* 1 (1972): 203–222.

10. Melvin Zelnik and John F. Kantner, "Sexuality, Contraception, and Pregnancy among Young Unwed Females in the United States," in U.S. Commission on Population Growth and the American Future, *Demographic and Social Aspects of Population Growth*, "Commission Research Reports," Vol. I (Washington, D.C.: USGPO, 1972), 355–374.

11. Melvin Zelnik, John F. Kantner, and Kathleen Ford, *Sex and Pregnancy in Adolescence* (Beverly Hills: Sage Publications, 1981), 65; Melvin Zelnik and Farida K. Shah, "First Intercourse among Young Americans," *Family Planning Perspectives* 15 (1983): 64.

12. Daniel Scott Smith and Michael Hindus, "Premarital Pregnancy in America, 1640–1971: An Overview and Interpretation," *Journal of Interdisciplinary History* 4 (1975): 537–570; *USNCHS-Series 21-15*, 38.

13. *Census CPS P20–385.*

14. Obviously, mothers *never* married are excluded, unfortunately.

15. Data not graphed here also pertain to marriages contracted at 14–17, a relatively rare phenomenon. Here, at essentially "deviant" ages for marriage, the differentials are rather more compelling among whites than among blacks.

16. Calculated from Martin O'Connell and Maurice J. Moore, "The Legitimacy Status of First Births to U.S. Women Aged 15–24, 1939–1978," *Family Planning Perspectives* 12 (January-February 1980), tables 1 and 2.

17. Calculated from *Census 1930–1*, 1181. The data pertain to females only, unfortunately.

18. These data unfortunately distinguish only between those mar-

ried *and with spouse present*, not simply married, as in 1930. Surely this does affect the conclusions. *Census 1970–3*, 255.

19. Here the data pertain to 1940 and 1970. *Census 1970–4*, 67–68.

20. These analyses rest on the detailed *retrospective* accounts of age at first marriage reported in the 1960, 1970, and 1980 censuses. There are, to be sure, some imperfections in the data, for our purposes. The most obvious is recollection, which surely becomes dimmer with the passage of years and more subject to distortion by divorce and remarriage. There is also an upward bias in estimated proportions marrying at any given age produced by the well-known tendency for married people to outlive those single, the more so the longer ago they married. This will be slightly offset by differential mortality by socioeconomic groups coupled with socioeconomic differentials in marriage timing. Note, too, that the censuses were gathered as of April and so do not strictly admit of the translation I here employ of years married into calendar year of marriage. *Census 1960–4*, table 2; *Census 1970–2*, table 2; *Census 1980–1*, table 16.

21. This is partly an artifact of shifting the source from the 1970 retrospect to the 1980.

22. Annual registration data are not subject to the distortion of memory to which retrospective materials are and avoid any biases produced by differential mortality. Lacking proper counts of single persons at single years of age for each year, however, we cannot calculate age-specific marriage *rates* and must content ourselves with examining year-to-year *trends* in *numbers of single men and women marrying* at particular ages. Data on New York State outside of New York City are published annually from 1921 to 1967 in S. V. De Porte, *Marriage Statistics, New York State, 1921–24* (Albany: State Department of Health, n.d.), and in New York State, Department of Health, *Annual Report.*

23. Amy Ong Tsui, "A Study of the Family Formation Process among U.S. Marriage Cohorts," (Ph.D. dissertation, University of Chicago, 1978). Tsui's findings are also based on the 1975 Current Population Survey public-use file.

24. The data are unfortunately not tabulated by age at marriage; so, instead, table 5 compares groups of women *currently* different in age and *married for equally long intervals*. Those currently 20–24 had been married as young as age 16 and as old as age 21. Those currently 25–29 had been married as young as 21 and as old as 26. Those currently 30–34 had been married as young as 26 and as old as 31.

25. Many southern black women, presumably the most prone to

prompt motherhood, married before age 20 and so have been excluded from table 5 because so few could have been married as many as three years at the time of the census.

26. Larry Bumpass, "Age at Marriage as a Variable in Socioeconomic Differentials in Marriage," *Demography* 6 (1969): 45–54.

27. These data, taken from *USNCHS Vital Statistics 1975*, Vol. III, table 2–1, present estimated national divorce totals as a ratio to currently married women.

28. Norval D. Glenn and Michael Supanic, "The Social and Demographic Correlates of Divorce and Separation in the United States: An Update and Reconsideration," *Journal of Marriage and the Family* 46 (1984): 571.

29. Samuel H. Preston and John McDonald, "The Incidence of Divorce within Cohorts of American Marriages Contracted Since the Civil War," *Demography* 16 (1979): 1–25.

30. Glenn and Supanic, "Social and Demographic Correlates of Divorce," 572.

31. Much of my discussion of trends in divorce-proneness is based on an examination of proportions of annual cohorts of marriages eventuating in divorce within nine years, compiled from the 1975 Current Population Survey. See Appendix 4. Such survey-based retrospects on divorce underestimate the amount of divorce, because many people choose to forget that which so distresses them. Perhaps, too, divorced people's mortality sufficiently exceeds that of those with lasting marriages that retrospective divorce estimates are biased downward. For comparative data revealing the bias, see *USNCHS-Series 21–34*, 20. Other tabulations of the CPS divorce data are found in *Census CPS P20–239*, *Census CPS P20–297*, and T. J. Espenshade, "Marriage, Divorce, and Remarriage from Retrospective Data: A Multiregional Approach," *Environment and Planning A* 15 (1983): 1633–1652.

32. Glenn and Supanic, "Social and Demographic Correlates of Divorce," 565–566; and see James A. Weed, "Age at Marriage as a Factor in State Divorce Differentials, *Demography* 11 (1974): 370–372.

33. Calculated from *USNCHS Vital Statistics*, III, annual.

34. For related reflections, see John Modell, "Historical Reflections on American Marriage," in Kingsley Davis, ed., *Contemporary Marriage* (New York: Russell Sage Foundation, 1986), 181–196.

35. Possibly unique Connecticut data bearing on the role of divorce in marriage sequences show that even since the end of the nineteenth century, the trend of remarriage probabilities for divorced persons has been markedly up, from a stigmatization of divorced peo-

ple in the marriage market which profoundly limited their chances of finding an acceptable spouse to something approaching parity with single people of like age by the end of World War II. The data also reveal a shift away from severely constricted remarriage rates for divorced *men* to one that by the 1910s regularly exceeded that of divorcees. Connecticut, State Board of Health, *Report*, annual; Connecticut, State Board of Health, *Registration Report*, 1884–1946, annual. The data given in these reports is of the number of remarriages in the state in a given year by sex and disposition of previous marriage. I divided these figures by a five-year moving average of the number: of divorces in the state. I thus assume no differential interstate migration for purposes of divorce or remarriage. During this period, probabilities of remarriage for widows grew slightly with the remarriage market, but not at all as rapidly as for divorcees; and probabilities of remarriage for widowers actually declined. So it was not *remarriage* that became increasingly acceptable but explicitly the remarriage of *people who had been divorced*.

36. *USNCHS Series 21–38*, Tables A, K.

37. *Ibid.*, 7. Also noted was a strong tendency (as of 1970) for states with *low* divorce rates to *have long* median intervals between marriage and divorce, where it does occur.

38. We can do nothing with the statistical problem introduced by the changing distributions of years since marriage in its interaction with proportions with any children and with propensity to divorce. We neglect this here, focusing on the most important crude trend.

39. One in ten did not report on their parenthood status. I would assume that these by and large had no children, but one cannot really be sure. The proportion not reporting parenthood declined gradually through the period we are considering, as registration of divorces slowly became more expertly accomplished.

40. *Census Marriage 1931*, 32; *Census Marriage 1932*, 6.

41. *USNCHS Vital Statistics*, annual, 1950–1975; *Census CPS P23–84*, 8.

42. The uncertainty is introduced by different modes of allocating those who did not report on whether or not they had children.

43. Based on the conservative assumption that the 1930 proportion was identical to that for 1940.

44. Kristin A. Moore and Linda J. Waite, "Marital Dissolution, Early Motherhood, and Early Marriage," *Social Forces* 60 (1981): 20–40.

45. *Ibid.*, 32.

46. *Ibid.*, 34.

3: Modern Youth: The 1920s

1. Robert M. Coen, "Labor and Unemployment in the 1920s and 1930s: A Re-examination Based on Postwar Experience," *Review of Economics and Statistics* 55 (1973): 46–55; H. Thomas Johnson, *"Postwar Optimism and the Rural Financial Crises of the 1920s," Explorations in Economic History* 11 (1973–74): 173–192, on the farm bust; Wesley C. Mitchell, "A Review," in Committee on Recent Economic Changes of the President's Conference on Unemployment, *Recent Economic Changes in the United States* (New York: McGraw-Hill, 1929), II: 841–910. But cf. Charles F. Holt, "Who Benefited from the Prosperity of the Twenties?" *Explorations in Economic History* 14 (1977): 277–289.

2. U.S. Department of Commerce, Bureau of Economic Analysis, *Long-Term Economic Growth 1860–1970* (Washington: USGPO, 1973), charts 2, 3, 4; Willard L. Thorp, "The Changing Structure of Industry," in Committee on Recent Economic Changes, *Recent Economic Changes*: I, 167–218; Frederick C. Mills "Price Trends" in *ibid.*, II, 603–656; Roland Marchand, *Advertising the American Dream: Making the Way for Modernity, 1920–1940* (Berkeley, Los Angeles, London: University of California Press, 1985).

3. Robert S. Lynd and Helen Merrell Lynd, *Middletown* (New York: Harcourt, Brace, 1929), Parts I, II; Daniel Horowitz, *The Morality of Spending* (Baltimore: Johns Hopkins University Press, 1985); Elaine Tyler May, *Great Expectations* (Chicago: University of Chicago Press, 1980), chap. 8.

4. Lynd and Lynd, *Middletown*, 130. The Lynds present an account of the 1920s family as ripe for overt change, yet so far reflecting this state only in subtle ways. As we shall see, the decade of the 1920s, by opening a range of new options, destabilized the youthful life course, restructuring patterns of family formation and altering thereby its tone.

5. *The Responsibilities of American Advertising* (New Haven: Yale University Press, 1958), 40–41; Simon N. Patten, *The New Basis of Civilization*, ed. Daniel M. Fox (Cambridge: Belknap Press of the Harvard University Press, 1968).

6. Daniel Pope, *The Making of Modern Advertising* (New York: Basic Books, 1983); Marchand, *Advertising the American Dream.*

7. Robert S. Lynd, "The People as Consumers," in William Fielding Ogburn, ed., *Recent Social Trends, II* (New York, 1932), 848; William E. Leuchtenburg, *Perils of Prosperity* (Chicago: University of Chicago Press, 1958), chap. 10; Marcus Felson, "The Differentiation of

Material Life Styles: 1925–1966," *Social Indicators Research* 3 (1976): 397–421; J. Frederic Dewhurst and Associates, *America's Needs and Resources: A New Survey* (New York: The Twentieth Century Fund, 1955), Appendix 4–5.

8. Paula Fass, *The Damned and the Beautiful* (New York: Oxford University Press, 1977); J. F. Steiner, "Recreation and Leisure Time Activities," in Ogburn, ed., *Recent Social Trends*, II: 912–957.

9. Edmund K. Strong, Jr., *The Psychology of Selling and Advertising* (New York: McGraw Hill, 1925), 170; Paul H. Nystrom, *Elements of Retail Selling* (New York: Ronald Press, 1936).

10. F. Thomas Juster, *Household Capital Formation and Financing, 1897–1962* (NBER General Series #83 [New York: NBER, 1966]); Edwin R. A. Seligman, *The Economics of Installment Selling* (New York: Harper and Brothers, 1927), 1: 263–264.

11. Blanche Bernstein, *The Pattern of Consumer Debt, 1935–36* (NBER, Financial Research Program, Studies in Consumer Installment Financing #6 [New York: NBER, 1940]), chaps. 2, 5.

12. By the end of the decade, two urban surveys found that around one-third of adolescent girls and somewhat fewer boys had a regular allowance. White House Conference on Child Health and Protection, *The Adolescent in the Family* (New York: Appleton Century, 1934), 292–93; Evelyn Dreser Deno, "Changes in the Home Activities of Junior High School Girls over a Twenty-seven Year Period" (Ph.D. dissertation, University of Minnesota, 1958), 51; Viviana A. Zelizer, *Pricing the Priceless Child* (New York: Basic Books, 1985), chap. 3.

13. Meeting of December 10, 1930, of Chapter 375 of Child Study Association of America. Child Study Association of America Collection, Social Welfare History Archives, University of Minnesota.

14. Lynd and Lynd, *Middletown*, 118, 131.

15. *Ibid.*, 121–122.

16. Robert Lynd and Helen Merrell Lynd, *Middletown in Transition* (New York: Harcourt, Brace, 1937), 152.

17. Lynd and Lynd, *Middletown*, 111.

18. *Ibid.*, 112.

19. *Ibid.*, 140; Lynd and Lynd, *Middletown in Transition*, 168.

20. LeRoy E. Bowman and Maria Ward Lambin, "Evidences of Social Relations as Seen in Types of New York City Dance Halls," *The Journal of Social Forces* 3 (1925): 288; Paul G. Cressey, *The Taxi-Dance Hall* (Chicago: University of Chicago Press, 1932).

21. Elon H. Moore, "Public Dance Halls in a Small City," *Sociology and Social Research* 14 (1930): 260; see also Gregory Mason, "Satan in the Dance Hall," *American Mercury* 2 (1924): 175–182. The dance

halls came under close scrutiny in the early part of the 1920s, charged with being the breeding grounds of a variety of immoralities, or at least their starting point, and proper rules of dance-floor decorum were prescribed informally and in law. American National Association of Masters of Dancing, "Rules, Regulations, and Suggestions Governing Social Dancing" (pamphlet, 1919), in American Social Hygiene Association Collection, Social Welfare History Archives, University of Minnesota.

22. Lewis A. Erenberg, *Steppin' Out* (Contributions in American Studies, no. 50; [Westport, Conn.: Greenwood Press, 1981]), 154, and chap. 5 generally; Kathy Peiss, *Cheap Amusements* (Philadelphia: Temple University Press, 1986), chap. 4.

23. Maurice A. Bigelow, *Adolescence* (National Health Series [New York: Funk & Wagnalls, completely rev. ed., 1937 [1924]]), 86.

24. Ella Gardner, *Public Dance Halls* (U.S. Department of Labor, Children's Bureau, Publication No. 89, 1929), 36–49; and see M. V. O'Shea, *The Trend of the Teens* (Chicago: Frederick S. Drake and Co., 1920).

25. Herbert Blumer, *Movies and Conduct* (Motion Pictures and Youth: The Payne Fund Studies [New York: Macmillan, 1933]), 195n.

26. White House Conference on Child Health and Protection, *The Adolescent in the Family* (New York: Appleton-Century, 1934), 292–293.

27. Bruce L. Melvin and Elna N. Smith, *Rural Youth: Their Situation and Prospects* (Research Monographs XV, Works Progress Administration [Washington: USGPO, 1938]). Chapter V is a fine review of the literature on the leisure and recreation of rural youth, before and during the Depression.

28. Alice Miller Mitchell, *Children and the Movies* (Chicago: University of Chicago Press, 1929), 123–124.

29. Lary May, *Screening Out the Past* (New York: Oxford University Press, 1980), chaps. 5, 8; Peiss, *Cheap Amusements*, chap. 6.

30. Edgar Dale, *The Content of Motion Pictures* (Motion Pictures and Youth: The Payne Fund Studies [New York: Macmillan Press, 1935]), 89, 94, 178.

31. Herbert Blumer and Philip M. Hauser, *Movies, Delinquency and Crime* (Motion Pictures and Youth: The Payne Fund Studies [New York: Macmillan Press, 1935]), chap. 5.

32. Although only one in five girls taking "personal hygiene" in a New York City high school in 1918 said that they would have wished further instruction in sexual matters, the sex-education proponent analyzing the survey concluded that many more would have said

so were it not "that what was uppermost in their minds could not find expression for reasons well understood." At least one response, quoted verbatim, could have been emblazoned on the banner of the sex modernizers and certainly indicates that at least *some* demand for school sex education existed ahead of supply. "Many girls feel that the sex relation is vulgar and is very repugnant to them. They have a wrong opinion which ought to be rectified by the hygiene teacher and told in a way that would not make us hate the other sex for this." Benjamin C. Gruenberg, "What Girls Want to Know," *School Review* 26 (1918): 753–755.

33. Mark Thomas Connelly, *The Response to Prostitution in the Progressive Era* (Chapel Hill: University of North Carolina Press, 1980).

34. Wallace H. Maw, "Fifty Years of Sex Education in the Public Schools of the United States (1900–1950): A History of Ideas" (Ed.D. dissertation, University of Cincinnati, 1950), 82–133.

35. "The Sex Questionnaire that Shocked the Nation," *True Confessions* (July 1929): 40+.

36. William G. Shepherd, "What Our Boys and Girls Think of Each Other," *Collier's* 74 (December 13, 1924): 48; Howard M. Bell, *Youth Tell Their Story* (Washington: American Council on Education, 1938), 90. In Maryland, black youth were especially supportive and far more likely to wish early instruction.

37. Michael Imber, "Analysis of a Curriculum Reform Movement: The American Social Hygiene Association's Campaign for Sex Education 1900–1930" (Ph.D. dissertation, School of Education, Stanford University, 1980); John C. Burnham, "The Progressive Era Revolution in American Attitudes toward Sex," *Journal of American History* 59 (1973): 885–909.

38. Joseph Kirk Folsom, *The Family* (New York: John Wiley and Sons, 1934), 230; Michael Gordon, "From an Unfortunate Necessity to a Cult of Mutual Orgasm: Sex in American Marital Education Literature 1830–1940," in James M. Henslin and Edward Sagarin, eds., *The Sociology of Sex: An Introductory Reader* (New York: Schocken, 1978), 68. Katherine B. Davis found in 1929 that four in ten of her married-women sample declared themselves to have been inadequately informed about sex at the time of their marriages and that *virtually all* of her unmarried-women sample favored sex instruction for both boys and girls. Davis, *Factors in the Sex Life of Twenty-two Hundred Women* (New York: Harper and Brothers, 1929), 63, 378.

39. D. C. Thom, *Guiding the Adolescent* (U.S. Department of Labor, Children's Bureau, Publication #225, 1933), 12. On parents' failings

in this task, see White House Conference on Child Health and Protection, *The Adolescent in the Family*, 192–211.

40. Quoted from the 1941 *Yearbook* of the Association in Maw, "Fifty Years of Sex Education," 130.

41. Laura Martha Myers, "A Study of a Personal Improvement Course for High School Girls" (M.Ed. thesis, The Pennsylvania State University, 1938), 34–41.

42. The expansion can*not* be laid to compulsory education laws. Almost all states that passed such laws in the 1910s had had more rapid rates of school expansion at the high school ages in the decade *preceding* the legislation. John K. Folger and Charles B. Nam, *Education of the American People* (1960 Census Monograph [Washington: USGPO, 1967]), 24–26. The White House Conference on Child Health and Protection, *Child Labor* (New York: The Century Company, 1932), Part IV, reflects both the difficulties of enforcing this shift in the construction of the youthful life course among working-class families and the strenuousness of efforts to accomplish that end.

43. Claudia Goldin, "The Changing Economic Role of Women: A Cohort Approach," *Journal of Interdisciplinary History* 13 (1983): 711.

44. U.S. Bureau of the Census, *Historical Statistics*, I: 379.

45. Tabulated from the Annual School Census of Philadelphia, in Philadelphia Board of Education, *Journal* and/or *Statistical Report*, annual.

46. Esther Mariel Cook, "The Relation between the Fluctuation of Juvenile Employment and the Enrollment of Pupils 14 and 15 Years of Age in Pittsburgh, 1923–1932," (M.A. essay, University of Pittsburgh, 1934).

47. Grayson N. Kefauver, Victor H. Noll, and C. Elwood Drake, *The Secondary-School Population* (U.S. Department of the Interior, Office of Education, "National Survey of Secondary Education," Monograph No. 4 [Washington: USGPO, 1933]), 8–26.

48. John Modell, "An Ecology of Family Decisions: Suburbanization, Schooling, and Fertility in Philadelphia, 1880–1920," *Journal of Urban History* 6 (1980): 397–417.

49. Folger and Nam, *Education of the American Population*, 8–9. For a fine, naive, contemporaneous expression of recent changes as they affected school life, see Olivia Pound, "The Social Life of High School Girls: Its Problems and Its Opportunities," *School Review* 28 (1920): 50–56. On economic aspects of school prolongation, see Howard G. Burdge, *Our Boys* (Albany: State of New York, Military Training Commission, Bureau of Vocational Training, 1921), chaps. 13, 23.

50. Duluth, Board of Education, *Annual Report*, 1921, 1926, 1937. In New Bedford, Massachusetts, in 1922, only 21 percent of sixteen-year-old boys were found in a single grade, and only 26 percent of the girls; by 1930 these figures had increased to 38 and 39 percent, respectively. New Bedford, *School Report*, 1923, 1931.

51. Clarence Long, *The Labor Force under Changing Income and Employment* (Princeton: Princeton University Press, 1958), tables A-2, A-3.

52. Winifred Wandersee, *Women's Work and Family Values, 1920–1940* (Cambridge: Harvard University Press, 1981), chap. 4.

53. Joseph A. Hill, *Women in Gainful Occupations 1870 to 1920* (Census Monographs, IX [Washington: USGPO, 1929]), 287.

54. Phyllis Blanchard, *The Adolescent Girl* (New York: Moffat, Yard and Company, 1920), 48, 50; Winifred Richmond, *The Adolescent Girl* (New York: Macmillan, 1936 [1925]), and *The Adolescent Boy* (New York: Farrar and Rinehart, 1933).

55. E. B. Hurlock and E. R. Klein, "Adolescent Crushes," *Child Development* 5 (1934): 80. It is striking that this excellent piece of research was uninterested in the "crushes" it did discover, obviously components of the teenage dating scene.

56. Scholarly observation of dating began with the inquiry into 1930s college dating carried out by the sociologist Willard Waller. Although Waller described dating as a special case of dissipation, he nonetheless established the crucial point that it was peer-supervised, rule-governed behavior. Waller, "The Rating and Dating Complex," *American Sociological Review* 2 (1937): 727–734; *idem.*, *The Family* (New York: The Dryden Press, 1938), chap. 9; Michael Gordon, "Was Waller Ever Right? The Rating and Dating Complex Reconsidered," *Journal of Marriage and the Family* 43 (1981): 67–76; Samuel Harman Lowrie, "Dating Theories and Student Responses," *American Sociological Review* 16 (1951): 334–340.

57. Reed Ueda, *Avenues to Adulthood: The Origins of the High School and Social Mobility in an American Suburb* (New York: Cambridge University Press, 1987), 132.

58. Fass, *The Damned and the Beautiful*; Bailey, *From Front Porch to Back Seat* (Baltimore: The Johns Hopkins University Press, 1988).

59. Fass, *The Damned and the Beautiful*, 262–273, 324–325.

60. Bailey, *From Front Porch to Back Seat*, 80.

61. Regina Malone, "Has Youth Deteriorated? II: The Fabulous Monster," *The Forum* 76 (1926): 29.

62. Bailey, *From Front Porch to Back Seat*, 78.

63. *Ibid.*, 21.

64. *Ibid.*, 16.

65. Lynd and Lynd, *Middletown*, 137–138.

66. E.g., Emory S. Bogardus, *The City Boy and His Problems* (Los Angeles: Rotary Club of L.A., 1926), 74–75.

67. Frederick T. Shipp, "Social Activities of High-School Boys," *School Review* 39: 773.

68. Edgar Schmiedeler, "The Industrial Revolution and the Home" (Ph.D. dissertation, Catholic University, 1927), 50–53.

69. Harvey C. Lehman and Paul A. Witty, *The Psychology of Play Activities* (New York: A. S. Barnes and Company, 1927), 55–57; Shipp, "Social Activities," 771; Sister M. Mildred Knoebber, "The Adolescent Girl" (Ph.D. dissertation, St. Louis University, 1935), 162; Albert Blumenthal, *Small-Town Stuff* (Chicago: University of Chicago Press, 1932).

70. Mildred B. Thurow, "Interests, Activities, and Problems of Rural Young Folk: I" (Bulletin 617 [Ithaca: Cornell University Agricultural Experiment Station, 1934]), 34.

71. Paul H. Landis, "Problems of Farm Youth—A Point of View," *Social Forces* 18 (1940): 502–513; O. Latham Hatcher, *Rural Girls in the City for Work* (Richmond: Garrett and Massie for the Southern Women's Educational Alliance, 1930): 52–53.

72. Frances Donovan, *The Woman Who Waits* (Boston: Richard G. Badger, 1920), chaps. 17–19; Frederick M. Thrasher, *The Gang* (Chicago: University of Chicago Press, 1927), chap. 13; W. I. Thomas, *The Unadjusted Girl: With Cases and Standpoint for Behavior Analysis* (Criminal Science Monograph No. 4 [Boston: Little, Brown, 1923]), chap. 4.

73. Peiss, *Cheap Amusements*, chap. 2.

74. William Foote Whyte, "A Slum Sex Code," *American Journal of Sociology* 49 (1943): 24–29; and see Dorothy Reed, *Leisure Time of Girls in a "Little Italy"* (Ph.D. dissertation, Columbia University, n.d.; Portland, Ore., privately printed, 1932).

75. Jane Synge, "The Way We Were: Farm and City Families in the Early Twentieth Century," unpublished manuscript (Department of Sociology, McMaster University, Hamilton, Ontario, n.d.), chap. 5.

76. Lehman and Witty, *Psychology of Play Activities*, 134–137.

77. Mary K. Holloway, "A Study of Social Conditions Affecting Stowe Junior High School Girls" (M.A. Ed. thesis, University of Cincinnati, 1928), 34, 40; Lillian F. Drayton, "Personal Problems of Adolescents in the Basin Area of Cincinnati" (M.Ed. thesis, University of Cincinnati, 1935), 104–106.

78. Quoted in E. Franklin Frazier, *Negro Youth at the Crossways* (Washington, D.C.: American Council on Education, 1940), 247; see also the balance of chaps. 8 and 9, and Drayton, "Personal Problems," *passim*.

79. Excerpt from response to query by Drayton in Drayton, "Personal Problems," 179.

80. *Ibid.*, 164.

81. Waller, describing dating at the Pennsylvania State University, far too cynically and simplistically characterized the date as incorporating mutual exploitation, with prestige and "thrills" in view. *The Family*, chap. 9; "The Rating and Dating Complex." And see Peiss's excellent treatment of working-class girls' choices of how far to go. *Cheap Amusements*, 108–114.

82. Fannie Kilbourne, "Pretend He's the Plumber," *Ladies' Home Journal* 46 (January 1929): 20+.

83. I read perhaps some 650 letters to two lovelorn columnists in three time periods—1920–21, 1925, and 1930–31—choosing and transcribing for closer analysis 326 of these, roughly divided among the three dates. Doris Blake was a syndicated columnist (first as "Doris Blake's Answers," later as "Doris Blake's Love Answers") in the New York *Daily News*, a pioneer tabloid appealing to relatively unsophisticated readers. Blake's column was the earliest I found which employed the letter-and-reply format (as contrasted with Dorthea Dix's essay-with-quotations format). Blake truncated her letters, obviously, and more so over time; Martha Carr's evidently local and nonsyndicated column from the St. Louis *Post-Dispatch*, unfortunately a newspaper of far higher tone, regularized grammar and spelling but allowed correspondents to ramble on at considerable length.

84. New York *Daily News*, August 7, 1920.

85. New York *Daily News*, December 27, 1920; April 29, 1925; February 19, 1925.

86. New York *Daily News*, May 10, 1925; November 8, 1930.

87. New York *Daily News*, October 16, 1930, and November 5, 1930; St. Louis *Post-Dispatch*, September 17, 1931.

88. New York *Daily News*, May 25, 1925.

89. Middle-class girls and those aspiring to middle-class status who did not prosper under the new system shortly became its victims. As early as 1924, a California high school dean of girls set up a program to help those girls (54 percent in her school, by her reckoning) who were left out. There were many reasons for failure, "yet it will be observed that all of these various types have something in common. The non-social individual centers all her thoughts and activity upon

herself." Caroline Power, "The Social Program for the Unsocial High-School Girl," *School Review* 32 (1924): 773.

90. Richmond, *The Adolescent Girl*, 53; cf. *idem.*, *The Adolescent Boy*. And for an unconventional statement of the conventional understanding on this point, see Ben B. Lindsey and Wainwright Evans, *The Revolt of Modern Youth* (New York: Boni & Liveright, 1925), chaps. 5 and 6. Lindsey and Evans hold that "the high-school boy is a much less dramatic figure than the high-school girl. Generally, she sets the pace, whatever it is to be, and he dances to her piping" (*ibid.*, 68).

91. "A School Girl's Misstep," *True Confessions* 6 (June 1925): 6+. A 1941 study of a St. Louis high school indicated that by senior year, two-thirds of the girls but just one in ten boys ordinarily dated persons from outside the school. Helen Moore Priester, "The Reported Dating Practices of One Hundred and Six High School Seniors in an Urban Community" (M.S. thesis, Cornell University, 1941), 41.

92. Waller's commitment to a conception of love in which idealization played a large part, I believe, blinded him to the affectionate element in dating and led him to believe that dating and courtship were wholly different activities. See Waller, "Rating and Dating"; Waller, *The Family*, chap. 8. See also Clifford Kirkpatrick and Theodore Caplow, "Courtship in a Group of Minnesota Students," *American Journal of Sociology* 51 (1945): 114–125.

93. Ernie to Martha Carr, St. Louis *Post-Dispatch*, April 3, 1931.

94. Computations from Kinsey data. See Appendix 4.

95. These trends pertain considerably more strongly to the informants who had attended college. We should recall that much of the apparent increase in the sexual content of life was captured within marriage, which was in accord both with received values and with the relatively new notion that the sexual pleasures of marriage were to be celebrated, not just tolerated.

96. Eleanor Rowland Wembridge, "Petting and the Campus," *Survey* 34 (1925): 394.

97. Folsom, *The Family*, 231–232.

98. Joseph Wood Krutch, "Love—Or the Life and Death of a Value," *Atlantic Monthly* 142 (1928): 207, 205.

99. "Observations on the Sex Problem in America," *American Journal of Psychiatry* 8 (1928): 529; Willard Waller, *The Old Love and the New* (New York: Liveright, 1930). Sapir spoke of trends he hoped would not overtake American culture.

100. Richmond, *The Adolescent Boy*, 192; R. H. Edwards, J. M. Artman, and Galen M. Fisher, *Undergraduates* (Garden City, N.Y.: Doubleday, Doran, 1928), 216–218.

101. White House Conference on Child Health and Protection, *Growth and Development of the Child, Part IV, Appraisement of the Child* (New York: The Century Company, 1932), 140–142.

102. Fass, *The Damned and the Beautiful*, 280, 294.

103. Folsom, *The Family*, 71, 408.

104. "One Girl" quoted in "To-Day's Morals and Manners—The Side of the Girls," *Literary Digest* 70 (July 9, 1921): 36.

105. George A. Lundberg, "Sex Differences on Social Questions," *School and Society* 23 (1926): 595–600; Daniel Katz and Floyd Henry Allport, *Students' Attitudes* (Syracuse, N.Y.: The Craftsmen Press, 1931), 252–253.

106. Folsom, *The Family*, 98, 412.

107. Caroline B. Zachry, *Emotion and Conduct in Adolescence* (New York: Appleton-Century-Crofts, 1940), 509. The study was conducted in 1934–1939.

108. Child Study Association, chap. 375, meeting of December 3, 1930.

109. Floyd Dell, "Why They Pet," *The Parents' Magazine* 6 (October 1931): 63.

110. For a classic expression of this conventional belief, see "A High School Boy Reveals Youth's Love Problems," *True Confessions* 12 (July, 1928): 34.

111. Quoted in Arthur Dean, "A Survey on Petting," *Journal of Education* 110 (1929): 414.

112. Jessie E. Gibson, *On Being a Girl* (New York: Macmillan, 1927), 141.

113. Fass, *The Damned and the Beautiful*, chap. 5, is splendid on the meaning of sexuality, if a little underemphatic about the gender dialectic.

114. "A High School Boy Reveals Youth's Love Problems," 107.

115. A mid-1920s *college* survey asked, "Is it right to kiss a man or woman you do not expect to marry?" Substantial minorities of 25 percent of the boys and 40 percent of the girls answered *no*, indicating that they still accepted sexual pleasure only in the context of courtship. Lundberg, "Sex Differences," 598. The classic 1920s exposition of cultural change in girls' sexual expressiveness is *New Girls for Old*, by Phyllis Blanchard and Carolyn Manasses (New York: The Macaulay Co., 1930). Theodore Newcomb's thoughtful conclusion that by the 1930s, a "less compulsive and more spontaneous demonstration of affection between boys and girls" was common suggests the only gradual accomplishment of this cultural change. "Recent Changes in Attitudes toward Sex and Marriage," *American Sociological Review* 2 (1937): 662.

116. "Miss Dateless" to Martha Carr, St. Louis *Post-Dispatch*, October 31, 1931. And see the exchange between Doris Blake and H. Ann and Peggy, "Doris Blake's Love Answers," New York *Daily News*, October 28 and November 27, 1930.

117. Gibson, *On Being a Girl*, 150.

118. Editorial, *St. Paul Central High Times*, December 16, 1927. And see letter from A.C., *Minneapolis South High Southerner*, April 13, 1921.

119. *Little Falls The Comet's Tail*, February 24, 1928, editorial. Also see Lynd and Lynd, *Middletown*, 162–164.

120. *Little Falls The Comet's Tail*, March 27, 1923.

121. L. C. in *Minneapolis South High Southerner*, February 29, 1919.

122. "One of Them" in *Minneapolis South High Southerner*, October 27, 1920.

123. *Minneapolis South High Southerner*, November 18, 1920.

124. Letter of E. D., *St. Paul Central High Times*, March 26, 1926.

125. Lehman and Witty, *Psychology of Play Activities*, 55–57; *Alexandria High Al-Hi-Nuz*, December 16, 1927.

126. "We are Bachelor Girls of 30," *True Confessions* 26 (June 1935): 38–39.

127. Russ Brackett, letter in *Minneapolis West High News*, May 2, 1924; and "One of the Many Sufferers," letter in *Little Falls The Comet's Tail*, February 11, 1930.

128. Quoted in Caroline B. Zachry, *Emotion and Conduct in Adolescence*, 121.

129. For all intents and purposes, the 1930 census data reflect the impact of the relatively booming 1920s rather than of the crash and certainly not of the Depression. Only about half a year had passed between the stock market crash and the census, and while some marriage decisions undoubtedly took this into consideration, most of the decadal changes, and even the changes in the changes, can be attributed to the "prosperity decade" rather than to its denouement.

130. *New Girls for Old*, 260.

131. *Ibid.*, 181. See also Wembridge, "Petting and the Campus"; Ernest R. Burgess, "The Romantic Impulse and Family Disorganization," *Survey* 57 (1926): 290–294; Alexander Black, "Is the Young Person Coming Back," *Harper's Monthly* 149 (1929): 337–346; and, for the parents' perspective, see Jessica H. Cosgrave, "Romantic Love," *Good Housekeeping* 81 (November-December 1928): 36.

132. Ann Bruce, *Love and Marriage* (Franklin Publishing Company, 1931), 66, 91. The overprudent male was a subject for gentle ridicule, however. Blanche Bruce, "The Adventure of the Lost Trousseau," *Ladies' Home Journal* 37 (1920): 14+.

133. A Family Doctor, "Youth's Greatest Problem: Wait or Mate," *True Confessions* 12 (October 1928): 113.

134. Eleanor Rowland Wembridge, "The Girl Tribe—An Anthropological Study," *Survey* 60 (1928): 198.

135. Temple Bailey, "Wait for Prince Charming," *Ladies' Home Journal* 43 (October 1926): 20 + .

136. *Census 1920–1*, 391–393; *Census 1930–1*, 846–847.

137. New York State Department of Health, Division of Vital Statistics, *Annual Report*, 1922–1930; S. V. DePorte, *Marriage Statistics, New York State . . . 1921–24* (Albany: State Department of Health, n.d.). These permit construction of the best series of single-year-of-age first marriages—based on registration data—that I have discovered.

138. The foreign born and to a lesser extent the children of the foreign born do provide a very striking counterexample, but this may easily be a result of compositional changes in these groups.

139. A like analysis, for the decade of the 1910s, was carried out as early as 1928 by William Fielding Ogburn, who, however, did not choose to analyze as narrow an age group as I and thus spent a great deal of the analysis worrying about changes in age distribution and in ethnic distributions in the state population. The results are reported extensively in Ernest R. Groves and William Fielding Ogburn, *American Marriage and Family Relationships* (New York: Henry Holt, 1932). Unlike Ogburn, I employ ordinary least squares multiple regression.

140. In part, this is to propose what is almost a demographic tautology, for by promoting early fertility, early marriage tends *per se* to be associated with relatively rapid population growth. But a look at the states in which population growth in the 1920s was especially rapid convinces one that other factors are at work as well, those that promoted immigration. The four most rapidly growing states during that decade were California, Florida, Michigan, and Arizona, with rates of growth all exceeding three in ten, well above anything that natural increase could explain. Nor were these states characterized by particularly high fertility. Many of the high-fertility states in the depressed agricultural South had rates of net population growth slow enough to suggest that natural increase was being offset by out-migration.

141. Obviously, one doesn't "search" for a mate across a whole state, or in a way limited by state boundaries *per se*. We may very reasonably suppose that the overall decline in the skewing of sex ratios also was reflected in declines within more meaningful *local* marriage markets.

142. Based on retrospective accounts taken in 1940 and published in Census 1940–4, 142–165.

143. Robert L. Hauser, *Fertility Tables for Birth Cohorts by Color: United States, 1917–73* (Rockville, Md.: U.S. National Center for Health Statistics, 1976), 424–425.

144. Too many years had elapsed since the vital events in question to expect very precise retrospective information on the 1920s from the 1975 Current Population Survey of marital and fertility histories, but the gross patterns discernible there fill out this picture usefully.

145. Regine K. Stix and Frank W. Notestein, *Controlled Fertility: An Evaluation of Clinic Service* (Baltimore: Williams & Wilkins, 1940), 25.

146. This study was carried out in 1941, asking about the family-building practices and beliefs of a near-representative sample of fecund white Protestants of native birth who had lived in cities for at least some years before their marriages (all in 1927–1929) and were living in Indianapolis at the time of the survey. See Appendix 4 for a discussion of machine-readable data files.

147. The relationship of schooling to fertility control was largely direct and not the product of a joint tendency for more educated women to marry older and for older-marrying women to practice more fertility limitation at this date early in their marriages.

148. James Reed, *From Private to Public Virtue* (New York: Basic Books, 1978), 124.

149. Stix and Notestein, *Controlled Fertility*, 53.

150. *Middletown*, 124; and see Reed, *From Private Vice to Public Virtue*.

151. Paul H. Gebhard *et al.*, *Pregnancy, Birth and Abortion* (New York: Harper & Brothers and Paul B. Hoefer, Inc., 1958), 70.

152. Data on contraceptive methods in Indianapolis rest on retabulations of data presented in Charles F. Westoff, Lee F. Herrera, and P. K. Whelpton, "Social and Psychological Factors Affecting Fertility, Part XX: The Use, Effectiveness, and Acceptability of Methods of Fertility Control," *Milbank Memorial Fund Quarterly* 31 (1953): 314, 317, 324.

153. Linda Gordon, *Woman's Body, Woman's Right* (New York: Penguin Books, 1977), chaps. 10–11.

154. P. K. Whelpton and Clyde V. Kiser, "Social and Psychological Factors Affecting Fertility, Part VI: The Planning of Fertility,"*Milbank Memorial Fund Quarterly* 25 (1947): 73.

155. F. I. Davenport, "Adolescent Interests: A Study of the Sexual Interests and Knowledge of Young Women," *Archives of Psychology* 66 (New York, 1923); Westoff, Herrera, and Whelpton, "Social and Psychological Factors."

156. Easily the greatest proportion of the variation in the propensity to use birth control was explained by wives' formal schooling, rather than by their ages at marriage. There was very little variation by husband's income at marriage or by Protestant sectarian affiliation.

157. Samuel A. Stouffer and Lyle M. Spencer, "Marriage and Divorce in Recent Years," *Annals of the American Academy of Political and Social Science* 188 (November 1936): 58.

158. Samuel H. Preston and John McDonald, "The Incidence of Divorce within Cohorts of American Marriages Contracted Since the Civil War," *Demography* 16 (1979): 10–11; USNCHS *Vital Statistics 1974*, III: 1–5, 2–5; William L. O'Neill, *Divorce in the Progressive Era* (New Haven: Yale University Press, 1967).

159. U.S. Bureau of the Census, *Marriage and Divorce 1930* (Washington: USGPO, 1932), 24, 35; Thomas P. Monahan, "The Changing Probability of Divorce," *American Sociological Review* 5 (1940): 536–545; USNCHS Series 21–34, tables 3, 4; USNCHS Series 21–38, table 1.

160. May, *Great Expectations*, 158–159.

4: In the Great Depression

1. Estimates based on Robert L. Heuser, *Fertility Tables for Birth Cohorts by Color* (Rockville, Md.: National Center for Health Statistics, 1976), tables 4B and 4C; Census 1930–1; Census 1940–1.

2. Clarence Long, *The Labor Force under Changing Income and Employment* (Princeton: Princeton University Press, 1958), 181–192.

3. Census *Population Trends*, 364–379.

4. Paul Osterman, *Getting Started: The Youth Labor Market* (Cambridge: MIT Press, 1980), 62–73.

5. In first-class cities in Michigan, where there was but little unpaid family work, 13 percent of boys 18 years of age were unemployed and seeking their first jobs, 7 percent were unemployed and seeking a replacement job, and 13 percent were not in school but not seeking work. State of Michigan, State Emergency Relief Commission, *Michigan Census of Population and Unemployment*, First Series, no. 10 (1937): 2–3.

6. Massachusetts Department of Labor and Industries, Division of Statistics, *Report on the Census of Unemployment in Massachusetts, 1934* (Public Document no. 15, 1934): 14, 84.

7. Samuel A. Stouffer and Paul F. Lazarsfeld, *Research Memorandum on the Family in the Depression* (SSRC Bulletin no. 29 [New York: Social Science Research Council, 1937]), 28–33.

8. *Census 1940–5*, 19; Walter F. Dearborn and John W. M. Rothney, *Scholastic, Economic, and Social Backgrounds of Unemployed Youth* (Harvard Bulletins in Education, no. 20 [Cambridge: Harvard University Press, 1938]).

9. Ruth E. Eckert and Thomas O. Marshall, *When Youth Leave School* (New York: The Regents' Inquiry, 1938), Part II, chap. 3.

10. Helen Wood, *Young Workers and Their Jobs in 1936* (U.S. Department of Labor, Children's Bureau Publication No. 249, 1940), 48, 69.

11. Dearborn and Rothney, *Unemployed Youth*, 131.

12. Census 1940–6, table 6; Census 1940–8, 92; Census CPS P60–7, 22, 30.

13. Tabulation from Census 1940–7, 28, inserting all children of the given ages in place of the private household population of those ages.

14. Census 1940–9, 16. And see Don D. Humphrey, *Family Unemployment* (Washington: U.S. Works Progress Administration, Federal Works Agency, 1940), 9.

15. Howard M. Bell, *Youth Tell Their Story* (Washington: American Council on Education, 1938), 26.

16. Bruce L. Melvin and Elna N. Smith, *Youth in Agricultural Villages* (U.S. Works Progress Administration, Division of Research, Research Monograph XXI [Washington: USGPO, 1940]), 65.

17. On this theme, see John Modell, "Public Griefs and Personal Problems," *Social Science History* 9 (1985): 404–409; Elder, *Children of the Great Depression*; E. Wight Bakke, *Citizens without Work* (New Haven: Yale University Press, 1940); Maurice Leven, *The Income Structure of the United States* (Washington, D.C.: The Brookings Institute, 1938), 166.

18. Dearborn and Rothney, *Unemployed Youth*, 96. And yet these were not the least successful or least apt students nor those least favorable to or engaged with school. The very best students tended to remain in school and out of the labor force, being thus neither employed nor unemployed. *Ibid.*, 98–120.

19. Similar patterns were present in other places for which such tabulations are possible, including cities and towns and villages with economies considerably different from Philadelphia. Humphrey, *Family Unemployment*, 91–110, Appendix A.

20. U.S. Federal Security Agency, Social Security Board, Bureau of Research and Statistics, *Statistics of Family Composition, 11: The Urban Sample* (Bureau Memorandum no. 45 [Washington: Federal Security Agency, 1942]), 165–167.

21. Henry F. Pringle, "What the Men of America Think of Women," *Ladies' Home Journal* (April 1939): 95; Pringle, "What the Women of America Think about the Double Standard," *ibid* (November 1938): 48; "The Fortune Quarterly Survey, VI," *Fortune* 14 (October 1936): 222.

22. Where the youth earned income, this tended to portray the family as of higher status, because total family income is the criterion used here. A fine New York youth study, conducted in 1935, found precisely the same differentials, using father's usual occupation to indicate socioeconomic background. The study found more current employment among children of professionals, proprietors, and managers as well as more school attendance and more unemployment (51 percent among sons of the unskilled) and housewifery among those whose fathers had less prestigious jobs. Nettie Pauline McGill and Ellen Nathalie Matthews, *The Youth of New York City* (New York: Macmillan, 1940), 64.

23. Roland S. Vaile et al., *Impact of the Depression on Business Activity and Real Income in Minnesota* (University of Minnesota Studies in Economics and Business, no. 8 [Minneapolis: University of Minnesota Press, 1933]), 45–46.

24. These data are found in the large national urban family budget studies conducted in prosperous times during and after World War I and during the middle of the Depression. Linear regression enables me to estimate for each period about how many cents per additional ten dollars of income went to these visible, symbolically significant items of personal adornment.

25. On the impact of the Depression on the position of clothes in the family budget, see Faith M. Williams, "Changes in Family Expenditures in the Postwar Period," *Monthly Labor Review* 47 (1938): 967–979.

26. Family composition, of course, had changed between 1918–19 and 1935–36, families now having somewhat fewer adolescent and young-adult children. This *could* affect the income elasticity of clothing expenditures, to the extent that the clothing expenditures detailed here were in large measure the purchase of goods needed, for warmth or decency, rather than in pursuit of reputation. But for this range of family incomes, this image is quite untenable.

27. "Youth in College," *Fortune* 13 (June 1936): 102.

28. *The Unemployed Man and His Family* (New York: Dryden Press for the Institution of Social Research, 1947), chap. 6.

29. Ethel S. Beer, "The Social Life of the Business Girl," *Social Forces* 17 (1939): 546–550.

30. James H. S. Bossard, "Depression and Pre-Depression Marriage Rates: A Philadelphia Study," *American Sociological Review* 2 (1937): 686–695. Bossard's study was based on a careful comparison of roughly age-standardized marriage rates for different areas of the city for 1928 to 1938.

31. Census 1930–2, 27; Census 1930–1, 557; Census 1940–7, 28. In New York City, and presumably elsewhere, this pattern was even more prevalent among blacks. Matthews, *Youth of New York City*, 34.

32. Census 1940–2, 4–5. And see Clyde V. Kiser, *Group Differences in Urban Fertility* (Baltimore: Williams & Wilkins, 1942), 112–113.

33. Ernest W. Burgess Papers, Boxes 60–63, Department of Special Collections, The Joseph Regenstein Library, University of Chicago.

34. Jessie Bernard, "The Differential Influence of the Business Cycle on the Number of Marriages in Several Age Groupings," *Social Forces* 18 (1940): 539–549.

35. Census 1950–3, 41–46.

36. Tabulated from AIPO 516. See Appendix 4.

37. Annual tabulations of Philadelphia marriages of white people, in City of Philadelphia, *Mayor's Report*, annual; Paul H. Jacobson, *American Marriage and Divorce* (New York: Rinehart and Company, 1959), 56.

38. Melvin Schubert Brooks, "Wisconsin Birth and Marriage Rate Trends by Occupations, 1920–1936" (Ph.D. dissertation, University of Wisconsin, 1941); Frances Meurer Deputy, "Marriages and the Depression" (M.A. thesis, University of Cincinnati, 1939), 103,122; James A. Bossard, "The Age Factor in Marriage: A Philadelphia Study, 1931," *American Journal of Sociology* 38 (1933): 536–547.

39. New York State, State Department of Health, Division of Vital Statistics, *Annual Report*, 1926–1941.

40. Massachusetts, *Registration Report*, Public Document 1, annual.

41. See, more generally, Stouffer and Lazarsfeld, *Research Memorandum*, 40–43.

42. Cincinnati Employment Center, Ohio State Employment Service, *The Population of Hamilton County, Ohio, in 1935* (Studies in Economic Security: II [Cincinnati: Cincinnati Employment Center, 1937]), 57–110, 210–215. The foreign born were surely too heterogeneous to analyze usefully, while the black population of Cincinnati was concentrated into too few census tracts to support a statistically reliable multivariate analysis of the sort possible with whites. The nativity of the parents of the native whites, unfortunately, is not distinguished in the 1935 Cincinnati census. I employ multiple regression as the statistical tool for this exploration.

43. Brooks, "Wisconsin Birth and Marriage Trends," 82, 159, and Methodological Materials in Appendix B. The annual occupation-specific rates compiled for a WPA project were based on a group of Wisconsin cities and depend on occupational statistics drawn from city directors as well as on a certain amount of uncertain record linkage, but they represent nevertheless a highly valuable source of trend data especially because of the very high number of certificates tabulated.

44. Census 1940–4, 58–62. And see Antonio Ciocco, "Studies on the Biological Factors in Public Health, I," *Human Biology* 12 (1940): 59–76; Clyde V. Kiser, "Recent Analyses of Marriage Rates," *Milbank Memorial Fund Quarterly* 15 (1937): 262–274.

45. These inferences are based on tabulations of proportions married among male workers 25 to 34, by occupation and employment status, from data in Census 1940–5, 107–110.

46. Ruth Shonle Cavan and Katherine Howland Ranck, *The Family and the Depression* (Chicago: University of Chicago Press, 1938); Stouffer and Lazarsfeld, *Research Memorandum.*

47. Elder, *Children of the Great Depression.*

48. Valeria H. Parker, "The Case of Youth *vs.* Society," *Journal of Social Hygiene* 21 (1935): 330–345.

49. "Ten Modern Commandments," *True Confessions* (1935).

50. Roy Dickerson, *When a Couple Are Engaged* (New York: Association Press, 1940), 8.

51. Oliver M. Butterfield, *Love Problems of Adolescence* (Contributions to Education, no. 768 [New York: Teachers College, Columbia University, 1939]), 124–125.

52. McGill and Matthews, *The Youth of New York*, 31–32. A fascinating tabulation of more than one thousand letters to popular marriage counselors in the 1930s, however, dealing with difficulties in courtship, indicated that only about one in eight of these had to do with inadequate income to contemplate marriage soon. Even at that date, the largest category of problems was parental obligations to the chosen man or woman, the second greatest, sexual matters. Antonio Ciocco, "On Social Biology, III: Elements Affecting the Formation of the Marital Group," *Human Biology* 11 (1939): 234–247.

53. Ernest W. Burgess and Paul Wallin, *Engagement and Marriage* (Philadelphia: Lippincott, 1953).

54. Carolyn Zachry, "The Adolescent and His Problems Today," in Sidonie Matsner Gruenberg, ed. *The Family in a World at War* (New York: Harper, 1942), 224–225.

55. Quoted in James Reed, *From Private Vice to Public Virtue* (New York: Basic Books, 1978), 190.

56. Bernarr MacFadden, "Why Not Marry?" *True Romances* 4 (March 1942): 4.

57. Paul Popenoe, "Two Million Lovers Are Desperately Asking: When Can We Marry?" *The American Magazine* 129 (June 1940): 22 +.

58. Hadley Cantril, *Public Opinion, 1935–1946* (Princeton: Princeton University Press, 1951). Computations discussed are based on AIPO 099. See Appendix 4.

59. Paul H. Gebhard and Alan B. Johnson, *The Kinsey Data: Marginal Tabulations* (Philadelphia: W. B. Saunders Co., 1979), 342; Paul Popenoe and Donna Wicks Neptune, "Acquaintance and Betrothal," *Social Forces* 16 (1938): 552–555.

60. James L. McConaghy, "Now That You Are Engaged," in William Frederick Bigelow, ed., *The Good Housekeeping Marriage Book* (New York: Prentice-Hall, 1938), 18.

61. Lemo D. Rockwood and Mary E. N. Ford, *Youth, Marriage, and Parenthood* (New York: Wiley, 1945), 102–104.

62. William S. Bernard, "Student Attitudes on Marriage and the Family," *American Sociological Review* 3 (1938): 354–361. And see Floyd Dell, "If They Want to Get Married," *Parents* 11 (December 1936): 14 +.

63. Quoted in Matthews, *The Youth of New York City*, 31.

64. N. K. to Martha Carr, in St. Louis *Post-Dispatch*, May 4, 1931.

65. William Mach and Donald J. Kiser, eds., *Corpus Juris Secundum* (Brooklyn: American Law Book Company, 1938), XI, 776–81; "The Law of Engagement Rings," *United States Law Review* 68 (1934): 342–351. In 1953, a Gallup Poll asked whether "when an engaged couple break off their engagement," the ring should be returned to the man or kept by the woman. Only 64 percent agreed with the legal doctrine that called for the ring's return. Eleven percent considered it an outright gift, while 17 percent said it was the woman's to keep unless it was she who broke the engagement, and 8 percent had no opinion. George Gallup, *The Gallup Polls* (New York: Random House, 1972), II, 1145.

66. Burgess and Wallin, *Engagement and Marriage*, 184; and see Manford Hinshaw Kuhn, "The Engagement," in Howard Becker and Reuben Hill, eds. *Marriage and the Family* (Boston: D. C. Heath, 1942).

67. Editors of *Vogue, Vogue's Book of Etiquette* (Garden City, N.Y.: Doubleday, Doran, 1936); Elinor Ames, *Book of Modern Etiquette* (New York: Walter J. Black, Inc., 1936); and see Paul Popenoe, "Betrothal,"

Journal of Social Hygiene 20 (1934): 444–448, and "Where Are the Marriageable Men?" *Social Forces* 14 (1936): 257–262.

68. Burgess and Wallin, *Engagement and Marriage*, 272.

69. Ernest R. Groves, *Marriage* (New York: Henry Holt and Company, 1933), 151.

70. Burgess and Wallin, *Engagement and Marriage*, 273, 282–295.

71. Willard Waller, "The Rating and Dating Complex," *American Sociological Review* 2 (1937): 727–734.

72. "The status of being steadies brings two persons into a relationship just short of actual engagement, one in which courtship may proceed intensively." Butterfield, *Love Problems of Adolescence*, 83.

73. Paul Popenoe, *Betrothal* (New York: American Social Hygiene Association, 1936), 4.

74. Anna Steese Richardson, *Standard Etiquette* (New York: Harper, 1925), 192.

75. Groves, *Marriage*, 145.

76. Norman E. Himes, *Your Marriage: A Guide to Happiness* (New York: Farrar & Rinehart, 1940), 96.

77. Gulielma Fell Alsop and Mary F. McBride, *She's Off to Marriage* (New York: Vanguard Press, 1942), 96.

78. Groves, *Marriage*, 146.

79. Margaret Sanger, *Happiness in Marriage* (New York: Blue Ribbon Books, 1926), 74–75.

80. Roy E. Dickerson, *When a Couple Are Engaged* (New York: Association Press, 1940), 10–11.

81. McConaghy, "Now That You Are Engaged," 22–23

82. Burgess and Wallin, *Engagement and Marriage*, 317; Lewis M. Terman, *Psychological Factors in Marital Happiness* (New York: McGraw-Hill, 1938.)

83. See Appendix 4.

84. Ernest W. Burgess and Leonard S. Cottrell, *Predicting Success or Failure of Marriage* (New York: Prentice-Hall, 1939), 406–407.

85. Little Girl to Martha Carr, in St. Louis *Post-Dispatch*, October 16, 1931.

86. "Love Hazards, *True Confessions* 26 (April 1935): 22 + .

87. Cavan and Ranck, *The Family and the Depression*, 168.

88. Quoted from the files of the National Council of the Protestant Episcopal Church, in Joseph K. Folsom, *Youth, Family, and Education* (Washington, D.C.: American Council on Education, 1941), 43.

89. Bernard, "Student Attitudes," 356.

90. Samuel H. Preston and John McDonald, "The Incidence of Divorce within Cohorts of American Marriages Contracted since the

Civil War," *Demography* 16 (1979): 1–25. The discussion does not consider the generally rising trend of divorce, looking rather at deviations from it.

91. Computed from the 1975 CPS retrospective data: see Appendix 4. Note that sample attrition and modest numbers for such old persons (in 1975) render these findings uncertain. But see also CPS P20–108, 33–39, and CPS P20–239, 17–39.

92. Pringle, "What Do Women of America Think about Birth Control?," 95.

93. Regine K. Stix and Frank W. Notestein, *Controlled Fertility: An Evaluation of Clinic Service* (Baltimore: Williams & Wilkins, 1940), 53; Stouffer and Lazarsfeld, *Research Memorandum*, 137; James Reed, *From Private Vice to Public Virtue* (New York: Basic Books, 1978).

94. Henry F. Pringle, "What Do the Women of America Think about Birth Control?" *Ladies' Home Journal* 55 (March 1938): 15.

95. Regine K. Stix, "Research in the Causes and Variations in Fertility: *Medical Aspects*," *American Sociological Review* 2 (1937): 668–677.

96. Paul H. Jacobson, "The Trend of the Birth Rate among Persons on Different Economic Levels: City of New York, 1929–1942," *Milbank Memorial Fund Quarterly* 22 (1944): 131–147; Evelyn M. Kitagawa, "Differential Fertility in Chicago, 1920–40," *American Journal of Sociology* 58 (1953): 481–492.

97. Frank Lorimer and Frederick Osborn, *Dynamics of Population* (New York: Macmillan, 1934); Kiser, *Group Differences in Urban Fertility*.

98. Edgar Sydenstricker and G. St. J. Perrott, "Sickness, Unemployment, and Differential Fertility," *Milbank Memorial Fund Quarterly* 12 (1934): 132. See also Helen C. Griffin and G. St. J. Perrott, "Urban Differential Fertility during the Depression," *Milbank Memorial Fund Quarterly* 15 (1937): 75–89.

99. Ruth Riemer and Clyde V. Kiser, "Economic Tension and Social Mobility in Relation to Fertility Planning and Size of Planned Family," *Milbank Memorial Fund Quarterly* 32 (1954): 190–193.

100. Clyde V. Kiser and P. K. Whelpton, "Social and Psychological Factors Affecting Fertility: Part XI: The Interrelationships of Fertility, Fertility Planning, and Feelings of Economic Security," *Milbank Memorial Fund Quarterly* 29 (1951): 41–122; Charles F. Westoff and Clyde V. Kiser, "An Empirical Reexamination and Intercorrelation of Selected Hypothesis Factors," *Milbank Memorial Fund Quarterly* 31 (1953): 421–435.

101. The data were published only for native white women. I have further limited the table to *urban* women, among whom fertility con-

trol was the most widely practiced and among whom, therefore, the patterns discussed appear most strongly.

102. Based on computations subdivided by year of marriage from Indianapolis Fertility data tape. And see Nancy Jean Davis, "The Political Economy of Childlessness and Single-Child Fertility among United States Women" (Ph.D. dissertation, University of Wisconsin, 1978), 225 and *passim.*

103. Ronald Freedman and P. K. Whelpton, "The Interrelation of General Planning to Fertility Planning, and Feeling of Economic Security," *Milbank Memorial Fund Quarterly* 29 (1951): 230–231; Riemer and Kiser, "Economic Tension and Social Mobility."

104. Marianne DeGraff Swain and Clyde V. Kiser, "The Interrelation of Fertility, Fertility Planning, and Ego-Centered Interest in Children," *Milbank Memorial Fund Quarterly* 31 (1953): 51–84.

105. Judith Blake, "Reproductive Ideals among White Americans," *Population Studies* 20 (1966): 190.

5: War and Its Aftermath

1. "The Fortune Survey," *Fortune* 24 (December 1941): 119.

2. "The Fortune Survey," *Fortune* 27 (June 1943): 16.

3. Selma Goldsmith *et al.*, "Size Distribution of Income since the Mid-Thirties," *The Review of Economics and Statistics* 36 (1954): 9–12.

4. Jerome S. Bruner, *Mandate from the People* (New York: Duell, Sloan, and Pearce, 1944), 163, 259–262.

5. U.S. Bureau of Labor Statistics, *Family Spending and Savings in Wartime* (Bulletin no. 822 [Washington: USGPO, 1945]), 88; Marshall B. Clinard, *The Black Market* (New York: Rinehart & Co., 1952).

6. Herbert Blumer, "Morale," in William Fielding Ogburn, ed., *American Society in Wartime* (Chicago: University of Chicago Press, 1943), 207–231; Francis E. Merrill, *Social Problems on the Home Front* (New York: Harper & Brothers, 1948); James H. S. Bossard, "War and the Family," in Howard Becker and Reuben Hill, eds., *Marriage and the Family* (Boston: D. C. Heath, 1942), chap. 24; Bossard, "What War Is Still Doing to the Family," in Howard Becker and Reuben Hill, eds., *Family, Marriage and Parenthood* (Boston: D. C. Heath, 1948), chap. 24; Leila Rupp, *Mobilizing Women for War* (Princeton: Princeton University Press, 1978).

7. Older soldiers, presumably because theirs were somewhat less resilient organisms and because they were likely to have served longer wartime hitches, were slightly more likely to receive disability benefits. Almost half the recipients of compensation had only "10% disabili-

ties," receiving annual pensions averaging $166 in 1947. Three-quarters of recipients were judged to have suffered no more than "30% disabilities." U.S. Administrator of Veterans Affairs, *Annual Report 1947* (Washington: USGPO, 1948), 148.

8. I. L. Kandel, *The Impact of the War upon American Education* (Chapel Hill: University of North Carolina Press, 1948), 77–79.

9. Ella Arvilla Merritt and Floyd Hendricks, "Trend of Child Labor, 1940–44," *Monthly Labor Review* 60 (1945): 762; Elizabeth S. Magee, "Impact of the War on Child Labor," *Annals of the American Academy of Political and Social Science* 236 (November 1944): 103–105; Sanford Cohen, "Teen-Age Student Workers in an Ohio County, 1940–49," *Monthly Labor Review* 77 (1954): 776–778. And see Alan Clive, *State of War: Michigan in World War II* (Ann Arbor: University of Michigan Press, 1974).

10. Theodore Levitt, "World War II Manpower Mobilization and Utilization in a Local Labor Market" (Columbus: OSU Research Foundation, 1951, mimeographed).

11. Lester M. Pearlman and Leonard Eskin, "Teenage Youth in the Wartime Labor Force," *Monthly Labor Review* 60 (1945): 6–17, table on p. 10.

12. Levitt, "World War II Manpower Mobilization," 267.

13. Pearlman and Eskin, "Teenage Youth," 12.

14. Calculated from City of Duluth, *Annual Report of the Board of Education*, "Age and Grade Report" Tables, 1941–42, 1942–43; Merritt and Hendricks, "Trends of Child Labor," 763, 771.

15. Golda G. Stander, "Young Workers in the Wartime Labor Market," *The Child* 6 (1944): 72–76.

16. Goldsmith *et al.*, "Size Distribution of Income," 15.

17. Melvin J. Williams, "A Socio-Economic Analysis of the Functions and Attitudes of Wartime Youth," *Social Forces* 24 (1945): 200–210.

18. Isidore Altman and Antonio Ciocco, "School Absence due to Sickness in the War Years," *Child Development* 16 (1945): 189–199.

19. See e.g., Kandel, *The Impact of War upon American Education*, chap. 4; Paul B. Jacobson, "High Schools and Manpower," *School Review* 51 (1943): 412–417; Harlan C. Koch, "Shifting Emphases in the Problems of Pupils in Certain Michigan High Schools," *School Review* 51 (1943): 79–84; Virginia M. Dewey, "War Comes into the Classroom," *Educational Record* 24 (1943): 93–104; Lloyd Allen Cook, "An Experimental Sociographic Study of a Stratified 10th Grade Class," *American Sociological Review* 10 (1945): 250–261.

20. Beverly Duncan, *Family Factors and School Dropout: 1920–1960*

(Cooperative Research Project No. 2258; Ann Arbor, University of Michigan, 1965, processed).

21. Robert C. Taber, "What's Ahead for the Teens," *Parents* 19 (July 1944): 104.

22. U.S. Department of Labor, Children's Bureau and FSA, U.S. Office of Education, *National Go-to-School Drive 1944–45: A Handbook for Communities* (n.p., n.d.).

23. Pearlman and Eskin, "Teenage Youth," 16.

24. Census P-S-9, 3.

25. "I Gave Too Much," *True Confessions* 41 (August 1942): 88; Ernest R. Groves and Gladys Hoagland Groves, "The Social Background of Wartime Adolescents," *Annals of the American Academy of Political and Social Science* 236 (November 1944): 26–32; George E. Gardner, "Sex Behavior of Adolescents in Wartime," *ibid.*, 60–66; and see Maurice A. Bigelow, "Social Hygiene and Youth in Defense Communities," *Journal of Social Hygiene* 28 (1942): 437–447; Charlotte Towle, "Some Notes on War and Adolescent Delinquency," *Social Service Review* 17 (1943): 67–73; John Slawson, "Adolescents in World at War," *Mental Hygiene* 27 (1943): 531–548; Dorothy Ellsworth, "Precocious Adolescence in Wartime," *The Family* 25 (March, 1944): 4.

26. "No Excuse for Immorality," *True Confessions* 41 (September 1942): 66.

27. Anne Maxwell, "This is Shocking," *Woman's Home Companion* 70 (January 1943): 34; "Companion Poll Question: Do You Favor Special Courses in Sex Education in High Schools as One Means of Reducing Juvenile Delinquency?" *Woman's Home Companion* 70 (November 1943): 32; Nelson B. Henry, ed., *Juvenile Delinquency and the Schools*, 47th Yearbook of the National Society for the Study of Education, Part 1 (1948); Kandel, *The Impact of the War upon American Education*, 55–60.

28. Paul Wiers, "Wartime Increases in Michigan Delinquency," *American Sociological Review* 10 (1945): 515–523.

29. U.S. Federal Security Agency, U.S. Office of Education, *Guidance Problems in Wartime* (Education and National Defense Series, Pamphlet No. 18 [Washington: USGPO, 1942]), 26.

30. U.S. Department of Labor, Children's Bureau, "Barometers of Wartime Influences on the Behavior of Children and Youth" (March 1943, mimeographed), 2–6.

31. *Social Statistics*, Supplement to *The Child*, vol. 8, no. 6 (1943). Retrospective data show that although premarital births were up slightly from 3 percent for the 1936–1940 marriage cohort to 4 percent for the wartime marriages (with a return to 3 percent after the

war), antenuptial conceptions were lower, at 4 percent, in the wartime marriage cohort; data from the 1978 Current Population Survey confirm the finding. Norman B. Ryder and Charles F. Westoff, *Reproduction in the United States, 1965* (Princeton: Princeton University Press, 1971); Martin O'Connell and Maurice J. Moore, "The Legitimacy Status of First Births to U.S. Women Aged 15−24, 1939−1978," *Family Planning Perspectives* 12 (January/February 1980): 18−19.

32. Caroline Zachry, "Preparing Youth to Be Adults," *National Society for the Study of Education 43rd Yearbook, part 1* (1944), 332−346.

33. Robert J. Havighurst and Hilda Taba, *Adolescent Character and Personality* (New York: John Wiley and Sons, 1949), 29ff.

34. See the classic statement, Kingsley Davis, "Adolescence and the Social Structure," *Annals of the American Academy of Political and Social Science* 236 (November 1944): 236.

35. D'Ann Campbell, *Women at War with America* (Cambridge: Harvard University Press, 1984), 73, 83, and chaps. 3 and 4 generally.

36. Leonard Eskin, "Sources of Wartime Labor Supply," *Monthly Labor Review* 59 (1944): 275.

37. Census CPS P60−2, calculated from tables 3 and 4.

38. *Ibid.*, table 7; Census P-S-22, table 3; Census, *Historical Statistics*, I: 296, 303.

39. U.S. Women's Bureau, *Women Workers in Ten War Production Areas and Their Postwar Employment Plans* (Bulletin no. 209 [Washington: USGPO, 1946]), 45.

40. Svend Riemer, "War Marriages Are Different," *Marriage and Family Living* 5 (1943): 84.

41. U.S. Public Health Service, National Office of Vital Statistics, *Monthly Marriage Report*, Series PM-4, no. 13 (April 21, 1947), table 2. The first of these years includes statistics estimated, evidently, by a jewelers' trade association.

42. U.S. Bureau of the Census, *Population*, Series P-S, no. 10 (1946): 3.

43. Constantine Panunzio, "War and Marriage," *Social Forces* 21 (1943): 445; see also the rather pompous theoretical interpretation of the same phenomenon by Jean Lipman-Blumen, "A Crisis Framework Applied to Macrosociological Family Changes: Marriage, Divorce, and Occupational Trends Associated with World War II," *Journal of Marriage and the Family* 37 (1975): 889−902.

44. Grace Sloan Overton, *Marriage in War and Peace* (New York: Abingdon-Cokesbury Press, 1945), 134.

45. Clifford R. Adams, "How to Pick a Mate," *American Magazine* 138 (December 1944): 32+; "Man Shortage," *True Confessions* 41

(January 1943): 24+; Gladys Denny Schultz, "Must We Ration Husbands?" *Better Homes and Gardens* 23 (November 1944): 10+. Beth L. Bailey believes this perception to have been considerably more widespread and longer-lasting than I do. *From Front Porch to Back Seat: Courtship in Twentieth-Century America* (Baltimore: Johns Hopkins University Press, 1988).

46. I rest these and subsequent statements on two sources, neither perfect, drawing confidence where—as generally—they coincide. These are first marriages registered in New York outside of New York City—which suffer from any racially differential migration patterns, since they are of *numbers* of first marriages and not of *rates*—and the white/nonwhite comparisons in the first-marriage retrospects reported in the 1960 U.S. Census, which overcome the migration bias but suffer from certain differential-mortality bias and probably differential-divorce bias. New York State, Department of Health, Division of Vital Statistics, *Annual Report*, annual; Census 1960–4, 38–43.

47. Theodore Caplow, "A Critical Study of American Marriage Rates" (Ph.D. dissertation, University of Minnesota, 1946).

48. A mythology of love appropriate to a nation at war held that both desperation and the inevitable haste of wartime marriage often produced socioeconomically mixed marriages, an assertion that I doubt but unfortunately cannot test. See, e.g., "For Always," *True Romances* (December 1942): 4+; "Brief Hours to Love, A Story in the Tempo of Today," *True Romances* (December 1943).

49. Calculated from Massachusetts, Department of Health, *Vital Statistics of Massachusetts*, annual. These data, unfortunately, are reported by five-year age *group* rather than by single year of age, as in New York State.

50. Rather than these representing a real change in who married who, I suspect that this represented a downward shift of the ages at marriage toward the lower bounds of the five-year age grouping of the Massachusetts data.

51. AIPO 377, available at the Roper Center Archives, University of Connecticut, Storrs. These data are explored at considerable length in Modell, "Normative Aspects of American Marriage Timing," 215–224.

52. Case #4551. Interviews are available in Ernest R. Burgess Papers, Regenstein Library, University of Chicago, typescript.

53. Case #2700.

54. Case #3001.

55. Case #3308.

56. Case #2705.

57. Case #2604.

58. Hazel Erskine Gaudet, "The Polls: Morality," *Public Opinion Quarterly* 30 (1966): 672; Robert J. Havighurst *et al.*, *The American Veteran Back Home* (New York: Longmans Green & Co., 1951), 38–41, quotation on p. 41; and see Reuben Hill, *Families under Stress* (New York: Harper, 1949).

59. Case #3004.

60. Case #3304.

61. Case #2601.

62. Case #4551.

63. "The Fortune Survey: Women in America," part 1, *Fortune* 34 (August 1946); *ibid.*, part 2 (September 1946).

64. *The American Veteran Back Home*, 84.

65. Hill, *Families under Stress*, chap. 5.

66. Karen Anderson, *Wartime Women: Sex Roles, Family Relations, and the Status of Women during World War II* (Westport, Conn.: Greenwood, 1981), 110.

67. *Wartime Women*, 111.

68. James H. S. Bossard, "Family Problems of the Immediate Future," *Journal of Home Economics* 37 (1945): 383–387; see also Francis E. Merrill's excellent summary and analysis of *Social Problems on the Home Front* (New York: Harper & Brothers, 1948.)

69. George Q. Flynn, *Lewis B. Hershey, Mr. Selective Service* (Chapel Hill: University of North Carolina Press, 1985), 96–110; Richard Malkin, *Marriage, Morals, and War* (New York: Arden Book Company, 1943).

70. Testimony of Paul V. McNutt, Federal Security Administrator, in U.S. Congress, House Committee on Military Affairs, *Hearings, Allowances and Allotments for Dependents of Military Personnel* (59th Congress, 1st Session, 1942), 2–3.

71. "Allowances for Servicemen's Dependents," *Monthly Labor Review* 55 (1942): 226–228; "Liberalized Allowances for War Service Dependents," *Monthly Labor Review* 58 (1944): 67–69.

72. Guglielma Fell Alsop and Mary F. McBride, *Arms and the Girl* (New York: Vanguard Press, 1943), 279–280.

73. "Love Is Worth Waiting For," *True Romances* (June 1941): 22+.

74. Quoted in Evelyn Millis Duvall, "Marriage in War Time," *Marriage and Family Living* 4 (1942): 73.

75. Ruth Burr Sanborn, "Hero Come Home," *Saturday Evening Post* 215 (September 12, 1942): 63.

76. "My Very Special Girl," *True Love and Romance* (February 1944): 24+.

77. Anne Maxwell, "Should Marriage Wait?" *Woman's Home Companion* 69 (November 1942): 58+.

78. Guglielma Fell Alsop and Mary F. McBride, *She's Off to Marriage* (New York: Vanguard Press, 1942). See also Leland Foster Wood, "Counseling on War Time Marriages," in Leland Foster Wood and John W. Mullen, eds., *What the American Family Faces* (Chicago: Eugene Hugh Publishers, 1943).

79. Available Selective Service records are surprisingly thin and document army inductees more fully than others, for the navy typically accepted volunteers only and only for a part of the war were these processed through Selective Service. The fullest table, dealing with the marital status of army inductees from November 1940 through September 1944, is in United States, Selective Service System, *Dependency Deferment* (Special Monograph No. 8 [Washington: USGPO, 1947]), 241.

80. To develop this latter story, I use three exceptional sets of survey data, gathered by the team of sociological and social-psychological researchers brought together to examine morale on behalf of the army. These data proved seminal in the history of American sociology and have been published in four volumes under the general title *The American Soldier* (Princeton: Princeton University Press, 1949), of which Samuel Stouffer was the senior author. Most of the surveys collected in this effort are available from the Roper Center Archives, Storrs, Connecticut, and at the National Archives. See Appendix 4.

81. Survey S-106EU and Survey S-144 included 9,892 white soldiers and 4,678 black soldiers, respectively. The selection of units involved purposive rather than strictly random sampling. Units were chosen such that each branch of service was represented in approximately correct proportions, and both more and less experienced soldiers were included. The black sample designated a subsample that was entirely comparable in sampling criteria to the parallel white study, but I elected to include the entire black sample, to conserve cases. The samples appear reasonably reliable in proportions married at induction, by comparison with Selective Service records. For discussion of these data, see John Modell and Duane Steffey, "Waging War and Marriage: Military Service and Family Formation, 1940–1950," *Journal of Family History*, forthcoming.

82. The model here is derived from an ordinary-least-squares multiple regression of age at induction and time since induction on nuptiality of those single at induction. As a model based on cross-sectional data, it represents *average* experience for the whole sample, not the experience of actual age-at-induction cohorts. Because of im-

precisions in calculating age at entry to the army at older ages, I present no estimates for their nuptiality here.

83. Overall, roughly equal proportions answered this way, the reverse, a middling position, and that they were undecided.

84. Stouffer *et al.*, *American Soldier*, I: 125.

85. Other *American Soldier* data show a counterinstance: when age is standardized, AWOLs were relatively more prevalent among those who had married during the war than among either the unmarried or those who were married when they began their service, except among those whose service stretched over two years, where preinduction husbands were the focus for AWOL. Stouffer *et al.*, *American Soldier*, I: 119.

86. The more exclusive navy was also more thorough in its limitation of black men to supporting roles, especially menial ones.

87. Robert R. Palmer, Bell I. Wiley, and William R. Keast, "The Procurement and Training of Ground Combat Troops," in *United States Army in World War II* (Washington: Historical Division, Department of the Army, 1948), Section I.

88. A measure of the disparity between branches is offered by tabulations of general-aptitude scores provided by Palmer, Wiley, and Keast. Thus, in March-August 1942, the air forces received 44.4 percent of its new men from the two highest aptitude classes and only 20.3 percent from the lowest, in comparison to the infantry's 27.4 percent high-scoring men and 43.6 percent low-scoring. Loud protest from infantry high command that it was hard to win a modern war with such poor material led to a modification that produced a 41.7 percent high and 27.0 percent low intake for the air forces in 1943, as compared with the infantry's 30.2 percent high and 37.2 percent low. Palmer, Wiley, and Keast, "Procurement and Training," 17–18.

89. This tendency was true among the black sample as well as the white, although the purposes and mechanisms undoubtedly differed.

90. Stouffer *et al.*, *The American Soldier*, I: 240; on comparisons between air forces and infantry in various aspects of morale, see chap. 5, Section II.

91. The infantry, I suspect, has a relatively more prestigious aspect among blacks, who typically received support rather than combat assignments. Yet figures comparable to those in the table appear when such characteristic black support branches as the quartermaster's corps and the engineers are tabulated in lieu of the infantry.

92. If we examine the *joint* effect of branch of the service and marriage during service on promotion, as we should because promotion was more likely within the air forces, we see that both branch and

rank were associated with white soldiers' marriage during military service, the latter substantially more so. A logistic regression model containing all of the above characteristics as explanatory variables accounts for approximately one-third of the variability associated with marriage during military service. Of this amount, over three-fourths is explained by the inclusion of years since induction. One-tenth is due to the subsequent (after years of service) inclusion in the model of age at entry to the armed forces. After these variables, rank, branch, and level of education enter the model with that relative importance. These variables contribute approximately 8, 3, and 2 percent, respectively, to the overall reduction in variance. The marriage process of soldiers depended both on the structure of the army and on attainment within the army, and these were not to be explained away by background, nor were they simply functions of the length of the military career. On discontinuities in the life course of blacks, see David L. Featherman and Robert M. Hauser, *Opportunity and Change* (New York: Academic Press, 1978), chap. 6; Michael D. Ornstein, *Entry into the American Labor Force* (New York: Academic Press, 1976), 173–177.

93. Based on a survey of American soldiers (excluding officers) in Italy, this study particularly closely probed sensitive personal issues because of its central concern with venereal disease and its prevention. "Seldom was a study under Research Bureau auspices planned and carried out with more meticulous care than this survey; the dangers of obtaining misleading information . . . were well understood in advance. . . . Questions were pretested with more than ordinary care." Stouffer *et al.*, *American Soldier*, I: 545–546. Study S-233 includes 2,685 cases. Blacks were intentionally oversampled.

94. Strong norms existed which supported thoughts and quasi-plans of marriage among soldiers. A careful survey of 750 undergraduates in schools all over the United States, conducted in 1945, concluded that "almost no conditions related to the war appeared to interfere with the girls['] willingness to become engaged," nor really to marry. Boys were a little less supportive of immediate marriage than girls (but were of course not themselves in the armed forces at the time they responded). Of girls, 79 percent favored immediate marriage if economic circumstances are adequate and 54 percent if the two had been "serious" about one another for at least six months (only 15 percent if they had not been well acquainted for so long a time); for boys, 55 percent supported immediate marriage if material circumstances permitted and 49 percent if the couple had been "serious" for half a year or longer. Engagement was much more feasible

for both young men and young women, and much of the differential about marriage was eliminated when the question was engagement. John H. Burma, "Attitudes of College Youth on War Marriage," *Social Forces* 24 (1945): 96–100.

95. Susan M. Hartmann, "Prescriptions for Penelope: Literature on Women's Obligations to Returning World War II Veterans," *Women's Studies* 5 (1978): 230.

96. Census P46–8, 9.

97. Calculated from USNCHS *Vital Statistics* 1974, III: 1–5, and USNCHS *Vital Statistics*, II, annual. The 1959 Current Population Survey retrospective accounts indicate that for white women married in 1940–1944, the pace of the transition to parenthood was virtually identical to that which had prevailed for white women at the end of the Depression, which was, of course, slower than that before the Depression. Census CPS P20–108, 38.

98. Ronald R. Rindfuss and James A. Sweet, *Postwar Fertility Trends and Differentials in the United States* (New York: Academic Press, 1977), 54–59.

99. David R. B. Ross, *Preparing for Ulysses: Politics and Veterans during World War II* (New York: Columbia University Press, 1969).

100. Bruner, *Mandate from the People*, 270.

101. Havighurst, *The American Veteran Back Home*.

102. Bruner, *Mandate From the People*, 270–271.

103. Keith W. Olson, *The G.I. Bill, the Veterans, and the Colleges* (Lexington: University Press of Kentucky, 1972); Census CPS P57–89, 8; *Veterans in Our Society*, 105; U.S. President's Commission on Veterans' Pensions, *Staff Report IX*, Part A (Washington: USGPO, 1956), 246–247.

104. Norman Fredericksen and W. B. Schrader, *Adjustment to College* (Princeton: Educational Testing Service, 1951). Most of the veterans studied had finished high school in midwar, and only half had begun to work full-time before entering the military.

105. For veterans and nonveterans alike, parental income was *negatively correlated* with the ratio of attained grades to predicted grades based on both high school grades and aptitude tests.

106. President's Commission on Veterans' Pensions, *Staff Report IX*, 55.

107. George Katona and Janet A. Fisher, "Postwar Changes in the Income of Identical Consumer Units," in National Bureau of Economic Research, *Studies in Income and Wealth*, vol. 13 (New York: National Bureau of Economic Research, 1951), 88. "Survey of Consumer Finances," *Federal Reserve Bulletin* 33 (1947): 957; "Survey of Con-

sumer Finances," *Federal Reserve Bulletin* 34 (1948): 774; "1949 Survey of Consumer Finances," *Federal Reserve Bulletin* 35 (1949): 16–18.

108. Census P-S-16, tables 3, 4A, 5. This relationship was present in *all* cities examined.

109. Census CPS P50–5, 9.

110. Mary Elizabeth Pidgeon, "Women Workers and Recent Economic Change," *Monthly Labor Review* 65 (1947): 668.

111. I here examine a subset of men in a random sample of the 1950 census who were of an age to have served in the military during World War II and who were not married before 1945. The subsample is of 4,955 men drawn randomly from the Public Use Sample of the 1950 individual-level population census. See Appendix 4.

112. The military, to be sure, excluded physically, mentally, and educationally deficient men, who were in any case probably not good candidates for marriage in 1945–1950 or at any time.

113. Calculated from Census CPS P50–14, table 1. See also Census CPS P20–10, 28.

114. Census P-S-16, 2; Thomas P. Monahan, "The Number of Children in American Families and the Sharing of Households," *Marriage and Family Living* 18 (1956): 201–203.

115. Census Housing 1947, table 4A.

116. We are here considering children fathered approximately between one year before Pearl Harbor and the Japanese surrender and thus point to a substantial amount of family-building during the war for soldiers and likely soldiers.

117. In each year, of course, those married with spouse present need not have been in this category at any earlier date, so that the apparent modest fertility increase among married ex-soldiers is in large part a product of the very great number of newly formed couples involving younger veterans between 1946 and 1947. For those who had not served, the period seems to have been one of modest, perhaps reduced, fertility. Census CPS P20–18, 19; Census CPS P20–46, 22.

6: The Baby Boom

1. "Coke for Breakfast," *True Love* (December 1959): 20+.

2. David Riesman, "Permissiveness and Sex Roles," *Marriage and Family Living* 21 (1959): 211–217; David Riesman, Robert J. Potter, and Jeanne Watson, "Sociability, Permissiveness, and Equality," in Riesman, *Abundance for What?* (Garden City, N.Y.: Doubleday, 1964).

3. By contrast, when a like sample was queried a decade later, the

results were drastically different: parents provided the prime frame of reference *only* for insurance policies and for 16-year-olds' choice of automobiles. Friends were prepotent for the great majority of items. Paul Gilkison, "Teen-Agers' Perceptions of Buying Frames of Reference: A Decade in Retrospect," *Journal of Retailing* 49 (Summer 1973): 25–37.

4. David Riesman and Howard Roseborough, "Careers and Consumer Behavior," in Lincoln H. Clark, ed., *Consumer Behavior*, II (New York: NYU Press, 1955). Vance Packard's muckraking *The Waste Makers* (New York: McKay, 1960) devoted a chapter to the role of advertisers in solemnizing domesticity in the baby boom and their effort to reach teenagers.

5. "The Exploding Youth Market—Do Ad Men Understand Teen-Agers," *Printer's Ink* 272 (July 29, 1960): 20–26. A pulp magazine, intriguingly, claims that young-singles resorts date from this period and were a product of prosperity. "So the boys went. And they did enjoy themselves. And the girls went, too. And they enjoyed themselves. It has been going on ever since." "Where and How to find a Man," *True Love* (December 1961): 35.

6. Janet L. Wolff, *What Makes Women Buy* (New York: McGraw-Hill, 1958), 267.

7. "The Fortune Survey," *Fortune* 35 (January 1947): 5–16.

8. On the relevance of this experience, see W. S. Woytinsky, "Postwar Economic Perspectives: I. Experience After World War I," *Social Security Bulletin* 8 (December 1945): 18–29.

9. Elmo Roper, "The Fortune Consumer Outlook," *Fortune* 37 (April 1948): 5.

10. *The Black Market* (New York: Rinehart & Company, 1952); George Katona, "The Human Factor in Economic Affairs," in Angus Campbell and Philip E. Converse, eds., *The Human Meaning of Social Change* (New York: Russell Sage Foundation, 1972), 229–262; Reuben Hill, *Family Development in Three Generations* (Cambridge: Schenkman, 1970); Bert G. Hickman, *Growth and Stability in the Postwar Economy* (Washington, D.C.: The Brookings Institute, 1960), 254–255, 323–325.

11. Janet Austrian Fisher, "The Economics of an Aging Population" (Ph.D. dissertation, Columbia University, 1950), 72, 76.

12. "A Case Study: The 1948–1949 Recession," in National Bureau of Economic Research, *Policies to Combat Recession* (Princeton: Princeton University Press, 1956), 27–53.

13. Hickman, *Growth and Stability*, 161.

14. *Ibid.*, 408 and *passim*.

15. Clinard, *Black Market*; Irwin Friend, "Individuals' Demand Deposits, June 1942–43," *Survey of Current Business* 24 (June 1944): 18, 20; Friend, "Personal Saving in the Postwar Period," *Survey of Current Business* 29 (September 1949): 9–23.

16. "A National Survey of Liquid Assets," *Federal Reserve Bulletin* 32 (1946): 574–580; Fisher, "Economics of an Aging Population," 155–156.

17. "National Survey of Liquid Assets," 717; "Survey of Consumer Finances," *Federal Reserve Bulletin* 33 (1947): 654.

18. "1949 Survey of Consumer Finances," *Federal Reserve Bulletin* 35 (1949): 639 and *passim*; see also the comparable surveys for 1946, 1947, and 1948 published *seriatim* in the *Federal Reserve Bulletin*; George Katona and Janet A. Fisher, "Postwar Changes in the Income of Identical Consumer United," in National Bureau of Economic Research, *Studies in Income and Wealth*, vol. 13 (New York: National Bureau of Economic Research, 1951), 94–97; Hickman, *Growth and Stability*, 254–255, 323–325; George Katona, "The Human Factor in Economic Affairs," 256 and *passim*.

19. George Katona and Eva Mueller, *Consumer Attitudes and Demand, 1950–1952* (Ann Arbor: Survey Research Center, University of Michigan, 1953), 40.

20. George Katona and Eva Mueller, *Consumer Expenditures 1953–1956* (Ann Arbor: Survey Research Center, University of Michigan, n.d.), 23.

21. "1954 Survey of Consumer Finances," *Federal Reserve Bulletin* 40 (1954): 249; Survey Research Center, University of Michigan, *1960 Survey of Consumer Finances* (Ann Arbor: Survey Research Center, University of Michigan, 1961), 222, 239.

22. Katona and Mueller, *Consumer Expenditures 1953–1956*, 27.

23. Gary Hendricks and Kenwood C. Youmans, *Consumer Durables and Installment Debt: A Study of American Households* (Institute for Survey Research, University of Michigan, 1972), 6; F. Thomas Juster, *Household Capital Formation and Financing 1897–1962* (New York: National Bureau of Economic Research, 1966), 65–67; U.S. Board of Governors of the Federal Reserve System, *Consumer Installment Credit*, II (Washington, D.C.: USGPO, 1957), 232–233; *Federal Reserve Bulletin* 37 (1951): 1517; *Federal Reserve Bulletin* 42 (1956): 702; Wharton School and U.S. Bureau of Labor Statistics, *Study of Consumer Expenditures, Incomes, and Savings*, XVIII (Philadelphia: University of Pennsylvania Press, 1957), 14, 26; United States Bureau of Labor Statistics, *Survey of Consumer Expenditures 1960–61*, Supplement 2, Part A (Bureau of Labor Statistics Report 237–38 [Washington: USGPO, 1946]), 4–8, 23–25.

24. Census Housing 1956, part 1, 18, 26–28; "1957 Survey of Consumer Finances," *Federal Reserve Bulletin* 43 (1958): 539; Louis J. Paradiso and Clement Winston, "Consumer Expenditure-Income Patterns," *Survey of Current Business* 35 (September 1955): 23–32; H. S. Houthakker and Lester D. Taylor, *Consumer Demand in the United States, 1929–1970* (Cambridge: Harvard University Press, 1966), chap. 4.

25. Alice Kessler-Harris, *Out of Work: A History of Wage-Earning Women in the United States* (New York: Oxford University Press, 1982).

26. Calculated from United States, *Employment and Training Report of the President* (Washington, D.C.: USGPO, 1979), 295. An excellent overview treating trends from 1940 to the mid-1950s is Gertrude Bancroft, *The American Labor Force: Its Growth and Changing Composition* (Census Monograph Series [New York: John Wiley, 1958]), chap. 5.

27. Mary M. Schweitzer, "World War II and Female Labor Force Participation Rates," *Journal of Economic History* 40 (1980): 89–95.

28. USNCHS Series 21–2, 32–33.

29. Citations to articles on juvenile delinquency in *Reader's Guide* expressed as a ratio to total pages rose to 40 per 1,000 pages in the 1943–1945 volume, declined to 12 in 1949–1951 and 14 in 1951–1953, and then took off: 47 in 1953–1955, 46 in 1955–1957, and a peak of 51 in the next two-year period, followed by a slight decline to 45, and then a sharp reduction back to its late-1930s level.

30. "Conditions Conducive to Youth Crime," *Congressional Digest* 33 (1954): 291+.

31. William Graebner, "Outlawing Teenage Populism: The Campaign against Secret Societies in the American High School, 1900–1960," *Journal of American History* 74 (1987): 411–437.

32. United States, Senate, Committee on the Judiciary, Subcommittee to Investigate Juvenile Delinquency, *Hearings*, part 8 (1955), 85.

33. H. H. Remmers and D. H. Radler, *The American Teenager* (Indianapolis: Bobbs-Merrill, 1957), 106; R. D. Franklin and H. H. Remmers, *Youth's Attitude toward Courtship and Marriage* (The Purdue Opinion Panel, vol. 20, no. 2; n. p., 1961), 4, 6.

34. "Self-Portrait: The Teen-Type Magazine," *Annals of the American Academy of Political and Social Science* 338 (November 1961): 15.

35. *Ibid.*, 20.

36. *Ibid.*, 21.

37. Elliot H. Drisko, "Parent-Teenage Codes" (Ed.D. Project, Teacher's College, Columbia University, 1960), *passim*; Ruth Carson, "A Code for Teen-Agers," *Parents* 34 (November 1959): 48+; Martha Grayson McDonald, "But Mom, All the Other Kids Do It!" *Parents* 40

(October 1965): 66+. A copy of the Philadelphia Parents' Council's social code for their teenage children, reproduced in *Parents* 30 (December 1955): 48–49, says gingerly about dating: "Home should not be forgotten as a possible place for dating. Public entertainment puts a strain on a boy's allowance. Parents could cooperate by providing an agreeable measure of privacy."

38. James B. Conant, *The American High School Today* (New York: McGraw-Hill, 1959), 37.

39. Census, *Historical Statistics*: I, 368; Census 1950–1, 1–210; Census, 1960–1, 1–37.

40. Beverly Duncan, *Family Factors and School Dropout: 1920–1960* (Cooperative Research Project No. 2258 [Ann Arbor: University of Michigan, 1965], processed), chap. 3; Beverly Duncan, "Trends in Output and Distribution of Schooling," in Eleanor Bernert Sheldon and Wilbert E. Moore, eds., *Indicators of Social Change* (New York: Russell Sage Foundation, 1968), 601–672.

41. U.S. Department of Health, Education and Welfare, *Digest of Educational Statistics* (Washington, D.C.: USGPO, 1965), 13. The trend accelerated through the 1960s.

42. Ralph H. Turner, *The Social Context of Ambition* (San Francisco: Chandler Publishing Company, 1964); James S. Coleman, *The Adolescent Society* (New York: The Free Press of Glencoe, 1961); C. Wayne Gordon, *The Social System of the High School* (Glencoe: The Free Press).

43. Graebner, "Outlawing Teenage Populism," 429.

44. "The School Class as a Social System: Some of Its Functions in American Society," *Harvard Educational Review* 29 (1959): 297–318, quotation at 314.

45. Computed from machine-readable data from Minnesota State Polls. See Appendix 4.

46. Samuel H. Lowrie, "Sex Differences and Age of Initial Dating," *Social Forces* 30 (1952): 456–461; and "Factors Involved in the Frequency of Dating," *Marriage and Family Living* 18 (1956): 46–51.

47. Ernest A. Smith, *American Youth Culture* (New York: Free Press of Glencoe, 1962), chap. 9; Samuel Harlan Lowrie, "Dating Theories and Student Responses," *American Sociological Review* 16 (1951): 334–340.

48. Computed from Roper Commercial Poll 15, Roper Center Archive, University of Connecticut, Storrs; Elizabeth Douvan, *Adolescent Girls* (n.p., n.d., but evidently 1956 or 1957, processed), 62. The questions were not identically phrased, but the gist was similar enough that we can make the comparisons with some comfort in view of the size of the differences. The 1939 poll asked about "different ideas from either one or both of your parents" about a variety of matters,

while the 1956 poll asked, "What disagreements do you have with your parents?" Each then proceeded with a list that included how often and where to go out; how late to stay out; and what opposite-sex friends are appropriate. Sampling methodology had changed between the survey dates. A large and carefully conducted poll from the state of Washington in 1948 shows that only about 8 percent of high school boys and girls said that they "often quarrel" or "always scrap" about the time of returning from dates or other evening activities. Forty-eight percent of the boys and 69 percent of the girls said they had more or less formal understandings about dating with their parents. L. J. Elias, *High School Youth Look at Their Problems* (Pullman: The College Bookstore, 1949), 20–22.

49. William A. Westley and Frederick Elkin, "The Protective Environment and Adolescent Socialization," *Social Forces* 35 (1957): 243–249; David Riesman, "Permissiveness and Sex Roles," *Marriage and Family Living* 21 (1959): 211–217; Margaret Mead, "Problems of the Late Adolescent and Youth Adult," in *Children and Youth in the 1960s: Survey Papers* (Washington, D.C.: Golden Anniversary White House Conference on Children and Youth, 1960).

50. For some details as seen by the girls themselves, see Coleman, *The Adolescent Society*, chaps. 4, 5; Douvan, *Adolescent Girls*, 98–101.

51. Coleman, *The Adolescent Society*, 43–50; Harold R. Phelps and John E. Horrocks, "Factors Influencing Informal Groups of Adolescents," *Child Development* 29 (1958): 70–86.

52. Arthur M. Vener, "Adolescent Orientation to Clothing: A Social-Psychological Interpretation" (Ph.D. dissertation, Michigan State University, 1957), 92–96, 109–112. Vener's study was administered to 782 public school students in Lansing, Michigan. Neither sex nor grade seems to have affected the conclusions I draw here.

53. Margaret Mooney Marini, "The Transition to Adulthood: Sex Differences in Educational Attainment and Age at Marriage," *American Sociological Review* 43 (1978): 498–499; and see Paul Ronald Voss, "Social Determinants of Age at First Marriage in the United States" (Ph.D. dissertation, University of Michigan, 1975).

54. Arthur L. Stinchcombe, *Rebellion in a High School* (Chicago: Quadrangle, 1964), 110–129. The study was carried out in the high school of a small logging and sawmill town.

55. *Ibid.*, 128–129.

56. Robert J. Havighurst *et al.*, *Growing Up in River City* (New York: John Wiley, 1962), 119, 129.

57. Clark E. Vincent, "Socialization Data in Research on Young Marriers," *Acta Sociologica* 8 (1965): 118–127.

58. *St. Paul Central High School Times*, March 14, 1954.

59. Franklin and Remmers, *Youth's Attitude toward Courtship*, 4–6.

60. Carlfred Broderick, "Social-Sexual Development in a Suburban Community," *Journal of Sex Research* 2 (1966): 1–24.

61. A large and methodologically excellent national survey conducted between 1966 and 1970, here mingling the responses of 12- to 17-year-olds of both genders, found about this degree of remaining socioeconomic difference by parental income and parental education. USNCHS, Series 11–153, 29.

62. Carlfred B. Broderick, "Social Heterosexual Development among Urban Negroes and Whites," *Journal of Marriage and the Family* 27 (1975): 200–203. USNCHS, Series 11–153, 29, finds a small excess of white daters that can easily be explained by the greater income of white parents and the greater propensity to date on the part of those from more prosperous families.

63. Warren Breed, "Sex, Class and Socialization in Dating," *Marriage and Family Living* 18 (1956): 137–144.

64. Joseph E. Lantagne, "Interests of 4,000 High School Pupils in Problems of Marriage and Parenthood," *Research Quarterly* 29 (1958): 410–412. These interests were still rather pressing among college students. Lantagne, "Comparative Analysis of Items of Interest in Marriage and Parenthood of 4,000 Students in Junior and Senior Colleges," *ibid.*, 27 (1956): 198–201.

65. Remmers and Radler, *American Teenager*, 80–85.

66. On this theme, see "I Was Looking for Dates," *True Confessions* (October 1957): 40+.

67. An excellent 1941 St. Louis high school study found that 24 percent of the senior boys and 8 percent of the senior girls were then going steady. Helen Moore Priester, "The Reported Dating Practices of One Hundred Six High School Seniors in an Urban Community" (M.A. essay, Cornell University, 1941), 41.

68. Lowrie's nonrepresentative 1948 high school junior and senior sample, gathered in middle-class urban areas, found that about half the boys and six-tenths of the girls who had dated before age 17 had gone steady before age 17. By age 19, about three-quarters of the boys who had dated had gone steady, as had eight in ten of the girls who had dated. Samuel Harman Lowrie, "Sex Differences and Age of Initial Dating," 456–461; Lowrie, "Factors Involved in the Frequency of Dating," 46–51.

69. Hazel Gaudet Erskine, "The Polls: Morality," *Public Opinion Quarterly* 30 (1966): 676.

70. Beth L. Bailey, *From Front Porch to Back Seat: Courtship in Twentieth-Century America* (Baltimore: The Johns Hopkins Press, 1988), 53.

71. Goldie Ruth Kaback and Margaret Albrecht," Going Steady. . . .

It's Not What It Used to Be," *Parents* 30 (July 1955): 37+. And see the letters in Abigail Wood, "Young Living," *Seventeen* (May 1963): 157+.

72. Elmer W. Bock and Lee Burchinal, "Social Status, Heterosexual Relations and Expected Ages of Marriage," *Journal of Genetic Psychology* 101 (1962): 43–51.

73. Claire Cox, *The Upbeat Generation* (Englewood Cliffs: Prentice-Hall, 1962), 37–38 and *passim*; "Teens on a Roaring Pajama Party," *Personal Romances* (December 1959): 18.

74. Smith, *American Youth Culture*, 201; William J. Cameron and William F. Kunkel, "High School Dating: A Study in Variation," *Marriage and Family Living* 22 (1960): 74–76; Charles D. Bolton, "Mate Selection as the Development of a Relationship," *Marriage and Family Living* 23 (1961): 238. See also Evelyn Mills Duvall, "Adolescent Love as a Reflection of Teen-Agers' Search for Identity," *Journal of Marriage and the Family* 26 (1964): 226–229.

75. John Richard Crist, "High School Dating as a Behavior System" (Ph.D. dissertation, University of Missouri, 1951), 242–243.

76. Quoted in Marion Le Count, "A Study of Certain Boy-Girl Relationships in a Group of High School Seniors" (Ed.D. project, Columbia University, Teachers' College, 1950), 159–160; and see Eugene J. Kanin, "Male Aggression in Dating-Courtship Relationships," *American Journal of Sociology* 63 (1957): 200.

77. Douvan, *Adolescent Girls*, 108–109.

78. Robert D. Herman, "The 'Going Steady' Complex: A Re-Examination," *Marriage and Family Living* 17 (1955): 36–40; Breed, "Sex, Class and Socialization," 139.

79. Ira L. Reiss, "Sexual Codes in Teenage Culture," *Annals of the American Academy of Political and Social Science* 338 (November 1961): 55.

80. Mead, "Problems of the Late Adolescent and Young Adult," 3–11; Svend Riemer, "Courtship for Security," *Sociology and Social Research* 45 (1961): 423–429; Ann Hartman, "Who Do I Love?" *True Love* (December 1961): 23.

81. *The Times*, October 31, 1952; February 6, 1953.

82. *Clarkfield (Minn.) High School Clarkette*, March 15, 1951; May 1953.

83. Le Count, "Boy-Girl Relationships," 273.

84. *Ibid.*, 273–274.

85. *Ibid.*, 165.

86. Remmers and Radler, *The American Teenager*, 80–85, based on a national poll from 1956–57; Elias, *High School Youth*, 38.

87. Le Count, "Boy-Girl Relationships," 166.

88. Crist, "High School Dating," 312.

89. Bailey, *From Front Porch to Back Seat*, 55–56.

90. Elizabeth Douvan and Joseph Adelson, *The Adolescent Experience* (New York: Wiley, 1966), 408–411.

91. The draw of marriage, often for reason of pregnancy, constituted a substantial portion of young women who did drop out before graduation—as much as one in four in small cities, according to one study. U.S. Bureau of Labor Statistics, *School and Early Employment Experiences of Youth* (Bulletin No. 1277, 1960), 66–69; David Segal and Oscar J. Schwarm, *Retention in High Schools in Large Cities* (United States Office of Education, Bulletin No. 15, 1957), 14.

92. On the whole, what small variation there was here paralleled going steady and overt marriage plans.

93. "I Want to Get Married," *True Confessions* 69 (December 1961): 19.

94. For a concerned parental response to the link of going steady with marriage, see Evelyn Seeley Stewart, "Why Teens Marry in Haste," *Parents* 37 (November 1962): 51+.

95. *The Roosevelt Standard*, October 14, 1954.

96. For girls, these elements of the adolescent social structure mattered a good deal more than such a critical life course variable *from the adult perspective* as pace of promotion through school. For boys, however, grade progress mattered rather more. Inferences from data reported in Marion F. Shaycroft *et al.*, *The Identification, Development, and Utilization of Human Talents: Studies of a Complete Age Group—Age 15* (Cooperative Research Project No. 566 [Pittsburgh: University of Pittsburgh Project Talent Office, 1963]), D-37.

97. Alan E. Bayer, "Early Dating and Early Marriage," *Journal of Marriage and the Family* 30 (November 1968): 628–632.

98. Harriet B. Presser, "Age at Menarche, Socio-Sexual Behavior, and Fertility," *Social Biology* 25 (1978): 100.

99. *Mate Selection: A Study of Complementary Needs* (New York: Harper & Brothers, 1958), 15.

100. "Marriage—Your Most Dangerous Decision," *Personal Romances* (October 1956): 20+. And see Luther E. Woodward, "Do Opposites Attract?" *True Romances* 51 (August 1950): 35.

101. Winch, *Mate Selection*, 287, xv.

102. "Is He a Man or a Boy?" *True Love Stories* 66 (September 1956): 41.

103. Census 1960–3, tables 1, 2.

104. For an instance, see Hilda Holland, comp., *Why Are You Single?* (New York: Farrar, Straus, 1949), which assumes that singlehood stems from psychological blockage.

105. Case #5180, National Growth of American Families Single Women Study, 1955, verbatim text file. See Appendix 4.

106. These inferences are based on the individual- and family-income-by-age data in Census, *Trends in Income*, based on the annual Current Population Survey income survey, and on Federal Reserve Board, "Survey of Consumer Finances," an annual sample survey published in installment in the Federal Reserve Bulletin. The latter provides tabulations for most years on income class by family life-cycle stage.

107. George Gallup, ed., *The Gallup Polls, passim*; Lee Rainwater, *What Money Buys* (New York: Basic Books, 1974), 53, and chap. 3 in general.

108. Calculated from Gallup Polls 377-K and 516-K; Henry F. Pringle, "What Do the Women of America Think About Money?" *Ladies' Home Journal* 55 (April 1938): 14; The Roper Organization, "Public Opinion Service News Release," July 23, 1949; Gallup, ed., *The Gallup Poll*, II, 904.

109. Peter Lindert, *Fertility and Scarcity in America* (Princeton: Princeton University Press, 1978), 161.

110. John Modell, Frank F. Furstenberg, Jr., and Douglas Strong, "The Timing of Marriage in the Transition to Adulthood," in John Demos and Sarane Spence Boocock, eds., *Turning Points* (Chicago: University of Chicago Press, 1978), S130–S133.

111. Marvin B. Sussman and Lee Burchinal, "Parental Aid to Married Children: Implications for Family Functioning," *Marriage and Family Living* 24 (1962): 320–332; Maureen Daly, "Subsidized Marriage," in Maureen Daly, ed., *Profile of Youth* (Philadelphia: Lippincott, 1951), 194–205.

112. "Everybody's Getting Married Except Me!" *True Love* (January 1963): 56–57; and see Abigail Wood, "Young Living," *Seventeen* (December 1962): 79+.

113. Reuben Hill, "Campus Values in Mate Selection," *Journal of Home Economics* 37 (1945): 554–558; John W. Hudson and Lura F. Henze, "Campus Values in Mate Selection: A Replication," *Journal of Marriage and the Family* 31 (1969): 772–775; John C. Flanagan, "A Study of Factors Determining Family Size in a Selected Professional Group," *Genetic Psychology Monographs* 25 (1942): 3–99; computations from AIPO 377.

114. What we are comparing is of course not strictly comparable. Although the ideals and behaviors are entirely contemporaneous, they are not the ideals and behaviors of the same people. Only single people are at risk of marrying for the first time. Unmarried individuals, net of their youthfulness, generally held somewhat older mar-

riage norms; but younger persons, net of the marital status, tended toward younger marriage ideals.

115. This statement applies a technique described in John Modell, Frank F. Furstenberg, Jr., and Theodore Hershberg, "Transitions to Adulthood in Historical Perspective," *Journal of Family History* 1 (1976): 7–32, to data in Dennis Hogan, *Transitions and Social Change* (New York Academic Press, 1981), 38–39, 52–53, 59.

116. Hogan, *Transitions and Social Change*, 44–61, 83; Margaret Mooney Marini, "Determinants of the Timing of the Transition to Adulthood" (Battelle Human Affairs Research Center Population Study Center Report, 1981), 23–25, 35, and table 3; Stanley Lebergott, "The Labor Force and Marriages and Endogenous Factors," in James S. Duesenberry *et al.*, eds., *The Brookings Quarterly Econometric Model of the United States* (Chicago: Rand McNally, 1965), 361. For a normative account, see Jeanne Sakol, *What About Teen-Age Marriage?* (New York: Julian Messner, 1961), chap. 5.

117. "Cradle Snatcher," *True Love Stories* 68 (October 1957): 5.

118. The ratio of IIIA deferments to inductions rose from 0.45 in 1952 to 0.48, 0.52, 0.60, and to 0.70 in 1956 and 1957. The ratio rose again even more sharply, reaching 0.81, then slightly exceeding unity, finishing the decade at 1.21. Computed from annual numbers of *Annual Reports of the Selective Service System*.

119. Census 1950–2, 100; Census 1960–5, 21–24.

120. "Components of Temporal Variation in American Fertility," in R. W. Hiorns, ed., *Demographic Patterns in Developed Societies* (London: Taylor & Francis, 1980), 40; Ryder, "Recent Trends and Group Differences in Fertility," in Charles Westoff, ed., *Toward the End of Growth* (Englewood Cliffs, N.J.: Prentice-Hall, 1973).

121. "A Model of Fertility Planning Status," *Demography* 15 (1978): 455.

122. Census 1960–3, table 36; Census 1970–1, table 29; Margaret Mooney Marini, "Effects of the Timing of Marriage and First Birth on the Spacing of Subsequent Births," *Demography* 18 (1981): 543.

123. Judith Blake and Jorge H. del Pinal, "The Childlessness Option: Recent American Views of Nonparenthood," in Gerry E. Hendershot and Paul J. Placek, eds., *Predicting Fertility* (Lexington, Mass.: Lexington Books, 1981), 235–264.

124. Adoptions of nonrelatives, in fact, outpaced even the growth of births during the baby boom, a pattern that did not reverse when fertility rates finally turned down late in the 1950s. U.S. Children's Bureau, Statistical Series no. 14, *Adoption of Children 1951*, 13; no. 39, *Adoptions of Children in the United States and Its Territories 1955*, 12; no.

51, *Child Welfare Statistics 1957*, 30; no. 88, *Supplement to Child Welfare Statistics—1966: Adoption in 1966*, 4.

125. The next several pages are drawn from a close textual analysis, by myself and John Campbell (now of the University of Arizona), of the quite open-ended questionnaires gathered from single women 18 to 24 years old in 1955 by the National Growth of American Families Survey. See Appendix 4. Modell and Campbell, "Family Ideology and Family Values in the 'Baby Boom': A Secondary Analysis of the 1955 Growth of American Families Survey of Single Women" (Technical Report No. 5 [Minneapolis: Minnesota Family Study Center, 1984], processed); Judith Modell, "Phrasing and Planning: A Rhetorical Analysis of Women's Statements about Family Formation," in David Kertzer, ed., *Current Perspectives on Aging and the Life Cycle*, vol. 2 (Westport, Conn.: JAI Press,1986), 237–266.

126. Based on computations from a larger national survey of both men and women carried out in 1953, also based on open-ended responses (N = 970) but coded by an earlier investigator. The study is the Survey of Consumer Attitudes and Behavior, Fall 1953 (SRC613). See Appendix 4.

127. Case #5156.

128. Case #5152.

129. Robert O. Blood and Donald M. Wolfe, *Husbands and Wives* (New York: The Free Press, 1960), 105.

130. *Ibid.*, 112.

131. U.S., Bureau of Labor Statistics, Bulletin 1977, *U.S. Working Women: A Databook* (1977), 23; Linda J. Waite, "Working Wives: 1940–1960," *American Sociological Review* 41 (1976): 65–80.

132. Richard A. Easterlin, *Birth and Fortune* (New York: Basic Books, 1980); Victor R. Fuchs, *How We Live* (Cambridge: Harvard University Press, 1983).

7: Modern in a New Way

1. "The choice of highly detailed, elaborate coding schemes for open questions in 1957 stood us in good stead when the 1976 coding began. . . . Had a different choice been made in 1957—for example, for more abstract, general, or inclusive code categories, the problem of comparability of coding in the two studies would have been considerably more thorny. . . . But in coding the interview questions, coders could follow the detailed categorization scheme established in 1957 with no apparent difficulties or problems. The specificity of the code designations assured comparability over time as well as high inter-

coder agreement [in each year]." Joseph Veroff, Elizabeth Douvan, and Richard A. Kulka, *The Inner American: A Self-Portrait from 1957 to 1976* (New York: Basic Books, 1981), 31.

2. None of the observations I will make about marriage on the basis of these data differed by marital status.

3. Larry Lee Bumpass, "Age at Marriage as a Variable in Socioeconomic Differentials in Fertility," *Demography* 6 (1969): 45–54.

4. Linda J. Waite and Glenna D. Spitze, "Young Women's Transition to Marriage," *Demography* 18 (1981): 691.

5. Karen Oppenheim Mason and Larry L. Bumpass, "U.S. Women's Sex-Role Ideology, 1970," *American Journal of Sociology* 80 (1975): 1212–1220; Beverly Duncan and Otis Dudley Duncan, *Sex Typing and Social Roles: A Research Report* (New York: Academic Press, 1978); Arland Thornton and Deborah Freedman, "Changes in the Sex Role Attitudes of Women, 1962–1977," *American Sociological Review* 44 (1979); Arland Thornton, Duane F. Alwin, and Donald Camburn, "Causes and Consequences of Sex-Role Attitudes and Attitude Change," *American Sociological Review* 48 (1983): 221–227.

6. James T. Carey, "Changing Courtship Patterns in the Popular Song," *American Journal of Sociology* 74 (1969): 720–731; cf. Donald Horton, "The Dialogue of Courtship in Popular Songs," *American Journal of Sociology* 62 (1957): 569–578.

7. The survey was carried out by the Roper Organization on commission from the Philip Morris Corporation as part of a promotion for their Virginia Slims cigarette, whose advertising featured stylized favorable references to change in women's gender roles. The sampling was stratified, with women trebly oversampled; in my computations, I weighted men trebly in compensation. See Appendix 4. For the results of this fascinating poll, see the Roper Organization, *The Virginia Slims Women's Opinion Poll*, Vol. III (New York: The Philip Morris Company, 1974).

8. *Birth and Fortune* (New York: Basic Books, 1980), 39. A number of careful critiques have indicated the failure of Easterlin's relative-income hypothesis (or of its operationalization, especially of the process of learning a taste for material goods) to explain variation in fertility. See Maurice M. MacDonald and Ronald R. Rindfuss, "Earnings, Relative Income, and Family Formation," *Demography* 18 (1981): 123–136; Arland Thornton, "The Relationship between Fertility and Income," *Research in Population Economics* 1 (1978): 261–290. Like Easterlin, however, these largely ignore the potential impact of anticipated income from wives' enlarged labor-force commitment.

9. The discussion of the circumstances of marriage on the next few

pages is based on data in the increasingly elaborate and inclusive annual *Marriage and Divorce* volume of USNCHS *Vital Statistics.*

10. The *coefficient of variation* offers a simple indication of the extent of "selectiveness" in the sense meant here. The coefficient of variation is calculated by taking the standard deviation of numbers of marriages (by age of bride and by age of groom) per month per year and norming this by the mean number of marriages per month. The larger the coefficient of variation, the more selective the monthly pattern of marriage over the year.

11. Melvin Zelnik, John F. Kantner, and Kathleen Ford, *Sex and Pregnancy in Adolescence* (Beverly Hills: Sage Publications, 1981), Appendixes A and B.

12. Data from the initial full edition (1976) of the annual Monitoring the Future survey. See Appendix 4. Lloyd D. Johnston, Jerald G. Bachman, and Patrick M. O'Malley, *Monitoring the Future* (Ann Arbor: Institute for Survey Research, University of Michigan, annual from 1976) is a fine code book with tabulations of each item.

13. This discussion is based on a multiple regression model. The impact of each independent variable is net of that of all others.

14. Paul R. Newcomb, "Cohabitation in America: An Assessment of Consequences," *Journal of Marriage and the Family* 41 (1979): 597–603; Eleanor D. Macklin, "Nonmarital Heterosexual Cohabitation: An Overview," in Eleanor D. Macklin and Roger H. Rubin, eds., *Contemporary Families and Alternative Lifestyles* (Beverly Hills: Sage Publications, 1983), 49–74.

15. Paul C. Glick and Graham B. Spanier, "Married and Unmarried Cohabitation in the United States," *Journal of Marriage and the Family* 42 (1980): 19–30.

16. Richard R. Clayton and Harwin L. Voss, "Shacking Up: Cohabitation in the 1970s," *Journal of Marriage and the Family* 39 (1977): 273–283.

17. *From Front Porch to Back Seat: Courtship in Twentieth-Century America* (Baltimore: The Johns Hopkins Press, 1988), epilogue.

18. Frances E. Kobrin, "The Primary Individual and the Family: Changes in Living Arrangements in the United States since 1940," *Journal of Marriage and the Family* 38 (1976): 233–239; Census CPS P20–212, table 2; Census CPS P20–289, table 2.

19. Robert T. Michael, Victor R. Fuchs, and Sharon R. Scott, "Changes in the Propensity to Live Alone: 1950–1976," *Demography* 17 (1980): 39–53.

20. Linda J. Waite, Frances Kobrin Goldscheider, and Christina Witsberger, "Nonfamily Living and the Erosion of Traditional Family

Orientations among Young Adults," *American Sociological Review* 51 (1986): 542.

21. There is some indication that the attitudes of cohabitants differed systematically by gender, with females more likely than males to believe (and presumably to act accordingly while in that relationship) that cohabitation should or does lead to marriage. In the Oregon county in which the University of Oregon is located, as the proportion of all couples marrying who had cohabited increased sharply during the 1970s, the association of cohabitation with *later* marriage grew more pronounced, although the pattern was already visible in 1970. Patricia A. Gwartney-Gibbs, "The Institutionalization of Premarital Cohabitation: Estimates from Marriage License Applications, 1970 and 1980," *Journal of Marriage and the Family* 48 (1986): 423–434.

22. Macklin, "Nonmarital Heterosexual Cohabitation," 59–63.

23. Alan E. Bayer and Gerald W. McDonald, "Cohabitation among Youth: Correlates of Support for a New American Ethic," unpublished paper, 1981, 16; data from Alexander W. Astin *et al.*, *The American Freshman: National Norms*.

24. A. Regula Herzog and Jerald S. Bachman, *Sex Role Attitudes among High School Seniors* (Research Report Series [Ann Arbor: Survey Research Center, University of Michigan, 1982]), 79.

25. Tabulations from Monitoring the Future 1976 data file. See also Herzog and Bachman, *Sex Role Attitudes*: 86, and Bayer and McDonald, "Cohabitation among Youth," 7–10. Among the college freshmen, considerably the most powerful predictor of assent to cohabitation was church attendance. Again, religious behavior mattered considerably more in helping to form attitudes toward cohabitation than did a range of socioeconomic and educational items. Alan E. Bayer, "Sexual Permissiveness and Correlates as Determined through Interaction Analyses," *Journal of Marriage and the Family* 39 (1977): 29–40, especially table 1.

26. I present it from the perspective of bride's choice of groom. The story for grooms is of course complementary in that as brides of a given age, on average, married younger grooms, so grooms of a given age married older brides. Because age at first marriage drops off far more gradually at its upper reaches than at its lower—because there are far more definite rules governing how young one *may* marry than how young one *should marry*—we would expect that as grooms married older brides their apparent "selectivity" would decline. This is so only to a very limited extent and only at the younger ages of grooms' marriage. For grooms marrying at age 25, for instance, the

standard deviation of brides' ages dropped markedly between the early and mid-1960s, then rose slightly and gradually to the mid-1970s, accompanying the rise of nearly half a year in mean age of brides. This amounts to powerful evidence for the genuinely increased age-selectivity of marriage in the 1960s and 1970s.

27. *Postwar Fertility Trends and Differentials in the United States* (New York: Academic Press, 1977), 99–101.

28. The figures are deviations from the means, in numbers of sub-three-year-old children, estimated by a multiple classification analysis.

29. Charles F. Westoff and Norman B. Ryder, *The Contraceptive Revolution* (Princeton: Princeton University Press, 1977), 56–58.

30. *Ibid.*, chaps. 2, 3; Christine A. Bachrach, "Contraceptive Practice among American Women, 1973–1982," *Family Planning Perspectives* 16 (1984): 253–259; Christine A. Bachrach and William D. Mosher, "Use of Contraception in the United States, 1982," *USNCHS Advancedata*; Koray Tanfer and Marjorie C. Horn, "Contraceptive Use, Pregnancy and Fertility Patterns among Single American Women in Their 20s," *Family Planning Perspectives* 17 (1985): 13–14.

31. Jane Riblett Wilkie, "The Trend toward Delayed Parenthood," *Journal of Marriage and the Family* 43 (1981): 583–591.

32. Census CPS P20–315, tables 27 and 28.

33. USNCHS Series 3–17, 18.

34. Amy Ong Tsui, "A Study of the Family Formation Process among U.S. Marriage Cohorts" (Ph.D. dissertation, University of Chicago, 1978), 102–103.

35. Data from surveys of mothers of legitimate children born in 1968, 1969, and 1972 give evidence that at least a part of the delay in marital fertility was accomplished by more satisfactory birth control practices. Between 1968 and 1972, *proportions* of mothers saying that they had not wanted a child or had wanted a child then decreased. Of course, there were progressively fewer among all married women of any given age who had had a child at all. USNCHS Series 21–32, table 1. And see Norman B. Ryder, "A Model of Fertility by Planning Status," *Demography* 15 (1978).

36. Veroff, Douvan, and Kulka, *The Inner American*, chap. 5; and see John Modell and John Campbell, *Family Ideology and Family Values in the "Baby Boom": A Secondary Analysis of the 1955 Growth of American Families Survey of Single Women* (Technical Report no. 5 [Minneapolis: University of Minnesota Family Study Center, 1984]).

37. Duncan and Duncan, *Sex Typing and Sex Roles* (1978): 213. Since the mid-1970s, high school seniors have increasingly reaffirmed their commitment to marriage and parenthood, without retaining the

younger marriage pattern that prevailed in the 1950s. Relatively heavy daters are most in favor of conventional marriage and are most eager for marriage relatively soon. Herzog and Bachman, *Sex Role Attitudes*; Richard R. Clayton and Harwin L. Voss, "Shacking Up: Cohabitation in the 1970s," *Journal of Marriage and the Family* 39 (1977): 273–283; Thornton and Freedman, "Changes in Sex Role Attitudes."

38. Judith Blake and Jorge H. del Pinal, "The Childlessness Option: Recent American Views of Nonparenthood," in Gerry E. Hendershot and Paul J. Placek, eds., *Predicting Fertility* (Lexington, Mass.: Lexington Books, 1981), 235–264.

39. Two of the items were couched in terms of skepticism about men's willingness to share in housework and in child care. The others dealt with attitudes toward women's employment, one asserting a nice fit of employment and mothering, the other relating mothers' own happiness to employment.

40. William Watts, "The Future Can Fend for Itself," *Psychology Today* 15 (September 1981): 40–41.

41. USNCHS Series 21–38, table A; cf. Arthur J. Norton and Paul C. Glick, "Marital Instability: Past, Present, and Future," *Journal of Social Issues* 32 (1976): 5–20.

42. Andrew Cherlin, *Marriage Divorce Remarriage* (Social Trends in the United States [Cambridge: Harvard University Press, 1981]), 49.

43. USNCHS Series 21–34, table 3. And see Robert T. Michael, "The Rise in Divorce Rates, 1960–1974: Age-Specific Components," *Demography* 15 (May 1978): 177–182; and Shiro Horiuchi, "Decomposition of the Rise in Divorce Rates: A Note on Michael's Results," *Demography* 16 (1979): 549–551.

44. Lenore J. Weitzman, *The Marriage Contract* (New York: The Free Press, 1981), 146–147.

45. Calculated from census data in Hugh Carter and Paul C. Glick, *Marriage and Divorce: A Social and Economic Study* (revised ed.; Harvard University Press, 1976), 432, 434.

46. Lynne Carol Halem, *Divorce Reform: Changing Legal and Social Perspectives* (New York: The Free Press, 1980), chap. 8.

47. Halem, however, concludes at about a five-year remove that "perhaps . . . because the reformers promised so much to so many [,] no-fault never lived up to expectation. It was publicized as a spectacular event—both a value reorientation and a systematic restructuring of the law." *Ibid.*, 281.

48. The table is based on data on persons still alive at the appropriate census date. The average elapsed time of these marriages is 7.5 years.

49. A good review of the literature on the role of women's work in recent changes in marriage is Sandra L. Hofferth and Kristin A. Moore, "Women's Employment and Marriage," in Ralph E. Smith, ed., *The Subtle Revolution* (Washington: Urban Institute, 1979).

50. This argument is developed at some length and with statistical documentation in John Modell, "Historical Reflections on American Marriage," in Kingsley Davis, ed., *Contemporary Marriage* (New York: Russell Sage Foundation, 1986), 181–196.

51. In Herbert J. Gans, ed., *On the Making of Americans: Essays in Honor of David Reisman* (Philadelphia: University of Pennsylvania Press, 1979), 221–234; and see Judith Blake, "Structural Differentiation and the Family: A Quiet Revolution," in Amos H. Hawley, ed., *Societal Growth* (New York: The Free Press, 1979).

52. Elwood Carlson and Kandi Stinson, "Motherhood, Marriage Timing, and Marital Stability: A Research Note," *Social Forces* 61 (1982): 258–267.

53. Veroff, Douvan, and Kulka, *The Inner American*, 191–192.

54. Ellen Gilliam, "Is Dating Outdated?" *Seventeen* (March 1973): 106.

55. Michael Gordon and Randi L. Miller, "Going Steady in the 1980s: Exclusive Relationships in Six Connecticut High Schools," *Sociology and Social Research* 68 (1984): 463–479; Randi L. Miller and Michael Gordon, "The Decline in Formal Dating: A Study in Six Connecticut High Schools," unpublished paper.

56. Bailey, *From Front Porch to Back Seat*, 87.

57. Lloyd B. Lueptow, *Adolescent Sex Roles and Social Change* (New York: Columbia University Press, 1984), 275. Lueptow's study combines a thoughtful review of the literature and a methodologically sophisticated replication study of 1964 and 1975 Wisconsin high school student samples.

58. John C. Flanagan *et al.*, *The American High School Student*, Cooperative Research Project No. 635 (Project Talent Office, University of Pittsburgh, 1964), 5–6ff.; USNCHS Series 11-147, 73.

59. There were some signs in later annual rounds of this annual survey of a slight increase in dating. Johnston, Bachman, and O'Malley, *Monitoring the Future*, annual.

60. Alan E. Bayer, "Dating and Early Marriage," *Journal of Marriage and the Family* 30 (1968): 628–632; USNCHS Series 11–147; David L. Larson, Elmer A. Spreitzer, and Eldon E. Snyder, "Social Factors in the Frequency of Romantic Involvement among Adolescents," *Adolescence* 11 (1976): 7–12; and see Dorothy C. F. Gregg,

"Premarital Sexual Attitudes and Behavior in Transition: 1958 and 1968" (Ph.D. dissertation, Purdue University, 1971); Johnson, Bachman, and O'Malley, *Monitoring the Future*, 1976.

61. Thanks to Martin Levin, Department of Sociology, Emory University, for a special tabulation on 17-year-olds in the 1966–1970 National Health Interview Survey. I computed comparable 1960 figures from the Project Talent public use data file.

62. Freddie Maynard, "The Real Relationship," *Seventeen* (December 1969): 100+.

63. This comparison and those that follow are computed from the public use file of Project Talent (eliminating all but the seniors) and from Monitoring the Future, 1976.

64. The questions were slightly different. Project Talent *first* asked, "On the average, how many dates do you have in a week?" And, *later*, "On the average, how many evenings a week during the school year do you usually go out for fun and recreation?" Monitoring the Future *first* asked, "During a typical week, how many evenings do you go out for fun and recreation?" and *then* asked "On the average, how often do you go out with a date?" The response categories supplied also differed slightly. The Project Talent public-use data file included 1,000 seniors; Monitoring the Future included a total of 3,353 seniors in 1976, although a complicated file structure reduced this number considerably in some of the tabulations to be reported in this chapter.

65. Trends in hours of study and college plans are present in the data. GPA is also, but the "grade inflation" of the period renders the observations noncomparable across time. Documentation for a decline in academic achievement can be found in the decline of SAT scores, which is, of course, an *achievement* test. College Entrance Examination Board, Panel on the Scholastic Aptitude Test Score Decline, *On Further Examination* (New York: The Board, 1977). Trends in after-school employment are found in *Census 1960–1*, table 197 and *Census 1970–4*, table 23. The downward trend in religious observation in the general population is documented in Smith, *A Compendium of Trends*, 14–15.

66. Inspection of the coefficients in the tables will suggest that this line of argument is overwhelmed by the distinctiveness and complexity of the black patterns, which I largely ignore here in favor of assessing trends among whites.

67. The expected-age-at-marriage question in 1976 was asked of a subset of the seniors who unfortunately were *not* asked the question about hours spent doing homework, so that this item must be dropped from the analysis.

68. "How likely do you think it is that you would stay married to the same person for life?"

69. Dating was *not* a magic key that unlocked all the aspects of variation in family values. A number of questions about parenthood—its salience, the preferred number of children, the pace of childbearing—were *unrelated* to frequency of dating, except for a positive relationship among boys with the salience item. So also were a number of questions probing how the high school seniors responded to aspects of feminism.

70. As one might anticipate, the partial correlation for involvement in religious organizations was strongly *positive*, at a .120 level, for instance, among white boys.

71. An interesting account of adolescents' preferred sources of advice based on local high school samples in 1963, 1976, and 1982 found a powerful turning from parents to peers (between the early 1960s and mid-1970s) followed by a modest turn back after that. Hans Sebald, "Adolescents' Shifting Orientation toward Parents and Peers: A Curvilinear Trend over Recent Decades," *Journal of Marriage and the Family* 48 (1986): 5–13. Adults, it seems, responded by fervently wishing that their authority was more substantial. Glen H. Elder, Jr., "Adult Control in Family and School: Public Opinion in Historical and Comparative Perspective," *Youth and Society* 3 (1971): 6–16.

72. Ira L. Reiss, *The Social Context of Sexual Permissiveness* (New York: Holt, Rinehart & Winston, 1967); Catherine S. Chilman, *Adolescent Sexuality in a Changing American Society*, DHEW Publication No. NIH 79–1426 (Washington: USGPO, 1979), chap. 6; Hazel Gaudet Erskine, "The Polls: More on Morality and Sex," *Public Opinion Quarterly* 31 (1967): 111.

73. Patricia Y. Miller and William Simon, "Adolescent Sexual Behavior: Context and Change," *Social Problems* 22 (1975): 58–76; Roy J. Hopkins, "Sexual Behavior in Adolescence," *Journal of Social Issues* 33 (1977): 67–85.

74. Catherine S. Chilman, "The 1970s and American Families (A Comitragedy)," in Eleanor D. Macklin and Roger H. Rubin, eds., *Contemporary Families and Alternative Lifestyles* (Beverly Hills: Sage Publications, 1983), 15–24, is one thoughtful synthesis of a large literature.

75. Melvin Zelnik, John F. Kantner, and Kathleen Ford, *Sex and Pregnancy in Adolescence*, 65; Melvin Zelnik and Farida K. Shah, "First Intercourse among Young Americans," *Family Planning Perspectives* 15 (March-April 1983): 64.

76. Hazel Gaudet Erskine, "The Polls: Morality," *Public Opinion*

Quarterly 30 (1966): 673; Tom W. Smith, *A Compendium of Trends on General Survey Questions* (Chicago: NORC, 1980), 151. And see Ira E. Robinson and Davor Jedlicka, "Change in Sexual Attitudes and Behavior of College Students from 1965 to 1980: A Research Note," *Journal of Marriage and the Family* 44 (1982): 237–240.

77. Virginia Venable Kidd, "Happily Ever After and Other Relationship Styles: Rhetorical Visions of Interpersonal Relations in Popular Magazines, 1951–1972" (Ph.D. dissertation, University of Minnesota, 1974), 28–31; John DeLamater and Patricia MacCorquodale, *Premarital Sexuality* (Madison: University of Wisconsin Press, 1979).

78. Shere Hite, *The Hite Report* (New York: Dell Books, 1976), 11, 59. Martin S. Weinberg, Rochelle Ganz Swensson, and Sue Kiefer Hammersmith indicate that by the mid-1970s, there had emerged in sex manuals a view of women's sexual *autonomy* that challenged the still more dominant "humanistic sexuality" notion presented in Hite. "Sexual Autonomy and the Status of Women: Models of Female Sexuality in U.S. Sex Manuals from 1950 to 1980," *Social Problems* 30 (1983): 312–324.

79. Murray S. Davis, *Smut: Erotic Reality/Obscene Ideology* (Chicago: University of Chicago Press, 1983).

80. Boston: Little, Brown.

81. Edward A. Tiryakian, "Sexual Anomie, Social Structure, Societal Change," *Social Forces* 59 (1981): 1025–1053; Ira L. Reiss, "Some Observations on Ideology and Sexuality in America," *Journal of Marriage and the Family* 45 (1981): 271–283.

82. Warren I. Susman, "'Personality' and the Making of Twentieth-Century Culture," in *Culture as History* (New York: Pantheon, 1984); Christopher Lasch, *The Minimal Self* (New York: Norton, 1985).

83. Ruth Brecher and Edward Brecher, *An Analysis of Human Sexual Response* (New York: New American Library, 1966), xiii.

84. David R. Reuben, *Everything You Always Wanted to Know about Sex but Were Afraid to Ask* (New York: David McKay, 1969), 4.

85. Sandra S. Kahn, *The Kahn Report on Sexual Preferences* (New York: St. Martin's Press, 1981), 212.

86. Davis, *Smut*, 193. And see Robert T. Francoeur, "Religious Reactions to Alternative Lifestyles" in Macklin and Rubin, eds., *Contemporary Families and Alternative Lifestyles*, 379–399, for a discussion of the now-dominant "process" view of sexuality.

87. Already in 1959, 73 percent of Americans queried believed that such information should flow freely, a proportion that has in-

creased in basically linear fashion at about one percent per year to a very strong consensus. Smith, *A Compendium of Trends*, 139.

88. Arthur M. Vener, Cyrus S. Stewart, and David L. Hager, "The Sexual Behavior of Adolescents in Middle America: Generational and American-British Comparisons," *Journal of Marriage and the Family* 34 (1972): 698; and Arthur M. Vener and Cyrus S. Stewart, "Adolescent Sexual Behavior in Middle America Revisited: 1970–73," *Journal of Marriage and the Family* 36 (1974): 728–735.

89. It is unfortunate that an inquiry into the number of *Saturday night* dates in the past four weeks, with no further explanation, is the only item about dating or socializing more generally on the Kantner-Zelnik survey.

90. The item read: "How about you? Which one of these statements best describes how you feel about sexual intercourse before marriage? a) Sexual intercourse before marriage is okay, even if the couple has no plans to marry. b) Sexual intercourse before marriage is okay, but only if the couple is planning to marry. c) Sexual intercourse is never okay before marriage?"

91. Reiss, *The Social Context of Sexual Permissiveness*.

92. *Ibid.*, 165.

93. DeLamater and MacCorquodale, *Premarital Sexuality*.

94. Cf. table 47, above. The difference may be between high school students and high school graduates.

95. Sorenson's 1972 adolescent survey is methodologically flawed but useful here because his respondents were younger than those of DeLamater and MacCorquodale. He presents a large number of tables in which quite a range of attitudes about sex and related phenomena are cross-tabulated with gender and with degree of sexual experience. By 1973 (in general conformity to the findings of DeLamater and MacCorquodale), items relating sex and marriage had largely ceased to be related to gender but were closely related to sexual experience. The linking of love and marriage, too, no longer varied systematically by gender. Robert C. Sorensen, *Adolescent Sexuality in Contemporary America* (New York: World Publishing, 1973).

96. Sorensen demonstrates this point overwhelmingly.

97. Herzog and Bachman, *Sex Role Attitudes, passim*.

98. Miller and Simon, "Adolescent Sexual Behavior."

99. Philip E. Converse *et al.*, *American Social Attitudes Data Sourcebook 1947–1978* (Cambridge: Harvard University Press, 1980), 272–277.

100. Easterlin, *Birth and Fortune*, Appendix tables 2.2 and 2.3.

101. Census 1960–1, table 197; Census 1970–4, table 23.

102. Noah Lewin-Epstein, *Youth Employment during High School* (Chicago: National Opinion Research Center, 1981, processed), 25–31, 40, 55, 131–133.

103. John C. Flanagan *et al.*, *The American High School Student*, (Pittsburgh: Project Talent Office, 1964, processed), 5–24; Jerome Johnston and Jerald G. Bachman, *Young Men Look at Military Service* (Youth in Transition Document No. 193 [Ann Arbor: Institute of Survey Research, University of Michigan, 1970]); Jerald G. Bachman, "American High School Seniors View the Military: 1976–1982," *Armed Forces and Society* 10 (1983): 88–89.

104. Kenneth Keniston, *Young Radicals* (New York: Harcourt, Brace & World, 1968), chap. 8.

INDEX

Designer: U. C. Press Staff
Compositor: G&S Typesetters, Inc.
Text: 10/12 Baskerville
Display: Baskerville